THE HEROIC EARTH

THE HEROIC EARTH

Geopolitical Thought in Weimar Germany, 1918–1933

DAVID THOMAS MURPHY

THE KENT STATE
UNIVERSITY PRESS
Kent, Ohio, and London, England

© 1997 by The Kent State University Press, Kent, Ohio 44242
All rights reserved
Library of Congress Catalog Card Number 96-38231
ISBN 0-87338-564-0
Manufactured in the United States of America

Library of Congress Cataloging-in-Publicaion Data
Murphy, David Thomas, 1960–
        The heroic earth : geopolitical thought in Weimar Germany,
    1918–1933 / David Thomas Murphy.
            p. cm.
        Includes bibliographical references and index.
        ISBN 0-87338-564-0 (alk. paper) ∞
        1. Geopolitics—Germany—History—20th century.   2. Germany—
    Politics and government—1918–1933.   3. Haushofer, Karl,
    1869–1946.   4. Germany—Historical geography.   I. Title.
    DD240.M86   1997
    320.943—dc20   96-38231
                                                                  CIP

British Library Cataloging-in-Publication data are available.

Contents

Preface   vii

Abbreviations   xiii

1   Rethinking Geography: *The Genesis of German Geopolitics, 1890–1914*   I

2   "The Product and Requirement of a New Age": *The Great War and the Transformation of German Geopolitics*   14

3   Struggle, Survival, Space: *The Language of Weimar Geopolitics*   24

4   The New Weapon: *Geopolitics in Weimar Culture and Politics*   43

5   The Geopolitical Minimum: *Seven Case Studies*   74

6   A Text for Imperialism: *Geopolitics and the German Student*   127

7   "The Suggestive Map": *Geopolitics and Cartography*   165

8   Space for the Third Man: *Geopolitics and the Weimar Crusade for Colonies*   191

9   Geopolitics and Republican Foreign Policy   215

10   The Legacy of Weimar Geopolitics   241

Notes   253

Glossary   305

Documentary Sources   307

Index   333

Preface

The myth of Nazi geopolitics has distorted scholarly understanding of the geopolitical movement in Germany for the last half century. The central elements of that myth were set forth during the Second World War when Western scholars, as they rallied to the fight against Nazism, identified geopolitical ideas as one of the many causes of Nazi imperialism. According to the myth, which persists in scholarly writing about political geography and German history to the present, the militarist geographer Karl Haushofer commanded from the mid-1920s an Institute for Geopolitics at the University of Munich. Using the institute as his tool, he gradually rose to become a sort of diabolical mastermind behind Nazi conquest. From Munich he influenced Hitler's follower Rudolf Hess and introduced Adolf Hitler himself to geopolitical concepts such as *Lebensraum* while Hitler was imprisoned at Landsberg. Under Haushofer's command a staff of "major German geographers" crafted imperialistic schemes that soon made him "the leading supporter and proponent of Nazi expansion" and allowed him to shape "German political and military strategies during World War II."[1]

Thus understood, this myth does more to mislead than to enlighten about the importance of geopolitics for interwar and wartime Germany. The facts of the myth as presented are half-truths at best. The idea that there was an institute with a staff of major geographers, for example, is quite deceptive. An *Arbeitsgemeinschaft,* or work group, did exist, but it was not founded until the 1930s; it served primarily to feed news articles to German and foreign press, had few major geographers affiliated with it, and was judged by Haushofer himself to be a failure.[2] The evil genius Haushofer is even more badly served by the myth. Although undoubtedly a respected scholar who sympathized with many National Socialist ideas and who played an important role in popularizing ideas of which the Nazis made ready use, he himself is remembered by those who knew him as an avuncular, slightly befuddled, former serviceman, "old Haushofer," "a retired Bavarian general of the friendly paternal type who had turned professor" and whose "hobby was geopolitics."[3] Most misleading of all is the idea that geopolitics, or Haushofer, somehow guided Hitler. The Führer followed his own instinct, using whatever justifications he wished; if those instincts happened to coincide with geopolitical theory, so much the better, but where they did not, most obviously in the invasion of the Soviet Union, it mattered very little to Hitler.[4]

The evidence presented in this study suggests, instead, that geopolitical ideas were most dynamic and significant in the years before 1933, when they prepared Germans to accept what came later, teaching them to think like geopoliticians and providing a convenient, seemingly scientific jus-tification for Nazi aggression. On the one hand, geopolitics flourished in the fertile pluralistic political setting of Weimar democracy, insinuating itself into Weimar's modernist discourse and capturing the imaginations of adherents across the political spectrum. On the other hand, geopolitical ideas ossified under the Nazis, losing under the new authoritarian order the dynamism and malleability that had lent them their earlier broad appeal. Though geopolitics certainly played a role in domestic propaganda under the Nazis, and helped shape *Raumforschung*, or Nazi spatial research and planning, in conquered territories, its importance for the formation of both foreign and domestic policy was greatly overshadowed by the imperatives of race. Therefore, this study is focused upon the develop-ment of geopolitical thought in Germany in the decade before Weimar democracy succumbed to national socialism. Geopolitical ideas will be reconsidered in order to understand their rhetorical dimensions and the sources of their appeal, the ways in which they were disseminated, and their place in German politics, culture, and foreign policy before 1933.

The title, *The Heroic Earth,* is borrowed from the works of a leading geopolitical thinker (Adolf Grabowsky) and was selected to focus at-tention on the theory of geocentrism, which was the central unifying concept of all geopolitical thought in the period. Geopolitical thinkers, ignoring the tautological and self-contradictory character of much geo-political theorizing, argued that geography determined the development of political and economic structures. The earth took the role of hero in political-geographic narratives of the geopoliticians, decisively shaping national histories, the characteristic qualities of ethnic groups, and even individual personalities. In this form geopolitical ideas were exploited by the nationalist Right during the Weimar years, but they also exerted a powerful magnetic attraction that reached beyond the confines of the political Right. Academics, writers, and journalists from the moderate Left to the far Right exploited key geopolitical concepts to popularize and support their views. By 1933, geopoliticians had succeeded in infusing geocentrism and other key geopolitical ideas into the Weimar public debate about Germany's political, economic, and cultural future. The natural historiographical urge to explain the catastrophe of national socialism has diverted attention from the socially and politically destructive quality of geopolitical thought during the Weimar years. This work represents an effort to revise historical understanding of the importance of geopolitical ideas in Germany by focusing attention on the years when they first transcended the bounds of German academia to enter the awareness of a broader public.

At the beginning of the 1920s the word *geopolitics* still retained a flavor of the exotic. It was first used in 1899 by the Swedish political scientist and journalist Rudolf Kjellén, whose prolific translated writings made the term known to German audiences before 1918.[5] Before Germany's defeat the Pan-German League and other imperialist organizations had used some ideas that would later be collected under the rubric of geopolitics, but the "science" of geopolitics and the ideas connected with it were largely confined to a small circle of writers and thinkers on the fringes of the German geographic establishment.[6] By 1928, however, writers such as Grabowsky were confident that it would be familiar to German readers. Geopolitics and its themes resonated among the literate German public, a fact the renowned geographer Alfred Hettner noted in 1929 when he wrote that "the word *geopolitics* has become popular, and if earlier one spoke of geographic position and the geographic contingency of political processes, so today the word *geopolitics* rolls off the tongue of every reporter and politician who takes himself seriously."[7]

A glance at the German media or into German schools or books in the late 1920s confirms Hettner's observation. The *Zeitschrift für Geopolitik,* founded by a group of academic geographers in 1924, within a few years enjoyed an annual circulation among people and institutions of influence that fluctuated between three and five thousand over the next decade.[8]

Geographical institutes at German universities offered lectures and seminars on geopolitics. Geopolitical theory and rhetoric figured prominently in the history and geography textbooks used in German elementary and middle schools. Geopolitics found its way into German homes on the radio, where academics and journalists, including Grabowsky, the geographer Karl Haushofer, and the journalist and geographer Arthur Dix, gave regular broadcasts, explaining the important political issues of the day in geopolitical terms.[9] Academic journals and intellectual magazines alike had a heavy geopolitical content, and German publishers offered their readers titles such as *Geopolitischer Typen-Atlas* (The atlas of geopolitical types), *Begriff und Aufgaben der geopolitischen Rechtswissenschaft* (The concept and tasks of geopolitical jurisprudence), and *Geographische Grundlagen der Geschichte* (Geographic foundations of history).[10] Rudolf Pechel, the informed conservative editor of the prestigious *Deutsche Rundschau,* who had close ties to many geopoliticians, recalled that geopolitics had been until the the early 1920s "largely unknown"; by 1926, however, an editorialist for the *Frankfurter Zeitung* wrote, "The press can note with satisfaction the gratifying degree to which an understanding for political geography has grown among the German people in recent years. The geopolitical view of political problems prevails more and more; the word *geopolitics* appears to have become a basic requirement of the modern editorialist."[11] Otto Maull, one of the founders of the *Zeitschrift für Geopolitik,* wrote with some pride in 1929 that "there probably has never been a time, probably not even in the time of the great discoveries, in which geographic thought has met with so much interest among those standing outside the science of geography as at present, thanks mostly to the high market value of geopolitics."[12]

This study is begun in the wake of the German military collapse and the revolutions of 1918 and 1919. Geopolitical theories gained ground slowly over the next few years, acquiring adherents in a variety of academic, political, and media settings. By the time the Republic entered its brief period of relative stability, beginning in 1924, the success of the *Zeitschrift für Geopolitik* provided an institutional framework for the dissemination of geopolitical ideas for the next two decades. The decision to conclude in 1933 recognizes the fact that an extensive literature already addresses many aspects of geopolitical thought during the Nazi era and reflects the conviction that geopolitics grew increasingly irrelevant to

German society and politics after 1933. Although the Nazis talked about geopolitical ideas, it is incorrect to say that they were guided by them. It seems more often the case that they saw in geopolitics popular slogans and convenient ex post facto rationalizations for courses of policy developed independently of strict geopolitical considerations. It is in the Weimar era, under an open and pluralistic political system, that geopolitical ideas flourished, exhibiting a broadly based appeal and a dynamism that could affect politics.

Conclusions regarding the dissemination of geopolitical ideas are based upon the extensive periodical literature of the era pertaining to geopolitics and the examination of contemporary historical and geographical works, textbooks, and other sources. Archival research focused on government support for groups that promoted geopolitical ideas, the promotion of geopolitics in Prussian schools, the papers of numerous journalists, academics, and geopoliticians, and the records of Weimar political parties and pressure groups. The project could not have been completed without the generous support of many individuals and institutions in the United States and Germany. Above all, I am deeply indebted for advice, criticism, and inspiration to Paul Schroeder and Peter Fritzsche, who guided the writing of the dissertation that provided the first foundations of this book. Both scholars read the manuscript carefully through many drafts and offered invaluable assistance. Without their creativity and vision this work would not exist. I am grateful to William Widenor, Peter Krüger, and Mark Bassin for their insightful suggestions. Thanks are due as well to Professors Donald M. McKale and Ken Calkins, who provided much helpful criticism, and Linda Cuckovich and Julia Morton of The Kent State University Press. The clarity of the text was improved enormously by Virginia McIntyre Barker's meticulous copyediting. Errors or oversights are entirely my own responsibility.

Means to pursue research were provided by the University of Illinois Graduate College, the MacArthur Foundation Program in Arms Control, Disarmament, and International Security, the Social Science Research Council Berlin Program for Advanced German and European Studies, and the Intercollegiate Studies Institute. Progress was greatly assisted by the efficient staffs of the Geheimes Staatsarchiv Preussischer Kulturbesitz, the Staatsbibliothek Preussischer Kulturbesitz, the Berlin Document Center, the former Zentrales Staatsarchiv in Potsdam, the Staatsarchiv

Marburg (particularly Inge Auerbach), the Universitätsarchiv Göttingen, the library of the Technische Universität Hannover, and the knowledge-able, friendly, and helpful staff at the Georg-Eckert-Institut für inter-nationale Schulbuchforschung in Braunschweig. This work could not have been written without the gifted assistance of Marcia Martin Murphy. It is dedicated to her and to my parents, Rosemary and Robert Murphy.

Abbreviations

AA	Auswärtiges Amt
AAAG	Annals of the Association of American Geographers
ADAP	*Akten zur deutschen Auswärtigen Politik*
ADV	Arbeitsausschuss Deutscher Verbände
ADZ	Arbeitsgemeinschaft deutscher Zeitschriften
AfG	Arbeitsgemeinschaft für Geopolitik
AHR	*American Historical Review*
AKOTECH	Arbeitsgemeinschaft für Auslands- und Kolonialtechnik
BAK	Bundesarchiv Koblenz
BAP	Bundesarchiv Potsdam
BDC	Berlin Document Center
BDHP	*Berichte der deutschen Hochschule für Politik*
CEH	*Central European History*
DA	*Deutsche Arbeit*
DAI	Deutsches Ausland-Institut
DBP	Deutsche Bauernpartei
DDP	Deutsche Demokratische Partei
DHP	Deutsche Hochschule für Politik
DHVK	*Deutsche Hefte für Volks- und Kulturbodenforschung*
DKG	Deutsche Kolonialgesellschaft

DNVP	Deutschnationale Volkspartei
DR	*Deutsche Rundschau*
DSB	Deutscher Schutzbund
DSVK	Deutsche Stiftung für Volks- und Kulturbodenforschung
DVP	Deutsche Volkspartei
DW	*Deutsche Welt*
EB	*Eiserne Blätter*
EG	*Europäische Gespräche*
FZ	*Frankfurter Zeitung*
GA	*Geographischer Anzeiger. Blätter für den geographischen Unterricht*
GB	*Grossdeutsche Blätter*
GG	*Geschichte und Gesellschaft*
GR	*Grenzdeutsche Rundschau*
GStA	Geheimes Staatsarchiv Preussischer Kulturbesitz, Berlin-Dahlem
GZ	*Geographische Zeitschrift*
HSM	Hessisches Staatsarchiv Marburg
HZ	*Historische Zeitschrift*
IGAD	Institut für Grenz- und Auslandsdeutschtum
KORAG	Koloniale Reichsarbeitsgemeinschaft
MGGH	*Mitteilungen der Geographischen Gesellschaft in Hamburg*
MGGM	*Mitteilungen der Geographischen Gesellschaft in München*
NG	*Die Neue Gesellschaft. Frankfurter Hefte*
NSDAP	Nationalsozialistische Deutsche Arbeiterpartei
PE	*Pan-Europa*
PGQ	*Political Geography Quarterly*
PJ	*Preussische Jahrbücher*
PK	Politisches Kolleg
PM	*Petermanns Mitteilungen*

RF	*Reichsflagge*
RKFDV	Reichskommissariat für die Festigung deutsches Volkstums
S	*Die Standarte*
SDVK	Stiftung für deutsche Volks- und Kulturbodenforschung
SM	*Süddeutsche Monatshefte*
SoM	*Sozialistische Monatshefte*
SPD	Sozialdemokratische Partei Deutschlands
UF	*Ursachen und Folgen vom deutschen Zusammenbruch*
UKZ	*Übersee und Kolonial-Zeitung*
USPD	Unabhängige Sozialdemokratische Partei Deutschlands
VB	*Volkswirtschaftliche Blätter*
VDA	Verein für das Deutschtum im Ausland
VDG	*Verhandlungen des Deutschen Geographentages*
VDR	*Verhandlungen des Reichstages*
VJHZ	*Vierteljahreshefte für Zeitgeschichte*
VR	*Volk und Reich*
VRa	*Volk und Rasse*
VVDH	*Verzeichnis der Vorlesungen der Deutschen Hochschule für Politik*
VVK	*Verhandlungen des Vorstandes des Kolonial-wirtschaftlichen Komitees*
VVM	*Verzeichnis der Vorlesungen, Philipps-Universität Marburg*
WW	*Weltwirtschaft. Monatsschrift für Weltwirtschaft und Weltverkehr*
ZfG	*Zeitschrift für Geopolitik*
ZGEB	*Zeitschrift der Gesellschaft für Erdkunde zu Berlin*
ZgU	*Zentralblatt für die gesamte Unterrichts-Verwaltung in Preußen*
ZfP	*Zeitschrift für Politik*

THE HEROIC EARTH

CHAPTER 1

Rethinking Geography

The Genesis of German Geopolitics, 1890–1914

> If we can no longer attribute all progress to the intervention of great personalities, as a more naive time did, and can, therefore, no longer profess a heroic world view without reservations, we can yet render the world itself a hero in the extent to which we can conceive it as the mighty foundation that man battles to subdue and upon which he remains, in the last analysis, ever dependent.
>
> Adolf Grabowsky, *Staat und Raum*

> History is geography in motion.
>
> Johann Gottfried von Herder

Adolf Grabowsky's proposal to replace "great personalities" with physical geography at the center of human history came in the midst of a flowering of geopolitical thought that took place in Germany in the wake of the First World War. German journalists and political activists, academics, patriotic students, and others eagerly embraced geopolitical ideas, using them to relocate the sources of German history, culture, and politics in geographic factors. The proposition that geography played a key role in a nation's history was not unknown in Germany before the war. Goethe, Herder, and others had called attention to the fact that geography exerted considerable influence over cultural and political developments. But the catastrophic trauma of the world war and the wrenching transformations it produced in German society and Germany's international position fed a new fascination with the role of geography in precipitating the tragedy. A heterogeneous circle of thinkers began to examine Germany's climate, topography, and landscape from a radically new perspective. They argued that geographic and spatial factors, properly understood, explained Germany's past triumphs and failures and held the key to national renewal. Building upon theories first sketched in the Wilhelmine era, the new advocates of a geopolitical perspective began to rethink the impact of geography on demographic change, international conflict, national frontiers, and the growth of state power. The door to a brighter German future, they argued, could be unlocked only by applying the truths of politics and geography revealed in the "science" of geopolitics.

The geopolitical theorists of the Weimar years were reaping a harvest sown decades earlier. The popular appeal and political utility of geopolitics during the Weimar years were founded in the Wilhelmine origins of German political geography. Long before the term *geopolitics* itself became common currency, geopolitical ideas had been influencing thinking about politics throughout the industrialized world. In all the Western nations, during the end of the nineteenth century a new concern arose with the connections between politics and geography, a concern undoubtedly stimulated by the so-called new imperialism of the period. The technological advantages conferred by steamboats, repeating rifles, and railroads strengthened Western dominance of worldwide trade and politics, intensifying colonial competition and accelerating global economic integration. Global expansion in these years fostered the formation of what has been called a "European planetary consciousness," and this, in turn, produced a new sensitivity to the political significance of geography.[1]

The geopolitical awareness that emerged in Weimar Germany was rooted in the nation's dramatic prewar political and economic expansion. Shaken in the final quarter of the nineteenth century by profound economic, political, and demographic transformations, German society proved receptive to explanations of change in which spatial factors played a large role. Such explanations were sprouting up all over the industrialized world at the start of the twentieth century. The American historians Frederick Jackson Turner and Alfred Thayer Mahan, the geographer Halford Mackinder in Great Britain, and social scientists elsewhere in Europe, including Rudolf Kjellén in Sweden and Friedrich Ratzel in Germany, all advanced theories of political, social, and historical change that centered on factors of space and physical geography. In the final decades of the Victorian era Mackinder and Mahan were particularly successful in conveying to responsive international audiences their vision of the decisive influence geography supposedly exerted over political relations.[2]

Mahan, in his day, earned global renown as a modern, maritime Clausewitz. A historian and captain in the United States Navy, he was hailed at the turn of the twentieth century as the prophet of the "new navalism." In his most famous work, *The Influence of Sea Power upon History 1660–1783,* which appeared in 1890, Mahan outlined a detailed thalassic analysis of national might against a panoramic historical backdrop. Those nations that had become wealthy and powerful, Mahan argued, had done so through control of the seas, and he insisted that maritime power would determine national greatness in the future as it had done in the past. Mahan's gospel of naval might, elaborated in scores of books and articles until his death in 1914, was enthusiastically welcomed in the United States, Japan, and England (where Queen Victoria entertained him and Oxford and Cambridge bestowed honorary degrees).[3] It was also acclaimed in Germany where it was greeted by political and economic elites as a particularly timely contribution to fin de siécle debate about the nation's place in the European political system. The kaiser, afire with his recurring nautical enthusiasm, "devoured" *The Influence of Sea Power upon History,* later receiving its author on the royal yacht and facilitating the work's translation for a German edition, which duly appeared in 1896.[4] Mahan's theories were seized upon as fortuitous expert testimony in the Naval League's campaign for a German battle fleet composed of capital ships (the *Reichsmarineamt* distributed more than two thousand copies of the massive work), and it had an important impact on the naval strategizing of Alfred Tirpitz although the precise nature of that influence remains the subject of historical argument.[5]

That Mahan is customarily numbered among the most influential originators of the German geopolitical approach to statecraft seems, upon first glance at his work, somewhat mysterious.[6] The great bulk of *The Influence of Sea Power upon History,* for example, is in the style of conventional military history, detailing the resources, diplomacy, and naval tactics of the various nations considered. Mahan was not a geographer, and he devoted only a few pages to an explicit discussion of "geographical position" as one of the "general conditions affecting sea power."[7] Mahan's work possessed inspirational qualities for a later generation of geopolitical enthusiasts, however, as a result of his implicit (and occasionally explicit) argument that spatial geographical factors played a crucial role in the expansion of political and military power. For Mahan the sea was a "great common" across which the strongest nations projected palpable but unseen lines of power from strategically located strongpoints, shipyards, and coaling stations.[8] In the Mahanian narrative of naval struggle the oceans and their littorals are cast as both settings for and actors in the global political struggle—favorable geographic positioning of bases was the sine qua non of his strategic analysis—anticipating a geographical determinism that would be one of the characteristic elements of later geopolitical discourse.

Mahan's British contemporary, the geographer Halford Mackinder, was less immediately influential but had a greater impact in the long run on the development of the specifically German (as opposed to British, French, or American) variant of geopolitical thought. In contrast to Mahan's maritime geopolitics, which located those geographical spaces crucial to political power on the oceans, Mackinder urged statesmen to look shoreward, to the earth's great land masses.[9] A product of the leading imperial power in an age of global empires, Mackinder's aspirations as a political geographer were ambitious, even grandiose: by considering the globe as a completed and now closed political system, he sought to find "a formula which shall express certain aspects, at any rate, of geographical causation in universal history."[10] Mackinder argued that such an analytical perspective left no doubt that global political dominance depended not on control of the seas but on mastery of the core of the Eurasian land mass, the region of western Asia and eastern Europe that he described first as the "geographical pivot of history" and, after World War I, as the "heartland."[11]

The world, according to Mackinder, had entered a new age at the dawn of the twentieth century. During the previous four centuries of what he called the "Columbian epoch" Europe had explored and expanded around the globe against comparatively little resistance. That era was now over. In the dawning "post–Columbian age" the last free spaces had been carved up and distributed. The nations of Europe would no longer be able to direct their dynamic power outward into fresh spaces, nor would they have new fields in which to acquire vital resources. Instead, the future would belong to those who had the most secure bases of population, agricultural space, and resources. The geography of the greatest such base, the Eurasian heartland, rendered it invulnerable to naval force—"The Heartland is the region to which, under modern conditions, sea power can be refused access"—and conferred incomparable material advantages upon its ruler: "The spaces within the Russian Empire and Mongolia are so vast and their potentialities in population, wheat, cotton, fuel, and metals so incalculably great that it is inevitable that a vast economic world, more or less apart, will there develop inaccessible to oceanic commerce."[12]

Mackinder's fame never approached that of Mahan, whom Mackinder viewed as a theoretical rival, and his impact on the development of geopolitics in Germany has been depicted in widely divergent terms.[13] Karl Haushofer, the best-known German geopolitician of the interwar years, was closely familiar with Mackinder's work, and there is no doubt that Mackinder's focus on control of the Eurasian heartland rather than of the seas was seen as vindication by many of those Germans who between the wars favored an eastern orientation to German foreign policy. It is easy, however, to overestimate Mackinder's role in shaping German geopolitical views. Influence there certainly was, and subsequent exaggerated evaluations of Mackinder's impact were fueled by Haushofer's testimony on the subject at the Nuremberg war crimes trials.[14] Despite important similarities, however, important differences on key issues, such as the likelihood of conflict between the Soviet Union and Germany, separated Mackinder's views from those of Haushofer and the German geopoliticians.[15] These had indigenous roots, and Mackinder's views are more accurately seen as reinforcement to the native pattern of development rather than as a decisive influence.

Although beginning their study of the relationship between politics and geography from the divergent disciplinary perspectives of history and geography, respectively, Mahan and Mackinder both arrived at geocentric conclusions. Geopolitics, thus, originated from a multidisciplinary heritage, a fact that would influence the development of the field throughout the Weimar years. Weimar geopoliticians were obsessed with political-geographical boundaries in every form, but they never succeeded in drawing clear academic boundaries for their science as an aspiring academic "discipline." The multiple lines of descent from which geopolitics emerged would lend the field a certain eclectic vigor, but they may also help to explain why geopolitics, despite attracting some thoughtful practitioners, never developed canons of theory or methodology that could lend it genuine coherence as a discipline. The complexity of the origins of geopolitics was further ramified by the legacy of the two most important continental geopolitical thinkers of the prewar years, Rudolf Kjellén of Sweden and Friedrich Ratzel of Germany.

Kjellén, a Germanophile political scientist and journalist, was schooled in *Staatswissenschaft,* an integrated field combining law, politics, economics, and history, which was nineteenth-century Germany's form of political science. He produced the earliest extended elucidation of geopolitics in 1916 in his book *Staten som lifsform* (The state as a life form), which was translated from its original Swedish into German the following year. Kjellén treated geopolitics as one of many aspects of what he intended as a synthetic "system of politics on the basis of a purely empirical conception of the state."[16] Kjellén anticipated the methods of Weimar geopoliticians by making geopolitics a purported practical guide to political action, a *Wegweiser.* In the geopolitical marriage of geography and politics the latter clearly played a dominant role. Geopolitical writing ultimately came to be devoted almost entirely to topical German political issues accompanied by precious little scientific geographical content. Kjellén, in his influential definition of geopolitics, helped ensure that from the start geography would play second fiddle to politics in the geopolitical equation:"Geopolitics is the teaching of the state as a geographic organism or a manifestation in space: therefore, the state as land, territory, district or, most obviously, as an empire. As a political science it has the state unit constantly in its focus and wishes to contribute to the understanding of the essence of the state; political geography, on the other hand, studies the earth as the site of human communities in their connections to the other properties of the earth."[17]

Kjellén offered his "empirically based" science of the state as an alternative to what he felt were the sterile abstractions and theoretical juridical concepts that dominated thinking about the state in his day. Geography, he hoped, would form one of the bases of the new science, anchoring it in the physical, the real, and empirically demonstrable facts of geography rather than in the airy legal theorizing on which traditional concepts of the state were constructed. Geopolitics would investigate and explain why a particular state occupied a given area and no other and how mountains, rivers, climate, access to the sea, and other geographical factors shaped the political life and cultural characteristics typical of its people. Kjellén's effort to create an "empirical" substitute for legalistic concepts of the state and to find an "empirical" rather than legal basis for relations between states would occupy geopoliticians throughout the Weimar era.

Mahan, Mackinder, and Kjellén each had an important influence on the origins of German geopolitics, establishing thematic concerns and linguistic formulations that would characterize the field. Undoubtedly, however, the Wilhelmine interest in the geographical roots of politics was articulated to Germans most clearly by one of their own, the zoologist, geographer, and journalist Friedrich Ratzel. Born in Karlsruhe in 1844, educated in the natural sciences at Heidelberg and Jena, Ratzel helped found German geopolitical thought with his *Politische Geographie,* first published in 1897 and reissued three times in the next thirty years (the last time, in 1923, by the Berlin geopolitical publishing house of Kurt Vowinckel).[18] The influence of this monumental work on the development of geopolitics cannot be overstated; German geopolitical writers and most German political geographers since have recognized in Ratzel the modern originator of their field.[19] Writing in the turbulent era of *Weltpolitik* (the popular Wilhelmine term for global policy) and the German quest for a "place in the sun," Ratzel blended a Darwinian emphasis on struggle with an organic concept of the state in his analysis of the links between politics and geography. By applying these theories to states within the framework of a marginalized but legitimate scientific subfield—political geography—Ratzel eased the way for their acceptance into the public discourse on politics and geography in Germany. As a result of his work, geopolitics was initially received as part of the field of political geography, which in relative obscurity had developed its own themes and analytical paradigms for German politics (especially the politics of foreign relations). Building on the Ratzelian base of geopolitical concerns limned at the turn of the twentieth century, postwar geopolitical writers would expand the range of their theoretical horizons far beyond the early boundaries set by Ratzel's political geography.

Ratzel's work defined a basic agenda and introduced many of the specific terms that would later occupy the geopoliticians. The preoccupation with colonies and access to maritime routes (in which Ratzel shows the influence of Mahan), the association of population growth with national vitality, the neo-Darwinian conviction of the inevitability of struggle between states, the emphasis on the formation of borders and the advantages of "natural" borders, these are all to be found in Ratzel.[20] Linking these themes logically, or apparently logically, was the central notion of the state as an organism. The use of biological metaphors and analogies in the description of state development did not, of course, originate with Ratzel. He went further than mere comparison, however, to construct a genuine morphology of states complete with a set of seven scientific "laws" of growth, development, and decay. Such a political morphology was Ratzel's goal (perhaps even more so the goal of Kjellén, who freely acknowledged his debt to Ratzel), and the ideas and terminology he developed in pursuit of this goal had an enormous impact on geopolitics.

It has been argued that Ratzel's view of the state as an organism was metaphorical rather than literal, but Ratzel's own background and writings suggest his organic state models were meant quite literally.[21] Educated in zoology, he chose journalism as his career and proceeded from these interests into a concern with anthropology and geography. That Ratzel was heavily influenced by Darwin's theories of natural selection and evolution is clear. In 1869, for example, he published a general description of Darwin's theory of natural selection written for lay readers. Throughout his political geography the Darwinian *Kampf ums Dasein* (struggle for existence) takes the form between states of a *Kampf um Raum* (struggle for space).[22] In the late 1870s and 1880s, however, Ratzel grew critical of what he considered a simplistic emphasis on racial competition in popular notions of Darwinism, and he explicitly distanced himself from vulgar Darwinist ideas. This retreat has led some later writers to argue that Ratzel's *Politische Geographie* was, in fact, an anomaly intended for a general audience, that he himself continued to view biological descriptions of the state primarily as convenient images, and that the degree of geographic determinism in his work was overstated by his later geopolitical followers.

This apology for Ratzel is misguided. His approach to political geography was beyond question founded in a combination of geographical and biological determinism, but the important point remains that he was no adherent of racist theories of statehood. "We know no stateless people!" Ratzel thundered, distancing himself from those prewar members of the Pan-German movement whose dreams for the creation of a German-dominated *Mitteleuropa* were based on unifying the settlements of ethnic Germans scattered through eastern and central Europe in the name of national self-determination.[23] To Ratzel, as to the majority of prewar Germans who were less than enthused by Pan-German propaganda, Germans beyond the borders of the Reich were simply citizens of other states.[24] In the radicalized postwar era many geopolitical theorists would shed Ratzel's reluctance to embrace racial theories, combining race and ethnicity with geographical determinism to make their case for renewed German hegemony in central Europe.

If Ratzel's work avoided the cruder racism of his time's intellectual ambience, it nonetheless in general bears out indictments of its biological-evolutionary nature. This is particularly true of Ratzel's analysis of the relationship between the state and its land or soil (*Boden*). The state was an "indigenous organism" on its piece of ground, Ratzel argued, insisting that "every state is a piece of humanity and a piece of ground."[25] It was, in fact, the land itself, according to Ratzel, that called forth the state. This fact had to be recognized in a much more elemental sense than was generally done in the "colorless" work of political scientists, however. State dynamics were based on "closer connections" between land and state, connections through which "all political forces take possession of the land, and precisely thereby become state-forming."[26] Between them, Ratzel made clear, state, land, and people formed a living being. "A nation does not remain immobile for generations on the same piece of territory," he wrote. "It must expand, for it is growing."[27]

The state, therefore, was an organic product of the land, provided it was occupied by a people possessed of sufficient political acumen to construct, maintain, and defend it. The strain of Hegelian exaltation of the state that remained characteristic of geopolitics through the Weimar era was already present in Ratzel's contention that the structures of geography exerted dynamic forces upon humanity and that these culminate inherently in state formation. The interaction of geography and humanity, in other words, was conceived as a narrative, whose plot resolves itself in state formation. "An inhabitable land promotes the development of states," Ratzel argued, "especially when it is naturally bounded." The nation in an ethnic sense, or *Volk*, was as essential as the land in Ratzel's concept of the interaction of politics and geography. From the symbiotic interaction between the two elements of *Boden* and *Volk* the state acquired its organic nature, its character as a life form. "The state is to us an organism not simply because it is a bond of the living nation with the inflexible land," Ratzel wrote, "but because this bond strengthens itself so much through mutual interaction that both become one and can no longer be imagined dissolved from one another without that life slipping away."[28]

Like other life forms, states possessed organs, which might or might not be sound and healthy. Chief among these organs, for Ratzel, was the *Grenze,* which may be interpreted as "frontier" or "border." This he described as the skin of the state, its "peripheral organ." The nature of the border and its correspondence to changes in topography, language, or culture could determine the character of the relations between the states separated by the border.[29] The geopolitical obsession with the injustice of Germany's borders during the 1920s, in particular the debate about Germany's "natural" borders in the east, drew heavily on Ratzel's concept of borders as naturally evolving organs of the state. Stable borders reflected the state's organic relationship between its people and its geography, and, therefore, they could not be arbitrarily redrawn as had happened at Versailles. The health of the state organism was also dependent, in Ratzel's estimation, upon population growth. A growing population was not only the source of national vitality and the visible indicator of a sound state organism it was the motor of natural state expansion through colonization.[30] Writing at the turn of the twentieth century, with Germany's population rapidly expanding and before the late-nineteenth century decline in the German fertility rate began to have noticeable demographic consequences, Ratzel saw no reason for pessimism in this regard. Two decades later, however, as German mothers continued to bear fewer children, the geopoliticians came to accept Ratzel's view that only a growing population was a healthy population and to look for the sources of Germany's declining birth rate in geographical factors, particularly a lack of living space.

The now infamous geopolitical term for the living space necessary to a healthy state organism, *Lebensraum,* also derives from Ratzel. Although *Lebensraum* would later be identified with the Nazis and symbolize arguments endorsing migrationist colonialism (and as such would involve an influential romanticized view of the peasantry as free, virtuous, and fecund), Ratzel originally intended it simply as a means of denoting the area necessary for a state to enjoy security in its independence.[31] Complete autarchy in terms of food and natural resource production was not one of Ratzel's criteria for adequate living space, but the question of whether Germany required a living space sufficient to provide autarchy gained currency with geopoliticians in the wake of World War I. Adequate living space, according to Ratzel, would guarantee social and political harmony and enable Germans to develop the cosmopolitan worldview required for the decisive conduct of international affairs. He buttressed his views with various natural "laws" that the state organism followed, most prominently the "Law of Expanding Spaces" or *Gesetz der wachsenden Räume*, according to which "law" the state strove "by its nature toward expansion and, candidly stated, toward conquest."[32] Furthermore, the state's ability to exercise this impulse toward expansion was a reflection of its size and cultural development: the more highly developed the culture, the greater the size of the state, and the more effective its efforts at expansion. "As the area of states grows with cultural advancement, so peoples at lower stages of cultural development tend to be organized into petty states. And in fact, the lower we descend in the level of culture the smaller states become, and the dimensions of the state represent one of the measures of cultural development. No primitive people (*Naturvolk*) has ever created a great state."[33] After the war, in a shrunken, defeated Germany faced with a declining birth rate, fears created by the correlation of state size, cultural development, and population growth with the health of the state would take on an intense urgency for the geopoliticians.

Ratzel was not entirely alone in exploring either the influence of geography on politics or the interaction of geography, politics, and culture before the war. Nor was he the only writer in the field trying to devise "laws" of geographic/political development. Kjellén, for instance, posited laws such as the *Gesetz der Genesung* ("Law of Recovery") whereby "amputated" states attempted to recover lost lands in other areas. Holland after 1830, he argued, demonstrated this law by recovering from the loss of Belgium through colonial expansion overseas.[34] He differed somewhat from Ratzel, however, in emphasizing an explicitly Darwinian approach to the competition between states and in a greater emphasis on racialism. Ratzel's essential focus on politics led him to conclude that race and ethnicity were less important than political factors in the interaction of geography and humanity. He argued that a people need not necessarily be bound by ethnicity or even by a common language but by the political bonds that grew out of cohabitation of a common space.[35] Kjellén, on the contrary, saw the four elements of race, space, culture, and state as the essential components of the political life form rather than simply the two elements of ground and humanity that dominated Ratzel's scheme.[36]

Other geographers and other influences helped lay the prewar groundwork for the later growth of geopolitics. Although most geographical research and writing at this time still concentrated on the description and classification of the earth's topography and not on anthropogeography or political geography, eminent geographers including the polar explorer Erich von Drygalski and Alfred Hettner turned more and more to the relationship between geography and politics. Hettner, who taught geography at Leipzig, Tübingen, and Heidelberg before the war and who edited the prestigious *Geographische Zeitschrift* after it, emphasized the dependence of culture and politics upon geography in his 1905 book *Das europäische Russland. Eine Studie zur Geographie des Menschen* (European Russia: A study of human geography). He argued, too, that the formation of states proceeded according to natural laws and that state size was an indicator of cultural development.[37] Political pressure groups such as the Pan-German League and the Naval League helped accustom Germans to the use of a deterministic geography to support political claims.[38] The influence of non-Germans was also, as has been seen, enormous. Mahan's emphasis on the geographic/political importance of maritime power helped stimulate Ratzel's 1900 book *Das Meer als Quelle der Völkergrosse. Eine politisch-geographische Studie* (The sea as the source of national greatness: A political geographic study), and the maritime theme retained its resonance into the 1920s.[39] Nonetheless, the key figure in the development of geopolitical thinking before the war was Ratzel, whose productivity and breadth of vision made him seem a towering figure in the field to those who came later. He was properly eulogized in 1928 as the father of the field by Otto Maull, who published his own *Politische Geographie* in 1925 with explicit reference to Ratzel's work. "The development of geopolitics is unthinkable without Ratzel," Maull wrote. "No one else, therefore, not even Kjellén, as is occasionally done from ignorance, can be characterized as the father of geopolitics. It is Ratzel."[40]

Even before the First World War, therefore, certain sectors of German academic and political culture had acquired a geopolitical awareness. Influential outsiders—Mahan, Mackinder, Kjellén—found German audiences sympathetic to their theories about the relationship between space and politics. Germans themselves—Ratzel, Hettner, and others—were generating a geopolitical design of their own, merging Social Darwinism, geodeterminism, and biological metaphors for the state in their narration of the interaction of geography and politics. Although these prewar writings set the stage for the later growth of geopolitics, however, their influence ought not to be exaggerated. Unlike Weimar geopolitical thought, which achieved a breakthrough into the popular consciousness and which attracted writers and political thinkers from every field, prewar political geography remained a small province of academic geography. It required total war followed by catastrophic defeat to attract a much broader range of thinkers to the uses of the geopolitical form of glamorized political geography.

CHAPTER 2

"The Product and Requirement of a New Age"

The Great War and the Transformation of German Geopolitics

The surge of life in the northern lands rises slowly, in their peoples, year by year, astonishing changes take place.

Arnold Zweig, *Der Streit um den Sergeanten Grischa*

More than ever, world order requires a German people again conscious of its inner strength. . . . The entire German people in Europe must remain constantly before the eyes [of the nation], regardless of state boundaries at the moment.

Helmut Göring, *Knaurs Weltgeschichte*

The Weimar-era geopolitical outburst, like the daring new fashions in women's clothing, the fevered nightlife of 1920s Berlin, or the industrial craft ethos of the Bauhaus, was a cultural consequence of the First World War. Its foundations, like those of so many other features of Weimar culture, date from the waning years of the Second Reich, when geopolitical theory first entered the German discourse about politics.[1] The war, however, was the crucial experience in preparing the ground for the explosion of geopolitical thought between 1924 and 1933. The catastrophic nature of total war imparted a graphic immediacy to geopolitical ideas that might have seemed mere academic exercises earlier. The unprecedented fluidity of the initial stages of the war on each front, followed by years of grinding attritional trench warfare in the west and the spectacular restructuring of states in the east, deeply imprinted the imaginations of German geographers and political scientists. The tragic drama of this war's politics, strategy, and technology—the struggle of German submariners to win control of oceanic shipping lanes, the discovery of the air as an avenue of offensive maneuver, the mechanization of human destruction by the machine gun—these and other elements of the wartime experience encouraged many German intellectuals to recast space and geography in ways that presented them as forces that were simultaneously static and dynamic.

On the one hand, Germany's wartime experience inflamed the fears of geopolitical thinkers. The enormous loss of life, the realization of the Bismarckian nightmare of a two-front war, and the blockade and starvation that succeeded the conflict inspired a traumatic sense of Germany's vulnerability, while the streetfighting and revolutionary unrest that accompanied the end of the war heightened fears about the fragility of the German social order. The war, therefore, augmented many time-honored anxieties of Germany's political and intellectual leaders. Just as certainly, however, the war also whetted some German ambitions. Germany's victory over the teeming Slavic hordes (as the geopoliticians saw them) on its eastern borders, the encounter with German-speaking settlements in distant regions of central and eastern Europe, and the short-lived but profound remodeling of east central Europe by the Treaty of Brest-Litovsk, fired the dreams and imaginations of journalists, academics, politicians, and others in the German opinion-making elites.

The schemes of Germany's wartime annexationists show considerable continuity with prewar spatial theorizing of the Ratzelian variety. Those who publicly fantasized about the possible consequences of a German victor's peace, however, normally justified their plans with economic and racial theories in which the prewar tradition of geopolitics played only a secondary role. Heinrich Class, chairman of the Pan-Germans, for example, in 1914 issued a memorandum that foresaw the eventual inclusion of Austria-Hungary, Rumania, the Netherlands, Scandinavian and Baltic territories, and a variety of overseas colonies in a German-led economic union. This was an ambitious program (it grew more so as the war progressed) but one that based its claims in Pan-German demands for the unification of ethnic Germans and the ostensible economic logic of such an arrangement rather than in geographic or geodeterminist reasoning.[2] Ratzel, by contrast, despite his support for German navalism and a generally aggressive German foreign policy had never favored efforts to link all ethnic Germans in regions such as the Baltic states or eastern Europe with the German Reich.[3]

The geopolitical tradition of the prewar years undoubtedly played a role in German thinking about what sort of world would emerge from the fighting. It was not coincidence that these years produced Kjellén's major work (and its German translation) on the state as a life form. Friedrich Naumann's *Mitteleuropa,* which appeared in 1915 before the collapse of Russia, provided an influential exposition of many prewar expansionist arguments, and Adolf Grabowsky, a publicist and teacher who would play an important role in popularizing geopolitics later, produced a geopolitically tinged analysis of eastern European politics entitled *Die polnische Frage.*[4] These works typify German wartime writing on the reordering of central Europe, however, in that they are focused primarily on the economic value of a central and eastern Europe organized under German economic and cultural leadership rather than on the geographic sense of such an arrangement. Wartime yearning for the economic security provided by a German-run Mitteleuropa and the short-lived effort to realize German hegemony in the east through the Brest-Litovsk settlement would inspire and inform more explicitly geocentric analysis of east European politics during the Weimar period.[5]

The unexpected loss of the war, culminating in the humiliation of the Versailles *Diktat,* or dictated peace, provoked a desperate search for answers to the question of why Germany lost. Bitter resentment of the peace settlement, particularly those paragraphs that deprived Germany of one-eighth of its prewar territory, stimulated a new approach in geography and helped popularize the use of geographic themes to explain Germany's vulnerability and to elucidate its new opportunities. In the geographic profession the response to defeat was manifested in a shift from natural geography, which had dominated prewar publications in the field, toward political geography. Many began to see the meaning of geography in its contemporary relevance, the contribution they felt it could make to ending the near state of emergency in which the German state was mired through much of the Weimar era. The signs of this change and its causes were unmistakably clear to contemporaries. Karl Rathjens, writing in 1927 in *Petermanns Geographische Mitteilungen,* explicitly recognized the war as the source of the transformation of geography: "The distinct (prewar) emphasis on geomorphological problems . . . was greatly weakened after the war. Provoked by the monstrous experiences during the war and in the postwar period . . . geographers began more and more to occupy themselves again with economic geography and political geography or, as one today chooses to name these fields of the science that have long been known and practiced, with geoeconomics, geoecology, and geopolitics."[6] Rathjens noted what was clear to other observers at the time: geographers had discovered new preoccupations since the war. Frontiers, cultural geography, and the sources of state power now excited more interest than vegetation, geology, or climatology. Disaster had stimulated in new forms a concern with ideas that had existed before the war but which had acquired a new urgency through the "monstrous experiences" arising from war.

In their pursuit of new truths about German geography Weimar geopoliticians viewed themselves as the vanguard of a new science. Their mission was clear. They intended to lay bare the hidden forces and unseen connections of geography and political processes that had destroyed Germany and whose apprehension would enable it to rise from the ashes of defeat and to assume its rightful place among the world's leading peoples. They attributed unseen formative powers to topography and climate, arguing that different geographic settings were "predestined to compel their inhabitants to a particular destiny."[7] Germany's rivers and mountains and plains in combination with the racial characteristics of the German people "had to make the German nation what it is today." Geopolitics, they argued, would "reveal the inner connections between historical change and the land in which this people lives."[8] Cognizance of these forces and inner connections was more vital than ever in the new historical era ushered in by the war, and geopoliticians, echoing Mahan, viewed themselves as heralds of the new global epoch. "Geopolitics is the product and the requirement of a new age" wrote Arthur Dix in 1926, "the (age) of transition from the so-called modern age, characterized as colonial-political, to our age, which we shall best have to characterize as the *global* age."[9] Only by understanding the geographical roots of Germany's failure in the war, as the geopoliticians saw it, could Germany adequately plan for the future, and they believed that it was "the young science of geopolitics which has sharpened the eye for these sorts of highly important but not always easily discernible facts."[10] As a geopolitical writer put it in 1931 in the *Geographischer Anzeiger,* the organ of the League of German School Geographers, geopolitics was a response to "an elementary need, a need for better scientific protection of political life forms . . . rooted in the bitter experience of an unjustified, unfounded, and senseless mutilation of our own living space by a peace treaty arising from a war that was the result of a complete disregard of geopolitical factors in the policy of the pre-war era."[11]

The accusation that prewar German statesmen had ignored the geopolitical realities of Germany's position did not apply to Bismarck, of whose geographical acumen the geopoliticians generally approved. Rather, they argued, his successors had failed to understand the value of the German overseas empire and ignored the lessons that ought to have been drawn from Germany's central position, or *Mittellage,* in Europe.[12] "How the expense of geopolitical education would have paid for itself, for example, with Bethmann-Hollweg and his people!" Haushofer exclaimed.[13] German intellectuals of the Wilhelmine era were also responsible for the debacle because by their omission of geographic factors from *Staatswissenschaft* they had failed in their duty to provide reliable guidance to policymakers and public alike.[14] To prevent a repetition of these failures geopoliticians believed they had to develop a new science that would demonstrate conclusively on empirical grounds the pure objective inadequacy of the peace settlement, to say nothing of its patent injustice, while simultaneously furnishing a reliable scientific guide to the future conduct of German foreign policy.[15] This guide they provided by evolving geopolitics out of political geography.

After the war, therefore, German geopolitical writers devoted considerable effort to distinguishing their field from the geographic subdiscipline of political geography. Whereas political geography before the war had been a stultifying intellectual backwater, "a withered skeleton of names and numbers" on whose methods and writing style "the educated reflected . . . with a mild shudder," the war cleared the fusty schoolbook aura from these issues by injecting a new urgency into the search for solutions to the "profusion of new geopolitical problems."[16] Although some geographers, Hettner, for example, carped that geopolitics was no more than vintage political geography in shiny postwar bottles, this assessment betrayed a lack of sensitivity to the tone and approach of the two fields.[17] The terms *geopolitics* and *political geography* were sometimes used interchangeably, and to many Germans they undoubtedly meant the same things. For the Weimar period, however, it is important to distinguish between the sweeping pretensions and popularized, often politically radicalized geodeterminism of geopolitics and the sober academic modesty of traditional German political geography of the sort practiced by geographers such as Hettner.

The relationship between geopolitics and traditional German political geography after the war was analogous to that between Charles Darwin's theories and the political and social ideas grouped under the rubric of Social Darwinism. Geopolitics may be seen as a sort of vulgarized political geography that attained a popularity never approached by its parent. Hettner's objection to the claims of geopolitics was significantly inaccurate in that it ignored important differences in the approach, rhetoric, and popular resonance of postwar geopolitics compared with the old political geography. Prewar political geography lacked the sense of pressing need, of immediate practical political utility, that the defeat and peace settlement imparted to geopolitics. Unlike geopolitics, which drew adherents from many fields and reached a broad audience through its penetration of the educational establishment, political geography had been largely confined to the geographic profession. Finally, geopolitics embraced a range of themes that political geography had only brushed, including but not limited to the impact of aviation, radio, and other modern technologies on geopolitical questions, antipositivism in understanding geography's political and cultural meaning and the relationship between geography and population.

Geopolitical writers certainly contributed to the criticisms against their discipline by the frustrating vagueness of many of the leading geopolitical writers, particularly the most famous of the Weimar geopoliticians, Karl Haushofer, whose byzantine style could at times appear willfully obscurantist.[18] The opacity of much geopolitical writing was attacked at the time, both by geopoliticians and others, and this aspect of geopolitics has drawn critical comment ever since. A recent historian of the movement has gone so far as to propose "lack of conceptual clarity" as a characteristic of the field in this period.[19] So far as it is not a manifestation of the "inbuilt tendency toward vagueness and lack of precision" of the German language, this evasive rhetorical blurriness may have reflected a nagging uncertainty about the "scientific" validity of geopolitics.[20] It may also be a product of the nascent stage of the field's development or an attempt to camouflage many of the internal contradictions of geopolitics, some of which are discussed below.

The apparently arbitrary nature of much geopolitical theorizing has been further complicated by the fact that geopoliticians frequently offered their own definitions of geopolitics when addressing this very issue. Some of the most prominent geopolitical writers of the time, Arthur Dix for example, candidly admitted that when they said "political geography" they meant the same thing as "geopolitics," and vice versa. When describing his 1922 book, *Politische Geographie,* four years later, Dix wrote that "the title 'Political Geography' was indeed still retained, but the essential label lay in the subtitle 'Worldpolitical Handbook,' which would indicate an introduction into geopolitics."[21] Otto Maull's *Politische Geographie* was described in reviews, accurately, as a work of geopolitics.[22] Maull himself would not have been bothered by this because he felt that attempts to distinguish between the two terms were foolish, arguing that "geopolitics is nothing less than applied political geography."[23]

Attempts to construct distinctions between the two fields by geopoliticians of the era generally hinged on the perceived "dynamism" and applicability or topicality of geopolitics as compared to traditional political geography. The "dynamic" aspect of geopolitics derived from its incorporation of a chronological perspective into political geography. Hermann Lautensach, a cofounder of the *Zeitschrift für Geopolitik* who would later teach geography at Braunschweig and "spatial research" (*Raumforschung*) at Greifswald, declared that the "conception of political geography is static, that of geopolitics dynamic," emphasizing the focus on political and historical change characteristic of geopolitics.[24] Richard Hennig, an academic who belonged to the Deutschnationale Volkspartei (DNVP), or German National People's Party, and the Stahlhelm and who became a prolific geopolitical propagandist in the late 1920s, tied this supposedly dynamic aspect of geopolitics to its role as the "science of the state as a living organism," which focused on analyzing changes in the organism rather than description of its static condition.[25] The difference between geopolitics and political geography could also be seen as a product of their divergent ancestries as Arthur Dix argued when explaining the two fields to the members of the German Geographical Congress in Breslau in 1925. He began by telling the assembled geographers that "exclusively descriptive" political geography and economic geography could still be considered branches of geography, whereas geopolitics and geoeconomics were "fruits in the neighbor's garden" that could be incorporated into the geographic tree only by grafting. The biggest difference in Dix's eyes was in the uses and purposes of geopolitics, which were clearly different from those of political geography: "Among the tasks that belong to geopolitics are the examination of political borders in comparison with the 'natural' geographic and with the ethnographic and economic (borders). The current borders of the German Reich, as they were drawn in Versailles, can in no way stand up to such an examination. Geopolitics is, therefore, our best advocate in the struggle over the revision of the central European border settlement."[26]

Dix's statement to the German geographers pinpoints how geopolitics was most clearly the fruit of the war in its sense of political mission. This will be the key to understanding it, and it is why those who focused on the applicability, as they saw it, of geopolitics in attempting to identify it as a unique field were on the right track. Prewar works such as Ratzel's and Hettner's had, of course, had political uses, but they were not overtly directed to solving pressing contemporary political problems through geographic analysis in the way that postwar geopolitical works were. Unlike earlier and later political geographers geopoliticians in the Weimar Republic presented their work as a kind of field guide to statesmen, intending not to impart general principles of understanding so much as to aid in the resolution of very specific dilemmas—Germany's "unfavorable" border settlement, the question of Alsace-Lorraine, and so on. Geopolitics would help German statesmen avoid the mistakes of the past while pointing out the road to a better future. Maull, for example, complained that geography was too apt to be treated as a purely theoretical science in Germany and that effective political action had to be based in geographical knowledge. "Genuine knowledge of the world," he argued, "is in good part geographical knowledge and, therefore, the best foundation for political ability."[27]

In a theoretical sense, the distinction drawn by geopolitical thinkers between their supposedly dynamic approach and the static description of traditional political geography revealed a faulty understanding of scientific investigation. Norbert Krebs, whose own work occasionally had geopolitical overtones, argued precisely this in reviewing the second edition of Hennig's *Geopolitik* in 1931. "I cannot allow that (geopolitics) distinguishes itself as an 'applied science' from political geography, that the latter is descriptive while the former is dynamic because every pure science must also study 'development and transformation'."[28] Geopolitics was "applied," however, in the sense that geopoliticians intended their works as contributions to the political, and less directly, cultural discourses of their period in a way that had not occurred to earlier political geographers. The sometimes acrimonious Weimar debate about the differences between the fields strikes later observers as academic; we can be reasonably confident, after all, that the merits and deficiencies of the various arguments remained arcana to the general public. The numerous testimonials to the popularity of the term *Geopolitik* suggest that investigations of the relationship between politics and geography in the Germany of the late 1920s and early 1930s were identified in the public mind as geopolitics, whether so called or not by their authors. Furthermore, even those professional geographers who were not swept up in the cruder forms of geographic determinism that characterized some geopolitics nonetheless used terms and ideas that were common to geopolitics.[29] The blurring of lines between the two fields was noted at the time by Karl Haushofer's son, Albrecht, a poet, geographer, and geopolitician in his own right who would later be murdered by the Nazis: "Geographers originally of the natural science school, such as Penck, Supan, Sieger and Hettner, Obst, Maull and Lautensach, turned their attention to the formulation of political-geographic questions; political self-assertion . . . demands goal-oriented scientific work treating the controversy about borders and Lebensraum. . . . Much has been written in German about the connection between the spatial environment and politics, partially under the name political geography and partially under the name geopolitics."[30]

Even more importantly, Weimar geopoliticians articulated a synthetic breadth of vision that was foreign to the traditions of political geography. Many of them, Haushofer, Hennig, Ewald Banse, and others, were positive zealots, converts to a new understanding of the world and of history bent on proselytizing among their people. Their pretensions and ambitions eclipsed the modest sense of limits revealed in the agenda of the old political geography, devoted as it was primarily to studying the geographic foundations of politics. Based upon the premise that geography determines the nature of far more than just relations between states, postwar geopoliticians revealed a catholicity of interest and a geodeterminism whose dimensions transcended whatever had come before. Their obsession with new technologies, their violent antiurbanism, the attempt to develop aesthetic or impressionistic geography, the attribution of legal systems, personality development, racial characteristics, and other phenomena to geographical factors all took hold in the geopolitical discourse only in the 1920s and went out from there to enter the main currents of the Weimar debate about politics, society, education, and culture.

The political and disciplinary heterogeneity of the thinkers attracted to geopolitics during the decade under consideration indicates that these years, not the Nazi era generally identified as the highpoint of geopolitical thought, represent the real "flowering" of geopolitics. In the ten years from the founding of the *Zeitschrift für Geopolitik* to Hitler's accession to power geopolitical ideas, despite their frequent pseudoscientific vulgarity and theoretical inconsistency, attracted thinkers from across the political spectrum. A group of conservative Social Democrats around the *Sozialistische Monatshefte* found in geopolitical ideas a useful rationalization for their dreams of a socially conscious confederated Europe. Democratic centrists such as Grabowsky saw them as the basis for a peaceful but assertive German foreign policy in central Europe. On the right geopolitics was used to explain to Germans how they had failed in the past and how they could rebuild a position of world power. To some it pointed to the inevitability of more unrest before the European state system could again regain its equilibrium.

Before the Nazis, in short, geopolitics meant many things to many people. After 1933, it meant one thing, the use of a certain kind of political-geographic rhetoric to justify the racial policies of national socialism. And the Nazis, whom many of the geopoliticians themselves welcomed, slowly revealed themselves to be the nemesis of geopolitics. After embracing a movement that ostentatiously paid lip service to their ideas, many geopoliticians found themselves with a state that used those ideas not to steer policy but instead to justify whatever course Hitler and his party found expedient. If, therefore, geopolitics acquired a somewhat greater prominence under the Nazis as it assumed the role of a quasi-official state foreign policy doctrine, it lost a certain vitality and diversity of thought that had made it popular in the Weimar Republic. Its flowering was over, and the advent of the Third Reich, as the eventual silencing of many leading geopoliticians by the National Socialists made clear, was the beginning of the long decay of geopolitics.[31] It is in the period immediately preceding the Nazi era, therefore, that one must seek to understand the forms of geopolitical ideas and the means of their dissemination, which lent them their popular resonance in Germany.

CHAPTER 3

Struggle, Survival, Space

The Language of Weimar Geopolitics

Characteristic of life, above all, are feeding and growth, the unconscious
urge to self-preservation and, among humans, the conscious striving
for safety as well as the impulse toward independence. It is basically no
different with states. One can even speak, in a certain sense, of
reproduction among them.

Johann Sölch, *Die Auffassung der 'natürlichen Grenzen'*
in den wissenschaftlichen Geographie

The bitter disappointment of defeat in the First World War ensured that
German geopolitical thought during the Weimar years remained focused
on the relationship between geography and the power of the state. According to the geopolitical analysis developed during the 1920s, Germany
was locked in a life-and-death struggle for survival, threatened externally
by the imposition of the disastrous terms of the Versailles treaty and internally by its declining biological energy and the geopolitical ignorance
of its citizens. The fate of Germany hinged upon restructuring the spatial
conditions of the state's existence, that is, its borders, and upon teaching
Germans to think geopolitically. Toward these ends Weimar geopoliticians emphasized the role space and topography played in fostering the
growth of states and in precipitating struggle between states. By combining this geographic sensibility with a model of the state as a living organism they hoped to explain the disaster that had befallen Germany and
to point out the course to national recovery.

The social and political setting was crucial in defining the thematic
parameters of German geopolitics in these years. The succession of domestic and international crises that confronted the nation—widespread

political violence, onerous reparations payments, hyperinflation, occu-pation—shaped a typical geopolitical agenda and lent the discourse of German geopolitics its characteristic defensive nationalism. The primacy of struggle in relations between states, the conditions under which states expanded or declined, the geographically determined biology of states, these were the broad themes to which geopoliticians returned again and again in the 1920s and early 1930s. The leitmotiv, however, was accom-panied by many refined variations through which a geopolitical perspec-tive was often used to frame important questions of contemporary culture and politics. Radical conservatives of the period, for example, used geo-political rhetoric to argue that geography had helped shape the racial and cultural characteristics of the Germans. This argument supported their demands for a geographical/racial reordering of central Europe under German auspices. Critics of Weimar culture and society used geopoli-tics to explain the accelerating urbanization of German society and to outline the perceived dangers of this trend as well. Geopoliticians em-bracing agrarian romanticism criticized Weimar culture sharply while celebrating German achievements in radio, aviation, film, and other new technologies that shaped that culture. Racial hygienists used geopolitics to help diagnose the causes of the drop in the German fertility rate, or *Geburtenrückgang*, and to find an antidote for it. The supporters of Pan-Europeanism made use of geopolitics, and although geopoliticians tended in general toward fanatical nationalism, they often adumbrated a sophis-ticated globalist view of political and economic processes. Many geo-politicians professed to admire anti-imperialist movements in places like India and North Africa (besides the achievements of non-Western cul-tures such as the Japanese) while vehemently demanding the restoration of Germany's own colonial empire and asserting the superiority of Euro-pean culture over all others.

An accurate understanding of the place of geopolitics in Weimar Ger-many must account for the impressive range of subjects to which geo-political ideas were applied. Woodruff Smith, in a perceptive study of the ideological roots of Nazi conquest, has argued that ideologies that suc-cessfully integrate broad sectors of the population must possess a degree of theoretical flexibility to accommodate contradictions without allowing those contradictions to become evident.[1] Geopolitical theory was suffi-ciently imprecise and, therefore, sufficiently pliable to prevent its internal contradictions from drawing undue attention. The theoretical opacity that lent a broad applicability to geodeterminist ideas therefore constituted both a strength and a weakness of geopolitical thought. Despite the widespread appeal of geopolitical ideas those ideas proved too diffuse to function as a unifying ideology. Instead, geopolitical concepts were adduced to bolster the arguments and claims of a variety of ideologies in the Weimar Republic.[2]

Geopolitics proved to be so useful and malleable, in fact, that it was exploited by groups ranging from Weimar's nationalist Right to the Social Democratic Left. The typical historical characterization of geopolitics as the tool of the reactionary Right consequently distorts the uses of geopolitics. This mistaken notion has, in turn, produced considerable misunderstanding about the place of geopolitics in Weimar culture. The following discussion will consider geopolitical ideas in a context that embraces more than the nationalist Right and trace their infiltration into a variety of political and cultural settings. A close examination of the ideas of geopolitics and of how some of these ideas were used in Weimar political life suggests that geopolitical thought validated and legitimated visions of German renewal across a much broader portion of the political spectrum than has been hitherto believed. Furthermore, the key to its attractive power seems to have been the optimism of geopolitics, the hopeful interpretation given geodeterminism by geopoliticians, which attracted conservatives, centrists, and some moderate leftists anxious about the perceived weakness of their state. A consideration of the main themes and rhetoric of Weimar geopolitics, keeping these facts in mind, suggests the outlines of a more accurate understanding of the relationship of geopolitics to broader currents of Weimar culture.

Raum and Struggle

The fundamental building block of the geopolitical understanding of the state was space, or *Raum*. Through the concept of Raum, geopolitical theory subordinated politics to geography. Geopoliticians insisted that under proper conditions the state grew naturally from its Raum. Translated into English as "space" or "area," the word is deflated, losing the thick layers of nearly mystical connotations with which it resounded for German geopoliticians.[3] They invoked Raum as a supranatural and elemental force in human affairs. Raum framed the state, Raum composed the state, in the final analysis Raum actually created the state. The path-breaking political geographer Otto Maull, for instance, endowed Raum with progenitive powers, seeing it as a diffuse, inchoate but, nonetheless, potent force that ultimately expressed itself through the formation of states. "The state in its total spatial structure and in its manifold incarnations must be the object of geographical research," Maull insisted, "not only as an organism *in* space, but in a much deeper sense as a spatial-organism grown *out* of space."[4] Maull and other geopolitical theorists who focused on political geography cast space as a dynamic element in the growth of states, and as a force that imparted to its inhabitants specific character traits. Raum, for them, was a sculptor of peoples. Wilhelm Volz, a geographer who had served as rector of the University of Berlin for a year during the First World War and later directed the Foundation for Research on German Ethnic and Cultural Soil at Leipzig, described the active role of space in bestowing national identity when he wrote, "Every space has its people, and history teaches emphatically that the space is co-determining for history where spaces and peoples pressure one another. . . . The people make the space their own, but the space also creates its people."[5]

This vision of space as shaper of peoples made Raum an extremely valuable concept for a resurgent nationalism. It broadened the appeal exerted by spatial explanations of the German catastrophe for a people who had seen in the lost war a crusade of Germanic culture against the soulless materialism of the West and the Asiatic barbarism of the East.[6] The unique Germanic soul, the inspirational fount of German culture, was now cast as a product of the equally unique Germanic space. Raum was thereby augmented and transformed. The old character of geographical space as a mere void punctuated by mountains, streams, plains, and other inert topographical features that furnished a passive setting for the unfolding of human agency was supplanted by a new identity as humanity's partner in the evolution of history. "Woods and plains and native sky create a feel for landscape," as one writer put it. "The soil, sand or swamp, or fertile earth, or the wide sea educate men. The state, whose essence . . . is power . . . grows from the landscape."[7] The Raum, in other words, became an active force in its own right, one that molded states and peoples. Raum in this sense was closely connected with other important geopolitical terms, Lebensraum, or living space, of course, but also Boden, literally "soil" or "ground." These terms signified geographic features, certainly, but they also evoked images of ethereal forces that defined states, gave peoples their distinctive national characters, and fired the engines of historic progress. "Because Europe appears as it does and not differently, history has developed in the way it has," Volz argued. "We could even consider historical destiny from the geographical standpoint. All geographical considerations depend upon the two basic concepts of position and Raum."[8]

As the historical example of Calvinism suggests, a belief in predestination or determinism need not result in pessimism, provided one is of the elect rather than the preterite. Faith in the power of geography did not mean giving up hope for a better future. On the contrary, the political implications of a belief in the deterministic formative powers of geography and space could be interpreted in an optimistic light, offering Germans solace for the humiliation of defeat by predicting their inevitable return to power. Confident in their "knowledge of the law," meaning in this case their geopolitical reading of how space functioned, geopoliticians argued that a geopolitically sensitive Germany had only to understand and submit to the historical force inherent in its space to rebuild German power. Despite all appearances, one wrote, Germany's enemies "have in reality not won at all because their victory was only an episode; they will soon realize that all the land that was taken from the German people simply could not be taken because it returns to them of its own accord. Raum is stronger than human caprice."[9] This was the view as well of Karl Haushofer, the era's most prominent geopolitician, who nicely captured the typical geopolitical sense of vulnerability and opportunity when he argued that Germans could best prepare for national revival by learning to think geopolitically, which would entail a "complete recognition of [Germany's] eternal and indestructible geopolitical power base, but no less of its weak and endangered position and most highly labile power balance."[10]

The concept of Raum was, therefore, a critical geopolitical formulation, one that permitted geopolitical ideas gradually to penetrate a broad range of venues during the Weimar era and for some years thereafter. It was presented to the masses in the popular political propaganda of the nationalist Right and to intellectuals not only in the writings of geopoliticians but also in the works of scholarly political and legal theorists such as Carl Schmitt. As early as 1926, for example, nationalist pressure groups such as the two million member strong Verein für das Deutschtum im Ausland (League for Germandom Abroad or VDA) were using mass-produced leaflets to remind Germans what the struggle to revise the

Polish border settlement was really about: "Over and above any unclear feelings, it is simply and soberly to be seen that the ethnic struggle over our borders is a struggle for self-preservation, a struggle over the German Lebensraum and *Arbeitsraum* (work space)."[11] Other groups, the right-wing veterans' organization called the Stahlhelm, for example, would continue in their propaganda to echo complaints that the Weimar regime "deprives us of any prospect . . . of winning the necessary Lebensraum in the east."[12] At the other end of the intellectual, it not necessarily the political, spectrum, Raum theories reached a different audience in the works of Schmitt in the late 1930s when he began to outline his concept of the Grossraum, or greater space. Schmitt differentiated his use of the term from geopolitics, arguing that it emphasized the dominant political idea of a given region (the American Monroe Doctrine in the western hemisphere, for example) rather than geographical determinism. Nonetheless, Schmitt's application of Raum concepts to international law and state relations had been prefigured in the 1920s by geopolitical thinkers, including Haushofer and Manfred Langhans-Ratzeburg.[13]

The centrality of Raum made it the natural focus of the geopolitical obsession with the struggle of the state organism for life and growth. The geopolitical concept of the relationship between Raum and struggle was revealing both for what it indicated about the geopolitical view of the state and for its implications for the geopolitical understanding of human nature as well. The intellectual debt geopolitics owed vulgarized Darwinism is seen most clearly in the concept of the state as an organism engaged in constant evolutionary struggle. "The biological process of the organism's struggle for existence," Maull wrote somewhat tautologically, "is always a struggle for space when considered from the spatial viewpoint."[14] In most geopolitical writing this struggle took the form of endless, apocalyptic combat among states for more living space.[15] The resulting geopolitical model of international relations is a fundamentally barbaric one in which racial or national extinction are constantly at stake in the endless mortal struggle for essential spaces. Geopolitical convictions about the nature of international relations had important implications for the geopolitical view of humanity as well. The dogma of the inevitability of violent conflict expressed a degraded view of the political human. The point that the human world was politically on a par with the world of beasts was occasionally made explicitly, as when Richard Hennig wrote that "Unrest, strife, and struggle dominate the animal—as the human—world from time immemorial and are woven into world history like a red thread. It doesn't profit us to ask why; the fact as such is given—we must accept it."[16] This struggle might be conceived in many ways: as a remorseless confrontation of worldviews, like that between Germany and the United Kingdom in the Great War, as a race to acquire vital colonial living space, or as an unending battle for economic and technological supremacy. The primary setting of the struggle, however, was between states framed by national boundaries, and these accordingly occupied an important position in the geopolitical worldview.

Boundaries

The point at which the state's struggle for existence was most tangibly manifested was at its border. Here, geopoliticians argued, the expansion that signified a vigorous state or the contraction of a decaying nation could be readily observed, and borders consequently attracted considerable attention. In general, the biological view of the state as a living organism led geopoliticians to reject notions of states and borders that rested on legal or political theories. Starting with the doctrine of the state as a living organism and, thus, subject to laws that operated independently of human agency, geopoliticians gradually diminished the role of law in considerations of the status of borders between states. They scorned the "conceptual fiction" of the border as a line drawn in space by human beings and maintained by legal agreements, and they hoped to subvert this "fiction" by propagating a geopolitical view of the boundary as a palpable and independent life form. The importance of the spatial perspective in boundary questions was reflected in the development of an extensive geopolitical literature on border structure, natural boundaries, and similar topics during the Weimar period.[17] Rather than simply being the "skin" of the state organism, borders were seen as organisms in their own right, related to the state and changing with it but possessing a separate organic identity nonetheless. "As [organisms], borders suddenly win a completely unique, emphatically independent life," wrote a commentator in the *Zeitschrift für Geopolitik*. "Out of lines on the map or in the landscape, out of purely conceptual fictions, the border becomes for us a living being, a play of alternating forces."[18] Haushofer voiced a vitriolic contempt for what he viewed as his era's hopelessly naive faith in legal guarantees for the border structure of Europe. In his book *Grenzen in ihrer geographischen und politischen Bedeutung* (Borders in their geographical and political significance), an exhaustive tome in which he analyzed scores of possible border structures according to geopolitical theory, Haushofer ridiculed the application of law to the understanding of borders:

> The fate of the world until now, and particularly that of Europe, shows the inability of the pure theoretical sciences (theology, jurisprudence, political science unrooted in the terrain or insufficiently rooted therein) to create biologically correct borders, that is, to a certain degree durable for centuries (secular, stable) and capable of transformation (evolutionary), instead of [borders that are] biologically false, labile and, therefore, inevitably productive of war and disruption. . . . Where, among the life forms struggling for existence on the surface of the earth, are all the proud, lofty and sombre words with which the theoretical sciences inflate themselves in the pauses in the struggle and which flee as soon as the struggle again begins to rage? *Civitas dei, Pax aeterna, liberum mare, jus gentium.*[19]

Haushofer's *Grenzen* (Borders) is noteworthy for his exhaustive treatment of a subject that, at first glance, seems simple and straightforward.[20] He considered at length various types of borders, such as those formed by seas, rivers, mountains, deserts, and drainage patterns, purely political borders, the "art of border drawing," and similar topics. Relying on the works of Robert Sieger, Albrecht Penck, and other geographers, Haushofer adopted an ambivalent attitude toward the doctrine of "natural borders" formed on the basis of geographical features. Geographical features could form natural borders, he conceded, but often enough the mediating effects of race, culture, politics, and will negated the importance of "natural" physical borders. This distancing from the idea of natural borders based on geographic features was particularly pronounced among those geopoliticians who had a commitment to the importance of Volk and the unification of ethnic Germandom in central Europe.[21] Theirs was a logical position. A belief in the right of all individuals of German ethnic descent scattered throughout central and eastern Europe to membership in a common political entity is incongruent with the idea that the geographical features separating these groups of Germans might "naturally" constitute legitimate political borders. A firm border, dictated by topography, was less appealing to many geopoliticians than the vision of a hazy ethnic or cultural *Grenzsaum,* or border seam, which left open possibilities of indefinite revision and expansion.

The inflections of geopolitical border doctrine were particularly clear in the geopolitical treatment of the Alps. Although they would seem to constitute the only natural barrier to German expansion southward, the Alps in some regions did not constitute an ethnic divider. Germans lived beyond the crest of the Alps, and this made a huge geopolitical difference. Haushofer, for example, wrote that "the Alps rise only apparently as a unified, protecting wall; three thousand years of geopolitical experience with the spatial body of the Alps tells us that it probably works occasionally as a hindrance but is still penetrable for political movement."[22] Sieger, too, attacked reliance on geography alone to draw borders if the borders and "those geographic factors that most directly affect state formation and life . . . diverge widely."[23] Other geopoliticians also retreated from a strict reliance on geography in the drawing of borders in the effort to be as inclusive as possible of areas of German settlement throughout central Europe. The organic concept of the state was a valuable tool here, which some used to construct a right to certain borders based on the supposed vitality of state organisms. Because the state and its people were alive, "there can, therefore, be no absolute organic border, only temporarily suitable frontiers, and these are always subjectively organic, that is, adapted to just that state body which pulses within them."[24] Even with such qualifications applied to the doctrine of "natural" borders, however, the general effect of geopolitical ideas was the same: "Natural" forces—geography, race, ethnicity—were being substituted for law and politics in the determination of legitimate borders.

Determinism, Contingency, and Environmentalism

In important ways the geopolitical commitment to the historical and political role of forces outside human control created a dilemma for many of its adherents. Geopolitical thought was always bedeviled by an inner tension between a longing for the certainties furnished by strict geographic determinism and the obvious implications of recent German history, that is, if political processes were, in fact, determined solely by geography, then there was no hope of reversing the historical verdict represented by Germany's defeat. The geopolitical reliance on cultural and racial factors in the determination of boundaries, not easily reconciled with strict geographical determinism, is a good illustration of the internal tensions that suffused the Weimar geopolitical discourse as a result of its topical political aspirations. Despite expounding the decisive role geography supposedly played in history and politics, many geopolitical theorists remained uneasy with a categorical spatial determinism and introduced a number of elements that supposedly mediated the effects of space on nations. The effect of such modification of geodeterminism was to make the state a product of symbiosis rather than a simple one-sided expression of the action of Raum on a particular ethnic group. This development in geopolitical thought had been mandated by the fact of German defeat. If physical geography had determined the defeat, there could be no basis for hope in the future because there had been no change in the physical geography of central Europe since 1918. Germany was locked into the role of eternal loser in state competition. Furthermore, geography, by putting rivers, mountains, and non-Germans in the spaces between the German settlements scattered throughout Slavic Europe, had permanently thwarted those volkish enthusiasts who desired a single state that would unite all Germans.

Despite its declared commitment to a geographical analysis, therefore, German geopolitics required mediators between geography and politics. Culture was the most important of these, and the ambiguity this introduced into geopolitical statements on geographical determinism was considerable. As a consequence, a geopolitician could argue, on the one hand, that "the state depends just as much on the people that inhabit it as upon the ground upon which it is erected; it cannot in consequence be properly understood if one does not take the human basis into account" while maintaining on the same page that "the human foundation of state formation is, however, just as much again determined by territorial, therefore geographical and historical-political, arbitrary tendencies."[25] Such tautological rhetorical maneuvers were commonly used to resolve the incongruence of geography with political aspirations.

The geopolitical approach to the impact of geographical factors on personality was less ambiguous. A pervasive climatic environmentalism played a prominent role in the geopolitical discourse of the interwar era, reinforcing the claims of nationalistic German geopoliticians for the uniqueness of the German people and German culture. Growing out of an environmentalist tradition that peaked in mid-nineteenth-century

European geography and was handed on by Ratzel, geopoliticians in general professed a strong belief in the supposed effect of climate upon "racial" and cultural attributes.[26] Inhabitants of the temperate zones of the earth were presumed to be, in terms of diligence, resourcefulness, and general intelligence, superior to inhabitants of tropical regions, according to geopolitical logic. Inhabitants of the German region of the temperate zones were particularly favored.

> In the humid air of the equatorial zone human work-energy drowses, an overabundant nature effortlessly satisfies the slight requirements of the people and spares them that significant physical and intellectual effort which the inhabitants of the temperate zones must expend in the life struggle. Quickly changing air pressure and weather variations and the rhythm of the seasons here have a stimulating effect on human physiology. The demands of housing, clothing, and nutrition are essentially higher here than in warmer lands, and preparatory organization must prepare for the unfavorable season into which nature moves. The person bound to the house for longer time seeks to occupy himself in a lively manner with profitable work or intellectual activity. This is the origin of the drive to high civilization and intellectual culture built upon heightened achievement and the patrimony of the fruits of the labor of ancestors. Man is here incomparably more deeply anchored in space and time than in the always hot and the always cold zones of the earth.[27]

This passage, taken from the writings of the geographer Hugo Hassinger, is especially noteworthy for the way in which climatic factors reinforce geography in rooting particular peoples in their spaces, working together to ensure that nations such as the Germans are particularly "deeply anchored in space and time." Such views of the effect of climate on character and racial characteristics were widely shared by other geopoliticians, who agreed that the qualitative superiority of the people of the nontropical regions was a product of geographical position.[28] Despite the geopolitical flourishes applied in Hassinger's presentation, the argument, reduced to its essentials, is an old one: the tropical climate renders its native inhabitants lazy. This belief that climate itself "contained compelling behavioral norms," a theory that enjoyed great currency not only in Germany but in late nineteenth and early twentieth century America and Great Britain, has been perceptively characterized as "climate's moral economy."[29] Geopolitical writers such as Maull and Hassinger could display considerable refinement in the discussion and application of environmentalist ideas, but the impact of such beliefs was prominent in the racialism of the German colonial revanchism of the period.

Raum and Demography

The geopolitical discussion of such subjects as natural borders, geodeterminism, and the influence of space upon society often reflected uncertainty and disagreement. Geopoliticians were also unable to agree about the precise nature of the relationship among population growth, the state, and geography. Weimar geopolitics was dominated by two seemingly mutually exclusive views about this relationship. On the one hand, Haushofer and other geopolitical writers argued that Germany's already high population density coupled with its expanding population threatened severe social dislocation unless new Lebensraum for settlement, food production, and the acquisition of raw materials was obtained. Those who used this argument generally felt that Germany was entitled to such new lands as a result of its national vitality (proven by population growth) and its imposing cultural achievements. The well-known cry of " *Volk ohne Raum!* " (people without space) is, thus, accurately identified with geopolitical thinking.[30] From the mid-1920s, however, geopolitical rhetoric about Germany's insufficiency of space in central Europe was increasingly supplemented by a trend to reverse the equation and portray Germany as the *Raum ohne Volk.* Hennig, Friedrich Burgdörfer, and others raised the warning that the fertility of German women was declining and that this would ultimately lead to a dangerous decline in German population. This fact was also used as proof that Germany needed more land, now for the settlement of peasants, who, it was believed, would return to their natural fecundity under the benevolent influence of simple country living. Ultimately, whether the number of Germans was growing or shrinking, geopoliticians were able to argue that the situation was proof of the need for territorial expansion.

Albrecht Haushofer and other geopoliticians who subscribed to the overpopulation theory pointed to the facts that, despite the enormous losses on the Eastern and Western fronts, the drastic wartime decline in the birthrate and the loss of one-tenth of the population through the drawing of new borders at Versailles, the German population in 1925 was, at 62.5 million, smaller by only 2 million than the population in 1910. By 1933 it had again surpassed its 1910 level, and because 13 percent of Germany's territory had been forfeited in the peace settlement, the population density per square kilometer was already in 1925 greater by thirteen persons than it had been in 1910.[31] They argued that as a result of population growth and the shortage of jobs caused by the economic upheaval of the early 1920s, Germany lacked space sufficient to accommodate all Germans.[32] To many, such as the volkish journalist Gerhard von Janson, it was evident that the peace settlement had pushed Germany into a state of demographic and spatial emergency: "We Germans remain the Volk ohne Raum. Not only has a vital part of our Raum been torn from us, we are crammed together in excessive population density upon insufficient Raum. Valuable fragments and splinters of our people and culture have been separated from the core people, chained to foreign national ethnic groups by the caprice of the Versailles victor-powers or long since robbed by the course of history of their most immediate connection with the German national state."[33]

By contrast, the sources of the decline in female fertility and "solutions" to the "problem" were also cast in geopolitical terms by geographers, demographers, and conservative writers. Geopolitical arguments were used to bolster theories of eugenics and so-called racial hygiene, which conjured up images of a German population whose quality and quantity alike were in decline. Geopolitical writers described a decaying German racial-genetic pool locked in mortal biological combat with hordes of fertile Slavs who were eternally threatening the German Lebensraum from its vulnerable eastern borders. One of the most prolific of the geopolitical prophets of biological doom was Friedrich Burgdörfer, a demographer and bureaucrat who played a key role in bringing geopolitical demographic theories into government circles in the Weimar period.[34] In a book published as a supplement to the *Zeitschrift für Geopolitik* in 1932 Burgdörfer warned that Germany faced a demographic crisis ("Who has youth has the future!") and argued that in central Europe "population changes of epochal significance sketch themselves . . . , which merit the most serious attention, from the German people especially, in its central European position and for its biopolitical border struggle in the East."[35]

More space would encourage Germans to have larger families, Burgdörfer felt, and this would stiffen the German ethnic border in the east.

The points of connection between the two geopolitical views of German demographic change are as revealing as their differences and tend to support the view that geopolitics was little more than a scientified justification for border revision rather than an analytical system possessing its own internally coherent rules. Both sides saw the sources of Germany's demographic crisis in urbanization, the decline of moral standards, and changes in the social role of women. Despite making what seem to be opposing claims about Germany's demographic predicament, both demanded new land to solve the problem. While those who feared the Geburtenrückgang and their conservative allies demanded new lands in the east of Europe for peasant settlements, however, those who subscribed to the overpopulation strain of geopolitical thinking generally emphasized a demand for a return of Germany's colonies.[36] Burgdörfer and Haushofer viewed the effects of urban life in similar ways, for example, despite embracing contrasting views of German population trends. "Like powerful suction pumps the great cities draw in the best strengths of the people, men and women at the best age for procreation and birth," Burgdörfer wrote, "and the end of all the abundance of blood, life, and power of the great city is more or less voluntary infertility, extinction of the families, and family branches loosed from the land in the first or second generation."[37]

That such views had manifest consequences for the position of women in German society is clear, but these were rarely addressed directly by geopolitical writers. Burgdörfer, for instance, argued that the birth decline was a result of the "rationalization of sex life," whereby family size was restricted in the interest of economic advantage, and declared that "the mother will decide in this struggle over the German *Volksboden*" (or ethnic soil). Although a great deal would be undertaken by the Nazis to compel women to take up their part in this biological struggle, Burgdörfer remained at the time content simply to call for moral renewal as a means of addressing the problem.[38] Lamentation over the decline of German moral standards was not unusual in geopolitical writing. Alois Fischer, for example, reminded readers of the *Zeitschrift für Geopolitik* that they must support "the moralistic combat of pleasure-seeking, greed, and laziness. The future of the white race is closely tied with religion."[39]

These views display a great similarity to some strains of eugenic thought evident in the period, and Burgdörfer was able to serve as a conduit between these geopolitical-eugenic ideas and official governmental bodies.[40]

Geopolitics, Expansion, and Racial Survival

The combination of geopolitics and population-angst usually produced a call for expansion, either in overseas colonies or in east central Europe. In both cases the acquisition of additional space was depicted as a prerequisite for the survival of the German "race." Despite the claims of some scholars that geopolitics was essentially hostile to the reacquisition of an overseas empire for Germany, many geopoliticians were committed to acquiring a new empire and based their claims on Germany's legal right, economic need, and the space requirements of the German population.[41] This is one of the aspects of Weimar geopolitics in which the continuity with prewar thought is clearest, particularly because the demand entailed a return of the old prewar overseas holdings of the German empire. Geographers and geopoliticians such as Arthur Dix, Walter Behrmann, Erich Obst, and the colonial propagandist and novelist Hans Grimm argued that overseas colonies were a geopolitical necessity for Germany.[42] In March 1926 the *Zeitschrift für Geopolitik*, dominated by the supposed "easterner," or continental expansionist, Karl Haushofer, devoted the entire issue to colonial questions. Under the title "Wir fordern unsere Kolonien zurück!" (We demand our colonies back!) Erich Obst and others argued with unmistakably minatory overtones that Germans could not wait indefinitely for colonial justice. "No other state of Europe is similarly hemmed in from all sides; none senses in the good as in the bad the central position in the heart of a balkanized continent quite as strongly as Germany," Obst wrote. "Without colonies suitable for the settlement of whites it is annually compelled to great sacrifice of blood to foreign lands and remains in consequence of its huge population pressure the source of inundation of foreign ethnic soil."[43]

Like the call for colonies, the argument for German expansion in central Europe had roots in the prewar era and in the German debate over war aims. That argument took on a new radicalism and stridency in the hands of postwar geopoliticians and conservative journalists, who presented it as a matter of life and death, a struggle for the existence of the German "race" in middle Europe. Whereas Friedrich Naumann and

the early adherents of a German Mitteleuropa had emphasized the economic and cultural rationale supporting such a construct, their descendants in the geopolitical and volkish movements of the Weimar era
had a perceived geographical and racial necessity in mind when they
spoke of Mitteleuropa. Europe would become "ever more Russian, ever
more Slavic," according to Burgdörfer, unless central European space for
German peasant settlements could be found. "Only a firmly established,
soil-entrenched, birth-friendly peasant population would be in the position to bear excess Slavic population pressure in the long run and to
successfully secure the German ethnic soil in the east."[44] Professional geographers embraced the grim prognostications of demographers such
as Burgdörfer and augmented them with their own arguments. In a review of Burgdörfer's *Volk ohne Jugend* in the *Geographische Zeitschrift,* for
example, the geographer Johann Sölch praised the work under the title
Raum und Zahl. Die Zukunftsfrage des deutschen Volks (Space and number:
The question of the future of the German people) and warned that "the
peoples of central, northern, and western Europe stand in a dangerous
condition of biological underbalance, 'in a condition of ethno-biological
sluggishness and hardening of the arteries' while on the other hand, the
Slavic peoples still demonstrate a powerful biological growth."[45]

Geopolitics and the Seas

Just as geopoliticians were divided over the nature of and proper response to Germany's demographic situation, so, too, their understanding
of the role of the sea in rebuilding German power led to divergence and
disagreement. In keeping with traditional geopolitical thought of the
Anglo-Saxon school, geopoliticians generally argued that maritime power
was a prerequisite to world power.[46] "Maritime strongpoints are absolutely indispensable to a power that conducts world politics today," wrote
the geopolitician Josef März, arguing later that "the seizure of (maritime)
strongpoints is, in the selection of geographic advantages, superior to expansion over broad areas; it is an expressly dynamic manifestation of the
constant political redistribution of the earth."[47] The seizure and consolidation of these strongpoints would proceed over maritime *Kraftlinien,*
or lines of power. Germany had once possessed such a strongpoint for
the extension of world power in Kiao-chow but had been blocked from
defending it by England's ability to cut German maritime lines of force

during the war.[48] The geopolitical advantages that maritime states possessed in the world struggle for power were considerable: they enjoyed greater freedom in selecting sites for the extension of state power than did continental states, Haushofer argued, and they could control global access to vital raw materials in times of crisis.[49]

The reality of Germany's geographic disadvantage in maritime competition, however, prompted one of two reactions among geopoliticians. Some called for the return of Germany's former overseas colonies to provide bases that would offset this disadvantage. Others, such as Haushofer and März, reluctantly concluded that the effort to gain maritime power was hopeless for Germany. Concurring with Mackinder's general analysis, they found Germany to be at an overwhelming geographical disadvantage in naval competition with those states that had more open access to the high seas—Great Britain, France, the United States—and they advised German statesmen to recognize this fact and concentrate on continental power. "The fundamental geographic fact for Germany," März wrote, "is the circumstance that it has no free access to the world ocean and that its connections with overseas possessions can always be blocked by a power that commands the English Channel and the North Sea."[50] As a result, Germans would have to use every opportunity to derive advantage from their continental Raum if they wished to regain world power.

This review of the themes of Weimar geopolitical thought is by no means exhaustive. No serious geopolitician of the period failed to address these central concerns—space, demographics, struggle, boundaries, and so on—but in their efforts to remain relevant to topical political and cultural questions geopoliticians turned their attention to a vast and eclectic array of subjects. The impact of technological progress on politics, economics, and international relations was frequently discussed in the pages of the *Zeitschrift für Geopolitik* and other geopolitically oriented journals, as were the League of Nations, the Pan-Europa movement, and other internationalist European political organizations and movements of the era.[51] On all these topics Weimar geopolitical analysis could be at times surprisingly perceptive. Geography does, after all, affect politics. Political, social, or cultural treatises that take this truism as their guiding principle are bound every now and then to arrive at accurate, if obvious, conclusions.

It is, nonetheless, difficult when reading widely in the works of Weimar geopoliticians to avoid a certain sense of detachment from reality, of lack of substance, as if the writer were trying, as an old saying puts it, to nail jelly to the wall. This sense of academic futility that hovers about a good deal of geopolitical writing may derive ultimately from the problems created by geographical determinism, however modified. Once it is conceded that geography plays some fundamental determining role in politics and culture—that the Sahara is unlikely to produce a thriving dairy economy, for example—it is not always easy to go further. All the efforts to sustain geodeterminist arguments proving the illegitimacy of the purely "political" German borders drawn at Versailles, for example, seem contrived when one looks at borders such as that separating Canada and the United States. By every canon of geopolitical thought of the Weimar period this boundary, a line arbitrarily drawn across thousands of miles of space, corresponding to no ethnic or geographic division for most of its length, ought to be a source of constant unrest. In fact, it has been stable since the 1840s.

With the passage of time many of the theoretical inconsistencies and logical shortcomings of Weimar geopolitics have become increasingly apparent. It is sometimes tempting to suppose that they were less evident to the many perceptive Germans who adopted them at the time and to view Weimar geopoliticians simply as intelligent men temporarily misled by artfully refined geopolitical argument. An examination of some of the geopolitical rhetoric produced in the fading years of the Weimar Republic reveals it to be of such a crudely deterministic character, however, that attempts to portray its widespread appeal as the seduction of confused and desperate individuals of good will by superficially logical arguments appear untenable. Geopoliticians were advocating an absurdly categorical determinism by 1932, arguing, for example, that "the racially determined composition of the population, with the formation of the terrain, the type of climate, the position of the Raum in the center of Europe, had to make the German that which he is today."[52] The shortcomings of such theories must have been apparent to even the most cursory objective examination at the time. The word *objective,* however, is the operative modifier. Although it is true that certain aspects of geopolitics were occasionally subjected to sharp criticism (e.g., by Alfred Hettner), geopolitics on the whole tended to receive a much more sympathetic hearing than its reductivist and determinist nature merited. Its currency in the Weimar Republic cannot, therefore, be explained by its internal strengths as an analytical tool. These were negligible. Instead, insight into the sources of the popularity of geopolitics is best gained by examining the currents of politics and culture within which the Weimar geopolitical discourse was embedded.

CHAPTER 4

The New Weapon
Geopolitics in Weimar Culture and Politics

Its development and rise is connected with the triumph of racial
thought; the racial and the geopolitical viewpoint of human community
in its temporal and spatial framework have the same sources and have
also risen out of the same preconditions, out of the preconditions of our
chaotically struggling present.

Otto Forst de Battaglia, 1932

In February of 1933, just one week after Adolf Hitler was named German
chancellor, Karl Haushofer remarked to a socialist acquaintance that the
Left would one day have to concede the geopolitical reality that Germany required greater living space. Regardless of political orientation, all
Germans would "have to come to the same compelling conviction from
the objectively accurate theory of geopolitics," Haushofer argued. "Precisely therein lies a demonstration of the impartially accurate utility of
scientific geopolitics."[1] Like much that Haushofer wrote, this statement
shrouded a grain of truth in distortions. There was, after all, precious little
objectivity to be found in geopolitical speculations about the role of geography in politics and history. But Haushofer was right to point out that
geopolitics had a nonpartisan utility, that its rhetorical pose as a science
lent it appeal to groups of quite varied political convictions. Because of
their spurious scientific credentials, geopolitical ideas made their way into
public debate about politics and foreign policy across a broad band of the
German political spectrum in the years preceding the rise of Nazism.
They thrived, of course, among the rightist organizations and intellectuals who dominated German radical conservatism during these years. Less

notice has been given, however, to the fact that geopolitics also played a significant role in the political discourse of moderate republicans and some leftist elements around the Sozialdemokratische Partei Deutschlands, or SPD (Social Democratic Party).[2]

The apparent explanatory power of geopolitical ideas, therefore, lent those ideas sufficient force to enable them to infiltrate the rhetoric of writers and activists across the Weimar political landscape. Far from being the exclusive concern of the far Right, geopolitical ideas about space, the state, and society were able to cut across the grain of the era's political discourse. Geopolitical language describing the organic nature of the state, the role of geographic setting, and the determining influence of geography on politics, social structure, ethnicity, and economics found adherents on the left and right and in the center as well during this period. Although always strongest on the right, geopolitics had a genuine if restricted influence elsewhere. Several factors may have contributed to this ability of geopolitics to gain a hearing throughout Weimar society. Whatever their political convictions, all Germans had in one form or another shared the shattering upheaval brought on by the war and its aftermath, and it may be that the resonance of geopolitics beyond the right derived from its attempt to address the sources of this harrowing shared tragedy. It could be as well that the resonance of geopolitics derived from the popular esteem enjoyed by science in these years. Despite Germany's international political weakness, German science retained enormous prestige, and Germans still took a justified pride in the achievements of the nation's scientists. Geopolitics may, thus, have gained legitimacy through its pose as an adjunct to the outstanding German tradition of scientific geography. Without question, the popularity of geopolitical ideas can only be understood in relation to the complex matrix of social and political forces that shaped Weimar culture and within which geopolitics was embedded. An understanding of the currency of geopolitical thought must, therefore, look to the relationship of geopolitics to other elements of Weimar culture.

Weimar Culture and the Allure of Geopolitics

Geopolitical language and ideas have thus far been discussed within the framework of a broad definition of the term *geopolitics* in its Weimar context. Theories that emphasized the determining influence of geographical factors upon international politics and the development of states, societies, racial groups, and individuals have all been characterized as "geopolitical." In the same way this consideration will focus on Weimar "culture" in a broad sense and the connections between this culture and geopolitical thought. Rather than examining the relationship of geopolitics to trends in the formal aspects of "high" culture (literature, music, the visual and plastic arts), the focus will be on its connection with other ideas that played important roles in the public discussion about society, politics, art, and the individual in Weimar Germany. What such an examination suggests is that the resonance of geopolitics derived in part from its links with elements of the "modernist" Weimar outlook. Geopolitical theorists boldly exploited their sudden popularity to outline a new concept of the nation for modern Germany, sidestepping divisive specifics of political organization to promote a vision of the German nation defined as an interactive unity of culture, race, and geography.

What were the attitudes and assumptions, then, that characterized Weimar modernism and in which geopolitical rhetoric and ideas were they embedded? Historical discussion of Weimar modernity emphasizes its heterogeneous, pluralistic, and often contradictory elements. Science and scientists were cast as the protagonists of a heroic quest for liberating knowledge, but the power of the will and the virtues of nonrationalism were equally exalted; modern capitalism and materialism were widely seen as the sources of German social fragmentation and cultural decline, but at the same time the technological products of capitalist industrialism—radio, aircraft, automobiles, cinema—were nowhere greeted more enthusiastically than in Germany; the new great cities were both exalted and vilified; the image of the sexually liberated new woman vied with traditional ideals of domestic, maternal womanhood.[3] These attitudes developed within the context of response to the political and social changes of the Weimar era, the economic uncertainty, widespread political violence, repudiation of traditional ideas of social order and gender roles, in short, to the crisis of German modernity that was ultimately resolved with force after the collapse of the German Republic. Within this context all the apparent contradictions of the cultural discourse assume such prominence that Detlev Peukert has argued they are, in fact, the key feature of Weimar as the twentieth-century archetype of modernism.

"Weimar attains classical modernity for our contemporary understanding," as Peukert puts it, "precisely in this multiplicity and contradictoriness."[4]

The effort to place geopolitics in the Weimar cultural brew is complicated by the difficulty of drawing clear political divisions based on attitudes toward various aspects of Weimar culture. As many historians have noted, it was and remains difficult to identify "reaction" and "progress" on the basis of ideas about German culture during this era, and the same applies to geopolitics. As a facet of Weimar intellectual culture it simply cannot be identified as the exclusive property of any single political faction.[5] It is by no means clear, furthermore, that those things viewed as progressive in the arts are necessarily linked to constructive or liberal political beliefs.[6] At the same time, many of those Weimar conservatives whose political views have been discredited since the Second World War delineated a critique of modern urban life that was at times perceptive and that was, in its admittedly critical response to the metropolis as one of the conditions of modern existence, itself a part of the modernist discourse. It may be more revealing of the sources of geopolitical appeal during the Weimar era, then, to focus initially upon the links between geopolitical rhetoric and the cultural discourse of which it was a part rather than upon the politics of specific geopoliticians. How did geopolitics, in other words, address German culture at the time? And how did it try to make sense of the world Germans faced during the Weimar era?

Geopolitics inserted itself into German public life, first and foremost, by attacking the Versailles peace settlement. Without Versailles, geopolitics would never have risen from obscurity. Germans of the time were divided, often violently, on many things, but they united in hatred of Versailles.[7] The goal of subverting or revising the treaty was a constant across the political spectrum, and this helped geopolitics break out of its potential confinement to the Right.[8] The geopolitical criticisms of the treaty—that its border arrangements violated the "natural" political geography of central Europe, that it unjustly excluded millions of Germans from their homeland, that the reparations settlement would destroy the economic cohesion of all Europe—were not significantly different from attacks launched on the treaty by other Germans, but as Haushofer and others argued, the geopolitical critique was scientific, presumably more objective than other critiques, and, thus, more credible to a diverse audience.[9]

Its congruence with the universal German judgment on Versailles, however, does not go very far in conveying the specific contours of the geopolitical appeal for the Weimar German imagination. Much more indicative of the geopolitical position in Weimar culture and revealing of the contradictions within geopolitical thought is the complex of geopolitical attitudes toward technology, rationalism, and the will. To the geopoliticians, technology was a promethean spark that would enable Germans to escape fate, to take control of the future, and to once again render space malleable. This perspective is also key to understanding why it is incorrect to see the geopoliticians as cultural pessimists, despite their attacks on Weimar civilization. German technological excellence, they argued, was the tool that would combine with German racial attributes to transform the significance of the Mittellage. Germany's centrality in Europe, previously a source of vulnerability, would be transformed by technology into an asset. Conversely, as a result of their geopolitical position and the historical effects of German geography on the German personality, the Germans were uniquely equipped to exploit technology without succumbing to soulless rationalist materialism. In combination with a rejuvenated German popular will the achievements of German technology would help them transcend dreary rationalism and redirect the forces inherent in the German Raum. Technology was the antidote to decline, the salvation from an otherwise ineluctable geographical fate.

This perception of technology was the geopolitical expression of a general German glorification of science in the period, which like geopolitics itself and many other elements of Weimar German cultural life predated the war in its origins. Novels such as Bernhard Kellermann's *Der Tunnel,* published in 1913, had glorified the feats of the modern engineer and depicted technology as the final guarantor of human triumph over nature.[10] The enthusiastic movie audiences of the Weimar Republic were regaled again and again with fantasies in which heroic German scientists and engineers exploited their superior technological acumen to thwart Germany's foes and often to acquire new lands.[11] In the art world the members of the *Werkbund* (crafts league) and Bauhaus movements and the followers of the Neue Sachlichkeit (New sobriety) busied themselves with the creation of a technological-functionalist aesthetic, believing they were helping to liberate the masses from drudgery. "Technology has sprung the gates of paradise," as one put it.[12] Geopolitical writers linked their theories to this current of German popular culture, glamorizing technology particularly through a close attention to aviation, the new significance of polar regions, radio, railways, ocean travel, and a new world economy.[13]

Geopoliticians coupled this technological appeal, paradoxically, with a simultaneous emphasis on the importance of nonrational factors that purportedly shaped technological progress. This geopolitical vision portrayed technology not only as an expression of human rationality but as an organic and nearly self-perpetuating outgrowth of the unique German character. Technology was a force of nature, a view expressed with laconic emphasis in 1927 by Max Krahmann in an essay under the lapidary title, "Kapital, Technik und Geopolitik" (Capital, technology, and geopolitics). "Technology wants to master nature. Technology is a continuation of nature in the spiritual, to which nature adapts itself. Technology is new creation or continuation of creation my man, by the ingenium, by the engineer. Technology is embodied capital, is tool, machine, explosive system, disciplined army, warship, press, routine, in short, means of power, new against old, human power against nature power, dominance over the earth, therefore—a powerful geopolitical factor." In the geopolitical concept of technology the power of this particular geopolitical factor influenced the meaning of geography and evolved continually with the advent of new technologies:

> "Politics is not the arbitrary behavior of individual men, groups, alliances or states," as has already been stated elsewhere in this journal, but "is decisively determined by the earth-space of a state with its natural resources, its flora, and its climate." Politics is the power deployment of stored capital of any type in the form of technology against resistant nature, including more natural, capital-deficient humanity without technology—for example, in the form of the ships of Columbus against America, or machine guns today against the rebellious Incas in Bolivia or future airplanes over South America to the fulfillment of the idea of the "engineer" Columbus.[14]

This is a chilling vision of technology focused in typical geopolitical fashion on struggle, violence, and domination. It also contains a paradoxical implication for geopolitics. Krahmann's picture of technology as a tool to master or dominate nature is conventional. More original and sinister is his depiction of technologically inferior groups of human beings as simply one aspect of "resistant nature," akin to rivers and mountains, the domination of whom is one of the accepted functions of technology. This view also represents a significant qualification of geodeterminism. Krahmann discusses the geopolitical view that the course of politics is geographically determined and then argues that this deterministic power of geography over politics may be refuted by the application of technology. Neither Krahmann nor most other geopoliticians explored this in any detail, however, because it threatens to undermine the frail logical structure supporting geographical determinism. If technology and culture offset the determining power of geography, after all, the effort to fabricate a nomothetic science of geopolitics such as that sought by the geopoliticians is doomed.

Geopoliticians were more interested in explaining the potential of technology for neutralizing the political and military liabilities of Germany's central position than in examining its implications for the logic of geodeterminism. They held high hopes that as technological change altered world politics it would also restore Germany to world power. Driven by the "technological achievements of the modern age," the world economy and world trade were gradually "breaking through geographic and linguistic borders of peoples" to create a "great living organism."[15] Western science, pioneered by the peoples of the Atlantic world and scientists from Kepler through Darwin, had restructured the globe. Thanks to its brilliant sons and "the great achievements of technology on the earth, through the seas, through the air, the West stands by this measure at the peak of human culture."[16] In the growing world organism "the German-speaking peoples are already directed by their geographical position in Mitteleuropa in a special way toward a balance between east and west."[17] New navigational and naval design technologies had revolutionized the role oceans played in politics; with the radio one could expect to see claims to sovereignty extended through hitherto open spaces by means of radio waves, with states laying claim to maritime broadcasting regions for the sake of their oceanic trade.[18]

Geopoliticians were astute in their assessment of the impact of new communications and media technology. The communications revolution, they were certain, was fraught with geopolitical significance. Historian Erich Maschke, a *Privatdozent,* or lecturer, at Königsberg, foresaw the unique propaganda potential of motion pictures, arguing in the pages of the *Zeitschrift für Geopolitik* that film as an art form was uniquely well adapted to portray the dynamic interrelation of "political will" and "natural spaces." He envisioned a film, to be entitled *Deutschland,* which would employ dramatic aerial shots to depict the German people filling the spaces of their borders to illustrate "the geopolitical demand for an organic formation of Germany's borders."[19] Arthur Dix used the term *the global village* as early as 1927, four decades before McLuhan, to describe the new intercontinental intimacy being created by communications technology and predicted that new technology would change the face of world politics.[20] "With the conquest of space through air travel and wireless news over the globe a new global age has dawned," Dix declared, a global age for which geopolitics would provide "the guidelines for world political objectives."[21]

Dix's words reflect the special role aviation technology played for the geopoliticians. They cherished a vision of flight as the key to transforming the significance of space for Germany. The crucial importance of aviation in the new world economy, they felt, created a special role for Germany, which "seems particularly suited in consequence of its central position" to take a leading role in implementing international air connections.[22] In a lengthy article entitled "Zur Geopolitik des Flugwesens" (On the geopolitics of aviation affairs) in the *Zeitschrift für Geopolitik* in 1930, Hans Hochholzer argued that Germany's world position and its internal geography accounted for its lead in the development of aviation. "German aviation today has two important roots: The general world position of Germany and the structure of its own economic regions. The world position inserts Germany between many large economic units. . . . Germany is the very state of Europe that conducts the most international lines over its territory. Germany's own economic regions are isolated from one another (e.g., in the valleys of the plain), and this as much as their separation by time-consuming mountain ranges is the chief cause of the vigorous German domestic air traffic." Hochholzer went on to write that "mastery of space is reduction of space" and that especially by changing the time between distances air travel was making the world spatially smaller. The pure technical advantages possessed by better airplanes accelerated this "spatial enclosure": "Airplanes possess a genuinely three-dimensional traffic space, and atmospheric hindrances can generally be flown around as well as be flown over. It is accurate to speak of a spatial reduction by air travel; the long-distance flight times show most emphatically that this analogy is correct. . . . The distance between western Europe and the west Sudan has become smaller 'chronologically', that is, relative-'spatially'."[23]

Hochholzer and other geopoliticians would have agreed wholeheartedly with the assessments of later historians who argued that aviation had "collapsed the vault of heaven," giving global political relations a new face.[24] The "conquest of space," as Dix called it, had softened geography, destroying the rigidity of topography and reducing the tendency of geography to isolate human populations. The outcome of this was to relativize the impact of geographical factors. Their significance now depended upon the forms of technology which the state could bring to bear upon them. Used properly, therefore, technology could transform the elements. It had changed the very essence of the atmosphere, for example, to which Weimar geopoliticians now began to refer as the "air ocean."[25] The analogy was well taken. Like the oceans, the atmosphere now served as a means for the exchange of goods and people via airships and airplanes, and of ideas via wireless. Germany was depicted as particularly fortunate to be in a position to exploit the new technology, and geopolitical writers again and again alluded to the advantages Germany's central location conferred, reminding Germans that even though they might lack access to maritime routes, the German state was, as one put it, "home harbor" to air vessels that ranged the world at will.[26] At the same time, they emphasized the military capabilities which aviation conferred on Germany's neighbors. By warning Germans that the diminished geographical dimensions of their postwar state made them open to enemy air power they added powerful security arguments to their demands for new land.[27] In this way both the opportunity and the vulnerability created by flight were put to service, creating a favorable domestic climate for revision of the peace settlement. For the geopoliticians, as for Germans generally, air technology opened broad vistas for fantasizing about the future, providing a "means of escaping from the confines of reality, a way of liberating the imagination."[28]

Nothing better demonstrates the geopolitical faith in the power of technology to transform geography than the geopolitical treatment of the poles. Romantic enthusiasm for polar exploration, spurred by polar zeppelin flights and the discoveries of the remains of the doomed André and Franklin expeditions, and by hopes of valuable mineral deposits as well, was a recurrent Weimar fad. Geopolitics linked itself to this polar interest, promoting a vision of the poles not as frozen and isolated wastes but as valuable virgin territory that would change the world political position of those able to use technology to exploit them. The lure of polar riches was provoking a new scramble for territory, geopoliticians argued, and

Germany's chances would worsen the longer it waited to begin asserting its place in the scramble for the poles.[29] "In short, the division of the
Arctic world, and probably soon the Antarctic as well, until now unruled
because disregarded as entirely worthless, is in full swing," wrote Richard
Hennig in 1928. "The wish to secure a favored position within the Arctic
air travel net is undoubtedly one of the chief motivating factors for this
surprising and unique tendency in the geopolitical picture of the present day."[30] Germans were exhorted to raise "their just claims" to those
areas first charted by German explorers such as Filchner and Drygalski in
the Antarctic.[31] Even more than the Arctic, the Antarctic was suspected of
concealing unimagined mineral wealth, and unless Germans took notice
of the implications of technological change it might be snatched from
under their noses. "The South Pole has become English on the quiet,"
warned Ludwig Quessel in the *Sozialistische Monatshefte.* "[British claims]
embrace most of the south polar regions researched 'till now and all access
routes to the Antarctic continent; they are rich in seals and whales, therefore capable of economic exploitation, and with the development of aviation are probably not without political significance for the future."[32]

Technology was thus extolled as a means of offsetting the liabilities of
German geography and of changing the political significance of space on
a global scale. Their professed affinity for the technological achievements
of modern science, however, confronted the geopoliticians with a philosophical dilemma. On the one hand, they were critical of the moral and
spiritual effects of modern industrial culture, particularly in their hostility to urbanization; on the other hand, they praised the material products of that culture as Germany's hope for the future.[33] Geopoliticians in
general attacked urban living as essentially unhealthy and un-German:
cities, they typically argued, fostered crime, moral decay, and infertility.[34]
This geopolitical antiurbanism and agrarian romanticism was strongly
influenced by Spengler's popularization of the organic view of states
(a view that geopolitics, of course, did a great deal to promulgate) and by
hostility to the rationalism of which cities were considered an expression.[35] Conservative geopoliticians looked for ways to separate the scientific, technological achievements they admired from the industrialized,
predominantly urban culture that produced them.

Geopolitical theorists circumvented the contradictions posed by their
hostility to the typically urban condition of modern life and simultaneously linked themselves with cultural trends of considerable potency

by emphasizing the role of the nonrational elements of race and will in German technological progress. In this way they implied that German technological prowess had no visceral link with the urban culture of Weimar Germany but was instead a product of deeper forces originating in geography. Arguing that Germany's geography had given the Germans racial qualities that allowed them to develop and use technology in a uniquely German way without sacrificing their German soul, geopolitical thinkers called upon Germans to realize those qualities with which they were imbued by Germanic geography and which were "bestowed by Germanic blood." Climate and topography had produced northern and southern Germans who complemented one another in ways that preserved the German soul from mechanization, according to Louis von Kohl:

> There predominate strength and manliness, here restlessness and variety. From this relationship grows the world mission of the German type because it makes it possible for the first time to make man and machine a living unity. It prevents the mechanization of the soul, the mass production of inconsequential people who are without individuality. It gives the era of the machine those higher ideals that prevent the decline of humanity. For a brief time the German Volk, of course, allowed itself to be confused by the madness of the machine era, but this illusion reached its fearful conclusion in the world war. Soon it will again recall itself to its type and become ripe to lead.[36]

Geopolitical belief in qualities that were at once inherent ("bestowed by Germanic blood") and yet a product of the influence of geography reflected a strand of racialism present in German geography that dated well into the nineteenth century and a pervasive racialism popular in the academic culture of Weimar Germany as well.[37] Both climate and geography, over the centuries, had bred into Germans a particular aptitude for technological endeavor, geopoliticians argued. The "cultural disposition of landscapes" of northern Europe generated the outstanding German technological achievement.[38] In this, as in all other aspects of geopolitical thought, struggle played a central role. Whereas peoples of the tropics were lulled into passivity by the natural abundance of their environment, the German character had been formed by its constant struggle with harsh surroundings so that Germans were "incomparably more deeply anchored in space and time" than peoples dwelling in more clement zones of the earth.[39] Because German racial qualities were specific to the German landscape ("The frequently heard comparison of the ancient Greeks with the Germans forces us to smile if we only throw a glance at the map and see how different from Greece is the structure and geography of Germany. To say nothing of racial qualities!"), urbanization was a danger that threatened to produce a politically dangerous debasement of the German nation.[40] "Today we are confronted with the fact," Albrecht Haushofer lamented, "that the broadest levels (of the population) are no longer intellectually capable of bearing the entirety of culture and civilization but by virtue of the right of democracy are entitled to decide its fate."[41]

The power of the will, German racial qualities, and German technology could reverse this cultural decay, rectify its temporarily weakened political position, and teach Germans how best to exploit their geographical position. Force of will and hereditary racial characteristics, however, were not considered to be subject to the dictates of reason. The geopolitical emphasis on such nonrational factors reflected a broader geopolitical skepticism about reaching truth through reason, a skepticism made all the more remarkable by geopolitical pretensions to wear the mantle of "science." All these elements in geopolitics—will, race, and faith in the power of nonrational qualities to guide action—represented links to other movements within Weimar society.[42] The belief in the importance of race, obviously, provided an entering wedge for geopolitical rhetoric to penetrate and eventually to find an important place in the conservative volkish movement.[43] The racial motif was often accompanied by an emphasis on "the great importance of the intellectual-spiritual attitude of a people. The will to self-assertion and to power is unconditionally *the* determining point for the rise or decline of a people."[44] All the faith in the transforming power of technology was qualified by the necessity for a strong will, and this, of course, had political ramifications, particularly in the call for a strong leader that was very popular with the geopoliticians.[45] Karl Haushofer liked to cite Rudolf Kjellén in arguing that "the great power is fundamentally a will, equipped with abundant tools of power. Great powers arise and pass precisely with their will to greatness."[46]

This is not simply to say, however, that certain aspects of geopolitical thought unconsciously reflected the influence of nonrationalism: There was instead a deliberate effort to incorporate the irrational in geopolitical thinking about the relationship between geography, humankind, and politics. German geographic science experienced a turn toward the impressionistic, the aesthetic, in this period, of which geopolitics was an essential part. In a different context Walter Benjamin has argued that fascism tended toward the aestheticization of politics by offering social groups new forms of expression about, rather than substantial changes in, property relationships.[47] Geopolitics in many ways revealed a similar tendency, over time, toward aestheticization of geography, offering images, impressions, and rhetorical forms of expression rather than substance in its analysis of the relationship between geography and politics. This aestheticization was especially clear in geopolitical cartography, much of which made little pretense to be any more than political propaganda rather than genuine cartography, but it was also evident in the increasing emphasis on nonrational thinking in geopolitics and geography.[48] The League of German University Teachers of Geography expressed this unambiguously in 1928 when they argued that good geographical education "does not depend in the first degree upon the formation of the reason by the communication of the most extensive possible knowledge in many subjects; the will must also be tempered, the sphere of emotion clarified, yes, even the irrational in man must be formed, because the harmonious personality can develop only from the collaboration of all these spiritual powers."[49]

At times the geopolitical conviction of the political significance of Germany's Mittellage between east and west could spill over from the geographical into the philosophical and result in attacks on both rationalism and "Russian" irrationalism. Hans Mühlestein, writing in the *Zeitschrift für Geopolitik,* argued that Nietzsche had shown Germans the way to a better future based on rebellion followed by a compromise between East and West. Nietzsche, he wrote, "embodied the rebellion—if also only the rebellion—of the autochthonous western soul against all Asiaticness (Jewishness, Christianity, Russianism) and against all Anglo-Americanism as well (John Stuart Mill, Spencer, Emerson, in short, common sense and democracy)." Germany had to follow the lead of Nietzsche ("the first German European of a new global age") in rebelling against the two dominant neighboring life philosophies, as befitted its central position, "if it wants to reshape the tragedy of its inner position between East and West to the greatest advantage."[50]

In a long discussion of the rationalization of modern economic life in the *Zeitschrift für Geopolitik,* for example, Colin Ross argued in 1930 that such rationalization had to be accompanied by "the realization that pure rationalism does not work, that man like the cosmos in which he stands is an irrational phenomenon . . . and that one must give full consideration to the irrational nature of man and his metaphysical requirements."[51] Ross characterized the irrational in man as closely connected with the religious impulse, which he explained correctly as a large part of the appeal behind the *Religionsersatz* of both fascism and bolshevism. The feeling that the age longed for a new religion appears repeatedly in geopolitical writing as when Heinrich Block argued that "our time is an epoch of dissolution. It recalls in many respects the collapse of the ancient and the age of the reformation and the renaissance. It is the longing for a new religion, which spills over into the social and the political."[52] This longing spilled over into the geographical as well. Here the gnostic pretensions of geopolitics were expressed in the effort to explain not only the apparent cruelty of the fates to Germany but the unseen forces shaping history, societies, and human beings as well. The search for new answers to replace obsolete or discredited ideas, which was such a large part of architecture, the visual arts, literature, and especially politics in the Weimar Republic, was reflected in the geographical sciences in the form of geopolitics.

Contemporary observers noted that geography reflected a general cultural trend toward the irrational in Weimar society. In an essay on geography written in 1925 for *Die Tat,* a conservative cultural magazine, Erich Günther recognized the shift toward the impressionistic, noting the significant role postwar geographers attributed to nonrational factors such as race and the will. Appearing under the title "Künstlerische Geographie" (Artistic geography), Günther's essay revealed a thorough familiarity with the geographical literature of the day, moving through discussions of the works of geopolitical writers, including Erich Obst, Wilhelm Volz, Friedrich Ratzel, and, the most important representative of the aesthetic impulse in Weimar geography, Ewald Banse.[53] He detailed the atomization of geographical studies by listing the sprawling branches of the field, including geophysics, climatology, and "racial and ethnographic geography."[54] Günther went on to argue that contemporary geography represented "not only a science but also not less than a science, but geography as a synthesis of science and art."[55] Günther here used the word *Kunst* in its sense as "art" rather than "craft" or "skill" and linked it to science in the attempt to describe what was happening to geography. This was a common motif of the geopoliticians, who frequently linked the two

terms, *Kunst* and *Wissenschaft* (science) in their efforts to describe geopolitical ideas. Hermann Lautensach, for example, one of the most influential German geographers of his day and one closely associated in the
early 1920s with geopolitics, could describe geopolitics as a *Kunstlehre,* a
"craft" or "skill doctrine."[56] In one of his earlier works, Karl Haushofer
had argued along similar lines that geopolitics represented "as much Kunst
as science, or at least a skilled craft."[57]

The most interesting and insightful contemporary examination of
the links between the nonrational elements of geopolitics and their place
in the broader culture of the period appeared in 1932 in *Europäische Gespräche,* the journal of the republican and pacifistic Institute for Foreign Policy in Hamburg, one of the many fascinating but ephemeral flora
spawned in the hothouse of Weimar political culture.[58] The author, the
Viennese intellectual Otto Forst de Battaglia, argued that geopolitics was
typical of its day in attempting to unite contradictory ideas drawn from
materialism and romanticism. He, too, recognized that it was tied in this
way to contemporary racialist thinking. "Unabashed materialism," Battaglia argued, was combined with the rise of "mysticism, of an irrational
world feeling" to create the "characteristic juxtaposition of ideas" of the
era. He cited Heidegger, Othmar Spann, and other thinkers as representative of this trend and concluded it was most visible in geopolitics, which
he said derived from history, political science, and geography.

> Its development and rise is connected with the triumphs of racial thought;
> the racial and the geopolitical viewpoint of human community in its tem-
> poral and spatial framework have the same sources and have also arisen out
> of the same preconditions, out of the preconditions of our chaotically
> struggling present. . . . We sense finally, most markedly, that geopolitics is
> a new, unfinished science. . . . This all signifies little next to the chief ob-
> jection that we will later pursue more closely: geopolitics claims to be the
> unique interpreter of facts, to whose understanding it indeed contributes
> much, which however must be discussed in a much broader framework
> than that which the youthfully impetuous new science has marked off.[59]

Battaglia's remarks here are revealing on a number of counts. First, his
insight into the links between the two forms of mystic thought, racialism
and geopolitics, is worth noting; his observation that the two derive from
common sources is accurate as is the implication that their currency in

Weimar culture springs from common roots.[60] The tone of the article is also interesting. Battaglia was writing a critical article in 1932 (at a time, therefore, of acute political crisis in Weimar society) for a republican, pacifist, and generally middle-of-the-road political journal, but he clearly believed that geopolitics as practiced in his day had a great deal to offer to an understanding of politics. He also pointed to a number of individuals whom he considered to be working in a geopolitical framework at the time, including, of course, Karl Haushofer, Hennig, Obst, Maull, and Lautensach (Battaglia calls them "the general staff of geopolitics") but also geographers and historians, including Hettner, Hassinger, Walther Vogel, Paul Herre, Albert Von Hoffmann, and others not ordinarily associated with geopolitics.[61] Finally, Battaglia suggested that geopolitics was ultimately weakened most by its claim to be a science along the lines of the so-called hard sciences endowed with a system of universally valid laws. If, instead, "geopolitics contented itself with 'furnishing equipment for political action', we would be grateful."[62]

As Battaglia accurately noted, the geopoliticians felt that the view of the state as a gigantic organism required them to provide a systematic framework for the prediction and analysis of changes in the structure of states. They expressed their nomothetic ambitions with a number of "laws" which purported to provide clear guidelines to the impact of geography on the state. The best-known example of such a law is the "Law of Expanding Spaces" first devised by Ratzel, who explained it briefly by arguing that "All state development proceeds under the law of progression from narrow to broad spaces."[63] This, of course, evokes an image of inevitable and eternal struggle for space between the state that is developing and those that happen to be in its sphere of "development." The popularity of such ideas among postwar German geopoliticians is not difficult to understand because it lent itself easily to making the domestic case for the revision of the peace treaties. If the state was not growing, it was obviously devolving, and this had to be considered a matter of life and death for all the members of the state. This law, which had close connections to Ratzel's ideas about Lebensraum, was used in conjunction with Germany's growing population to help make the case for the inevitability of Germany's renewed growth in Europe. This attempt to regularize the geopolitical analysis of state relations led to Haushofer's claim that politics was 25 percent geography, emphasizing what he liked to call the "one-quarter of scientific clarity in the mechanism of politics."[64] As with so many of their attempts to systematize the interaction of geography and political processes, the geopoliticians were here dogged by the fact that culture clearly influences politics and that states with sometimes similar geographical circumstances had differing political problems and histories. Consequently, they had recourse to transparent expedients such as the "Law of the Mutability of Connections between Nature and Man," an especially wooly geopolitical law designed to provide a way out of the culture/geography dilemma.[65]

It seems clear that the geopoliticians in their treatment of technological and racial questions were attempting to present a hopeful, optimistic vision of Germany's future by fashioning a definition of the state which was not cast in political terms but instead as a dynamic unity of culture and race shaped decisively by geography and animated by will. Such an image of the German nation not only furnished hope for an improved future but provided geographic, cultural, and ethnic foundations for a reassertion of German power in central Europe. The Germany of the geopoliticians was not a helpless one, fated to remain a "coolie nation with mutilated borders and completely insufficient living space" as Karl Haushofer depicted Germany's postwar condition.[66] If Germans only paid attention to the lessons that geopolitics could teach them, if they could learn to see their space as an active element and power-political ally, they could again attain "freedom and self-determination, sufficient breathing-space on the earth."[67] Like the Nazis after them, many geopoliticians displayed an ambivalent attitude toward modernity. In the hope of revitalizing Germany and revising the peace settlement they often combined enthusiasm for technological progress with political reaction and a brutal view of international relations.[68] The tactical acumen many geopoliticians displayed in avoiding any but the vaguest of discussions about what political form this reinvigorated and enlarged Germany would take, however, permitted them to expand the appeal of their ideas by evading the divisiveness this topic would inevitably raise.

Weimar Geopolitics, Right, Left, and Center

The political culture of the Weimar years, characterized as it was by fragmentation and instability, proved receptive to geopolitical spatial/political theories, to groups both to the right and left of the political center and among moderate democratic supporters of the Republic as well. On the left, a circle of Social Democrat colonial enthusiasts made extensive use of geopolitical rhetoric to argue their claims. In the center, committed supporters of Weimar democracy such as Ernst Jäckh and Adolf Grabowsky followed geopolitical tenets in their analysis of Republican foreign policy. The influence of geopolitical ideas on political theory was most evident during the Weimar years, however, as part of the radical conservative upheaval characterized variously as the new Right, the volkish movement, or the conservative revolution. To those radical conservatives influenced by the writings of Arthur Moeller van den Bruck, Othmar Spann, Edgar Julius Jung, and other conservative theorists, who agitated throughout the Weimar years for revision of Versailles in the name of the German *Volkstum* scattered throughout east-central Europe, geopolitics proved to be a propaganda weapon of enormous value.

It is sometimes argued that Weimar-era geopolitical revanchism was distinguished from racialist, or volkish, arguments for a reordering of central Europe by the primary emphasis in the former upon geography and the centrality of racial/biological considerations to the latter.[69] In an abstract sense this distinction is valid. Geopolitical thinkers in general explained postwar Germany's political and economic instabilities as consequences of the violation of geographical law in the peace settlement. A basic theoretical conflict, furthermore, exists between the Darwinian evolutionary environmentalism of geopolitics, with its focus on change, and the focus of racial or volkish theory on the permanence of blood and hereditary factors; logically, unchanging racial nature collides with environmental geographical nurture.[70] In practice, however, no conflict existed between the two until well into the Nazi era. Before 1933, the dictates of logical consistency notwithstanding, the rhetoric of radical nationalists harmonized geodeterminist environmentalism with racial theory. This successful resolution of two apparently incompatible concepts is particularly evident in the rhetoric and literature of Weimar Germany's nationalist and volkish groups.[71]

There were, in fact, good grounds for the popularity of geopolitics with volkish propagandists despite potential theoretical differences concerning the significance of race. The geopolitical blend of geographic and demographic rationalizations for German predominance in central Europe dovetailed nicely with already current ethnic and racial arguments, and they rapidly became a welcome addition to the propaganda arsenal of volkish writers. In the mouthpieces of the *Volkstum* movement—*Grenzdeutche Rundschau, Volk und Reich,* the *Süddeutsche Rund-schau,* propaganda sheets such as the *Grossdeutsche Blätter,* and others—the use of terms such as *Volkssterben,* "dying of the people" or "race," popular in geopolitical circles, was current throughout the era. Radical conservatives justified German expansion by blending a geopolitical sensibility with racial concerns to insist that "the population maintains itself or grows only where new land can be acquired under favorable conditions."[72] Conservative nationalists argued, as did many geopoliticians, that "the struggle for a healthy and numerous posterity is for us the struggle over Lebensraum. Again and again one sees that a central question of population policy is the creation and maintenance of a healthy peasantry, and the settlement question has rightly taken its place in the foreground."[73] In the final analysis, therefore, the struggle to preserve the race was a struggle to acquire space. In this fashion, through the common emphasis on struggle and expansion as prerequisites of national survival, the arguments of geopolitical revanchists were wedded with those of racially motivated German revanchists.

Conservative thinkers took care, however, to reject proposals to find the needed space within Germany through redistribution of the large estates in the east, a scheme discussed among some circles on the German Left. To geopolitical thinkers, these large landholdings were a "*Realpolitik* necessity."[74] Instead, they concentrated on exploiting geopolitical concepts to elaborate their own ethnic and biological arguments for a revision of borders eastward to create a German Mitteleuropa. As one observer has noted, "ethnically oriented border revisionism stood in immediate connection with geopolitics."[75] Volkish writers argued that "Raum and volk are the two poles" of state life, and they welcomed signs that the significance of race as well as space was beginning to impress itself upon the German people.[76] They hoped that a racial understanding of history would highlight "the symbiosis between earth and race from which arises every land's primeval essence" and which would help Germans "know [the land's] inner possibilities."[77] Geopolitical ideas could be a powerful instrument of persuasion for conservative thinkers who stressed the importance of German ethnic identity as Rudolf Pechel, editor of the influential *Deutsche Rundschau,* pointed out in an appreciation of Karl Haushofer's work on the occasion of the geopolitician's sixtieth birthday: "An intellectual student of Ratzel and Kjellén, whose teachings he took up and built upon with the strongest admixture of his own knowledge, he has become a catalyst in the grand manner for the science of Raum, geopolitics. His work, set down in many books, in a widely read journal, in lectures and addresses, leads Germans of our day to an indispensable realism. . . . He furnished a new weapon for the ethnic German armory by his consideration of the big picture."[78]

The "new weapon" to which Pechel referred, the geopolitical understanding of geographical space was potent indeed in the form in which racialist writers developed it. Geopolitical writers resolved the apparent conflict between volkish genetic racialism and the geographical environmentalism of geopolitics by combining the two. "The old concepts of nature and population have been displaced by the new concepts of landscape and ethnicity," argued one, "and between both, which appear to be linked to one another by climatically determined characteristics of the blood, a bridge begins to form which establishes a definite unity between landscape and volkhood."[79] The combination of biological views of the state with geographical determinism and volkish racism (expressed in phrases such as "climatically determined characteristics of the blood") produced a virulent rhetoric of a central European imperial mission among radical conservative writers quite early in the 1920s. Arguing that Germany was prevented by geography and ethnicity from expanding elsewhere, these geopolitically and racially influenced writers declared that only in the east were there no barriers to the acquisition of necessary Lebensraum. Freiherr von Gayl (accurately characterized by Gordon Craig as "a rather primitive *Junker* backwoodsman"), who would later serve as minister of the interior under Franz von Papen, did not hesitate to draw the most sinister conclusions from geopolitical and ethnographic "facts":[80]

> The German east is the foundation and object of German ethnic policy. The double task, therefore, is to maintain the German east and strengthen it in order to be able to use it as one of the essential pillars for a successful German ethnic policy. Toward the west and the south the German Volk ohne Raum is forever blocked off; over the sea only minor possibilities of activity exist; in the North we are closed in by blood-related German tribes. Only toward the east does the view for the German people remain free, only toward the east can it project its economic and cultural powers.[81]

Gayl's lack of sensitivity to the anxieties of Germany's Slavic neighbors is not surprising, but many more sophisticated theorists used very similar

ideas, if expressed differently, to voice German claims to the east. Geopolitical rhetoric was used to link race, culture, and Raum in arguments
for German predominance in central Europe by professional geographers,
geographic literati, including the likes of Ewald Banse, and sophisticated
conservative propagandists such as Martin Spahn and Edgar Julius Jung.[82]
Geopolitics bolstered their arguments that Germans beyond the borders
of the postwar German state were still part of Germany and entitled to
membership in the German polity. Such thinking broke with both prewar
geopolitical traditions and with the wartime Mitteleuropa theorizing
of Friedrich Naumann, whose vision was denounced for being merely
economic, hence materialistic, and thus lacking in those transcendent
elements that gave ethical justification to German claims.[83] Spahn, for
example, repeatedly attempted to define a German vision of *Grossdeutschland* and *Mitteleuropa,* which used the terms interchangeably and which
emphasized the role of geographic factors in melding German "racial characteristics." "What, therefore, does *Grossdeutsch* mean to us? The
combination of the German *Volk* and the central European *Raum* in the
Reich, hence, the sustenance of the yet unbroken growth-powers of our
Volk so that we can again renew the natural link with its root soil. At the
same time, it denotes careful work toward preserving its uniqueness, and
struggle for the foundation of a living community between this Volk and
the other populations of Mitteleuropa."[84]

Here as elsewhere, Spahn characterized the links between the German
space, its inhabitants, and the geographical location of Germany in the
center of Europe in organic terms. The "roots" of the "growth-power"
of the Germans depend on a "natural" connection with its territory,
which includes regions outside the political bounds of the German state.
Spahn, Gayl, and others who employed geopolitical ideas felt that Germany needed land and that geography and race dictated that it be found
in the east where the organic relationship developed over centuries between German settlers and their Raum bestowed paramount rights in the
region upon the German people. The supposed effect of landscape and
geography on the development of racial or ethnic characteristics is treated
below in the discussion of the writings of Ewald Banse, but Spahn's
geopolitical views on this issue were typical. "The historical development
of every Volk, its emergence, fulfills itself by the manner in which it
roots itself ever more firmly in its terrain, grows with its terrain and takes
it into its disposition. The Boden works reciprocally upon the Volk and
forms itself with it. The state creates the law, oversees the conditions,

orders the connections under which the process of the growing together of Volk and Raum is carried out."[85]

This emphasis on the connections of the German volk with its Boden and the German position in the plains of north-central Europe led to a geopolitical vision of a Germany whose borders stretched along axes from the North Sea to the Black Sea and from the Baltic to the Alps.[86] According to the geographer M. Friedrichsen in the *Zeitschrift für Geopolitik,* these were the borders that best reflected "the laws of 'natural' landscape definition apart from all politics and under purely scientific viewpoints."[87] This view did not strike other writers as far-fetched. As early as 1923 Arthur Dix had pointed out what he called "the naturally bestowed economic unity" of this region, and conservative racialist theorists echoed this view. "German borders in the west have hardened themselves in the thousand years of German history that lie behind us," wrote one. "Yet the lands between the Baltic and the Black Sea form a great unity. . . . The growth and historical development of the German people has left German settlements throughout this entire region. This has created an indigenous power source for an all-German political will."[88]

This assessment of the consequences of Germany's position in the center of the continent was common currency among geopolitical writers, who liked to dwell on the fact that Germany bordered more states than any other nation in Europe. The implications of this fact for German foreign and domestic policy were clear, they felt, because "only a powerful foreign policy, supported by a unified domestic political will, can offset the disadvantages of the central position. For the central position of the German Reich the words of Friedrich Ratzel still apply: 'Germany exists only if it is strong'!"[89] Geopoliticians rarely reflected upon the fact that states such as Poland and Switzerland had histories very different from that of Germany, despite a similar central position.[90]

The links between radical conservatives, volkish groups, geographers, and geopolitics were extremely close during this period. Karl Haushofer in the mid-1920s distinguished a geopolitical "school" of ethnic geographers who used geopolitical methods to ensure "the maintenance of the threatened *Volks- und Kulturboden* (Ethnic and cultural soil) through the means of comprehensive scientific penetration."[91] He singled out Robert Sieger, Albrecht Penck, one of the towering figures of modern geographical science, and Wilhelm Volz as the most prominent members of this school and with good reason. All were active in using geographic and

geopolitical arguments in support of the revisionist aims of the movement to unite all ethnic Germans in central Europe. Volz, for instance,
had been instrumental in founding a Central Office for Middle European Questions (*Mittelstelle für zwischen-europäische Fragen*) in 1922, which
was intended to promote "the intimate cooperation of all scientists active in ethnic politics, that is, in the area of the care of Germandom
domestically, and in border and foreign lands."[92] Volz was the group's
first chairman, but, despite his considerable exertions, it never developed into a particularly productive or active center. Other conservative revanchist groups with an ethnic orientation, such as *Verein für das
Deutschtum im Ausland* (League for Germandom Abroad) did much more
to integrate various strands of contemporary science with the geopolitical
movement, especially at German universities.[93] The links between geopolitical and volkish thought were manifested especially clearly in two other
conservative propagandizing groups, however, the *Deutscher Schutzbund*
(German Protective League or DSB) and the *Arbeitsgemeinschaft deutscher
Zeitschriften für die Interesse des Grenz- und Auslandsdeutschtums* (Workgroup
of German Journals for the Interests of Border and Foreign Germandom [ADZ]).

The German Protective League was founded in 1919 out of a number
of smaller groups interested in preserving the sense of German nationality among ethnic Germans in the lands Germany forfeited in the Treaty
of Versailles.[94] It grew into an umbrella organization for more than 120
conservative ethnic organizations, becoming in the process the "intellectual center" of the volkish movement in the period.[95] The DSB was
headed by Karl Christian von Loesch, a Privatdozent from Silesia, and,
with the financial support of both the Reich Ministry of the Interior and
the Foreign Office, ran its own publishing house, through which it propa-
gandized on behalf of border revision and German expansion throughout
the era.[96] League activities were wide-ranging and effective and displayed
a shrewd appreciation of the value pseudoscientific geopolitical arguments
held for revanchist propaganda. Under the League's auspices, for example,
Albrecht Penck produced his famous "Map of the German Volks- und
Kulturboden," which was drawn by the geopolitical cartographer A. Hillen
Ziegfeld and published by the DSB in 1925 in a collection of volkish
essays entitled *Volk unter Völkern. Bücher des Deutschtums.*[97] (See fig. 1.)

The map discarded the traditional reliance upon language as the hall-
mark of cultural paramountcy, using instead agricultural methods, house

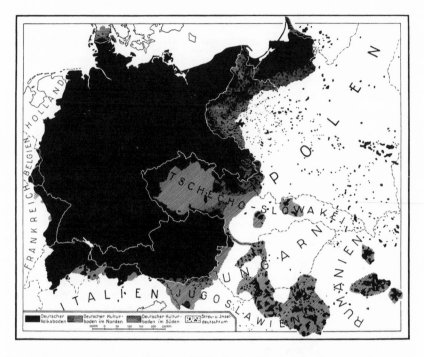

Fig. 1. *Karte des deutschen Volks- und Kulturboden* (Map of the German ethnic and cultural soil), from *Volk unter Völkern*, ed. K. C. v. Loesch and A. H. Ziegfeld (Breslau: F. Hirt, 1925).

design, techniques of forest management, language, and a range of other criteria to trace the spread of German cultural influence. The concept of the *Kulturboden*, or cultural soil, judged by this broad and often nebulous range of criteria, proved to be a very useful pseudoscientific political concept. Penck's creation gave scientific legitimacy to arguments that even regions of central Europe where German was not the dominant tongue, Bohemia for example, were areas of Germanic culture, making a case for German preeminence far into eastern Europe. Penck used it to persuade his readers that Germany's cultural soil, although clearly defined in south and west, stretched indefinitely into the east as far as central Russia.[98] While Penck was careful to point out that this resulted as much from human activity as from geographically determined factors, the map soon began appearing in German geography texts as an illustration of the effect of geopolitical forces on both the dissemination of German culture and on central European politics.[99]

The DSB also served as an important nexus, linking geopoliticians and geographers with volkish theorists and propagandists. Both *Volk unter Völkern* and its companion volume published the following year, *Staat und Volkstum,* featured articles by Karl Haushofer, Penck, Ziegfeld, the geographer Oswald Muris, and the borderlands scholar and sociologist Max Hildebert Boehm.[100] The meetings of the DSB brought together publicists, geopoliticians, colonial activists, and volkish thinkers including Boehm, Pechel, the colonial activist Heinrich Schnee, politicians including von Gayl, and many others.[101] And geopolitical concerns had an unquestionable influence on the rhetoric with which the DSB defined its volkish mission and its aims in central Europe. The league described its most important goal, for example, as the creation of a "new order of states" in the "chief tremor zone" of Europe; "the core district of the European new order is the zone of ethnic mixture between the east border of the German settlement area and the west border of the Russian."[102] This, league officials argued, would incorporate the border Germans into "the entire German organism" and provide "the middle European economic space necessary to self-sufficiency" for Germany, for which they would prepare by "regular political investigation of the situation (geopolitically)."[103] The DSB also adopted a geopolitical approach to the population question, arguing that the fertility of German women was falling as a response to lack of space and publishing the geopolitical demographic works of Friedrich Burgdörfer to popularize this view.[104] Karl Haushofer also helped convey the geopolitical perspective on racial issues to the members of the DSB, sitting as a member of its Border German Committee and addressing the annual conventions of the DSB on topics such as "The Significance of the Southern Border Zone for German Ethnic Activity."[105]

The links between the DSB and geopolitics in these years were put to good propaganda use on behalf of conservative politics through the ADZ, Workgroup of German Journals, the brainchild of the conservative journalist Pechel. He sat on the governing committee of the DSB, and his prestigious and widely read magazine functioned during these years as the league's house organ.[106] Pechel proposed the formation of the ADZ in June 1921 with the aim of orchestrating a clandestine propaganda campaign that would present the appearance of a spontaneous expression of public enthusiasm for border revision and the unification of ethnic Germans.[107] The ADZ, sponsored by heavy government subventions, proved quite successful in its aims, and geopolitics was an integral part of its propagandistic arsenal. Pechel told Haushofer he hoped the "geopolitical impulse could be deployed in the field" on behalf of the revisionist cause, and Haushofer responded by publishing geopolitical revanchist articles in magazines such as *Die Grenzboten* at the suggestion of the ADZ.[108] At the biannual meetings of the ADZ, where as many as fifty-nine journals were represented, geopolitical enthusiasts including Karl Haushofer, Albrecht Penck, the geopolitical publisher Kurt Vowinckel, the geopolitical historian Walther Vogel and Adolf Grabowsky, editor of the *Zeitschrift für Politik,* mingled with radical conservatives and racialist activists such as Martin Spahn, Pechel, Johann Wilhelm Mannhardt, Gottfried Traub, and editors of magazines from a broad range of fields.[109] Other geopolitical geographers and theorists who were members of the ADZ included Arthur Dix, Wilhelm Volz, Hugo Hassinger, Norbert Krebs, and Robert Sieger.[110]

While geopolitical ideas were, thus, finding an enthusiastic and well-organized audience on the nationalist and revisionist right in these years, pro-republican centrist and leftist writers were also pursuing the implications of their own encounters with geopolitics. Although geopolitical thought never attained an influence on the Left comparable to that it achieved on the Right, it was far from unnoticed. The most important examples of geopolitical influence on the Left were its use by the circle of moderate Social Democrats around the *Sozialistische Monatshefte* and the attempt of the Social Democrat Georg Graf to use geopolitics as a complement to Marxist historical materialism. Even the most famous Marxist rebuttal of geopolitical ideas from the period, however, that penned by Karl Wittfogel, betrays a significant admixture of geopolitical theory.

At its worst, Weimar geopolitics appears as an often vague and sometimes self-contradictory theoretical grab bag, whose appeal to Marxists may at first seem surprising. There are, however, a number of logical points of affinity between the geopolitical and Marxist worldviews. Both, for example, were based in materialism and determinism. Both donned the mantle of "scientific" truth and both attempted to justify their policy proscriptions by promising a better future. Like Marxism, geopolitics purported to reveal the forces that propelled historical change and that remained concealed from the uninitiated or uneducated. Important differences in perspective of course remain, but the epistemological similarities between the two are sufficiently pronounced to suggest that the more important question may be not why some Marxists incorporated geopolitical thought in their work, but why more failed to be attracted to the geopolitical point of view. The strain of mystic nonrationalism evident in geopolitics may have repelled many Marxists, and, as Wittfogel complained in 1929, geopolitics paid too little attention to the economic factors that mediate the relationship between state and soil to satisfy Marxists.

For a circle of socialist thinkers around the *Sozialistische Monat-shefte (SoM)*, however, geopolitics exercised considerable attraction in these years. Founded by Joseph Bloch in 1895, the *SoM* became during the Weimar era the organ of a group of moderate SPD Reichstag deputies.[111] To these writers and politicians the adoption of geopolitical ideas was entirely consistent with the effort to reach a scientific understanding of human society:

> The combination of two sciences, anthropology and geography, within the framework of a socialistic concept of the world leads us to evaluate the results of both sciences socially as this has already occurred, in part, in geopolitics. . . . All results of these sciences of the physical and intellectual-spiritual constitution of human groups and their forms of expression are now to be set in connection with the soil on which these groups live and to the climate that acts upon this soil. The facts to which geographic and climatological science introduce us are of the highest significance for the understanding of the social manifestations of human groups.[112]

No writer in the *Zeitschrift für Geopolitik* could have put it better. Some of the goals in whose service geopolitical rhetoric was used by the *SoM*, furthermore, were distinctly similar to its uses on the right. They argued, as did many geopoliticians, that geography had made Africa the logical spatial and economic complement to Germany and Europe and that Europeans had to turn their attention to united exploitation of that continent.[113]

Geopolitics influenced the approach of the *SoM* to other contemporary issues as well. The favorite foreign policy motif of the *SoM*, which was justified with reference to the geographic imperatives of Germany's continental position, was the call for a peaceful extension of Franco-German hegemony over the continent.[114] Apart from the cooperation with France, abhorrent to conservative geopolitical enthusiasts, this program was quite similar to the geopolitical foreign policy espoused by many rightists. While expressing little interest in eastern Europe, socialist geopolitics argued, as did the geopolitics of conservative revisionists, that the postwar *Kleinstaaterei* (particularism) was a curse to Europe and, in common with conservatives, it distinguished England as the chief foe of German ambition. The Young Plan, for example, was depicted as a "work, which was created by and for the Anglo-Saxons, against Germany and against Europe."[115] Except that they lack the acid bitterness of conservative revisionists, these sentiments mirror many of those expressed in the *Zeitschrift für Geopolitik* regarding adjustment of the German reparations payment plan.[116] Even more indicative of the geopolitical tone of the *SoM* was its analysis of the decline in the birthrate, which was attributed to a lack of space precisely as was done by many rightist geopoliticians. Like the geopolitical right, writers for the *SoM* blamed urban living for the "catastrophic decline in the birthrate" and advocated the acquisition of space in colonies and settlement on eastern estates to offset the drop. Indeed, these moderate socialists evinced a cold-blooded utilitarianism concerning population questions whose brutality equaled anything found on the geopolitical right in these years, endorsing legalized euthanasia, eugenic measures to control "population quality," and other forcible and voluntary population control measures, which "can counter the unrestricted increase of the socially undesirable."[117]

The thinkers around the *Sozialistische Monatshefte* were not alone on the left in arguing that the truths of geopolitics could aid the rise to power of the working class. In 1924, for example, the Social Democrat Georg Engelbert Graf argued in an essay entitled "Geographie und materialistische Geschichtsauffassung" (Geography and the materialistic conception of history) that Marx had consistently ignored the enormous impact of geography on historical processes. Graf's essay, published as part of a *Festschrift* (commemorative volume) dedicated to Karl Kautsky, argued that by omitting geographical factors from its calculations the Left deprived itself of a powerful tool in the acquisition and wielding of power. "It is precisely the proletariat as a rising class that has an interest in geopolitical thought and geopolitical education," Graf insisted, "because the rise of a class takes its course to political power through conquest. And political power will always be faced with the resolution of geopolitical problems. An education for democracy must, therefore, also be an education to geopolitical thought."[118]

Graf remained loyal to the chief precepts of orthodox Marxism ("The mother soil of history is the society in the Marxist sense, the economic society"), but he linked these to geographic determinism. The *economic society,* as Graf described it, was "necessarily rooted in the material," which he defined as geographical conditions.[119] These had to be the subjects of research and teaching in order to prevent "illusionary claims to power" and to combat exaggerated nationalism by revealing the interdependence of working classes around the world. The proper "geographic conception of space," therefore, would serve to promote peace and worker solidarity.[120] Although Graf's attempt to win converts for geopolitics on the Weimar left was not notably successful, it is extremely interesting both in its own right and for the response it provoked. Graf saw what he believed to be logical connections between Marxist historical determinism and the similarly reductive historical determinism practiced by some geopolitical thinkers. And his account of Marx's shortcomings provoked a famous response from Karl Wittfogel who, in attacking geopolitics and defending Marxism, actually tried to co-opt many geopolitical ideas for the Weimar left.

Wittfogel, whose post–World War II opus *Oriental Despotism* became the subject of intense controversy among geographers, was in the 1920s and 1930s "a typical and prolific Marxist intellectual of the Weimar Republic."[121] His response to Graf was published in 1929 as "Geopolitik, geographischer Materialismus und Marxismus" (Geopolitics, geographic materialism and Marxism) in a scholarly organ of the German Communist Party, *Unter dem Banner des Marxismus.* Wittfogel harshly attacked geopolitics in its Weimar form. Geopolitics, he claimed, ignored societal conflict of interests, and he correctly pointed out that it accorded far too much importance to formal criteria of state size, position, and border structure. He concluded his analysis by arguing that "we believe our work has created clarity over the worthlessness of the geopolitical method."[122] At the same time, however, Wittfogel paid tribute to what he clearly felt to be the truth of some key geopolitical propositions. He argued, for example, that Marxists had always believed what geopoliticians now taught as a new science, that geographic factors were determinant for the form taken by the society that was occupying a particular space. "We must never forget (lest we repeat the mistake, only with a reversed pattern, of the intuitive materialists censured by Marx), that all human social activity is bound to a specific material substratum, in the last analysis to 'nature,' the character of which determines the direction of human labor activity, if the society progresses, whether upward or downward, that is, to lower or higher forms of productivity of human labor."[123]

This view is not all that distant from Graf's, the object of Wittfogel's scorn. Like Graf and geopoliticians from more remote political regions, Wittfogel argued that the dependency of society upon the natural setting, although mediated by economic systems and forms of production, was a real dependency nonetheless. "The dependency upon conditions of nature takes on an ever more mediated character, but the dependency itself remains."[124] Although such a view reflects geographical determinism only in the broadest sense, the organic idea of the state and the emphasis on the creative power of geographic space characteristic of geopolitical rhetoric had found its way into the worldview of this orthodox Marxist geographer. This view was reflected in tones reminiscent of Otto Maull, for example, in Wittfogel's argument that geographical spaces and structures "call political life forms into life."[125] The heresy implicit in Wittfogel's defense of Marx was not lost on the vigilant German communist clerisy of his day, who anathematized his work for its unorthodox contention that geography matters in the social sciences.[126]

The characteristic attributes of German geopolitical thought during the Weimar era may be broadly summarized as follows. Geopolitical doctrine depicted states, societies, and even individual personality characteristics as the direct or indirect products of geographical conditions. It emphasized a crude Darwinistic faith in natural selection through struggle, and it applied this faith particularly to relations between states. Germany had to have space to expand, either overseas or in the east, or face insurmountable problems, including a gradual decline in population. To attain this expansion the Versailles agreements had to be revised. Geographic and racial factors mandated German preeminence in a very broadly defined central Europe. Modern German culture and society as manifested in the Weimar regime were, on the whole, bad, whereas technology, will, and the German soul were good and could serve as antidotes to the former evils. Society faced a crisis and was in decline, but timely perception of the geopolitical realities facing Germany coupled with grim resolve to act upon these realities could yet avert the otherwise inexorable and tragic decay of the German volk.

Culturally, some of these geopolitical attitudes are clearly part of the stream of thought of the period generally perceived as "modern," including the geopolitical exaltation of technology, faith in science, and Darwinian "scientific" racism. Other characteristics are clearly part of a grouping of ideas identified with reaction and hostility to modernism, for example, the view that cities are evil or, at least, have evil consequences for individuals and nations. Detlev Peukert and Marshall Berman, for example, both suggest that the metropolis is the modern experience par excellence, and it could be concluded that geopolitical hostility to this experience is by definition "antimodern."[127] One of the conclusions to be drawn from this examination of geopolitical themes, however, is to suggest that geopolitical ideas were less reactionary and antimodern than is ordinarily believed, in fact, that they could have arisen only within a "modern" society. Furthermore, they were clearly embraced by many who were sympathetic to the Republic of Weimar, Adolf Grabowsky, for example. As a manifestation of a response to modernity, geopolitical ambivalence about Weimar society should, perhaps, be considered one aspect of modernism even though it often expressed opposition to the trend of modern life.[128] These remarks are intended heuristically, however, and not as a definitive judgment on the distinctions between "modern" and "antimodern." They do attempt to reposition geopolitics and to modify the traditional view that it was a reactionary element of right-wing, antimodern Weimar thought by showing its affinities with other modernist currents in Weimar culture and by questioning traditional concepts of modernism and antimodernism. A brief examination of several writers who used geopolitical ideas illustrates the diversity, cultural function, and political characteristics of geopolitical thought in this period.

CHAPTER 5

The Geopolitical Minimum

Seven Case Studies

To return to a normal existence, to work and to eat, that was now the
wish of most Germans. But how they would work and eat and live, how
the young would grow, the old live and die, depended only in part upon
themselves; it depended too upon the public destiny, German politics,
and world politics. There were also restless spirits who found the chief
goal of their lives not in their own development but awaited fulfillment
from the state in the realization of beautiful or wild dreams. There are
always such spirits. In quiet times they remain constrained and unheard;
in unquiet, they find a place.

> Golo Mann, *Deutsche Geschichte des 19. und 20. Jahrhunderts*

The Weimar Republic was home to more than its share of such "restless spirits," and many of them found in geopolitics a theoretical focal
point in the public debate about the future of Germany and Europe.
Writers working in a variety of disciplines helped disseminate geopolitical
terms and concepts while using geopolitics to frame their own visions
of German recovery. Professional geographers were particularly likely
to be drawn to geopolitics, of course, but historians, jurists, journalists,
statisticians, and political scientists also discovered applications for the new
science. These writers often disagreed about important political issues and
in their judgments on how geopolitical insights ought to be applied in the
arena of practical politics. Despite their differences, however, all shared a
geodeterministic understanding of historical, political, and social change.
To a greater or lesser degree they all believed that a nation's cultural and
"racial" characteristics were contingent upon the geographical form of
the Lebensraum.

This broad commitment to incorporating geographical and spatial factors into various fields drove an impulse toward interdisciplinary integration that characterized much geopolitical writing.[1] The men whose ideas are examined here and scores of others like them constituted an informal geopolitical movement, the unarticulated aim of which was to make geopolitical understanding of politics, state development, and state relations an integral part of the Weimar political discourse. To that end these writers exploited the German media, higher education, and links to German popular culture to sensitize Germans to the geopolitical forces shaping their national destiny. Geodeterminism, however modified, provided a sort of geographic lowest common denominator, a geopolitical minimum, which united geopolitical writers of otherwise disparate interests and beliefs. Driven by a faith in the power of geopolitical ideas, these writers explored the importance of geographic factors in the life of the German nation. They believed that poor geopolitical judgment, combined with the unjust peace settlement, had robbed Germany of its political autonomy and, hence, of its international importance. Once propagated through education and the media, they felt that geopolitical ideas would mobilize German society so that it might reassert its control over Germany's destiny, control that had been lost with the war. The features of this shared geodetermist faith are most clearly revealed through a brief but detailed investigation of the use of geopolitics in the works of a number of representative geopolitical writers.

Ewald Banse, Geopolitics and "Expressionist Geography"

Ewald Banse's writings ordinarily play only a small role in studies of Weimar geopolitics.[2] At first glance, the reasons for this seem fairly obvious. Although he was extremely prolific, publishing more than one dozen geographical books and pamphlets and literally scores of articles between 1924 and 1933, Banse did not publish in the *Zeitschrift für Geopolitik* during this time, and he was never identified with the relatively small coterie of hard-core geopolitical propagandists who made geopolitics a household word in the era. Nor was his work concerned with politics for most of the period, which may also have encouraged his omission from the literature on geopolitics, which tends to focus on international relations and the geopolitical approach to foreign policy. Instead, Banse devoted himself to what he termed *gestaltende Geographie* (formative or developmental geography) and *Länderkunde,* or "regional geography." Banse's admirers and detractors sometimes used the term *aesthetic geography* as well to describe his mix of popular anthropology, psychology, and impressionistic description of landscape and topography. Given the political emphasis of most studies of geopolitical thought, therefore, Banse's relegation to second rank is understandable. His works deserve closer consideration for several reasons, however. Banse's writings were widely known and provocative in geographic circles at the time. His voluminous and popular travel writings, infused with geodeterminism and frequent use of geopolitical terms and ideas, helped popularize geopolitics with segments of the Weimar public who were removed from academic geography. And his fusion of impressionistic, mystical, and irrational elements with geopolitics makes him an outstanding representative of the links between geopolitical thought and broader Weimar cultural trends.

Banse was born in Braunschweig in 1883 and as a young man studied geography, zoology, and other subjects at Berlin and Halle. He pursued a doctorate in geography for a few years at Halle, but he was a dreamy student (he later wrote that he could never sit through an entire lecture without his thoughts drifting out the window) who was dissatisfied with what he regarded as the sterility of conventional geography, and he left Halle in 1906 with his dissertation unfinished.[3] He spent the next several years writing and traveling widely, especially in the Middle East and North Africa, and supported himself and his wife through his writing and with the help of his parents.[4] His prewar publications were mostly travel writings about Turkey, Libya, and other "oriental" areas, which appeared in geographic journals and books. He also contributed to works such as the *Enzyklopädie des Islam,* which appeared in 1913. These writings were often highly subjective and lyrical, already demonstrating traces of what he would later attempt to systematize programmatically as *seelische Geographie,* or "spiritual geography."

After the war Banse began to describe his idiosyncratic brand of geographical writing as "milieu portrayal" and argued that it was, in fact, "nothing other than expressionism."[5] By this Banse meant the mingling of *Wissenschaft* and *Kunst,* a juxtaposition of terms later to become a familiar part of the rhetorical repertoire of geopolitics, which would allow geography "to consolidate by means of art, in essential images, the multiple forms of reality, by which it illuminates the hidden side of things."[6] This statement, from Banse's 1920 work *Expressionismus und Geographie,* captures an important recurring theme of geopolitical thought in Weimar Germany, that is, the belief that uncovering hidden geographical forces was the key to understanding political and social structures and the processes by which they changed. The statesman, politician, or even the ordinary individual who acted in ignorance of these forces moved in a perilous blindness. For Banse himself the conviction that these hidden forces could be uncovered by interpreting geography though the mediating influence of artistic sensibility would henceforth play a determining role in his geographical thought.

Exactly what Banse meant by this emphasis on the mediating role of artistic sensibility became clear in his writings over the course of the following decade. His approach to geography was outlined in greater detail in his book *Landschaft und Seele. Neue Wege der Untersuchung und Gestaltung* (Landscape and soul: New methods of investigation and development), published in 1928. Here he reiterated his earlier arguments for a melding of Wissenschaft und Kunst in order to obtain a true understanding of the human significance of geography. "This concerns the question; do the means of science (analytical investigation and description) suffice to portray a region, or must the weapons of art (intuition, synoptic presentation, configuration) be taken in help to let a land come alive?"[7] For Banse this was clearly a case of a new geographic paradigm challenging a moribund geographic orthodoxy as he made clear with a return to organic imagery: "The old geography jumped around a region like the anatomist with a cadaver, who cuts right through with abandon—the patient feels nothing any longer! The new geography works on a living body; it investigates not just the tissue but also its activity and emotional life."[8]

The application of art and science to the understanding of topography would culminate in "developmental geography" and unify knowledge of geographic form and its impact on human spiritual development.[9] Development in this sense "aims at unity," Banse argued, "imparts perspective, indicates the sense that stands behind the scenes, the soul."[10] He was convinced, as were other geopoliticians, that geography exercised a decisive formative role in shaping human character. In this sense he declared that typical cloud formations, for example, have an effect on the development of national character (the precise nature of which he never explained, presumably because of the inherent futility of the endeavor), and he urged readers to observe "the sharply delineated, mythical beast-like, concentrated cloud armies" of the German coastal regions and to

compare these with the "characterless heaps of clouds of the German interior, which wander aimlessly about."[11] Topographical features such as
steppes, deserts, and mountainous wastes produced "dread and loneliness"
in their inhabitants, whereas in the absence of a distinct horizon at sea or
under the influence of visual distortions created by hot air in deserts "we
become insecure, and we lose hold of our entire concept of nature."[12]
As did geopoliticians in general in the era, Banse distrusted the modern
city. Products of humans in the country (bridges, lone castles, etc.) might
become organic components of the landscape, and old cities that had developed over centuries, growing organically, adorned the landscape like
precious stones. No city that had grown since 1860, however, could be
considered an organic part of the local geography because the modern
city "no longer 'sits' in the landscape of which it is a part but prowls
around in it."[13]

It is difficult when reading such passages to escape the sense of
watching Sisyphus at work; what Banse was getting at kept slipping out
from beneath his analysis and description. No doubt geographical factors
profoundly influence the form and progress of human activity, but the
relationship between the two is far too complex and amorphous to be
captured by the glib generalizations and simplistic "laws" of Banse and
other geopoliticians. Banse's faith that applying the proper method would
enable scholars to reify the intangible was a common operating assump-
tion among geopoliticians. Their belief that the effects of geography on
the course of political processes could be precisely defined is mirrored in
Banse's belief that the application of "formative" methods to the analysis
of geography would reveal the "spiritual climate" created by a particular
environment.[14] This and his geodeterministic view of character and social
development constitute fundamental conceptual links between Banse and
geopolitics. He exhibited as well a typical geopolitical racialism, arguing that geography played a decisive role in the formation of typical
"racial characteristics." The "Mongol race," for example, as a result of
the contrasting climatic and topographic extremes of its homeland, could
adapt itself to nearly any region of the globe—not so the European, who
required a climate like that of northwest Europe. As for Africans, Banse
wrote, "their physique and intellect stand closest to the animals, their
pigment- and sebum-rich skin make them less sensitive than the other
two races to high temperatures and humidity—in short, [they are] the

expression of a nature that overpowers man and allows him to live only as a shy and powerless beast among beasts."[15] This view contrasts interestingly with the "overabundant nature" view held by Hugo Hassinger and other environmentalist geographers and geopoliticians, who argued from precisely the opposite starting point to the same conclusion. Although they argued that the environment was too kind to Africans, thus robbing them of initiative, and Banse argued that it was too harsh, both concluded that African geography had constricted the mental development of the continent's inhabitants.

Banse's approach in this period may be seen in a representative form in his 1926 work, *Das Buch vom Morgenlande* (The book of the Orient). The title refers to *Orient* in the sense of *Levant,* not "Far East," and the book contains Banse's impressions of the interaction of geography, race, and culture in the lands of Islam that border the Mediterranean from Syria to Morocco. Banse divided the world between the Urals, the Atlantic, and the Sahara into three regions: the *Abendland* (literally, evening land, or west) including all of Europe north and west of the Alps and Pyrenees, the *Mittagsland,* or "midday land," embracing a belt of mostly mountainous land from Iran through Turkey, Greece, the Balkans, Italy, and Spain, and the *Morgenland* (literally, morning land) consisting of the Islamic lands of North Africa and the Arabian Peninsula (see fig. 2). For Banse, this categorization was justified by the fact that the characters of the peoples of these lands and of the institutions that they erected reflected each region's indigenous topography and vegetation.[16]

In the Abendland, although geography was dominated by the plain, the variety of geographic, climatic, topographic, and vegetative phenomena formed creative but stable personalities. The characteristic alternation of woods, meadows, fields, rivers, and lakes provided a stimulating variety of landscapes to which the seasonal change in climate added variations.[17] Agriculture rested here upon a firm natural foundation and, in common with other geopoliticians, Banse argued that the West's technological achievements were the result of the response of Western people to their relatively harsh climate. "The struggle against the cold gives the entire culture of the West its character," he wrote, arguing that Western humans responded to and dominated their environment through technology.[18]

In the Orient, by contrast, human society was given its character by the flat wastes of the desert, "a bright plain without character," whose in-

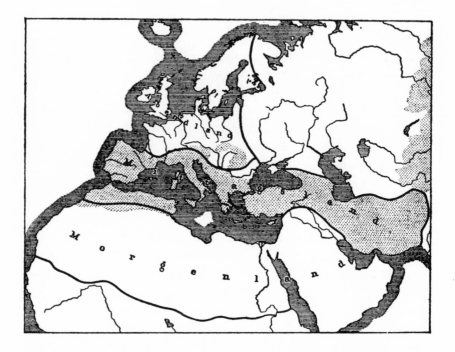

Fig. 2. *Morgenland* (The levant), from Ewald Banse, *Das Buch vom Morgenland* (Leipzig, 1926).

habitants struggled in vain against the heat and which imparted to the local population a lethargic equanimity.[19] Apparently, Banse believed the technological response to harsh environmental conditions could be called forth only by those kinds of extremes found in the European temperate zone, not those encountered in the Sahara, the Arctic, or central Asia. In any event there was a heavy racialist element in this as in all Banse's geographical writings. The lethargy induced by landscape and climate, for example, had historically rendered the peoples of the Orient "playthings in the hand of Nordic potentates, be it a Cyrus or Alexander, a Mehmet Ali or Lord Cromer."[20] Their own sense of racial purity was so degraded, Banse argued, that eastern sultans willingly gave their daughters as wives to black Africans; this was almost to be expected, however, since in the last analysis the Orientals were themselves only lighter-complexioned blacks:

> The depth of the Western soul, with its plenitude of possibilities and successively revealed beauties encounters in the Orient a bare, undifferentiated

surface. . . . To creative transmitting instinct there, which pours forth bless-
ings as from Nordic rain clouds, corresponds here a readiness to receive,
exactly as the dry earth of the south awaits fertilization. The impassive
slave, the Pascha with crossed legs who sucks his hookah, the odalisque with
naked body and jingling gold bangles, black eyes expectantly glimmering,
these are the representatives of the Orient, all finally nothing but light
Negroes.[21]

Banse here took to a rhetorical extreme the geopolitical project of revealing the formative power of spaces. Engendering as male the creativity
of the "Nordic" lands of Western Europe, whose fertility "pours forth"
upon the passive and waiting south, engendered as female, his imagery
provided an explicitly gendered geographical apology for Nordic domination of other lands. This is of a piece with the geopolitical project as a
whole, which sought to justify political action by endowing geography
with the characteristics of organic life forms. In Banse's case specifically
the passage is a good illustration of the praxis of "formative geography,"
which looked to intuition, artistic representation, and sensory impressions
rather than the empirical methods of traditional geography to convey a
living sense of the interplay of landscape and humanity. Banse insisted
that his own method was indicative and suggestive rather than descriptive. "This is a fundamental difference, and it has been decisive for my
entire conception of geography," Banse said, "not so much to describe
causally but to suggest instinctively."[22] In practice "instinctive suggestion"
meant for the most part simple descriptions of aspects of life and nature
encountered on his travels interspersed with passages of forced lyricism as
in the following description of starlit desert nights from his chapter on
caravans in *Das Buch vom Morgenlande:*

> Oh, you bright, star-sparkled nights of the Orient. By your light
> the eternal pyramids of Egypt were built.
> Beneath you the patriarchs stood before their tents.
> Beneath you the ten thousand marched down the broad-flowing
> Euphrates.
> You saw the curved sword of Mohammed spring through the land
> against East and West.
> You take in the hearth smoke of the Bedouin camp and let it drift
> into eternity.

> You heard the death sighs of uncounted slaves on their
>   sorrow-journeys
> from night to day. . . .
> Oh, you living nights, which reached for me with small-limbed,
>   white hands.[23]

Here Banse's anthropomorphization of landscape was freighted with momentous political implications. The oriental nights were shown as levellers of class and status into which disappeared patriarchs, soldiers, and slaves alike: Gender roles and family life, "the hearth smoke of the Bedouin camp," were also swallowed up in the landscape. Not all the passages in the book plumb similar depths of sentimental romanticism, but they are sufficiently frequent to set the book clearly outside the mainstream of what was then (or now) considered pure geographical investigation or travel reportage.

That Banse's effort to fashion a new form of geography was rooted in the geodeterminism that characterized geopolitics is clear from his views of the effect of Raum on supposed racial characteristics. By the early 1930s his work revealed an unequivocal racist crudity that made his earlier writings seem tame by comparison. In an essay written in 1932 for *Volk und Rasse,* a volkish periodical with heavy eugenic overtones, Banse argued that climate and landscape had given Africans their dark skins while retarding the development of their nervous systems. "Thus the black remains on a lower level, and his entire character remains bound to the simple prolongation of more animalistic, if you will, vegetative tasks," Banse wrote. The "powerful jaw" and "smaller cranial capacity" of the African were also a product of his Raum. By contrast, "The white race arose in its Raum and is unthinkable without it" although the characteristics of this space imparted an ability to master a variety of climates through the application of European technological culture.[24]

Like more overtly political geopoliticians, Banse also urged a new concept of geography and history based on an organic understanding of the links between nature and humankind. "The older statistical and thoroughly materialistic approach will be replaced here by an organic one, which penetrates into inner processes and attempts to render the dead material living," Banse wrote.[25] One aspect of this approach was the attempt to understand the psychical effects of landscapes. "The plain is culture—sea and mountain, nature;" he wrote, "the one compulsion, necessity, working day, the other two freedom and festivity."[26] His concept of nationality also reflected the general postwar geopolitical friendliness to racial-geographical concepts of volk, which departed from the political emphasis of prewar geopoliticians such as Ratzel. *Volkheit,* or "nation-hood," he described not in political terms but mystically as "a community of destiny of people of the same or related blood (living) within a distinct landscape style."[27] Despite the topographical variations of the German land Germans met the criteria for nationhood because of the effects of racial factors and relatively uniform climatic conditions.

That Banse's work was familiar to better-known geopoliticians is certain. His connections with Erich Obst, a distinguished geographer and cofounder of the *Zeitschrift für Geopolitik,* for example, were very close. When Banse founded the magazine *Die Neue Geographie* in 1922 to spread the gospel of formative geography, Obst visited him in Braun-schweig and, as Banse later recalled, expressed opinions "completely in accord with my views." Obst also wrote the first and introductory article for the magazine, which failed after four years. Throughout the 1920s, when Banse's lack of a doctoral degree prevented him from obtaining a desired geography post at the technical university at Braunschweig, he requested assistance from Obst, Haushofer, Hassinger, and other geo-politicians. His efforts were finally rewarded in 1932 when he received an honorary professoriate (*Honorarprofessor für Geographie*) at Braunschweig to teach courses in gestaltende Geographie. He was relieved of the po-sition the following year after an international outcry against the Nazi propaganda of his 1933 book, *Raum und Volk im Weltkriege,* but was then awarded an equivalent position at Hanover.[28] Banse was also the editor of the ambitious *Lexikon der Geographie,* which appeared in 1922 and 1923 (and in a second edition ten years later) and whose contributors included, among others, Hassinger and Haushofer.

Banse's theories provoked both heated criticism and impassioned defense among his geographical and geopolitical contemporaries. Con-demnations of his approach, on various grounds, came from Hermann Lautensach, Hugo Hassinger, and Alfred Hettner, among others. Has-singer, for example, refused to review a copy of Banse's *Buch der Länder* (Book of lands) despite his friendship with Banse, saying there was too much in the book "against which I would have to raise the sharpest disagreement as a scientist and a person."[29] Lautensach also attacked the subjectivity of Banse's approach and his "pharasaical" conviction of the superiority of the Nordic races, arguing that there would have to be "as many spiritual geographies of the same landscape as there are embodiers who bother themselves to consciously recognize it and compose it in words. . . . [Banse's geography] necessarily lacks that which is and must be inherent in science, evidence for the objective truth of that which is claimed."[30] Banse's defenders included Haushofer's mentor, Erich von Drygalski, who wrote he was "gratified at the beautiful and exact synthesis of man and landscape" he found in Banse's work, and Max Eckert and Oswald Muris, who praised Banse at length:[31] "We school geographers, who in addition to pure science strive also for artistic expression in teaching, will only be able to learn from E. Banse if we want to bind young souls to us and excite them for the subject. . . . We go forth to the dynamic, and Banse's style is also dynamic. . . . [He] wants to portray [geography] artistically on a firm scientific basis."[32]

The criticisms leveled against Banse by Hassinger and other geographers were undoubtedly justified. His approach, whether it is called formative geography, aesthetic geography, or any of various other names, amounted in practice to little more than tricked out travel writing masquerading as a blend of anthropology and geography. While paying attention to topographical features and, in an anecdotal and offhand fashion, to local customs and ethnography, Banse's main goal was the creation of a mood, capturing the "barely perceptible milieu," as he freely admitted. And this repudiation of science in the name of advancing the science of geography was, as noted, a source of his popularity among those geographers who accepted him as it was among those outside professional geography who embraced his works. One of these was Erich Günther, who wrote in the magazine of radical young conservatism, Die Tat, that Banse's work represented geography as a "synthesis of science and art," citing with approval Banse's estimation of his own work as "expressionistic in the best sense," and arguing that his followers included Volz, Obst, and Hassinger.[33] And whether they would have accepted this themselves or not, it was true that these academic geographers shared many of the same preconceptions relating to the effect of climate on society and "racial" characteristics. By the early 1930s and through the Nazi period Banse abandoned gestaltende Geographie for the more conventionally geopolitical Wehrgeographie, or military geography.[34] Banse's was the dubious distinction, however, of bringing together "expressionism" and geo-determinism in the Weimar setting. More than any other geopolitical writer of the period, Banse tried to give concrete expression to the geo-political conviction that geography determines individual and national character.

Friedrich Burgdörfer, Declining Fertility, and the Inversion of Lebensraum

For many thinkers influenced by Weimar geopolitics Ewald Banse's concern with the effects of geography upon the inner person must have seemed dangerously frivolous. The overriding question of the moment was not mere personal development but the German demographic struggle for existence, which was integrally linked to German space and German geography. Anxiety about the future of the German "race" had been a key source of the geopolitical demand for an expanded German Lebensraum since the First World War. In the late 1920s, however, this element of geopolitics was challenged by growing awareness of a relatively new demographic reality, that is, a sharp and apparently lasting decline in the surplus of births over deaths in Germany. Young German women were having fewer babies, and although the mortality rate continued to fall, birthrates were declining even faster. It was clear that if this decline, which began around the turn of the twentieth century, were to continue, the German population over coming decades would not only cease growing but would in time begin to shrink.[35] Such a course of events would vitiate the logic of the geopolitical demand for more space, which was founded in part in Germany's demographic preponderance among the peoples of central Europe. This newly perceived state of affairs posed a critical challenge to geopolitical Lebensraum theory and to its adherents in the volkish movement. Volkish writers and leaders such as Hans Harmsen and Karl Christian von Loesch, the head of the German Protective League, wrote prodigiously on the topic.[36] No German of the period, however, occupied himself with the Geburtenrückgang with greater fervor or constancy than Friedrich Burgdörfer, who as a writer, demographer, and influential bureaucrat tried to persuade Germans to see the declining birthrate as an emergency and to cast that emergency and its solutions in geopolitical and geodeterministic terms.

Burgdörfer was born in the Rhenish Palatinate in 1890 and attended the university at Munich where, like Rudolf Kjellén and others ultimately attracted to geopolitics, he studied Staatswissenschaft. He received a doctorate in political economy in 1916. An ambitious and intellectually precocious statistician, Burgdörfer had begun work with the Bavarian State Statistical Office while still a gymnasial student in Kaiserslautern. He rose rapidly through the ranks there until 1921 when he joined the Reich Statistical Office in Berlin as government councillor (*Regierungsrat*). He assumed the directorship of this bureau in 1929, a notable and politically sensitive position that he held for the next ten years, serving simultaneously as the leader of the office's Section for Population, Business, Agricultural, and Cultural Statistics.[37] He lectured during this period as an honorary professor at the University of Berlin and was a member of the International Statistical Institute and advisor to a variety of governmental agencies, most having to do with population questions. Burgdörfer's only formal political affiliation before joining the National Socialist party in 1937 was a brief membership (from 1917 to 1918) in Admiral Tirpitz's short-lived German Fatherland Party.[38]

In 1929, Burgdörfer published *Die Geburtenruckgang und seine Bekämpfung. Die Lebensfrage des deutschen Volkes* (The birth decline and its control: The life question of the German people), a book that would prefigure his position (and that taken by geopolitics in general) on this issue for the next several years.[39] In it he warned that the apparent continued growth of the German population was "mechanical," that is, the result only of the working out of earlier trends and not of a sustained or increasing birthrate in combination with a falling mortality rate. In fact, the German birthrate seemed to be trapped in a slow but steady decline, casting doubt on the chances for the future of Germany because "only a growing people is healthy and full of hope."[40] Far from arguing that this new trend obviated the need for more room for the now or soon-to-be shrinking German population, Burgdörfer performed a neat inversion of the conventional geopolitical perspective on Lebensraum to that point. He developed the ingenious approach that infertility was itself a symptom of insufficient *Lebensspielraum,* a variant of Lebensraum meaning, roughly, "elbow room." Germans, crowded into densely populated cities, were intentionally restricting family size because they had little prospect of providing decently for their families in the new, mutilated Germany. He contrasted the "infertility of the great city population" with the "fertility of the country population."[41] Not only would the "shrinking and aging

German ethnic body" not be able to provide economically for German needs but it might not be able to protect Germany from being inundated in a wave of fecund Slavs.[42] Burgdörfer cast the demographic trends of eastern and central Europe in Darwinist terms to raise the spectral vision of an apocalyptic demographic struggle with the German people, envisioned as a single body, or *Volkskörper,* locked in a struggle for survival with the Slavic tide to the east. For Germans to emerge victoriously from this struggle more land would be vital. "Only an indigenous, procreative peasant population, tied to the soil, would be in the position to resist the excess Slavic population pressure and successfully secure the German ethnic soil in the east."[43]

Because of their geodeterminist approach to the German birth decline, Burgdörfer's writings quickly attracted the attention of geopolitical and volkish circles. He spoke with considerable authority from his post as a prominent federal statistician, and other statisticians, including Harmsen and K. Saenger, president of the Prussian Statistical Office, had early on developed a sophisticated use of statistical argument to support geopolitical propositions in geopolitical propaganda.[44] In the same year *Der Geburtenrückgang* appeared Burgdörfer published an essay in a special issue of the mainstream *Süddeutsche Monatshefte.* In it he argued that Germany required a dam of settlers to fend off Slavic population pressure from the east, worrying that "the time does not appear to be far off . . . where the biological weakness of the interior of Germandom will undermine our ethnopolitical front in the east."[45] Burgdörfer forecast an equally grim development in an essay entitled "Die schwindende Wachstumsenergie des deutschen Volkes im europäischen Raum" (The dwindling growth energy of the German people in the European area) which appeared in a supplement to the *Zeitschrift für Geopolitik,* and three years later the geopolitical Vowinckel press of Berlin published his book *Volke ohne Jugend. Geburtenschwund und Überalterung des deutschen Volkskörpers* (People without youth: Birth atrophy and overaging of the German ethnic body), as a supplement, or *Beiheft,* to the *Zeitschrift für Geopolitik.*[46]

By this time Burgdörfer's message was cast in ever more urgent and sensationalist terms. His title, *Volk ohne Jugend,* was in deliberate contrast to Hans Grimm's colonialist novel *Volk ohne Raum.* The work, which appeared in several editions during the Nazi era and which Burgdörfer personally presented to Benito Mussolini in 1938, was dedicated to dispelling what Burgdörfer saw as the dangerous popular notion that there were too many Germans.[47] Instead, he insisted, there were too few, having too few children. He again evoked the notion, shared by both pre- and postwar geopolitical writers, that the German social order was particularly fragile, and he argued that the social and economic divisions arising from the Versailles settlement were both a cause and symptom of the birth decline.[48] The emphasis on the fragility and instability of Germany's social structure and the attempt to link this to population trends provided an implicit justification for eugenic regulation to maintain the health of this important source of political power, that is, the population, of German society. Darwinist imagery of a ceaseless mortal struggle between two rival Volkskörper also played a central role in his repeated evocation of a "biopolitical border struggle in the East."[49]

Burgdörfer's approach to the Geburtenrückgang had relevance from the geopolitical perspective above all, however, because he related the causes, consequences, and solutions of the birth decline to the German Raum.

> The German people, above all others, has occasion to take these dangers seriously; since, because of its central European location, it is threatened by them most immediately. Germany forms the center of a demographic low pressure zone. At the same time it borders immediately in the east upon a demographic high pressure zone. Therefore, ethnopolitical tensions necessarily appear here most immediately and sharply. The struggle of Germandom in defense of the German ethnic soil has been complicated especially by the political and world-economic disruption conjured up in the peace settlements in the Paris suburbs. This is seen above all in the unexampled national splintering of Germandom.[50]

Burgdörfer's vocabulary here, explicitly scientific in its use of meteorological analogies, suggested a buildup of natural forces beyond human control. He presented the *Völkermischzone* (zone of ethnic mixture) of eastern Europe as a threat to ethnic Germans, who, as subjugated minorities in the new national states of the region, were threatened with de-Germanization. Germany's colonies overseas also had to be returned, he insisted, because as an extension of German Lebensraum they contributed to the survival of the German Volkskörper.[51] As in his earlier works, Burgdörfer argued that only a peasant population with organic connections to the soil could provide the necessary demographic dike against the building Slavic flood.[52] His "scientific" antiurbanism, founded in what he argued was the threat posed to German demography by urbanization, may also have helped to endear him to generally conservative and antiurban geopolitical circles.[53]

Burgdörfer's message found a wide and ready audience among nationalist conservatives and among professional geographers and geopoliticians.[54] Johann Sölch, an eminent Austrian geographer attracted to geopolitical arguments against Italy's postwar acquisition of the South Tirol, reviewed *Volk ohne Jugend* in the influential *Geographische Zeitschrift*, calling it a concise warning of the impending decline of the German people because "a centrally located space like Germany can least of all remain empty."[55] The work was likewise hailed in *Petermanns Geographische Mitteilungen* as a timely admonition that Germans could not afford to ignore because it showed that "the German people are already today no longer in the position to maintain stability for the future on the basis of their own strength—a result that must produce surprise and despair even among pessimists!"[56] At the same time other geographers, such as Herbert Barthel, began to occupy themselves with demographic issues in terms that clearly reflected the influence of Burgdörfer's analysis. In an article entitled "Der Geburtenüberschuss in Polen" (The birth surplus in Poland), for instance, Barthel argued as did Burgdörfer that the shortage of births in Germany's eastern districts created a tempting demographic vacuum that would naturally provoke the land lust of the bordering Poles and, of course, inevitably produce a struggle. "It seems all too likely, therefore, that the interest of Poland will direct itself to the relatively thinly settled German eastern districts with their, by Polish standards, flourishing agriculture," Barthel wrote. "The marked birth surplus of Poland thereby threatens to become a source of danger for the German east."[57]

As a result of his governmental position, Burgdörfer's influence upon German perceptions of the declining birthrate was not confined to professional geographers but could make itself felt in official and quasi-official circles as well. In 1929 he worked with the Population Policy Committee of the German Protective League (under the leadership of Harmsen) to produce for that body a population pamphlet distributed under the title of *Der Geburtenrückgang und die Zukunft des deutschen Volkes* (The birth decline and the future of the German people).[58] Burgdörfer was also a member of the official Reichsausschuss für Bevölkerungsfragen (Reich Committee for Population Questions) formed in December 1929 under the auspices of the Ministry of the Interior. Here he worked with writers, politicians, and activists interested in population and eugenic questions, such as the socialist Alfred Grotjahn, a prominent professor of social hygiene at the University of Berlin, and liberal Deutsche Demokratische Partei (DDP) Reichstag deputies, including Gertrud Bäumer and Willy Hellpach, studying the "health, national economic, social and state political consequences" of the birthrate decline.[59] In his position at the Reich Statistical Office Burgdörfer had already helped prepare a document entitled *Denkschrift über den Geburtenrückgang und seine Bekämpfung* (Memorandum on the birth decline and its control) for the Ministry of the Interior, which argued that "among the consequences of the war and the inflation . . . the contemporary nadir of the birthrate is to be conceived as a natural reaction to the links between population density and the livelihood and nourishment opportunities at the disposal of the people." Only "a healthy Volkskörper" would be able to resist "hypertrophy through neighboring, in themselves culturally inferior peoples with higher birth numbers." The outlook for the German people was grim, but "a situation of improved prospects from various perspectives would naturally arise through the acquisition of German colonies, which would afford the population remaining in the motherland greater elbow room and amelioration of the conditions of existence."[60]

This particular memorandum went on to argue that the causes of the falling birthrate were to be found less in decaying ethical and moral standards, as some contended, than in "hard necessity" arising out of post-defeat conditions. Germany was especially threatened because its "eastern frontier runs up against Slavic peoples who do not share the nearly general European birth decline but have a fertility [rate] twice as high as we Germans. East Prussia, the border land, is already too thinly populated." Among the proposed solutions a centrally planned and vigorously prosecuted eastern settlement policy took a prominent place.[61] Such arguments found wide currency in governmental circles to the extent, at least, that it became popular to call for measures to protect the growth of the German population. The Reichstag passed a resolution early in 1928, for instance, stating that "in view of the birth decline, which severely threatens the future of the German people, the Reichstag declares that the viewpoint of the maintenance and increase of the German population power (*Volkskraft*) shall henceforth be given effective consideration in all legislative measures under consideration."[62] Although it is not clear that such concern frequently translated into effective legislative action, Reichstag deputies in the late 1920s and early 1930s cited both the dangers of the Geburtenrückgang and Burgdörfer's Reich Committee for Population Questions to support demands for more effective settlement policy and support for the German family. One of the Zentrum (Center Party's) deputies, arguing in June 1930 for increased spending on youth and restrictions on working hours for mothers, cited the Reich committee's research as evidence that German infertility threatened national security and was rooted in unhealthy notions of family life and women's roles.[63] Members of the Deutsche Bauernpartei (German Farmers' Party) used the committee's work and general fear of the birth decline to call for increased efforts to prevent flight from the land where peasants raised large families and particularly to help the border districts with Czechoslovakia.[64]

Such public and political expressions of a geopolitically influenced view of Germany's demographic "crisis" clearly reflect Burgdörfer's success in injecting his concerns into the mainstream of Weimar public life. Burgdörfer was a crucial link in the Weimar geopolitical network, using his media connections (including occasional radio lectures) and influential political position to popularize the geopolitical interpretation of Germany's changing population structure and family patterns.[65] By the early 1930s, clearly, Burgdörfer had helped to make the Geburtenrückgang and his geopolitical interpretation of it an accepted part of the public discourse with fateful consequences for the political development of Germany in the next decade.

Arthur Dix and Geopolitical Colonialism

Speaking to the German Geographic Congress in June 1925, Arthur Dix greeted the dawn of a new era in world history. "With the conquest of space through air travel and wireless communication around the world, a new, a global epoch has broken," Dix told the geographers assembled in Breslau, "distinguished world-politically from earlier eras by the fact that extra-European powers have entered fully into the ranks of the determining factors." The new period would bring not only greater economic interdependence of all states but would also require a new way of thinking about the links between states, geography, and economics.

"This new global age demands not only earth-spatial thinking but also careful evaluation of the earth spaces according to their own quality and according to the value-creating quality of their inhabitants." The two most reliable tools for meeting the conceptual demands of the new age, according to Dix, were "geoeconomics" and geopolitics.[66] Unlike the apocalyptic demographic disasters envisioned by Burgdörfer or the middlebrow geographic aestheticizing of Banse, Dix was a voice of a somewhat theatrical and hopeful colonial geopolitics.

Dix was also, in 1925, a rather unlikely harbinger of an impending new phase in world history. At fifty he was somewhat old for the role of herald, and little in his background would suggest an affinity for dramatic political transformations. Born near Berlin (in Kölln), and educated at Königsberg, Berlin, and Leipzig, Dix had been a prominent journalist and editor active on behalf of the Nationalliberale Partei (National Liberal Party) before the war. Afterward he joined Stresemann's Deutsche Volkspartei (DVP, or German People's Party) and in 1930 the Konservative Volkspartei (Conservative People's Party), both more comfortable as pillars of order than as arbiters of change. His remarks to the geographic congress seem, in some ways, rather incongruous. Despite many geographic publications, for example, Dix was not a geographer at all, but educated in economics. He described himself as a "geographic autodidact," and he was always concerned at least as much with questions of economics as with strictly geographical issues.[67] Above all, however, Dix's idea of what the new age portended seems paradoxical. For while proclaiming an often very perceptive vision of an emerging new world community, Dix devoted his entire career from the end of the world war to his death in 1935 to the proposition that the solution to Germany's problems in the new age lay in a return to Germany's colonial past in Africa. Dix thus presents perhaps the most ironic image in the interwar geopolitical milieu, a political moderate who clearly perceived the impending devolution of Europe's global hegemony but who was unable ultimately to break from obsolescent colonialist concepts of world order.

Dix was the most active and impassioned colonial advocate among those thinkers and writers identified with geopolitics in the Weimar era. Like Banse, Haushofer, and others, he was an extremely prolific author. He published, for example, geopolitical works such as his 1922 book *Politische Geographie* (Political geography), reissued the following year in a second edition, and the introductory text *Geopolitik. Lehrkurse über die geographischen Grundlagen der Weltpolitik und Weltwirtschaft* (Geopolitics: Teaching course on the geographic foundations of world politics and world economics). At the same time, he produced a steady stream of propagandistic colonialist works, such as *Was geht uns Afrika an?* (What matters Africa to us?) in 1931 and *Weltkrise und Kolonialpolitik. Die Zukunft zweier Erdteile* (World crisis and colonial policy: The future of two continents) in 1932. His links to colonialists, geographers, and geopoliticians were broad and varied, and he enjoyed ready access to a wide range of media outlets for his views.[68] He wrote articles for newspapers and colonialist periodicals such as the *Übersee- und Koloniale Zeitung* and authored the brochure *Was Deutschland an seinen Kolonien verlor* (What Germany lost to its colonies) for the Arbeitsausschuss deutscher Verbände (Working Committee of German Associations, or ADV), an alliance of nearly two thousand conservative organizations headed by the colonial activist and former governor of German East Africa Heinrich Schnee.[69] Dix founded and edited the journal *Weltpolitik und Weltwirtschaft* (World politics and world economics), which in 1927 was absorbed by the *Zeitschrift für Geopolitik*.[70] He lectured regularly on colonial and geopolitical topics over the radio, at schools, and to military and academic organizations.[71] Through his membership in the Staatswissenschaftliche Vereinigung (Political Science Union), the Gesellschaft für Erdkunde zu Berlin (Berlin Geographic Society), the Kolonial-Wirtschaftliches Komitee (Colonial-Economic Committee) and other organizations he was associated with a broad circle of influential men, including geographers such as Norbert Krebs, Albrecht Haushofer, and Albrecht Penck, political scientists such as Adolf Grabowsky, the writer Hans Grimm, and politicians and bureaucrats, including Erich Koch-Weser, party leader of the German Democratic Party, the socialist Max Cohen-Reuss, and Friedrich Burgdörfer.[72] Dix was, in short, an important nexus, linking geographical, political, academic, and popular circles with geopolitical and colonialist ideas.

Dix argued that technological change, especially aviation, had eased the conquest of space (*Raumüberwindung*) and, thus, given geography new meaning for politics. Geopolitics, which Dix felt was more closely related to Staatswissenschaft than to geography, met the new need for analytical geographic perspective by examining the "earth-spatial foundations" of state power.[73] But geopolitics, he argued, was more than simply a method of analyzing and understanding the world; it was praxis, a form of conducting state policy. Here Dix displayed a common and persistent fundamental confusion in geopolitical thought, using the term to denote not only the analytical approach embodied in the "science" of Raum-conscious analysis of state growth but also to describe a particular type of policy.[74] Geopolitics, for Dix and others, was an analytical tool and guide, which achieved broader importance in the age of democratic states because "precisely through the natural foundations with which geopolitics works, the masses can also be led closer to a state-political understanding; the, so to say, spatial natural history of the state can be grasped, so in our age of democratic suffrage . . . the great voting masses also receive some understanding of the conditions under which the state to which they belong exists, and which natural efforts it must pursue toward the secur-ing of its existence."[75] In good geopolitical fashion Dix insisted that the state and its economy were a fusion of volk and Boden, and he was con-vinced, like Ewald Banse, that "the physical properties of the soil and the psychic properties of its inhabitants belong together, and in their commu-nion produce the geopolitical overall image."[76]

That Dix was an informed and perceptive observer of world politi-cal trends is beyond question. He clearly discerned the centrifugal forces that were operating on the international system in the 1920s and 1930s, weakening European dominance and initiating a less-centralized global political/economic system. Much of his analysis of the interplay of tech-nology and global politics became common parlance by the late twentieth century. Geopolitical insights revealed that the world had progressed from a colonial age in which the earth was dominated by the European powers, according to Dix, to an age in which state powers all over the globe were able to project their interests. Dix invoked the common geo-political image of an earth imbedded in a navigable "air ocean" and accu-rately predicted, long before Marshall McLuhan popularized the term, that technological change would create an increasingly interdependent "Global Village."

I have in another place coined the phrase "The Global Village," in which everyone can look in his neighbor's window. We live—I cannot neglect the opportunity to repeat—on the threshold of a new epoch or already in a new age. . . . Earlier [we saw] the promotion of transmission of thought from person to person through the entire people: Gutenberg with his printing—today transmission of thought over the entire earth in seconds by broadcasting, by radio, by wireless telegraphy and telephone and transmission of thought in a propagandistic sense also by the cinema. . . . As before the world seas were conquered and all five continents converged in the further course of navigation, so today the decisive step has been taken to convergence, to the further shrinking of the globe by airship travel and the airplane, through the conquest of the air ocean.[77]

For all his insight, however, Dix remained committed to European colonial preeminence. As he told Germans again and again in the seventeen years between the end of World War I and his death, the advent of a new age by no means portended the end of the old colonial mission of European and other world powers. Precisely on geopolitical grounds and precisely because of the intensification of state competition caused by technological changes Germany above all still required colonial land for the German economy to be healthy and competitive. "We live in a time of the greatest world-economic interconnection," Dix wrote, "and in a time of the strongest striving for world-economic independence of the individual economic bodies, and we must necessarily adapt to this time. . . . We suffer spatially under the harshest restrictions. . . . Our economic body is in every possible direction amputated. We are actually, seen as a whole, an economic cripple."[78] The nation could be restored to vigor, however, by renewed German colonial activity in Africa, the one area of the world that was still *kolonialreif,* or ripe for colonization.

Dix never espoused a simple return to the colonial status quo ante bellum, however. The notion that Germany in the mid-1920s could simply resume governance of all its old colonies as if nothing had happened in the intervening decade smacked of fantasy, even for a nostalgic colonialist like Dix. He proposed a more sophisticated vision of the German twentieth-century colonial future in the form of a joint European condominium over the continent to the south. This would be grounded in the common good of both Africans and Europeans, but even here his thinking was based more in the past than in the future. "We must only return to the concept, already suggested many times before the war, of a *Flurbereinigung* [enclosure of land] in Central Africa," Dix wrote, "eventually in the South Seas also, but above all in the huge areas of Central Africa where very small lands such as Portugal and Belgium dispose of very large colonial possessions, whereas Germany now lacks land there for production that it urgently needs for its home economy."[79] In the new interdependent world, however, neither Germany nor any other developed power could confront the huge tasks of colonizing alone. "Colonial land, the use of whose products stands at Europe's disposal, is shrinking," he wrote, "and new land is no longer to be won, sooner old to be lost. What remains must be used all the more intensively—by the application of all suitable powers."[80]

Characterizing the era of German colonialism as the "golden marriage" of two continents, Dix argued that German colonial activity would prove a great beneficence to all, Africa as well as Germany and Europe.[81] Again, his thinking used new terms and ideas, but it linked these to earlier notions of the "white man's burden," or the "civilizing" mission of Europe in Africa that must have heightened the resonance of this colonialist appeal for its German audience. "Let us summarize in a few words what Africa needs. . . . Under current conditions, as has been proven, Africa needs European administration, European work on the reorganization of its population, on the struggle against the shortage and the surplus of water, on the lack of means against human and animal epidemics, European transport, European economic leadership."[82] Dix also cherished the fond notion, common in the colonial movement at the time, that the natives "yearned for the return of proven German economic leadership."[83] For Germany, renewed colonialism would remove not only the "unbearable manacle" of its exclusion from access to its own colonial raw materials and export markets but it would also help remove the causes of German population constriction. Dix shared the geopolitical obsession with the Geburtenrückgang, and he, like Burgdörfer, was convinced that it had its sources in economic misery and want of land. Tropical lands would solve both problems by improving the economy and offering space for German agrarian expansion.[84] A "twilight of the Germans" threatened, Dix argued, if appropriate measures were not soon taken: "We are, viewed from the densely populated industrial centers and large cities, Volk ohne Raum," Dix wrote. "We have at the same time, with the unfavorable contemporary development of the agricultural economy, Raum ohne Volk. We must fill the unpeopled space and must procure new land for the spaceless people."[85]

A variety of geopolitical laws and tendencies dictated that Germany seek the solutions to its problems by augmenting its space. Although conceding that these laws were not of "unconditional validity,"

Dix's geopolitical scheme of the world presented them as reliable guides to how states would and, indeed, how they must behave. He posited, for example, a "Law of Struggle toward the Sea," the strongest of the "transport-geographic laws," and a "Law of Movement in the Direction of Least Resistance," according to which states with insufficient "*Nahrungs-mittelspielraum*" (roughly, "nutritional elbowroom") naturally began to seek more from weaker neighbors whose lands would readily complement the economic structure of the expanding state.[86] Other laws included the "Law of the Development of Borders," which followed a Ratzelian scheme whereby indefinite border seams (*Grenzsaum*) developed into precisely defined border lines (*Grenzlinie*) over time, or the "Law of Struggle toward Ethnographic Consolidation."[87] For Germany's role in Europe these laws meant that it strove naturally toward the unification of the lands between the Black Sea and the Baltic. The image of these lands as a "natural" field for German expansion was a popular geopolitical motif. Dix presented German growth here as an ineluctable tendency fueled by the ethnographic reality of scattered settlement of large numbers of ethnic Germans and by the unity of transport created by the river systems of the Rhine, Elbe, and Danube.[88] In colonial terms such laws meant that "in every national group there is the tendency to possess politically in its own hands those sources of nourishment necessary to its survival."[89] Furthermore, because geography determined cultural development, there was little likelihood of the native inhabitants of Africa objecting to the ownership of their lands by Europeans. "The peculiarity of property relationships among the blacks lies mainly in the surplus of land in which all firm arrangements are lost. Because they have so much land, they little value its possession."[90]

Dix was convinced that if a sufficient number of Germans were apprised of the essence of geopolitics and of the geographical realities of the German position in Europe, general cognizance of the need for colonies would follow. He was consequently gratified by the progress that geopolitical thought was making in learned circles in 1927 and of the results that he anticipated from this: "We see at various universities how the geopolitical perspective penetrates more and more and how professional scholars turn more and more to the geopolitical discipline. Among young academics, so far as I have been able to observe on many journeys through German university towns, the understanding for the necessity and for the tasks of geopolitical thought is already extraordinarily widespread. . . . Precisely the entering into, the familiarizing with space, in its conditions, limitations, and possibilities also stimulates economic thought in the direction of recognition of the great community of interests of an economic body in a given space and in given dependencies from foreign spaces."[91] Dix's reading of the growing resonance of geopolitical ideas at German universities was accurate, and his own work had contributed in significant measure to this trend. When the preparations for Dix's new age began to bear fruit for Germany, however, these ideas were applied not in Africa but in the European east, and the promise of empire overseas, despite all Dix's efforts, was to remain a mirage.

Adolf Grabowsky: Geopolitician for the Republic

Adolf Grabowsky's relationship to geopolitical thinking in the Weimar era was, like that of Arthur Dix, suffused with paradox. Grabowsky approached theories exploring the links between geography and politics with a cold, critical eye that was conspicuously absent in the writings of most of his geopolitical contemporaries, none of whom shared his interest in puncturing the inflated claims, pretensions, and dangerous mysticisms fostered by geopolitical enthusiasts. His criticism of the patron saint of Weimar geopolitics, Karl Haushofer, could be devastating, and he was succinct in pointing out many of the theoretical shortcomings of geopolitical thought in general.[92] At the same time, Grabowsky articulated a geopolitical and spatial approach to German politics and foreign policy, and his conviction of the analytical utility of geopolitical concepts made him the most persuasive adherent of geopolitical thought among Weimar Germany's democratic political thinkers. Ironically, Grabowsky's very objectivity, his judicious criticisms of the flaws of "vulgar" geopolitics and his political standing as a good, if conservative, democrat, lent a credibility to his own geopolitical commitment that promoted the dissemination of geopolitical ideas in genuinely republican circles where they might otherwise have been rejected out of hand.

Grabowsky was a native of Berlin, born of middle-class parents (his father was a businessman) in 1880. In common with many others who embraced geopolitical ideas in the period he had no formal geographic training, having studied law instead in Geneva, Freiburg, and Berlin. In 1905 he gave up the practice of law to pursue a career in research and literature, and two years later he founded, with Richard Schmidt, the

Zeitschrift für Politik. For the next three decades, until he fled Germany for Switzerland in 1934, Grabowsky produced a substantial body of written work, including poetry, plays, and political books and essays.[93] It is to the last of these that he owes his continuing historical significance and reputation. Grabowsky's political writings provide what has been described as the "first systematic exposition of 'theoretical politics' in Germany," and taken as a whole they reflect a preoccupation with questions of international relations and foreign policy.[94] Politically, he was a moderate conservative before the war, later characterizing his approach with the motto "Stand right, think left." He embraced a refined paternalism, idealizing society under the leadership of a democratic, service-oriented intellectual aristocracy, conscious of its political responsibilities.[95] During the First World War Grabowsky served with German forces in the east, an experience that stimulated his 1916 book, *Die polnische Frage* (The Polish question), one of his first works to show signs of what became a lasting preoccupation with the role of spatial and geographical elements in state relations. After Germany's defeat Grabowsky found a secure institutional platform for the dissemination of his geopolitical views in democratic circles as leader of the geopolitical seminar at the Deutsche Hochschule für Politik (German University for Politics) in Berlin where he taught from 1921 to 1933.

Grabowsky published his most programmatic description of the relationship between politics and geography in 1928 in *Staat und Raum. Grundlagen räumlichen Denkens in der Weltpolitik* (State and space: Foundations of spatial thought in world politics), but the outlines of his subsequent approach to space and the state can be discerned in his wartime work of twelve years earlier, *Die polnische Frage* (The Polish question). Grabowsky is accurately remembered in Germany as an advocate of a compromise peace settlement, but his ideas of compromise were not, from a Polish nationalist point of view, likely to be very gratifying.[96] The only just solution to the Polish question, he argued, would be a joint German/Austro-Hungarian condominium over Poland with cultural and local political autonomy for the Poles, a proposal he grounded in historical and ethnographic but also geographical/political arguments.[97] His argument from history and ethnicity maintained that much of Polish life and society had been decisively formed by its contact with German culture and that postwar arrangements were unfair to the large German ethnic minority still living in Poland. This position anticipated volkish and geopolitical arguments used to advocate revision of the borders with states influenced by German culture (interpreted as all the states in eastern Europe) after the war's end.[98] Its geographical position, furthermore, made a Polish state unfeasible because a weak Poland would naturally become a plaything manipulated by the greater powers surrounding it, whereas a strong Poland would present a danger in its own right as a result of its inevitable expansionistic strivings for outlets to the sea. "A [Polish] empire dependent upon itself must seek an outlet to the sea by expansion, which such a [powerful] Poland would merit," he wrote. "The Polish tendency to expand toward the mouth of the Weichsel is well known."[99] Grabowsky's analysis of the position of Poland in the state system thus anticipated the geopolitical view in three ways: a sense of state relations as an arena of eternal and inevitable struggle reflected in the view that no mere legal agreements could either restrain or guarantee a geographically doomed Poland, the belief that the historically proven influence of German culture in eastern Europe had political consequences for the present, and the view that certain strivings inhere naturally in states as a result of geographical setting.

The geopolitical approach to state relations outlined here blossomed in Grabowsky's writings after the war and received their most detailed exposition in *Staat und Raum* (State and space). This book was the first volume in a series entitled the *Weltpolitische Bücherei* (World-political library) of which Grabowsky was the editor. The series was favorably received by the geographical press of the period, and as general editor Grabowsky came in contact with Otto Maull, Walther Vogel, Richard Hennig, Walther Pahl, Franz Thorbecke, Josef März, and other prominent geopoliticians and political geographers of the period.[100] Grabowsky made it clear from the outset that Germany's failures in the past had been failures of spatial vision and that his goal was pedagogic, if not propagandistic, in that he intended to heighten the German people's sense of the role of space in politics. "It will soon seem inconceivable to us that world politics could once have been pursued without actually knowing the actual substance of the world, space," he wrote. "One speaks much today of people without space; one should also speak of world politics without space as a thing that must be overcome." The means of achieving this was "the so-called geopolitics, no panacea but a decisive method."[101] He went on to describe geopolitics as a "new science" that, in response to a naive rationalism and individualism, emphasized the group and its relation to space, thus focusing upon the importance of the volk. "It is basically nothing other than the conviction that the gradual development of the whole, the nationality that bears the individual and from which he first receives all his rights, is more important than the passing individual. To the counterforces against individualism and rationalism belong now also the sensitivity to the value of space for the fate of mankind."[102]

Unlike Maull and other geopoliticians, he credited Kjellén rather than Ratzel with being the father of geopolitics by introducing the concept of the state as a living organism. Although Grabowsky argued the state was not exactly comparable to a biological organism, it possessed, nonetheless, an organic nature in more than a simply metaphorical sense.[103] As a life form the state originated in the symbiosis of volk and Raum. Because space left an indelible imprint on the volk, the impact of space always had to be considered in light of what might be called cultural volkish factors. The analytical application of this concept of volk, space and culture would explain seeming paradoxes, such as the different natures of the seafaring Phoenicians and their neighbors the Jews, who despite a setting on the Mediterranean littoral never developed a maritime culture. The Phoenicians, according to Grabowsky, were a *bodenständiges Volk,* or indigenous people, who had developed out of their space and in dependence upon its resources, whereas the Jews (like the Turks) were a wandering people of plains origin (*Steppenherkunft*) who had brought their old culture and habits into their new space. This did not mean they were forever fated to ignore the potential resources of their new space but that it would be more difficult for them to recognize and exploit them.[104]

Although this is a reasonably sophisticated point of view, his commitment to volk and space as forces shaping the state as an organism made Grabowsky, like many more conservative geopoliticians, skeptical about the power of legal agreements to regulate relations between states. If such agreements failed to accord with what he saw as "the geographic and ethnographic perspective," they were doomed to fail. Treaties, according to this approach, were "merely the expression of specific living forces," and this was particularly true of treaties like that signed by Germany at Versailles, which regulated border arrangements. Grabowsky described such negotiated boundaries as "mere treaty borders" and argued that "a border can rest on the conditions of space and on conditions of ethnicity. In both cases it is no artificial, no mere treaty border, but a natural one, since ethnicity is, just as we have seen, every bit as much the natural underpinning of the state as is the space."[105] He went on to develop an entire phylogeny of borders, including many types of cultural borders, geographical borders (both are "natural" border types) and "artificial," purely legalistic borders. This had obvious implications for the postwar arrangement of borders in eastern Europe, which Grabowsky did not overlook.

Grabowsky's theories as developed in *Staat und Raum* shared many other elements of the general geopolitical rhetoric of the time. Like Banse, for example, he argued that the aesthetic impression created by a landscape helped determine the character of the people who inhabited it, and he deployed a lexicon of pseudoscientific geopolitical jargon terms to describe the "typical" forms of state evolution. States, for instance, followed *Kraftfelder* and *Kraftlinien,* or fields of force and lines of force, in their expansion, and these were the areas where conflict would usually arise. Certain landscapes functioned as "glacis" landscapes, others as "bridgehead" landscapes for future expansion; the latter role was also filled by "growth points." He described as well "ballast landscapes," regions where a state reached beyond its natural borders to envelop parts of a different ethnic group, as the Habsburg empire had done in Lombardy and Venetia.[106] In common with a whole school of Weimar geographic thinkers he favored a renewal of German colonial activity on grounds that it would benefit Africans (by placing them in "a deeper relation to their soil") and the Germans alike.[107] Unlike Dix, Banse, and many other geopoliticians, however, Grabowsky's motivation on the colonial issue seems to have been untinged by racism. In his play *Der Neger,* for example, a white European character (Senechal), repelled by European materialism, abandons her connections to Europe and casts her lot with Africans so that "the black shall again be proud of himself. He existed in prehistory before the whites and will exist after the whites."[108]

Over the Weimar era Grabowsky developed a critical aversion to the treatment of geopolitics as an independent discipline. The crux of his criticism of the "Haushofer circle," as he termed the dominant geopolitical school, was their contention that geopolitics was an independent science. Instead, he treated it as a method, as a certain spatial approach that had to be fitted into an analysis of politics, history, medicine, jurisprudence, and other fields.[109] "The isolated geopolitician behaves like a surveyor who measures a section of earth without considering its connections and dependencies. . . . But if one considers that in the interpretation of spatial destiny (*Raumschicksal*) the ancillary considerations are quite the main thing, the insertion of the spatial factor in the other factors, this leads to the deduction that geopolitics is in no way a science but only a method—one method of historical interpretation beside other interpretive possibilities."[110] This was a departure from his earlier characterization of geopolitics as the "new science," and he went on to argue that the oversimplified geodeterminism of Haushofer and his disciples led to a form of "geographic materialism" akin to the "blood materialism" of the racial fanatics, which left only space and the hero as explanatory factors for historical change.[111] This methodological definition also solved the vexing dilemma of the difference between political geography and geopolitics for Grabowsky. Whereas political geography was concerned with static geographical structures that shaped the state, geopolitics analyzed the state as a "struggling spatial subject" (*kämpfendes Raumsubjekt*). Geopolitics as a method focused upon the understanding of the dynamic state and its active response to the "overpowering weight of space": "A simple spatial view is not promoted, as in geography, but dynamic and simultaneously statist spatial thought."[112] Unlike political geography, in other words, geopolitics focused not on the physical characteristics of the earth's surface but on man's political construct, the state.

Grabowsky's theoretical sophistication in no way weakened his commitment to a geodeterminist approach. The destructive effects, from the point of view of state relations, of Grabowsky's geodeterminism and his geopolitical view of the state as an organism, are clear in his essay "Der Primat der Aussenpolitik" (The primacy of foreign policy), which he published in 1928. The essay was a rebuttal to Eckart Kehr's seminal essay on the domestic political sources of the First World War, "Englandhass und Weltpolitik" (Hatred of England and world politics), and it was published together with Kehr's famous article in Grabowsky's *Zeitschrift für Politik*.[113] Grabowsky argued that Kehr (who was Grabowsky's colleague at the prestigious German University for Politics) failed to understand the state as an organism embedded in Raum following its own laws, and, hence, he misunderstood the sources of German foreign policy. "The state is a vital essence, which is composed above all of space and nationality, its natural foundations, but which cannot be comprehended through a simple summation of these elements but only by a combination and juxtaposition of space and nationality in a higher form."[114] This meant, of course, considering the state as an organism that possessed a life of its own ("*Das Gemeinsame von Staat und Organismus ist das Leben aus eigenem Recht*"). Considered in this way, the course of prewar German foreign policy acquired an entirely different aspect from that proposed by Kehr, one which to a certain extent reflected forces beyond human control.

> If we examine the fleet policy and the tariff policy around the turn of the century from this point of view, we find that they are, in fact, not explained by domestic power struggles but that they derive in the first degree from an entirely different sphere, namely the advance of Germany in the modern world of states. The geographic factor is decisive for this, the situation of Germany, its borders, the formation of its natural landscape, but then also the ethnographic factors. . . . The will to self-assertion is the supreme quality of the state just as it is the supreme quality of the individual. Here space and nationality combine, the space wishes to be preserved, the people to be maintained.[115]

This striking passage illustrates clearly how the acceptance of an organic and geodeterministic framework for analysis of state relations resulted in the validation of raw power as the legitimate final arbiter of relations between states. Although Grabowsky accurately pointed out the central weakness in Kehr's interpretation, that is, his failure to consider forces inherent in the same structure of the competitive state system that acted upon Germany from without, Grabowsky, for his part, attributes too much influence to these forces and sees them as manifestations of nature rather than what they in fact are, manifestations of international politics. Furthermore, despite his declarations against the use of Raum as an apology for partisan political ideas Grabowsky argued cogently that Raum justified the redrawing of German borders in the East: "Because Germany as a whole is a living unity, based upon a space and a nationality, the robbery of the Polish corridor is an amputation on a living body, an amputation that the patient cannot overcome and that makes him sick until the earlier condition is recreated. This is fortunately possible in the life of the state, unlike in physical life."[116]

As a journalist writing for the *Berliner Tageblatt, Das Neue Deutschland,* and other newspapers, Grabowsky was very active in applying his ideas of space and politics to the political issues of the day, focusing in his writing on questions involving eastern Europe and the League of Nations, which he criticized as a passive product of capitalism unsuited to solving the dynamic problems created by spatial dislocation in central Europe.[117] He felt that the German media could help overcome Germany's central European dilemma, however, by using geopolitics as a "means of education" to create "the geographical conscience of the state."[118] An active and effective foreign policy had to be based upon "knowledge as the predecessor of ability. More than any other nation, the German, so oriented toward the literary, needs world political ability, to somehow bring itself to rights in the world."[119] In promoting this knowledge Grabowsky was active as a lecturer on radio, to geographical groups, and to the general public in Berlin.[120] His greatest influence, however, may have been through his activities as a lecturer at the German University for Politics.[121] The university, which derived its funding from the federal government, the Carnegie and Rockefeller foundations, and the contributions of wealthy industrialists such as Robert Bosch, has been seen as a bastion of solidly liberal democratic thought in the Weimar era, but some recent scholarship suggests that it became increasingly nationalistic and rightist over the course of the Republic's history.[122] Grabowsky's duties included teaching the course "Introduction to Politics" and leading the "Geopolitical Seminar with World Political Exercises." The seminar was intended "as a practical supplement to the lectures on geopolitics and geoeconomics. It will thereby proceed not from geography but fundamentally from political science and politics; it concerns itself, therefore, not with political geography but with actual geopolitics in closest connection with world politics and world economics."[123]

The university's impact on the political life of the Republic was significant. By 1930 more than two thousand students had attended the university at various times, and although it remained small, it had the distinction in 1930 of offering the only diploma in political science available from a German university.[124] And because Grabowsky's courses were required in two of the most popular of the five courses of study offered (general politics and political history, and foreign policy), it seems likely most students came into contact with his ideas at one time or another.[125] At the same time larger circles came into contact with the ideas of Grabowsky, the democratic geopolitician, through his magazine, essays, lectures, and broadcasts. There is evidence that others in democratic circles, for example, Ernst Jäckh, Grabowsky's influential colleague and head of the German University for Politics both before and after the Nazi era, adopted elements of his approach. In his collection of lectures published in 1928 as *Deutschland. Das Herz Europas* (Germany: The heart of

Europe) Jäckh refers specifically to Grabowsky's seminar and uses many of his ideas in his discussion of the geographical factors determining the German role in Europe.[126] The future did not belong to Germany's democratic geopoliticians, however, and the events of the next few years would lend a tragic irony to Grabowsky's confidence in the divining power of geopolitical insights. "Like all political studies, geopolitics strives for the prognosis as the ultimate goal. Not prophecy, not, therefore, any kind of particulars of future development, but the prognosis, the overall course of future development as the product of insight in the over-all structure of historical destiny."[127] The inaccuracy of his own geo-political prognosis must have become painfully clear for Grabowsky only two years after writing these words when he fled national socialism for Switzerland.

Karl Haushofer: Geopolitician of the Airwaves

As German armored columns began rolling into Russia in the summer of 1941, many of the Wehrmacht's soldiers were initially uncertain of their ultimate mission. Speculation varied from the plausible to the fantastic. Some felt they were marching on a short preemptive campaign against Stalin; others argued the soldiers were only passing through the Soviet Union on their way to establishing a Nazi empire in India and Asia. Still others, guided by geopolitics, had sound scientific foundations on which to base their speculations, and they argued that Germany was setting forth to gain "bread and wheat fields" by force of arms. "One (sol-dier) had read Haushofer," a participant recalled later, "and gave a talk about geopolitics."[128] The common soldier's effort to make sense of his orders by reaching back to the teachings of Haushofer illustrates both how closely the name of Haushofer was associated with geopolitics in the German popular mind by 1941 and how successful Haushofer had been in using the German media to propagate his geopolitical message.

Haushofer was a ubiquitous presence in the German media during the two decades before the Second World War, spreading the message of Germany's shortage of living space "by a thousand channels."[129] He published more than five hundred articles and reviews and scores of books.[130] His association with some of the most influential journalists of his day, Rudolf Pechel, for instance, was close, and his work was widely published. In addition to his own journal Haushofer's writings appeared in mainstream publications, including the *Deutsche Rundschau, Deutsche*

Allgemeine Zeitung, Frankfurter Zeitung, and *Schwäbische Merkur,* and a host of lesser venues as well, including *Das Neue Reich, Deutsche Republik, Deutsche Wehr,* and more.[131] Haushofer may have had his greatest impact not through his abundant writings, however, but through his facility in adopting the new medium of radio as a means of heightening the geopolitical awareness of Germans. Radio was the second (after the telephone) of the many revolutionary communications technologies to reach a mass audience in the twentieth century, and its popularity during the Weimar years was phenomenal. The first German radio exhibition took place in Berlin in 1924, and by 1929 three million receiving sets in German homes were providing simultaneous access to an audience of unprecedented proportions.[132] And, beginning in 1924 and lasting through the fall of the Weimar Republic (with a brief interruption in 1931), Haushofer reached some portion of this audience with regular monthly broadcasts on political and geopolitical topics.[133]

Haushofer's flexibility in adapting to the new medium seems in some ways at odds with the rest of his character, which always retained a flavor of stolid, unimaginative pedantry, of Professor Unrat and the Kaiserreich, reflected in, among other things, his baroque literary posturings.[134] He was, nonetheless, a learned and widely traveled man. Born in 1869, Haushofer became an army officer and served as a German military observer in Japan from 1908 to 1910 where he acquired a lasting admiration for the spatial and geopolitical acumen of the Japanese. He also traveled in India, China, and Russia. After the war (which he ended as a divisional commander) Haushofer earned his doctorate in geography at Munich under Erich von Drygalski and was made an honorary professor in political geography, military geography, and East Asian studies there in 1921. His lectures, like his writings, were remarkable for their opacity, with the result, as his most thorough biographer has written, that "at the end of his lectures many (of his students) may have asked themselves, 'And what, in fact, did he just say'?"[135] Haushofer has entered history as the man who introduced Adolf Hitler to the concept of Lebensraum, but there is no agreement on when he first met Hitler. By 1924 at the latest, however, Haushofer had made Hitler's acquaintance through his pupil and friend, Rudolf Hess, and Haushofer certainly visited Hitler during his incarceration in Landsberg Prison.[136]

Haushofer was not the only advocate of geopolitics to recognize the utility of radio. Dix, Grabowsky, Banse, and Hermann Lautensach all made geopolitical broadcasts during this period.[137] No other geopolitician made the airwaves as regularly as Haushofer, however. He used his radio broadcasts, carried on *Deutsche Welle, Bayerischer Rundfunk,* and other networks, to define geopolitics for a broad audience and to alert Germans to the practical utility of the science. In two successive broadcasts carried on *Deutsche Welle* in 1929, for example, Haushofer treated the topic "What Is Geopolitics?" and described for his listeners the origins of the field and its contemporary relevance:

> Kjellén wanted [with geopolitics] to lead those in charge of political education to the conviction that no struggle for the maintenance, distribution, and shifting of political power on the earth . . . may proceed without constant regard for the earth-determined fundamentals, such as inhabitability and arability of the soil, its forms, its precipitation, its vegetation, and other life, if it wishes to be meaningful and have permanence. . . . And, on the other side, there is still in the prefix "Geo" something of the ancient mysticism that shrouds the holy name of mother earth.[138]

Haushofer here united two of the dominant rhetorical aspects of Weimar geopolitical thinking, its pose as a science (which placed geopolitics "above all party beliefs"), which it merged with references to mystical powers (exercised by race or environment) that could not be comprehended through science. For Germany geopolitics revealed the inequity of the distribution of Lebensraum among the world's great nations. Germans had to support 135 people per square kilometer of land, Haushofer argued, a population density far greater than that of the other advanced nations and one which world population trends would only make worse the longer Germans waited to revise it. "Our goals mean nothing less than the effort to produce a just distribution of living space on the earth, safeguarding against the fearful overpopulation of the earth (which is coming) in three hundred years at most."[139] Haushofer's listeners were reassured that their diligence and cultural excellence made the German revisionist cause a just one: "Thus geopolitics, properly understood, is one of the most powerful weapons for the just distribution of breathing and living space on the earth, according to the work ability and cultural achievement of peoples, not according to the violent dictates of a skillfully constructed firm for the maintenance of an unjust spatial distribution, a distribution that was only wangled and seized (*erlistet und errafft*) by war and force."[140]

Haushofer did not leave his listeners guessing as to the practical utility of geopolitics. As with any other science, geopolitics was meant to be a means of prediction and prescription, "naturally with a certain leeway for misdiagnoses, just as is the case with meteorology and medical science!"[141] If Germany's politicians had paid attention to geopolitical forces before the war, for example, the gross underestimation of the war's duration that formed the basis for many of their decisions would have been avoided. "[The duration] had to do, to a certain degree, with a purely geopolitical problem: the recognition that certain broad political spaces will necessarily need almost two years before they reach their full military exertion—as with the British and Russian empires—and that they naturally require another year to understand that this exertion of power cannot lead to the intended success."[142]

Nor did Haushofer shrink from prophesying, on the basis of geopolitical insight, a grim future for the European state system. "The more complicated, cramped, and illogically one builds life forms, like the twenty-seven small states of Europe, too small for world concepts, the more dangerous geopolitically predictable collisions around the world become for them."[143] This attempt to convince Germans, in 1931, that the European state system could not be stabilized in its present form because of geopolitical shortcomings was succeeded by an encouragement to revanchism in the form of a condemnation of "bad boundaries . . . which will always be felt as an open wound, until either all restrictions and hindrances fall or national countrymen of the same language on both sides of the border are again united."[144]

The close scrutiny devoted to Haushofer in the historiography of geopolitics is justified both by his contacts with the Nazis and his prolific contributions to the Weimar and Nazi German media popularizing geopolitics.[145] Haushofer's geopolitical beliefs led him to welcome the Nazis as the embodiment of a government that could vigorously pursue geopolitical principles in its foreign policy, which by following "Hitler, with his political-scientific instincts" would relieve the "fearful population density" of the German state.[146] The appalling lack of political insight that allowed him to see Nazi brutality as a force for the rejuvenation of Germany was shaped by his geopolitical convictions, and it is entirely possible that his writings and ideas contributed to similar misjudgment on the part of many of his fellow Germans. Haushofer's radio broadcasts, rarely examined because they are preserved only in his papers, provide a

vivid glimpse of what may have been his most effective venue of propagandizing. Because the size of radio audiences could only be estimated
in a day before ratings and surveys, one can only speculate about how
many Germans heard Haushofer's message. Still, with a potential audience over the years in the millions, thousands of Germans, many more
than the *Zeitschrift für Geopolitik* was able to reach, must have been exposed to Haushofer's geopolitical perspective. Years later, some looked to
geopolitics and Haushofer as they marched toward disaster in Russia.

Manfred Langhans-Ratzeburg and Geojurisprudence

One of the most unsettling of the many sinister characters portrayed in
Erfolg, Lion Feuchtwanger's novel of the triumph of reaction in Weimar
Bavaria, is the fictional Bavarian justice minister, Otto Klenk. Writing in
1930, Feuchtwanger depicted Klenk as an urbane and cynical reactionary, fortified in the cheerful practice of arbitrary judicial violence by a
glib faith in a peculiarly Bavarian form of justice. "It is grown, organic
Bavarian justice," Klenk explains to a challenger at one point. "Law and
ethics, maintained a certain north German philosopher by the name
of Immanuel Kant, were (important) beyond all proportion. Law and
Boden, however, law and climate, law and Volk, thinks he, Otto Klenk of
Munich, are two in one, indivisible. . . . Justice is the foundation of states,
but precisely because of that each state's justice must be out of the same
material as the state itself."[147] Although Feuchtwanger clearly condemns
the relativistic, or more properly particularistic, legal ethic expressed by
Klenk, there is little doubt that Klenk's sentiments would have found the
whole-hearted approval of many geopoliticians. They saw the law as yet
another aspect of state life that had its deepest roots in geography, and
they had a term for this relativist, localist, and "organic" approach to legal
theory, referring to it as *geojurisprudence.* The "organic" legal theories advanced under this name, and attacked indirectly in Feuchtwanger's cele-
brated novel, found their most articulate and prolific proponent during
the Weimar era in Manfred Langhans-Ratzeburg. His effort to integrate
law and geopolitics drew considerable notice from geographers and legal
theorists and demonstrated the limitations of the geopolitical claim to
applicability in every discipline.

Although Langhans-Ratzeburg was trained in the law, in which he
held a doctorate, his interest in geography came naturally. He was born in

1902 as the son of the famous geographer Paul Langhans. In addition to being one of the preeminent geographic and cartographic experts of his day the elder Langhans was also the editor through most of the Weimar period of *Petermanns Geographische Mitteilungen,* one of Germany's most prestigious geographic journals. It was in his father's journal that Manfred Langhans-Ratzeburg began publishing work on the links between geography and law with an article in 1924 entitled "Reichtliche und tatsächliche Machtbereiche der Grossmächte" (Legal and actual spheres of influence of the great powers). In this essay Langhans-Ratzeburg discussed the relationship of informal political or economic dominance which would today be called *neocolonialism,* and he argued that this relationship between the leading economic powers and less-developed states throughout the world had to be depicted on maps to convey an accurate picture of the state of world politics. The dominance of the weaker states by the stronger, even though informal, was a concrete part of international relations.

> In the wake of economic or intellectual penetration modern statecraft allows the more powerful [sovereign state] to erect a protective relationship in many essential points the equivalent of annexation over the weaker [protectorate state], the former carefully avoiding, however, allowing itself to appear as the actual ruler of the area it dominates. It is all the more an urgent geopolitical necessity, therefore, to track down all these often skillfully concealed but still existing connections and according to the acquired knowledge to draw a world image that corresponds to the actual power relations.[148]

This was, of course, an entirely reasonable view of the condition of relations at that time between the United States and much of Latin America, Great Britain and parts of the Middle East, and many other areas where the influence of powerful states eclipsed the self-determination of nominally independent but weaker states. To help foster the more accurate world image he hoped to see in future Langhans-Ratzeburg provided a double world map purporting to contrast de facto and de jure power relations around the globe. Nominally independent regions of Latin America dominated by the United States, for instance, were pictured in color schemes that ignored the official borders and portrayed them as colonies of the United States. He enlarged on the same theme two years later with a map and article entitled "Karte des Selbstbestimmungsrechtes der Völker" (Map of the self-determination rights of peoples). This work, which also appeared in *Petermanns,* betrayed a more immediate political purpose than was evident in his analysis of global spheres of interest. The goal of the map, he wrote in the accompanying essay, was to depict "together those peoples and lands that correspond in their international law and geopolitical positions and, thereby, to acquire a map of the self-determining and the partially and wholly oppressed living spaces."[149] He argued that geopoliticians, particularly Karl Haushofer and Otto Maull, were his predecessors in this endeavor, and he went on to divide the world's peoples into two groups, "peoples with self-determining states," and "peoples without self-determining states."[150] These two major categories were in turn divided into subgroups with Germany occupying a place in the lowest subgroup of the self-determining category, "third stage: partially self-determining externally, with full internal self-determination." This put Germany in a group with Bulgaria, Hungary, and other states that were subject to observation by organs of the League of Nations; only five countries, the United States, Japan, Russia, France, and England, had attained the most advanced stage of self-determination, "first stage: self-determining with influence on foreign states." Considered as a whole, Langhans-Ratzeburg argued, the map showed "with frightening clarity how little the high ideal of legal equality of peoples has till now been attained, despite the League and pacifism, and how far separated the internationalist daydream yet remains from its goal. For the German people this map also has an educational effect because with its stages it draws emphatic notice to how deep it has actually sunk in relation to other peoples."[151]

Both geopoliticians and other intellectuals at the time took positive notice of the effort to link geography, law, and international law. A relativistic legal tradition had existed in Germany since at least the early nineteenth century, and Langhans-Ratzeburg's efforts to bring geographic considerations into legal theorizing had similarities with the Grossraum legal theoretics of Carl Schmitt.[152] Otto Köllreuter, teacher of constitutional law at Jena and author of influential legal studies, including *Grundriss der Allgemeinen Staatslehre* (Political parties in the modern state), reviewed Otto Maull's *Politische Geographie* (Political geography) in the *Archiv des öffentlichen Rechts* in 1925, praising the geopolitical concept of the state organism and arguing that the "various qualities of land and people doubtlessly play an important role" in the formation of constitutional law.[153] Karl Haushofer took this idea further in an article in the *Zeitschrift für Völkerrecht* in 1928 entitled "Geopolitik und Geojurisprudenz" (Geopolitics and geojurisprudence), in which he indicted German legal studies for its lack of geographical grounding and blamed it for helping mislead Germans about the nature of their struggle in the First World War. Invoking the sainted Kjellén, Haushofer argued that the great geopolitician had worried often about "the thin, sterile air of legal scientific concepts and the fraudulent, political scientific, treaty-waving political posture of the so-called central powers in their struggle for existence, which was recognized too late by the masses."[154] Haushofer continued that geojurisprudence, as presented in the work of its chief representative (*Hauptvertreter*) Manfred Langhans-Ratzeburg, offered a way back to the essentials of German law that would avoid the mistakes of the past. The German concept of legal relations between states, by incorporating a geographic perspective, would reveal to Germans that the only durable legal structures (e.g., borders) were those that accorded with the dictates of geography. Geojurisprudence would, thus, contribute to the geopolitical revanchist mission by helping Germany to renew its law "from solid ground outward on the back of the real earth and again to expand the extent of its ethnic and cultural soil."[155]

Just what Haushofer meant by founding the study of law "on the back of the real earth" is clear in Langhans-Ratzeburg's major exposition of the theory of geojurisprudence, entitled *Begriff und Aufgaben der Geogaphischen Rechtswissenschaft (Geojurisprudenz)* (The concept and tasks of geographical legal science [geojurisprudence]: A systematic approach to the connections of legal science to geography, cartography and geopolitics). The book was published by the Kurt Vowinckel house in 1928 as a companion volume to the *Zeitschrift für Geopolitik* (Journal for geopolitics), and Langhans-Ratzeburg was clear, at least in his own mind, that law and geography were inseparably linked. He correctly identified the attempt to integrate disciplines as one of the keys to the geopolitical approach, praising works of Hettner, Karl Haushofer, and the historians Walther Vogel and Albert von Hoffmann for their attempts to link the study of geography, history, politics, and culture. Then he argued that the same approach would be fruitful in the study of law. "The geographic method is applicable to all, even purely intellectual, manifestations, and should, therefore, be placed at the disposal of law. Jurists, too, ought to have long since overcome their pronounced, disadvantageous prejudice in view of the excellent knowledge collected through similar cooperation, for example, in the border discipline of legal history or in geopolitics. Thus, it requires in fact only a bit of stouthearted confidence to raise the demand for a geographic legal science, or geojurisprudence.[156]

This new discipline would be a branch of law, not geography, because the application of legal approaches to geography promised to yield little for geography, whereas the application of geographical knowledge and methods to law promised to yield a great deal.[157] Langhans-Ratzeburg was always particularly sensitive to the meaning of cartographic symbols, as his comments on maps in his articles on self-determination and spheres of influence would suggest, and he envisioned the creation of a new cartography as one of the primary tasks of the field. Geojurisprudence would help produce maps of regional variations in criminal, private, and commercial law, the extent of various legal ideas and procedures, historical maps of the regional evolution of legal practice, and international maps that indicated neocolonial relationships. He explicitly recognized the reifying function of cartographic imagery, arguing that geojuridical maps would reveal "the spatial jurisdiction of legal phenomena," the geographic extent of Roman law in Europe, for example, and would, thus, serve as tools to expedite change.[158] Cartographic geojurisprudence would expose the hypocrisy of conventional cartography by portraying the true state of political relations between states. "Geojuristic maps allow the colonial political character of the continent of Africa and the peripheral position of its few independent states to stand out," he wrote, complaining later that "all political maps, in a completely deceptive manner, present the 'free states' of Panama, Haiti, Nicaragua, and so on, as completely independent, even though their complete dependence upon the United States . . . is well known."[159]

Geojurisprudence would also be responsible for articulating the "earth dependency (*Erdgebundenheit*) of constitutional law." Because the consideration of law had been for so long loosed from its moorings in soil and ethnicity, "the very sense for the mutual interconnection of constitutional law and geography has until very recently remained largely undeveloped." And, although the role of historical forces might at times supersede that of geography in elucidating legal developments, the processes of historical, state, and constitutional development themselves were geographically conditioned. Langhans-Ratzeburg pointed to the problem of conflicts between particularistic and centralizing forces in German legal and political development as an issue to which geojurisprudence could contribute a new dimension of understanding. Only by considering the interplay of geography and the "ethnic diversity of the German tribes" over the last thousand years of German history could one develop a meaningful appreciation of the problem and hope to devise a lasting solution.[160] Other cases that a geographical approach would illuminate were the development of the legal relations of metropole and colonies in the British empire and the development of democratic forms in various geographical settings. "The example of direct democracy shows equally clearly how thoroughly the type and formation of the [geography of the] state influence the shaping of governing forms because its actual application is possible only in small states [Swiss cantons]."[161]

Langhans-Ratzeburg's primary research interest was in applying geojurisprudence to interstate relations and international law, and he argued that geojurisprudence had special contributions to make to these fields and to geopolitics in general. Geographic international law could serve as a source of geopolitical knowledge because he felt it was "the essence of geopolitics to investigate political processes through a dynamic method of consideration within the chorographic perspective of earth dependency, thus it treats primarily international legal processes."[162] This could mean in practice a number of things, such as drawing "on a map of middle Europe over the course of the Danube and its tributaries those stretches internationalized in the treaties of the suburbs of Paris . . . [thus gaining] a concept of how widely ramified and spatially large is the geopolitical Danube problem."[163] It could explain the sources of conflict in "contested areas," regions of the earth "in the actual possession of one power while another refuses officially to recognize existing circumstances, and each according to occasion and circumstance more or less frequently and more or less loudly justifies its own legal claim." This aspect of geojurisprudence had particular geopolitical significance because "in [these areas] the spatial conflicts of the states struggling for possession intersect so that they usually represent characteristic geopolitical properties of national border struggles," and such conflicts generally arose "in geopolitical friction belts."[164] Other significant efforts to synthesize a geographic view of international legal relations included his study from 1929, *Die Volgadeutschen. Ihr Staats- und Verwaltungsrecht in Vergangenheit und Gegenwart* (The Volga Germans: Their state and administrative law in past and present). This work appeared as an imprint of the German Society for the Study of Eastern Europe, whose organ, *Ost-Europa,* was edited by Otto Hoetzsch.

Ultimately, the work implied, law could in some cases triumph over geography. Langhans-Ratzeburg concluded from his investigation that though the Volga Germans were geographically isolated from their homeland, the increased legal autonomy they had received from the Bolshevik regime would preserve their cultural integrity and that "precisely we Reich Germans can and should be glad of the rescue of a small island of German ethnicity from sinking in the great Slavic sea surging around them."[165]

In his last major work written in the Weimar era, *Die grossen Mächte geojuristisch betrachtet* (The great powers considered geojuristically), Langhans-Ratzeburg argued that Germany as a state still belonged among the great powers by virtue of its natural resources, population, and development but that its position in international law as a result of defeat by the Allies was that of a "handicapped great power." In common with geopolitical thought in general, in this book he emphasizes the importance of national will in determining the fate of states. It was, in fact, primarily the power of will, supported by geographical factors, that bestowed Germany's continued status as a great, if diminished, power. This was proven, he wrote, "by the gratifying fact that no German government, whether right or left, has recognized by an eastern Locarno the Polish corridor created by the extorted peace treaty and that every government till now has characterized the *Anschluss* of Austria as desirable. And Austria and Danzig announce at every opportunity their will to Anschluss. One must, therefore, characterize Germany as a whole . . . as a handicapped great power."[166] Langhans-Ratzeburg also used the book to argue, like Feuchtwanger's character Klenk, that German conditions dictated a decentralized and particularistic brand of jurisprudence within the Reich. "The French landscape, with its structure friendly to transit is everywhere easily reached from Paris, the Russian landscape is characterized by the radial river and canal network fanning out from Moscow; in both cases the unitary state is a given, as we have already said. The German Reich has no such central gathering space. Therefore, the German state, if it is to harmonize with the form of its living space, cannot be centralized in the French or Russian sense, but must, following the cue of nature, assume a decentralized form."[167]

Despite its occasional successes (such as heightening the general awareness of informal hegemonic international relationships) geojurisprudence on the whole was a failure, the result in large part of the same weaknesses that undermined geopolitics in general. As reflected in the work of Langhans-Ratzeburg, geojurisprudence was never able to devise a convincing reconciliation between its claims for geodeterministic development of law and the realities it was attempting to explain. This is apparent in the effort to explain centralization and particularism in Germany and Japan. Langhans-Ratzeburg argued that geography and ethnic composition shaped German legal and political development along particularistic and decentralized lines because of the lack of a central "gathering space" (Sammelraum). Leaving aside the entire issue of whether Russia presented any kind of ethnic unity or whether it actually offered a geographically determined natural gathering point (created in part by a network of canals), Langhans-Ratzeburg's explanation for the development of Japanese centralism conflicted with his analysis of the sources of German particularism. He cited Japanese ethnic homogeneity and the harmony of the Japanese national landscape as elements tending to make a unitary and centralized state as the most natural form for Japan.[168] Although it is possible that the Japanese population is ethnically more homogeneous than the German, and that this may ease the task of welding a centralized governing structure together, it can scarcely be said that the geography of the Japanese archipelago, scattered across one thousand miles of ocean, divided by rugged mountain ranges into a series of valleys, and subject to considerable climatic variations, is more "naturally" or inherently conducive to centralization than are the North German Plain and the German plateau to the north of the Alps. As with the geopolitical approach to the relation of politics and geography, the reliance of geojurisprudence on geodeterministic forces to account for legal developments lacked consistent explanatory power. Viewed from a distance of nearly seven decades, it seems clear that the temptation to turn to geography for the sources of law was as much a chimera as was the effort to derive the sources of politics from geography.

Walther Vogel and the Function of Geography in History

The relationship between geopolitics and the study of history was always intimate. Attempts to apply geopolitics in case studies of specific regions usually took on a strongly historical cast, and as the writings of many geopoliticians make clear, a primary goal of German geopolitics was to explain Germany's history and international position before, during, and after the First World War through geography.[169] The works of Walther Vogel, a historical geographer who used geopolitical ideas extensively in understanding history, provide a revealing case study of the forms in which geopolitics penetrated historical writing and teaching at German universities in the Weimar era. Born into an industrialist's family in Chemnitz in 1880, Vogel spent his early academic career writing on the history of the Hansa, editing the *Hansische Umschau,* and publishing in 1915 the *Geschichte der deutschen Seeschiffahrt* (History of sea travel). During the Weimar era he taught as professor (*ördentlicher Professor*) for historical geography and state science at the University of Berlin (a position created in part at the urging of Albrecht Penck) and served as chairman and co-founder of the university's geopolitically oriented Council for Foreign Studies from 1920.[170] Popular as a teacher at Berlin (participation in his seminars averaged between forty and sixty students per semester from the mid-1920s to the early 1930s), Vogel was also a prolific author of widely read books, essays, and reviews.[171] His most important work of the era, *Das neue Europa und seine historisch-geographischen Grundlagen* (The new Europe and its historical-geographical foundations), went through three printings within four years of its publication in 1921. Vogel was also active as a lecturer outside the University, and he published articles in a variety of geographical, colonial and geopolitical journals.[172] With the possible exception of the writings of Hugo Hassinger, Vogel's work represents the most thoroughgoing and sophisticated attempt to apply geopolitical ideas within a historical framework, and he was recognized by contemporaries as one of the foremost historical advocates of geopolitical ideas.[173]

Das neue Europa was the product of a series of lectures on political geography that Vogel delivered after the war at Berlin. The purpose of the book was to make readers aware, as Vogel put it, of "the deeper foundations of the present new ordering of the European state system."[174] These deeper foundations were, as he explained, geographical, and Vogel elucidated an extremely long-term view of German history, arguing that the events of everyday political activity and historical change were a mere superstructure, froth on the submerged geographical currents that really determined history. The determinist aspect of geography in history held promise for the German nation. The unfolding of geographic destiny in human history was an ineluctable process and one that would ultimately restore Germany to its position of power in central Europe. It was the duty of historians, imbued with a consciousness of the political meaning of geography, to expose the elemental causes of history, "since through the colorful procession of daily excitement and the immediate prehistory of the world war, in which we ourselves have taken passionate part as contemporaries or even as participants, we forget all too easily the deeper, slower currents of national life and the barely changing geographical circumstances that, with pitiless force, determine the destiny of states much more effectively than the alarm and agitation of everyday life would permit one to believe."[175]

An understanding of history grounded in these forces revealed, Vogel argued, that a new age had been called into being by the war, "the turning point has already been passed," and the process of adjusting and resolving all the newly created conflicts might take decades before stability was reintroduced into the economic and political life of the European state system. This was to prove, in the event, an accurate prediction although it is not clear whether it was the result of the ineluctable ethnic and geographic forces singled out by Vogel or of political failures and obsolete ideologies. Vogel offered Germans an analysis of these events that was, "to use the technical expressions coined by Kjellén, essentially a geopolitical and demopolitical study."[176]

What such a study revealed about the state in general and about Germany specifically, according to Vogel, was the organic nature of the state. Vogel echoed Haushofer and other geopoliticians in asserting that the state was the living expression of the symbiotic relationship between the land and its people. He thus objected to any concept of the state that was merely legal, or which saw in the state only the protector of order and rights, claiming instead that it was "just as much a naturally grown combination of people, an ethnic-organism, which clings to a particular piece of soil, a power manifestation, which means a natural being, which, therefore, like men behaves not only according to reasonable rules as the representative of morality, but organically instinctively, according to instincts of will."[177] For Vogel as for Adolf Grabowsky, the geopolitical concept of the state as an organism led to a repudiation of political and historical theories that argued that peoples and states create their own destiny independently of geography, a view denounced by Vogel as "an extraordinarily harmful prejudice." Organic state theory and geodeterminism also promoted a conservative, corporatist approach to politics that, like the political theory of Adolf Grabowsky or the jurisprudence of Manfred Langhans-Ratzeburg, glorified the state and stressed the primacy of the group over the individual. Relying, for instance, on Othmar Spann's corporatist writings, Vogel argued, "One grasps the true essence of the state only when one proceeds from the supra-individual whole as the primary, the truly essential."[178]

Applied to the history of Germany and central Europe, these ideas suggested to Vogel that the cause of the region's unsettled history was the contradiction between geopolitical and demopolitical tendencies resulting from the mixing of roughly twenty nationalities in an area of two million square kilometers devoid in many places of significant natural barriers. The area between the Oder, the Adriatic, the Black Sea, and the Dnieper was "a confusion of nations and tribes," an ethnogeographic Gordian knot that offered little chance for the creation of ethnically homogeneous, unified nation-states. By casting the issue of central European political ferment in such terms, suggesting that ethnic heterogeneity was the primary problem, Vogel left a dangerous theoretical opening in his historical scheme. It is but a step from the identification of multiplicity as the root problem to the conclusion that the elimination of multiplicity is the solution.

For Germany itself, Vogel argued, disunity and defeat were problems created by geography rather than ethnicity. The German lands were characterized by lack of harmony, with variations in climate between north and south, east and west, and rivers that served as axes of division for German trade and politics rather than avenues of easy exchange. The state created by Bismarck was, therefore, fissured along lines of local state and confessional loyalties, which the political pressures created by Germany's central position had exacerbated by inducing Germany "to look simultaneously east and west like a Janus head."[179] These internal divisions had helped bring on the German defeat, which had left the state in an infinitely worsened political-geographical position. Because of territorial losses in west and east, "the population of Germany is not only painfully cut on its borders and constricted upon narrower space but has also been robbed of precisely the most promising agricultural colonization areas on the broad, thinly settled fields of the east Elbian landowners (the average population density risen from 120 to 130 per square kilometer)."[180]

Like others who embraced geopolitical ideas, however, Vogel lacked the courage of his convictions in one respect: he was unwilling to accept his own pronouncements concerning fate and the determining role of geography because history suggested they could condemn Germany to the role of predestined loser. Geodeterminism was a handy means of exculpating Germans of their defeat and earlier disunity, but it could also be a trap. The geography of Germany, after all, was essentially the same in 1921 or 1925 as it had been before the war when it had helped cause Germany's defeat. Vogel, like other geopoliticians, felt compelled to seek an escape from the trap of his own geodeterminism. For Arthur Dix, technology had provided the key to escape. For Manfred Langhans-Ratzeburg legal mystification and superficiality had provided it. Vogel, like Haushofer, found this escape in will. Human will, if applied with proper understanding and with sufficient resolution, could overcome the dictates of geography, could even transform them into assets. Will, for example, could change the Lebensraum required by a nation by helping to modify living standards or through the application of cultural methods of improving the productivity of the living space.[181] "The majority of the nation shrank from the will to national unification against the outside," Vogel wrote in explaining the psychic causes of German defeat. "It requires only this unified national will to reacquire freedom; all technical-military, economic, and other measures and considerations are in comparison of relatively minor significance."[182]

The sources of this national failure of will were to be found not solely in geography but also in politics and ethnicity, Vogel argued. Specifically, this meant Socialists and Jews. As with his analysis of political instability in central Europe, Vogel here identified ethnic heterogeneity as a source of Germany's problems. He now carried his analysis further than he had done earlier, however, by calling for action to limit the problems created by the alien ethnic element. The "claim for national independence," as Vogel described German postwar revanchism, foundered because it intersected with the strivings of socialist workers to "maintain and expand their acquired political-social power position in the state." And the selfish concerns of socialist workers for their own well-being, a selfishness evident in democrats in general, were most fervently defended by an ethnically alien element, German Jews.

A great difficulty lies in the fact that these obsolete but still powerful international or antinational views are borne in the social-democratic (and overall democratic) leadership in the nation primarily by members of an alien ethnicity, namely by Jewry. That the Jews, apart from their economic involvement in the national body, are unable to enthuse themselves for national German requirements and ideals is indeed understandable from the entire historic position of this people, but it makes all the more serious their power position in the state, which stands in crass incongruence with their numbers.

Vogel was willing to concede that Jews could be useful as movers and shakers for the "often somewhat ponderous German type," provided they "kept in their place." However, he unequivocally denounced the prominence of Jews in Weimar society: "Their adopted master role is unbearable, and to topple them [is] one of the first preconditions for Germany's renewal."[183]

Vogel completed his comprehensive analysis in *Das neue Europa* with a call for a form of economically federalized Europe. Because of German productivity, this would provide a safeguard for German political and cultural power and a means of escape from the League of Nations, which he denounced as a tool of the victor powers for the suppression of Germany.[184] Vogel's federalized Europe would allow Europeans to resist pressure from the behemoths on their flanks, the Americans and Russians, while maintaining their autonomy within the individual nation-states of Europe. But he made it clear that the nation-state as such, which he said had arisen as a specific response to the conditions of European geography and the small continent's multiplicity of languages and ethnic-cultural groups, had exhausted its utility.[185] At first glance such a federalistic scheme might appear inconsistent with Vogel's attacks on Jews and socialists for their "obsolete" internationalism and inability to warm up to the necessary "national" approach to Germany's recovery, but Vogel's European federalism was primarily a vehicle for the reassertion of German power rather than a means to end international conflict.

Not surprisingly, Vogel was also hostile to the peace settlement in the Rhineland.[186] Both in *Das neue Europa* and elsewhere he devoted a great deal of attention to the geopolitical importance of the Rhine in German history. This was not because Vogel felt that the Rhine had historically possessed a central political role in linking the German peoples along its course. Despite the great economic importance of the Rhine, the topography of the river valley, the presence of other navigable rivers nearby and the patterns of settlement along its banks had prevented it from serving, as the Danube served Austria, as a political-economic backbone for a unified Germanic state.[187] To Vogel, however, the main trunk of the European continent formed what he described as a "trapeze," over which the course of history (in the form of political, economic, and military power) swung back and forth. This trapeze stretched roughly along lines from north central France in the west to Moscow in the east, and from the Baltic in the north to the Balkans in the south. It was pierced by four great throughways for exchange of which the Rhine was one, and from this fact the river derived its importance for the German future. Despite the geographic and political factors that had combined to limit its political significance in the past, river traffic as a supplement to rail had been on the increase before the war, and it was clear that the river was again reverting to German influence. "The internationalization of the German rivers established in the Versailles peace extortion, particularly that of the Rhine, is in the present form infeasible for the long run," because France was a "foreign body" on the Rhine.[188] To help draw it further under German influence and to help it realize its political potential for Germany Vogel proposed the construction of a Rhine-Danube canal.

As a historian, Vogel was always sensitive to the potential for a geopolitical analysis to become too heavily geographical, and he cautioned against this tendency.[189] He was also a professional educator, however, and he was enthusiastic about the potential benefits of educating Germans to a geopolitically influenced view of history. Such teaching could, for example, contribute to the realization of a kind of "Prussian socialism," which Vogel idealized as the optimum relationship between German workers and their leaders, a relationship which would relegate Jews to their "proper place" in German society. Decades of education in a geopolitical-historical view of German development would lead workers to realize "completely on their own, that violent eruption out of the course of national tradition brings its own consequences, that the proper place for them is at the side of the representatives of genuine old Prussianism, and that in the old Prussian spirit is contained more concession to the whole, more true sense of community, truer socialism than in the verbose Jewish-Marxist ideology."[190] At his death in May 1938 Vogel was at work on what he hoped would be the pedagogical culmination of his life's work, the *Historische Atlas von Deutschland,* a project begun under Vogel's leadership in 1930 with the financial support of the Notgemeinschaft der deutschen Wissenschaften.[191]

Vogel assigned readings from his own work, from Maull, Hettner, Fritz Jaeger, Ratzel, Kjellén, and others in his courses to illustrate his views to his students.[192] Both in his own courses and in the seminars that he organized as chairman of the Council for Foreign Studies at Berlin Vogel's focus was on political power, and he felt geopolitics was an essential part of such a study. "The question that will be answered here," he wrote, "and indeed not generally and theoretically but concretely and in each individual case is 'How is political power formed; how is political will embodied? Which components contribute to the formation of power?'"[193] During years of lecturing he had found that the teaching of the state laid out by Kjellén was a reliable method of educating students in these questions. "I have found Kjellén's division into geopolitics, ecopolitics, demopolitics, sociopolitics, and cratopolitics proven and use it as the foundation, often somewhat simplified, for the consideration of individual states." Within the framework of a consideration of each of the "active great powers," Vogel proceeded to represent first "the genesis and the geopolitical character of the state being, particularly the development of the territory," considering at the same time significant nongeographical historical factors."[194] Geopolitics thus played a role in his explanation of the origins of states to his students, as well as informing his delineation of their historical development.

Like other geopoliticians, Vogel's pedagogical approach was integrative. Speakers, exercise leaders, and participants in the language and culture courses he implemented for the Council for Foreign Studies were drawn from all the faculties of the University of Berlin, an unusual approach at a time when German university life was characterized by sharp and carefully maintained divisions between disciplines. This was a logical consequence of his own historical practice, which attempted to blend elements of history, geography, law, and other disciplines. Although his analysis of the consequences of the war and his prediction that Europe would need decades to settle into a peaceful state system proved accurate, his reading of the sources of European turbulence in geography and demography is only a part of the story. Ideology and politics operated in ways not directly derived from either geographic or demographic factors to influence the course of events, as Vogel himself occasionally admitted. Despite his warnings against slipping into geographical determinism, Vogel's analysis in the end did precisely that, proving unable to find any satisfactory way around the dilemma that his own geographical emphasis created for Germany. Thus the focus on will, and the hostility to groups (socialists, Jews) who "threatened" the unity of that will. Vogel predicted in *Das neue Europa* that Germany would not find peace for years: He was right, and his own writings contributed to the fulfillment of his prophecy.

Germany's postwar misery intensified the appeal of geopolitics for thinkers from many disciplines and political backgrounds. The geocentrism expressed in Grabowsky's concept of the heroic earth is key to understanding this appeal. The notion that geographic space, the earth's topography, was an active force that Germans had ignored at their peril supplied seemingly plausible explanations for the disaster that had befallen Germany, and it suggested there were ways to reverse the verdict of the war. Each of the men examined in this chapter, for example, hoped geopolitical education would catalyze the social mobilization of the German nation so that they could press with a united front for revision of the peace settlement. Dix and Haushofer were tireless in taking their case to the German people through every channel possible, believing that the scientific validity of geopolitics would convince Germans, regardless of their political background, of the pressing need of the moment. Vogel hoped a geopolitically sensitive Prussianism could replace socialism and unite workers in support of the patriotic cause.

The appeal of geopolitics as revealed in the works of these writers also had a curiously double-edged quality. Although an optimistic note was provided by the claim that geography, properly understood and acted upon, promised salvation to desperate Germans, the geopolitical analysis of racial and demographic issues rested more than a little in an appeal to fear. Geopoliticians promised that technology and the new concept of geography would lift Germans out of their humiliation, but they also incited undercurrents of racial and class antagonism in German society. Fear of Slavs, Jews, and, in the case of Vogel, Socialists was invoked to add potency and attraction to geopolitical rhetoric. For Burgdörfer and Dix the specter of a demographic racial catastrophe, the sources and solutions of which were cast in geopolitical terms, was used to emphasize the need for united commitment to geopolitically founded settlement programs. For many of these writers, including Grabowsky, Haushofer, and Vogel, the perceived necessity for national unity led to a political emphasis on the needs and rights of groups over those of individuals, which in the cases of the latter two men approached a geopolitical apology for corporatism. Their geopolitics, taken as a whole, exalted the state, promoted fear of Germany's Slavic neighbors, and justified German imperialism. Even in the hands of an intelligent and perceptive moderate such as Adolf Grabowsky, geopolitical rhetoric implicitly subverted the rationale for a peaceful and internationalist foreign policy. When translated into political action, the nationalistic expansionism elucidated in theory by these geopolitical and geopolitically influenced intellectuals could have an important impact on the German domestic political scene as the history of the German colonialist movement in the interwar years suggests.

CHAPTER 6

A Text for Imperialism

Geopolitics and the German Student

From the standpoint of national-political education few words are
required about the necessity of pursuing geopolitics in teaching.
The school as a portion of the entire people cannot isolate itself from
the destiny of the age. It has to take up the new ideas that inhere in
geopolitics as a science and must incorporate these suitably in its structure.

Johann Thies, *Geopolitik in der Volksschule,* 1932

The ceaseless publicizing activities of individual geopolitical theorists—
the radio broadcasts of a Haushofer, the lectures of an Adolf Grabowsky,
or the journal articles of an Arthur Dix—played a key role in elaborating
geopolitical ideas for a wide public audience. Despite the notable success that such individual proponents of geopolitical ideas enjoyed, however, geopoliticians themselves were never satisfied with such haphazard
methods of reaching their audience. They sought, instead, a permanent
institutional base for the dissemination of geopolitical ideas, and they
found this base in the Weimar Republic's schools, particularly its universities. The use by German elementary and secondary schools of maps,
rhetoric, and concepts taken from geopolitics during the Nazi era is fairly
well known.[1] Less widely recognized, but certainly as significant, is the
extensive promulgation of geopolitical ideas in German schools—in
many subjects—during most of the Weimar era. Because of the inroads
geopolitics made in German schools between 1924 and 1933, there can be
little doubt that most young Germans schooled during these years were
already perfectly familiar with geopolitical rhetoric and ideas by the time
the Nazis assumed control over the German educational system.

No aspect of German social life during the Weimar period interested geopolitical thinkers more than the education of German youth.

Geopoliticians were especially interested in what Germans learned of geography and history, for obvious reasons. If the applied science of geopolitics were to have any practical value, they reasoned, it had to be able to use a systematic means of influencing the mental image Germans held of topography, politics, and the past. It had to overcome German narrowness of perspective—*Kirchturmschattenbeschränktheit,* Haushofer called it, or church steeple parochialism—and impart a broad, spatial view of the world.[2] Such expansion of German horizons, they believed, was a necessary prerequisite to any rebirth of German power in central Europe. It was natural for geopoliticians to look to schools as promising channels for the dissemination of the geopolitical perspective, in part, because many of the geopoliticians were themselves professional educators. The classroom was attractive, too, because it offered an impressionable captive audience, and geopolitical thinkers enjoyed considerable success in their efforts to ensure that this audience was exposed to the message of geopolitics. School administration was a power reserved to the states, not the central government, under the Weimar constitution. The schools of Prussia may be taken as broadly representative of German education in general, because these instructed two-thirds of all German students and tended in some ways to serve as a model for schools in the Republic's other states. The geopolitical penetration of Prussian schools was so thorough that by the time the Nazis seized power Prussian students had been instructed in geopolitical ideas and rhetoric through their entire formal education from elementary school to the university. Three factors combined in Weimar Prussia to ensure that geopolitics assumed a place in school curricula. The first of these was an ongoing movement within the discipline of geography to reform geographic instruction. This movement, in turn, provided an opportunity for geopolitical geographers and historians to influence the course of these reforms and to introduce geopolitics into schools through their texts. Finally, the sympathetic intervention of state educational authorities gave these efforts the official sanction that guaranteed a significant geopolitical presence in Prussian schools.

Constructing a "National" Geography

A movement within the geographic profession to reform instruction in geography provided a springboard for the infusion of geopolitical ideas into Prussian education. Since the closing years of the nineteenth century professional geography in Germany had struggled both with its self-definition as a discipline and with the question of how best to teach geography to students in secondary schools. The two issues were obviously related. Geography as a field of study was plagued by an ambiguous self-image. German geographers viewed their subject, on the one hand, as a natural science with links to geology whose primary emphasis was on mathematical geography and the study of variations in topography. On the other hand, cultural or, in contemporary parlance, human geography, imparted a strong flavor of the humanities to much geographical writing, imbuing it with an emphasis on cultural landscapes that in practice produced a blend of descriptive geography, history, and anthropology.[3] By the turn of the twentieth century this had created a widespread feeling within the profession that geographers had lost any clear sense of their pedagogical priorities, and that they had to narrow their focus in order to give greater definition to geography as an independent discipline.[4] This epistemological confusion prompted a series of calls for reform of the field and its teaching methods.

One of the first and most successful such calls came from Hans Harms, who criticized the amorphous nature of geographic studies in his *Fünf Thesen zur Reform des geographischen Unterrichts. Ein Vortrag.* (Five theses for the reform of geographic teaching), published in 1895 and sufficiently well received to go through seven editions in the three succeeding decades. "Geographic instruction has become too all-embracing," Harms warned. "It must consolidate itself as a geography of the fatherland."[5] Harms called for a greater patriotic and contemporary political emphasis as a means of sharpening the focus of the discipline for educational purposes. This struck a receptive chord among many of Harms' colleagues and anticipated the calls for reform of geographic and historical teaching that the geopoliticians would raise after World War I. The material to be taught by geographers had become "boundless as the globe," Harms complained, and he suggested that the best way to reduce and give shape to this mass of material was to make Germany alone the focus of geographical education which, properly developed, would ensue in "a complete cultural geography."[6] "Let us make the fatherland the core and hub of geographic teaching! The French have done so, as far as I know, long before us."[7] Geography would thus define itself by moving away from cosmopolitanism, acquiring purpose by outlining a national geographic narrative. Nationalism would shape both the form and content of geography, functioning for the geographic profession in the same way nationalist historians like Friedrich Meinecke hoped it would for the historical profession.[8]

These arguments were echoed and amplified fourteen years later in the *Reformvorschläge des deutschen Geographentages für den erdkundlichen Unterricht an den höheren Schulen* (Reform proposals of the German geographic Congress for geographic instruction in the higher schools). The proposals, presented in a series of essays by some of the most prominent academic geographers of the day, emphasized the contemporary political uses and aims of a proper German geographical education. Alois Geistbeck, a geographer who composed a series of important geography texts used throughout the Weimar period, argued that geography ought to make Germans aware of their interests in sea power and colonies and serve as "teacher and guide to the present, as history is for the past." Geistbeck's call for geographic renewal in terms of political utility cited Ratzel and anticipated Weimar geopoliticians by arguing that "all politics, all trade and exchange rest finally on geographic ground, and the state not only outwardly but in its inmost essence is connected with its Boden."[9] The profession as a whole reiterated its support for this approach at its convention in Strassburg in 1914, adopting a model teaching program that emphasized the dualistic nature of geographic teaching (pairing physical geographic and anthropogeographic instruction) and called for two hours of geographic education at all levels rather than the one hour permitted by the Prussian educational guidelines of 1901.[10] At the time, however, these proposals were not taken up at official levels.

Professional perplexity about geographic education was intensified by the results of the war. Reform-minded geographers began to incorporate geopolitical theory, which had its own pedagogical program and goals, to produce a persistent and ultimately effective call for the reform of geographic instruction in Prussian schools. Erich Obst warned in 1923 that splintering into a variety of specializations was creating a "tragedy of general geography" that could end in the disappearance of the profession. "Geography runs a very real danger of becoming a superficial science of the earth if it does not specialize itself as quickly as possible according to particular regions."[11] Like Harms before the war, Obst was proposing that geography resolve its crisis by attempting to create a geographical narrative of Germany. This "crisis of geographic science" would be surmounted only on the basis of a new synthetic and integrative geography, which would draw the various geographic specializations together into a geography of the "landscape as a complex phenomenon."[12] This new geographical awareness would be regional in focus, hence the name Länderkunde, or regional geography, and it would be "the geography of the future." Echoing Harms's comments from nearly three decades earlier, Obst argued that the precondition to the survival of the field was a constant awareness of geography as a "science of the present," sensitive to every natural and artificial, including political, change in landscape. The illumination of geographical causes of political and social processes would be not an end in itself but a means to the end of "representing all the more clearly, deeply, and concisely the essence of the area under consideration."[13] This would then be presented to the German people in the form of an "artistic geography," a synthesis of science and impression like that being developed by Ewald Banse. "Let us not prove ourselves small-minded in this fateful hour," Obst exhorted his colleagues. "This concerns not just the maintenance of the lofty status of geographic science in Germany, but it quite plainly concerns the future of the German people, its culture, its economy, its politics."[14]

Obst's call for synthesis, integration, and service to the German people in its hour of need as the key to the survival of geography converged with the prescriptions of other geopoliticians who demanded the inclusion of geopolitical ideas in German education. Thus, as professional geographers were seeking to reform their discipline, their reasoning and arguments were exploited by geopoliticians to expand the role of geopolitics in schools. Again and again, for example, they lamented the lack of spatial awareness and sophistication displayed by Germans in comparison with the British, the French, and other peoples. The "fearful incomprehension of the masses" in Germany for questions of space, power, and geography was contrasted with the "natural political-geographic understanding" displayed by the English and French. The superior geopolitical consciousness of Germany's rivals was attributed to the effect on popular thought of their far-flung imperial holdings.[15] The geopolitical ignorance of the masses was not the only source of German weakness, however. Those who stood in "politically responsible positions, who could be of use or harm," had also failed Germany by their lack of geopolitical understanding. No architect or builder would proceed without knowing his ground, but "how many jurists and students of public affairs in the Germany of today unfortunately follow such a procedure, building their state on paper instead of upon the soil."[16] Such shortcomings of spatial knowledge had been dangerous before the war, indeed, had precipitated its disastrous conclusion, but they were even more threatening now because of the new democratic system, which allowed all citizens to participate and throw "the dark shadow of their disharmony on the entire conduct of the state."[17]

The outlook of geopolitical thinkers, on this as on other topics, was decisively conditioned by the shattering tragedy of the lost war and the traumatic peace settlement that followed. Until the nation was resolved to educate young Germans to think geopolitically, they warned, it would not be in a position to exploit opportunities to better Germany's position. "How utterly different was the position of the French people in this connection in 1914," lamented one in 1932. "Since the lost war of 1870-71 a deliberate national education on a geopolitical basis was promoted in France."[18] Geopoliticians were confident that geopolitical truth would provide a sound foundation for the recovery and unification of the nation. The impulse to unite Germans "can only come from within through a healing of political life, and this is only possible if a common platform can be found" for German political action. This would "depend on a living understanding for the fundamental external and internal political connections under which the fatherland stands," which it was the function of geopolitical education to reveal.[19] This education for geopolitical sensitivity, for "a first feeling for the state as a living organism," should begin as early as possible in the elementary grades and proceed "from the geopolitical questions of a general sort to geopolitical regional geography" by considering the geopolitical aspects of contemporary political questions, such as "Why must we strive for colonies?"[20]

The geopolitical call for reform here transcended the merely geographical, however. Geopoliticians hoped instead to use the geopolitical perspective to illuminate a broad range of fields, including but not restricted to geography. Germany's educators, they felt, bore responsibility for the failures of the past in the degree to which they had omitted the geographical foundations from all fields. This was true for myopic educators in "geography, history, sociology, law and political science, stuck too narrowly in their depths and unable to create links with the foundations of political knowledge, as our opponents created the 'political science' of the Anglo-Saxons or the 'école des sciences politiques' in Paris."[21] Correcting these oversights of the past, geopoliticians argued, was "a matter of giving a geopolitical shading to historical, geographical, or whatever subjects."[22] In other words, their approach was to introduce a geopolitical perspective into existing disciplines rather than to attempt the establishment of an entirely new field. Because of its integrative nature as a discipline, "Geopolitical discussions are particularly well-suited to build bridges between instruction in geography, history, and the languages . . . and one can almost say that if geopolitics had not existed it would have had to be invented for the present day higher schools with their emphasis on concentration."[23] The consequence of the inclusion of this spatial perspective in German schooling in a variety of subjects would be a reinvigoration of foreign policy. "Schooling in geopolitical thought is the best preparation and a constant source of strength for a well-founded world-political outlook," wrote one. "Through geopolitics to world politics!"[24]

The infusion of a geopolitical coloration into geography, history, law, medicine, and other fields was supposed to do more than just serve the reinvigoration of the geographic discipline, heal the divided German polity, or teach "spatial-political thought."[25] It was to build character as well, to promote the formation of will in German students by introducing a new understanding of the landscape and its effects on the individual. Geopoliticians sought to foster a mystical sensitivity to the formative power of the landscape along the lines promoted by Banse and advocated as "aesthetic geography" by Oswald Muris and others. Coupled with a sounder sense of the political significance of geography, this would help the new generation of Germans to acquire a deeper inner life and greater love of the homeland. Geopolitics in the schools would transform young Germans, making them active participants in preparing Germany to face modern challenges that had caught the nation unawares in the war. This view of geography and education was rooted in the consciousness that a new age with new requirements had arisen out of the ruins of war and that geography could no more exempt itself from the demands of the new age than could the arts and sciences generally. "A new age dawns, and it will bring forth a new geography," Obst predicted, "as it has created the new in poetry, painting and sculpture, philosophy, and history." He insisted on a synthesis, "intermingling and interweaving the individual geographic landscape factors to a representation of the greatest possible animation and vividness."[26]

Even those who disagreed with Obst's optimistic evaluation of the new age joined him in calling for a remade geography able to prepare Germans for the new conditions faced by their nation. Geographers and geopoliticians who lamented the dehumanizing factory work and "crass materialism" of modern Germany hoped that geopolitics could strengthen the will and "sharpen the view of the more mature youth for world-political questions."[27] The combination of geopolitical ideas with a deeper spiritualization of thought, *Verinnerlichung,* would end the sterile "intellectualism" that had characterized geographic instruction up to the present. The League of German University Teachers of Geography adopted a geographical educational agenda that reflected geopolitical goals in its call for a geography that would not only "steel the will" but "clarify the sphere of feelings, even shape the irrational in the person, because only from a combination of all spiritual powers can the harmonious personality develop itself."[28] In the form of Länderkunde or *Heimatkunde,* regional or local geography, geopolitical reformers argued that geographical teaching would in this way acquire a new effectiveness. "In combination with the rise of a new sense of homeland (*Heimatsinne*) the age after the war has produced a new movement in the geographic sciences, which speaks of the 'spatial and earthbound tendency in history,' namely geopolitics. . . . Geography has, thus, been given a new task, namely to grasp the living space of a people, which gives direction to all politics."[29]

Under national socialism, these trends in thinking about geopolitics, geography, and education would follow an entirely predictable course. What had been a relatively moderate call for the use of geopolitics in "civic education," as Hermann Lautensach had put it, was quickly vulgarized and made into a call for unabashed geopolitical and political propagandizing in German schools. Geopolitically oriented geographers themselves were at the forefront of this movement under the Nazis. Throughout the Weimar period the geographic profession's response to the call for geopolitics in the schools had been positive. The *Geographischer Anzeiger,* for instance, in its role as the organ of the League of German School Geographers, had published from the mid-1920s on a regular series of articles on "Geopolitical Questions in Geographic Instruction." Usually written by Georg A. Lukas, these explained to teachers how to give a geopolitical cast to subjects such as the "South Tyrol question," the "unity of the German eastern front," and "middle Europe's geopolitical axis," by focusing on the geographic distribution of ethnic Germans in central Europe.[30] Within one year of the Nazi seizure of power the *Zeitschrift für Geopolitik* had published a call for the combination of geopolitics with geography, history, biology, law, and other fields to create a "national state science," advance the "German new order," and awaken "love for and inclination toward the tasks of the nation."[31] The ease of the Nazi *Gleichschaltung* of the geographic profession owed a great deal to the popularity of nationalistic geopolitical theories before 1933.[32] The call to incorporate geopolitics in the schools as a national state science was soon echoed by educators in other fields, often those who had been interested in geopolitical education before the advent of Nazi rule.[33]

State Promotion of Geopolitical Education: The Prussian Case

Instruction in Prussian higher schools during the early years of the Weimar Republic still followed teaching guidelines compiled by the Ministry of Education in 1901. These guidelines conceded a place to geographic instruction in the higher grades, but only as part of a one-hour course of instruction taught in conjunction with history. The goals promoted for geography in these guidelines were formally apolitical and intended to impart "knowledge of the physical properties of the earth's surface and the spatial distribution of people thereupon as well as knowledge of the basis of mathematical geography."[34] Konrad Hänisch, the right-wing Socialist who served as the first Republican Prussian minister of education, began to formulate new guidelines for Prussian education at the end of 1920. The reformed guidelines were to include a new plan of geographic instruction, and opinions were solicited from geographers of rank, including Albrecht Penck and Hermann Wagner, on ways to improve the teaching of geography.[35] This effort at reform culminated in 1925 with the promulgation of new and entirely revised *Richtlinien für die Lehrpläne der höheren Schulen Preussens* (Guidelines for the curricula of the higher schools of Prussia) in which, as one commentator has described it, "the geopolitical concept of geography was taken over uncritically."[36] The crucial event in consolidating official support for the inclusion of geopolitical ideas in geographic (and historical) instruction, however, occurred when Otto Boelitz succeeded Hänisch as Prussian minister of education in 1921.

Boelitz ran the Ministry of Education until 1925, and under his leadership it issued a series of policy statements concerning geographical education that gave official sanction to geopolitical education in Prussian schools. In addition to recommending geopoliticized textbooks for use in geography courses the ministry under Boelitz repeatedly admonished Prussian teachers to emphasize the politically and culturally determining effects of geography in the life of the state. "It is desirable that geographic instruction also contribute to the training of our youth for practical life," according to a proclamation from 1924. "It is, therefore, necessary to emphasize more than has heretofore been the case (1) the connection between the nature of the land and the economy, (2) the political side of geography, the dependency of states, their borders, and their world power on the geographic, ethnic, and economic conditions of their territories."[37] The ministry followed these instructions later the same year with directives that geography lessons stress the importance of colonies to the nation. They should, furthermore, be shown the "mutual connections" between "the German landscapes, ethnic groups, and states in their uniqueness" so as to foster an awareness of "the connection between Boden and state" and "represent the regularity (of this connection) and make the students ready for functional thinking, educate them to a genetic understanding, and deepen their civic understanding through reliable concepts of the connections between state and soil, between earth and humanity."[38]

Geographic education in Prussia, therefore, was already moving toward an emphasis on politics and geodeterminism characteristic of geopolitical thought in the years before the 1925 curriculum guidelines formalized this trend. The guidelines, promulgated on 6 April 1925, mandated the incorporation of geopolitics not only into geography but into history as well. In addition to repeating the goals established for geographic instruction in the guidelines of 1901, geography was now to be elevated to the status of a core subject to prepare the student better for "German citizenship." It was also to familiarize the student with "the spatial distribution of humanity according to races and peoples, economic stages and forms, and state forms as well in its dependence upon its position and the natural attributes of its Lebensraum."[39] At the upper levels, this could take the form of discussion of news articles or daily events, which would lead to the "discussion of world economic and geopolitical problems," and questions of geology or physical geography.[40] Geographic instruction was to begin in the lower grades by emphasizing descriptive and physical geography (although cultural and political geography were included as topics even in the lower grades) and to culminate by passing from "the natural properties of the earthspace through a consideration of its economic-, political-, and cultural-geographic effects to a contemporary image of the earth."[41] This would include comparison of the ethnic and political configurations of central Europe, which in this context could scarcely be other than politically revisionist in nature. The recommendations of geopoliticians and geographers to concentrate on Germany (Heimatkunde) clearly had an effect with geographic study intended to conclude in the political and cultural geography of Germany.[42] The geography guidelines set forth for the highest grade, the Oberstufe I, were devoted almost entirely to topical issues of politics, culture, and economics:

> Cultural geography of Germany. The German soil as the basis of the landscape and its reworking through the labor of the German people. German settlements. The various forms of German economic life.
>
> The ethnographic and political conditions of Mitteleuropa. The interconnection of German economic life with neighboring states and the outside world. The geographically discernible cultural influence of Germans on other peoples. Germandom in the world.
>
> Deepened consideration of the homeland. A summarizing consideration will conclude with a brief overview of the entire geographic image of the contemporary earth.[43]

The emphasis at this level on ethnicity ("ethnographic conditions," "Germandom") and its relation to the political conditions of central Europe is striking. Geographic instruction in this form and with these goals would have conformed almost completely to the ideal concepts of the geopoliticians. Indeed, these goals might have been written and prescribed by them, so much so that although the geographical profession as a whole praised the guidelines for their attention to geopolitical issues, the fact that they made geography a "core subject," or *Kernfach,* and that they introduced geographical study at all grade levels, they also stimulated complaints that they were too much guided by the contemporary fashion for geopolitics.[44] The guidelines did not entirely reflect the pedagogical mission of teaching students the superiority of German life and the geographic sources of this superiority. They endorsed a lukewarm cultural relativism, for example, arguing that "insight in the natural-law dependency of foreign life forms will guard the youthful mind against uncritically measuring foreign conditions by those in the homeland."[45] Taken on the whole, however, the Prussian curriculum directive expressed an unequivocally nationalistic pedagogic ethic designed to produce in students a mental world map that would have conformed to that drawn by Weimar geopoliticians.

The provisions for the teaching of history put forth in the guidelines presented an even more striking view of the congruence between the geopolitical agenda for education and that promoted by the Prussian authorities. History was to be taught in an integrative, interdisciplinary fashion, incorporating a strongly geodeterminist approach to questions of historical change. "The connections between history and geography are ultimately manifold," according to the guidelines. "By a thorough division of work between the subjects historical structures will be traced back to forces of the landscape that condition them, the relation of culture and nature will be explored, the view for natural dependencies in the system of settlements, the establishment, spread, and decline of states will be sharpened."[46] The inclusion of such geographical perspectives would also heighten awareness of struggle in history, reinforcing the geopolitical emphasis on struggle and conflict as the normal condition of relations between states. Geography would add to historical instruction in the degree to which it depicted "struggle for rivers, passes, seas, sources of raw materials, and export markets, trade routes, and exchange routes of the entire earth."[47] This, in turn, would foster a sounder historical understanding of borders in all their varieties, including "natural, political, ethnographic, and linguistic borders."[48]

As Boelitz himself later explained, the new instructional plan was intended to promote identification with German ethnic groups outside the border, foreign Germandom or *Auslandsdeutschtum,* and the geopolitical slant of geographic instruction was to play an important part in this. "In addition to historical instruction, teaching in geography is especially significant for a clear concept of border and foreign Germandom," Boelitz wrote. Before the war these questions had been treated in German education in an "all too perfunctory" fashion, usually by giving "a couple of meager numbers." Because, in part of the geopolitical presence in the instructional plans, however, this situation had improved in recent years, he argued. "It is gratifying to see how settlement geography, anthropogeography, and geopolitics have acquired their place in the new Prussian guidelines and how they produce the evaluation of Germandom in the world as one of the natural goals of geographic instruction in our higher schools."[49]

In Prussia, therefore, the policy of the state was to promote geopolitics and geodeterminism in geographic and historical instruction as a means of fortifying nationalism in Prussian students. To the considerable extent that this included teaching these students to think of ethnic Germans outside Germany's borders as still somehow a part of the homeland, this was an education for revisionism and foreign political instability. This was as true at the grade and middle school levels of Prussian education as it was at the high school level. New guidelines meant for the middle schools, also issued in 1925, replaced a teaching plan in effect since 1910. The new guidelines instituted two mandatory hours (rather than one) of geographic instruction in boys' and girls' schools, and emphasized political geography (*politische Erdkunde*), the study of the former colonies, "Germans" outside the borders and, in keeping with the ideas of many geopoliticians, focused on "the German fatherland" as an organizing principle for the mass of information to be treated.[50] Grade school guidelines, issued between 1921 and 1923, followed suit by making geographic instruction a means of preparing Germans for the work of national rejuvenation.[51]

The call for the inclusion of geopolitics in education was not unanimous. A few geographers warned against the campaign to geopoliticize German students, most prominently Franz Thorbecke. He repudiated both geopolitical geography and the demand for a focus on Germany, cautioning that "geopolitics does not belong in the school, the task of geographic instruction is to [give] the student fundamental facts of the earth's surface" and that "an exaggerated concentration of geographic instruction on Germany alone is also no good. . . . No doubt we should bring the student closer to the homeland, but he should also know that Germany is not the world."[52] Others, such as Walter Behrmann of Frankfurt, felt that although "geopolitics and the natural dependency of cultural manifestations" certainly belonged in geography course exercises and should without question be addressed by university geographers, the theory of these fields was as yet insufficiently developed to support entire courses of study at the lower levels.[53] This was distinctly a minority point of view among geographers, however, and accounts by teachers of overcrowded geopolitical courses and geopolitical study groups forced to turn away students give reason to believe it was not the general point of view of German students either.[54] The campaign for geopolitical education, therefore, enjoyed the support of the overwhelming majority of German geographers and teachers who addressed the issue, and it appears to have enjoyed success among students. The eventual acceptance of geopolitics in Prussian higher education, however, owed as much to the explicit support of the authorities as to the enthusiasm of teachers and students.

The focus of this examination has been on Prussia, but there is no reason to believe that Prussian education was more deeply imbued with geopolitical thought than was education in the other states. On the contrary, educational programs in Saxony, Bavaria, and Braunschweig were frequently extolled as models of effective inclusion of geopolitics in education.[55] The Saxon Ministry for Public Education, for example, issued an educational memorandum in September 1926 calling for a greater emphasis on historical geography (using Kjellén's work as an example) and geopolitical questions, which was warmly praised by geographers, including the textbook author Paul Wagner.[56] Braunschweig issued new guidelines for its schools in 1928, reviewed and praised in the same year in the *Geographischer Anzeiger,* which characterized their "chief goal [as] showing the connection of the German people and its culture with the German soil and to waken patriotic and civic sensibility. . . . The end goal is the acquisition of geopolitical understanding."[57] The crucial tool to attain this goal was the textbook. By the end of the 1920s German teachers of geography or history enjoyed an abundance of sources to help them convey the geopolitical contours of the German nation.

State Organisms and Provisional States: Geopolitics in Weimar Geography and History Texts

The world that geography texts depicted for German students during the Weimar era was one characterized by struggle and instability. Conflict among peoples, and between humanity and nature as well, was central to their picture of geography and human civilization. In general, they presented a globe that was divided into states and empires, all products of a natural, "organic" evolutionary process of constant struggle with one another and with the natural conditions created by their geography. In some places the boundaries of these states were determined by topographical features, in others by politics, ethnicity, or language, but they were in the final analysis maintained by force, not law. Borrowing terms from nineteenth-century German anthropology, they divided the earth's peoples into Naturvölker, whose relationship with geography was passive and receptive, and *Kulturvölker,* who were active in developing the higher forms of culture and technology that enabled them to manipulate their natural environment and their relationship with geography.[58] The former peoples were slowly dying out, losers in the struggle for survival, whereas the latter were increasing. Germany's position in the center of the European state system entailed both advantages (when the German state was strong enough to secure and safeguard its needs) and dangers (when it was not).

Although this picture of the explicit and implicit messages contained in texts of the period is simplified, it is not otherwise distorted. Proceeding from a conviction that the state was a living organism in a very literal sense, history and geography schoolbooks offered students a concept of geographic space as an entity imbued with meaning by human struggle. Constant striving for advantageous boundaries, for a more favorable space, were the natural conditions to which geography subjected human societies, and the sources and outcomes of such struggles were portrayed as the natural subjects of geographic study. The logical student could draw similar conclusions from Weimar history texts as well. In treating their central themes—the interaction between states and geography, Germany's diplomatic situation, the new states of eastern Europe, and global political competition—both history and geography texts promoted a geopolitical worldview of dynamic space, political impermanence, and sociopolitical change decisively conditioned by geography.

The concept of the state as an organic, living entity was one of the key images of political geography in grade school and high school texts of the period. This biological model of the state furnished a direct link to geopolitics and laid a foundation for the development of further geopolitical insights. Alexander Supan's popular *Leitlinien der allgemeinen politischen Geographie: Naturlehre des Staates* (Manual of general political geography) typifies the progress made by the organic concept of the state in the teaching of geography in Weimar schools. First published in 1918, the 1922 edition was recommended by the Prussian Ministry of Education for use in secondary schools.[59] The work was based on manuscripts left by Supan after his death that were subsequently compiled and edited by Erich Obst.[60] Although Supan tried to distinguish his political geography from geopolitics, the work was later cited by Hermann Lautensach as an outstanding example of a text that incorporated geopolitical themes in its treatment of political geography. Lautensach's praise provides some indication both of the considerable extent to which questions of ethnicity and nationality were integrated into geopolitics during the period and also of the degree to which distinctions between geopolitics and political geography were blurred by their practitioners.[61]

Lautensach was a perceptive critic of the text. Although Supan repudiated the simple application of organic models to states, indeed discussed the shortcomings of both Ratzel's and Kjellén's organic concepts of the state, in the end he reverted to the following definition of the function of political geography: "Political geography, or the natural philosophy (*Naturlehre*) of the state, considers it as a natural body."[62] Although Supan attached a string of qualifications and modifiers to his definition of the state as a "natural body" ("it is a phenomenon sui generis"), it is not at first glance easily distinguishable from Kjellén's study of the "geographic organism" or Hauschofer's "science of the political life form in its natural living-space," and one can wonder whether or not the average young reader followed Supan's subtleties. Supan's language and imagery, in fact, could only reinforce the notion that the state was a natural organism. For political geography, the state was a human community "bound to a piece of the earth's surface," which, "considered as a spatial creation is a natural essence." Furthermore, this spatial phenomenon was "no empty space, but filled with people, therefore a solid body," whose "natural foundations" had to be investigated by the political geographer.[63]

In typical geopolitical fashion Supan devoted a great deal of his political geography to the study of borders, and here the image of the state as an organism is just as vivid although, like his objections about organic models of the state, it never sheds an air of blurred ambiguity. On pragmatic nationalistic grounds, Supan's text declared that Germans could not acquiesce in the idea of "organic" borders because "the theory of organic borders delivers the German Bohemians to Czech, and the German south Tyrol to Italian, domination." The term could, thus, "excuse any mischief," but even his disclaimer went on to strengthen the organic image of the state and to reach an ambiguous substitute term for *organic* or *natural* borders. "Even the name 'organic' border is misleading," Supan argued, "because it awakens the appearance that it is grown with the inmost essence of the state." He suggested instead the term *Naturgrenze,* or "nature borders," while emphasizing that all borders were inherently mutable and transitory.[64] "The momentary form of a state is always the product of a phase of development. . . . No state has yet over the course of long periods maintained its form unaltered."[65] Supan found himself confronted by the structural dilemma of geopolitics, which forced its adherents to devise a way around the fateful implications of geodeterminism. Although he was uncomfortable with some of the unpleasant consequences, for Germany, of organic theories of borders, Supan proved unable to break out of the organic model to suggest a convincing alternative rhetoric or analytical scheme.

His ultimate reliance on an organic model of the state is particularly clear in Supan's explanation of the practical value of political geography. Here states were presented as persons, or as developing personalities, with all the characteristics of a living being. The more highly developed states were described for students "as essences with conscious wills, as personalities." Political geography was meant to reveal "the degree to which the natural situation strengthens or hinders the will."[66] As presented in Supan's work, political geography, just like geopolitics, was an applied, practical, and present-centered science. As regional geography develops into the geography of the state, he argued, "it becomes a practical science, immediately directed at life."[67] The acquisition of state power was the object of this practical science because only through the use of power was the state's will freed. "Strength and weakness are only expressions for varying degrees of intensity of power to realize our conscious will," Supan argued. "External freedom is the necessary precondition to this; the slave is impotent. Only if the state has power can it unfold its personality freely, can it expand."[68] If Supan was ambiguous in his treatment of the issue of the state's organic nature, his point here is unmistakable: the state needs to be powerful so that it may work its inherent will to expand.

Supan's geopolitical emphasis on struggle and organic models of the state had destructive consequences. Peace between states, for example, could only be envisioned as episodic, and because the struggle between states was presented as both eternal and mortal, the acquisition of power had to be the constant and primary goal of the state. Views similar to these, derived from geopolitical theories, were reflected in most texts on political geography. The authors of these texts were generally less sophisticated than Supan in their presentation of the subtle quandaries raised by an organic concept of the state. Rudolf Reinhard, *Weltwirtschaftliche und politische Erdkunde* (World economic and political geography), also recommended by the Prussian Ministry of Education, took an unequivocal approach to the issue of natural borders. "Boundaries resting in historical events and economic relations, established in numerous treaties over the course of centuries, are always artificial and usually take a very complex course," Reinhard wrote. "They are, therefore, easily blurred in thinly populated or inaccessible regions, such as large swamps, high mountains, deserts, which leads then to border controversies."[69] Natural borders, or borders that were connected to "outstanding characteristics of the earth's surface," were more likely to be stable and lasting. They could be one-sided (where no states bordered one another directly, as at coastlines) or two-sided, as where states bordered in impassable mountain ranges.[70] Ethnic borders, where two races or nations bordered, also constituted a form of natural border, according to Reinhard. In the context of Germany in the 1920s Reinhard's doctrine of borders constituted a justification for revanchism, juxtaposing stable borders, determined by ethnic or geographic divisions, with unstable borders resulting from mere political agreements, such as those constructed at Versailles.

The geopolitical influence in Weimar geography texts was especially clear in their treatment of eastern Europe. In a work such as Johannes Wütschke, *Unsere Erde. Erdkundliches Lehrbuch für höhere Schulen auf der Grundlage des Arbeitsunterrichts* (Our earth: Geographical textbook for higher schools on the basis of practical instruction), the area between the Rhine and the Soviet Union, made up in its eastern sections largely of states created in the wake of the war, was denoted in a long section on "geopolitical regional geography" as *Zwischeneuropa*. This term was first used by the volkish geographer Albrecht Penck in 1916 and soon became a staple of geopolitical writing on the region.[71] Literally, it means "between-Europe," but the sense of the term as used by geopoliticians was as much chronological as spatial, and may be more accurately rendered as "interim-Europe" or "provisional-Europe." It was, in fact, so defined by other writers.[72] German geographers described the region as Europe's "tremor zone," invoking geological metaphors to convey the natural inevitability of earthshaking upheaval in the area.[73] Its use in Wütschke's text emphasized the ephemeral nature of the current political arrangements of the area, an emphasis heightened by his use of the term *staatliche Splitterzone*, or "national fragmentation zone," for the region. This region was defined in the west by a relatively stable geographic "border seam" along the Alps and the Rhine, but it was indistinct in the east. As a result, "the plains here did not lead to political stability and the creation of a unitary Slavic nationality. . . . The zone forms an essential part of the region of ethnic mixing that has been characterized as the 'critical zone'

(Kjellén) and that since the World War has become Europe's national fragmentation zone and thereby its political danger zone."[74]

Wütschke's conclusions were unequivocal. Because of their lack of geographic and ethnic closure, "none of the successor states is really viable." This was true throughout the region but especially in the north where the Baltic states, Finland, and Poland were doomed not only by the dictates of geography and ethnicity but also by their inherent cultural decadence, because, Wütschke argued, they had borrowed "the foundations of their cultural life" from Germans and Swedes.[75] Here, as elsewhere in eastern Europe, ethnic and geographic factors combined to foment unrest. Geography, in fact, had compelled Russian expansion in the region: "The breadth of the east European spaces and the connecting parts of northern Asia, as well as the isolation of the land from the open sea, compelled the Russians to imperialism."[76] The rhetoric employed by Supan, Reinhard, Wütschke, and other textbook authors is noteworthy for the determining political influence it accords geography and for its nonchalant acceptance of the apparent inevitability of aggression and warfare between states. It becomes all the more remarkable when one recalls that this rhetoric was directed at an audience of young students.

Similar geopolitical approaches to the effects of geography on human populations, with a heavy overlay of racial theories, are found in what may have been the most popular series of geography texts and school atlases published during the era, the Fischer-Geistbeck texts.[77] This series had first appeared before the war and during the succeeding years and through the Weimar period was reissued several times by its Munich publisher, R. Oldenbourg, in revised forms edited by various academic geographers. It included workbooks, texts, and atlases for most levels of instruction up to the university and, under the editorship of geographers including Paul Wagner, Friedrich Littig, and Hermann Vogel, the series acquired a pronounced geopolitical flavor. These texts, too, used the term *Zwischeneuropa,* now denoting not the parts of central Europe that included Germany but only those regions inhabited primarily by Slavs and lying between Germany and Russia from the Baltic to the Adriatic.[78] These states were, furthermore, depicted as threats to Germany: "The new Polish state is a part of Zwischeneuropa pushed far forward toward the heart of Germany."[79]

The Fischer-Geistbeck texts were intended largely for middle and high schools. The books were issued in a series divided into volumes devoted to a specific topic or region, such as cartography, Germany, Europe, and so on. The sixth volume, treating general geography, and the ninth, dealing with the formation of states and world-political questions, carry an especially heavy geopolitical imprint. The volume devoted to cartography, for instance, in its treatment of anthropogeography (or human geography), divides humankind into the two broad categories of natural and cultural peoples. Culture is here defined as "the loosing of mankind from the compulsion of nature through physical and mental work, the results of which are handed on to posterity."[80] The Fischer-Geistbeck works argued that the economy was the basis of culture, and the development of this culture was presented as being closely determined by geography. Although the foundations of European culture were in Mediterranean antiquity, the land and climate of northwestern Europe exerted a decisive influence in its formation. One could not speak in northern Europe as one did in the Mediterranean region, for example, of climate shaping a "merry and generous" people. "The raw Nordic forest must first be cleared and settled from the few open stretches of land, long and cold winters, much fog and rain must be taken into account and overcome at all seasons."[81] Students learned, as geopoliticians wrote, that geography and climate were the sources of German technological excellence.

These texts argued directly that geography had formed the European "discoverer soul" (*Entdeckerseele*), which propelled the age of navigation and discovery, precipitating the advent of true world history. Although the Chinese, for instance, had developed the telescope, printing, gunpowder, and porcelain long before the Europeans had, they lacked the "Germanic-Romance" cultural values to employ these in a productive conquest of nature. Unfavorable geography was seen as the source of the lack of initiative deemed characteristic of the Chinese. "It has been decisive for this system and this development of character that the western European continent with its extraordinary articulation and simultaneous nearness to the ocean compels its inhabitants toward the sea." With the discovery of the new world and the European development of technological advances in transportation, the world was remade into a global system. Although this brought with it the advance of industrial society, which rendered humans "nearly a slave of their creation," it had more positive results as well. "Geographically, this development of European culture has worked itself out according to two perspectives. It has led from discovery to development to the progressive Europeanization of the earth. It has expanded the economic life of the cultural peoples to a world economy." In all these developments, the reference to Europe is largely to the Germanic-Nordic and southwestern portions of the continent. Everything east of a line from the Balkan Peninsula through eastern Poland is subject to a different set of ethnic and geographical conditions and, thus, is "not unjustly called Half-Asia."[82]

Geodeterminism was made to serve a revisionistic and vehement nationalism in the Fischer-Geistbeck political geography text. The book's epigraph set its tone: "Every science has the duty to place its knowledge and possibilities in the service of life and of the fatherland."[83] The quest for space was a dominant theme of the text, which distinguished between "organic" and "inorganic" expansion of states on the basis of correspondence to natural borders. Expansion within naturally enclosed territories whose properties were similar to those of the expanding state was depicted as organic. The text's subordination of scientific principle to political expediency, always characteristic of geopolitics, was particularly egregious. The German seizure of Alsace-Lorraine in 1871, for example, was justified as "reconquest" and an example of organic expansion: "In the extent to which this (reconquest) advanced to the Vosges, it won a land that in regard to population as well as to natural properties belonged to Germany. On the other hand, the renewed appropriation of this land by France must be characterized as unorganic growth because not the Rhine but the Vosges forms France's natural eastern border."[84]

Space itself became an important indicator of a state's viability. Its acquisition produced political power; its diminution denoted decline and loss of power. Size, however, was necessary but not sufficient to ensure national security: Not all space possessed the same value. Distinctions were drawn between "active" and "passive" space, the latter being that in which population density fell below one person per square kilometer. Passive space could be rendered active through a combination of human activity and population density, however, and states possessing great spatial reserves such as Canada and the Soviet Union were lucky indeed. Even more important than the acquisition of space, however, was the mastery of space, or *Raumbewältigung*. Mastery consisted of the application of technology to topography in the form of railroads, roads, canals, and aviation and promoted utilization of the possibilities otherwise dormant in passive space.

After dwelling upon the importance of geographical location (latitude, hydrography, soil, etc.) and political situation (central or peripheral) of states, the text concluded with an assessment of Germany's position that was extraordinarily vehement in tone. The peace settlement was denounced as an English and French conspiracy aimed at the "total destruction" of Germany, the "heart" of Europe.[85] Germany's just ambitions for world influence were frustrated both by the hostile designs of its enemies and the "disadvantage of the position, the lack of freedom of movement born of the central position between great states, which required consideration of her watchful neighbors at every step of German policy."[86] The text is most striking, however, for its violent hostility toward the Slavic peoples and states east of Germany. The Czechs and other peoples of eastern Europe were depicted as cultural parasites engaged in "a war of destruction against Germandom, to which they owe the best of their culture and economic welfare."[87] Their inability to rule themselves was proof of their cultural degeneracy: "The incapacity of the Slavic peoples for the formation and flourishing development of independent states is sufficiently demonstrated by the history of the Poles, Czechs, Slovenes, and Serbs. Russia seems, or seemed, to be a monumental exception, but Germans stood at its cradle as well."[88]

Weimar geography texts, through their absorption and use of geopolitical ideas, conveyed a message to German students that in the international system of the 1920s could only have disruptive consequences. Students were taught that central and eastern Europe were regions of German cultural hegemony where only the armed might and unnatural malice of Germany's enemies propped up states that neither culture, geography, nor ethnicity legitimated. Nor were these states, as the students learned, legitimated by history. Weimar history texts, influenced by a view of geopolitics as a marriage of history and geography, also emphasized the political, economic, and cultural decadence of the Slavs. Regardless of political arrangements in the east, they argued, there were no clear geographic bases for the existence of the Slavic states, and culturally the area between Germany and eastern Poland was all part of the German *Kulturboden*. This term, like *Zwischeneuropa,* owed a great deal of its currency to the work of Albrecht Penck.[89] One out of every three Germans, one such text argued, was forced to live outside German borders in Slavic areas "that German labor, German industry, German intellect created. With greater care than anywhere else in the east, the land is worked, the forest tended, the streets are better maintained, houses and villages cleaner. The towns and their culture are German: Posen, Brünn, Olmütz, Prague, and others."[90] Within one year of the appearance of Hans Grimm's famous colonial novel, the same text declared the Germans a Volk ohne Raum.[91] States were depicted historically as having followed the "laws" laid down by their "geographical position," according to which, among other things, Russia had been historically compelled to seek a warm port and the Polish corridor must vanish.[92] Like geography texts of the period, they referred to the area between the Rhine and Russia as Zwischeneuropa and emphasized the transitory nature of many of the political settlements reached in the region.[93] Geopolitical border theory and terminology were used to argue that the borders with the new states to Germany's east could only be temporary while these states continued to govern large German ethnic minorities.[94] Arguments like these, with an obvious debt to geopolitical thought, contributed to the geopolitical project of revitalizing German nationalism. The instability of the east to which they continually returned was simply the political expression of the geopolitical malleability of space. By constantly referring to this instability these texts reminded the German people of the opportunity that geography and politics had placed to their east.

All these trends in the gradual inclusion of geopolitical ideas in schoolbooks intensified at the close of the Weimar period, and many texts of the early Nazi period differed more in style than in substance from their Weimar predecessors. Textbooks such as Franz Knieper's *Politische Geographie (Geopolitik) für den Unterricht* (Political geography [geopolitics] for instruction) and Johann Thies's *Die Staaten als völkische Lebensräume. Für den Erdkunde- und Geschichtsunterricht bearbeitet* (States as national living spaces, adapted for geographical and historical instruction), both first published in 1933, descended to a crudely reductivist plane of geodeterminism. Thies, a tireless and prolific advocate of geopolitical propaganda in teaching throughout the Weimar years, offered students an unequivocally national socialist geopolitics. In his book, introduced by an epigraph from Adolf Hitler, Thies defended the efforts of states to expand to "natural" geographical and ethnic borders as an inevitable part of state life because it was "to be understood as part of a strong national life will that a state is imbued with the striving to attach itself to its national comrades living in the peripheral districts of neighboring states."[95] Just as the Fischer-Geistbeck geography texts had done throughout the Weimar era, Theis's work endorsed expansion to so-called natural borders as "organic growth" or "organic spatial expansion," concluding that even if Germans exploited every opportunity for internal settlement, they would remain the Volk ohne Raum and retain "a particular claim to expansion."[96]

In his popular book, which went through four printings in the decade after its initial publication, acquiring in the process a fulsome foreword by Karl Haushofer, Knieper is even more blatant in subordination of the "science" of political geography to partisan political ends. Purporting to reveal to students the "causal connections between history and geography" based on the works of Haushofer, Dix, Obst, Vogel, Maull, and others, he argues that because of its geography Germany "cannot loose itself from the fluctuating play of geo- and world-political forces."[97] Germany's position in the war was undermined by its central position in Europe, surrounded by states bent on thwarting Germany's aspirations, and the position of its industrial districts on the fringes of the German state, which invited the aggression of neighbors.[98] After examining the natural boundaries of the German regions of central Europe, Knieper led students to the conclusion that Germany ought to extend, in the west, to a line running from the channel through the Ardennes and the Vosges and in the east through east-central Poland.[99] The borders proposed by Knieper, in fact, would have nearly restored Germany to the borders of the Holy Roman Empire in the east, west, and north, although not the south.

Considered as a whole, the emphasis on the putatively provisional nature of the border arrangements in eastern Europe must be considered one of the most damaging aspects of these texts. The dangerous implications of the organic concept of the state and of a geodeterminist approach to history and society here bore their most poisonous practical fruit, helping to persuade a generation of German students to regard the new states to their east as abnormal, unnatural, unfair, and inherently transitory. As with so much else involving geopolitical thought in the period, an aspect of paradox inheres in this treatment of the successor states and their borders. If borders and states in this part of Zwischeneuropa were, in fact, provisional, no more than an interim settlement resulting from the lack of outstanding topographical features or the intermingling of ethnic groups, then the only possible source of legitimacy for borders in the region could be the political agreements that these texts frequently decried as artificial. If this were the case, they might have been right to attack the legitimacy of the new borders from the point of view that Germany's political consent had been obtained only under duress, but this was not, in fact, the point of view usually taken to challenge the borders. Instead, they were indicted on supposedly objective, "scientific" grounds for failure to conform to nature while it was conceded that nature provided neither geographic nor ethnic grounds for the drawing of borders. The point of geopolitics in schoolbooks, however, as in the larger society to which the books were to be an introduction, was not rhetorical or logical consistency but the propagation of a new mental picture of Germany's place in Europe and the world.

The New Science Matriculates: Geopolitics in Weimar Academia

The efforts of Weimar geographers and historians to include geopolitics in education proved to be most productive at the highest levels of the German educational system, that is, in German universities. Geopolitical thought influenced Weimar academic life through a variety of institutional channels, which may be grouped in three interrelated categories. At the universities themselves, many ordinary, or tenured, geographical faculty members adopted geopolitical themes in their course offerings as the Weimar era progressed.[100] Quasi-independent institutes affiliated with universities, such as the Institut für Grenz- und Auslandsdeutschtum (Institute for Border and Foreign Germandom, [IGAD]) at Marburg or the Foundation for Research on German Ethnic and Cultural Soil at Leipzig, formed a second institutional conduit for the geopolitical penetration of German academia. Finally, specialized schools founded to promote the study of specific fields, such as the famous German University for Politics and its conservative counterpart, the University for National Politics, also did a great deal to familiarize a generation of German intellectuals with geopolitics.

The academic career of Erich Obst at the Technical University of Hannover illustrates the role committed faculty members played in establishing the academic legitimacy of geopolitics. Although the Technical University had existed for ninety years when Obst was called to Hannover in 1921, the school had up to that time offered no regular instruction in geography. The first German university chairs in geography had been established only in the 1870s, so the field as a discrete discipline was, in any case, relatively new.[101] Geographic instruction at Hannover had consisted until the 1920s of occasional lectures by mineralogists, physicists, and others sponsored by the Geographic Society of Hannover. It is reasonably safe to assume, given the backgrounds of the scholars involved, that these lectures generally addressed questions of physical geography, mathematical geography and other technical aspects of the field rather than political geographical issues.[102]

Obst's arrival in Hannover in October 1921, however, to occupy the brand new chair in geography, rapidly transformed geographic instruction there, stimulating a new interest in geography with a geopolitical flavor. Obst, the son-in-law of the geographer and textbook author Alexander Supan, had enjoyed a varied and distinguished career in geography before this appointment.[103] After lecturing on geography at the Colonial Institute in Hamburg, he led the Hamburg Geographical society's expedition to East Africa from 1910 to 1912, and during the war taught geography at the University of Constantinople as director of the Imperial Ottoman Central Institute for Meteorology.[104] He was hired at Hannover as professor for economic and transportation geography, and he quickly imbued geography there with a geopolitical perspective. Beginning with one room and a single assistant whose time was divided between geography and public economics, Obst had by 1928 created a new Geographic Institute at Hannover. By 1930 it employed in addition to Obst two lecturers, an assistant, a draftsman, and a secretary and was outfitted with a considerable library, many of whose holdings, according to Obst, derived from his affiliation with the *Zeitschrift für Geopolitik*.[105]

During this period, when Obst helped found the *Zeitschrift* and served as one of its coeditors, the courses he and his assistants taught frequently reflected his geopolitical preoccupations.[106] In addition to basic general courses such as Fundamentals of Political Geography the seminar (and later institute) offered such politically oriented courses as "Geography of Border and Foreign Germandom," "The Colonial Problem, with Particular Consideration of the German Proctectorates," and (taught by Obst's assistant, Kurt Brüning) "The Polar Lands and Their Development."[107] The geography of global economic systems figured prominently in Obst's course offerings. It is, of course, difficult to know precisely what was taught in the lectures themselves, but in some cases there are grounds for making reasonable guesses. Beginning in 1925, for instance, Obst taught a course entitled "Growth and Decline of the British World Empire," which is almost certainly based on work prepared for his book *England,*

Europa und die Welt (England, Europe and the world), a historical-geopolitical analysis of England's place in the world system. The Vowinckel press published the book in 1927 in which Obst called for a loose European continental confederation against the flank powers of the United States and the Soviet Union.[108] His course, on "The Great Powers of the Present," first offered during the winter semester of 1929–30, was likewise based on Kjellén's *Die Grossmächte vor und nach dem Weltkriege* (The great powers before and after the world war), a seminal geopolitical tract, revised with the help of Obst for a new edition that appeared in 1932.[109] Obst's geopolitical approach to colonialism, furthermore, is well known and was undoubtedly reflected in his teachings on the subject at Hannover. Every aspect of Obst's career in this period, therefore, his teaching, research, writing, and editing, all centered on geopolitics.

Obst's ultimate plan for the institute, as he himself explained it, was to establish separate research sections for "all important world-economic large spaces."[110] Such a regional approach conformed to geopolitical research schemes suggested by Arthur Dix and other geopoliticians, who emphasized regions as the important units of economic and political activity to legitimate their theories of German regional hegemony in central Europe.[111] It also prefigured the research strategy for geography later institutionalized by the Nazis in the guise of a myriad of "area" or "spatial" research work groups.[112] This approach seems to have gained the support of the Hannover student body and the local community, but it also won for Obst's efforts, in his own words, "the constant, complete support" of the Prussian Ministry for Science, Art, and Public Education.[113] Beginning in 1927, students could sign up for geography as a major at Hannover as part of a course of training for high school teaching. Although the numbers who did so each year—twenty to thirty—remained modest, Obst's lectures were a popular feature of Hannover academic and civic life throughout the period. "His lectures and talks on current geographic and geopolitical questions," according to the University's history, "attracted citizens outside the university as well so that these functions developed into an integral part of the cultural life of Hannover."[114]

Obst was far from being an isolated instance. He was simply one among many German academic geographers who incorporated geopolitics into their university offerings. Walther Vogel's seminar on political geography at Berlin, for example, was essentially a course in geopolitics, relying heavily on the works of Kjellén, Otto Maull, Arthur Dix, and Karl Haushofer to teach its members that the "Raum embraced by a state is much more than a mere stage. . . . The Boden in its broadest sense exerts an extraordinarily deep influence on the life of peoples."[115] At Munich, as might be expected, Haushofer himself introduced a heavy focus on geopolitical themes into the university's geography offerings. The trend toward a geopolitical discussion of issues in political geography was also evident in the teaching of geographers such as Otto Maull at Frankfurt, Wilhelm Volz at Leipzig, Erich Wunderlich at the Technical University of Stuttgart, Richard Hennig at Düsseldorf, and J. Ernst at the Handelshochschule (Commercial University) of Leipzig and across the border in Austria in the courses of Robert Seiger at Graz and Hugo Hassinger at Vienna.[116] Throughout Germanophone Europe, advanced geographic instruction was deeply imprinted by the geopolitical sensibility of the era.

As Obst's career at Hannover shows, geopolitics sometimes found its way into university course listings through the advocacy of regular faculty members. Other paths, however, could also confer academic legitimacy. The activities of special foreign studies institutes attached to universities, of which a prominent example is the Marburg Institute for Border and Foreign Germandom, made geopolitics *salonfähig* (presentable) in academic circles by uniting it with interest in ethnic Germandom. The Marburg case illustrates the natural affinity that existed between geopolitics and those conservatives whose primary interest was in defining the political and cultural dimensions of the German volk, the ethnic Germans of central Europe. The institute was part of a project initiated by a number of state governments to promote foreign studies at German universities that originated during the Kaiserreich and had produced, among others, the Colonial Institute in Hamburg (1908) and the Institute for Maritime Exchange and World Economy in Kiel (1913). During the war other universities were helped to set up institutes to study specific regions, such as Scandinavia (Greifswald) and southeast Europe (Leipzig).[117] Marburg was entrusted with the study of the Auslandsdeutschtum, or "foreign Germandom," an assignment that, with the defeat in the war and the separation of large German populations from the German state, was supplemented with the study of *Grenzdeutschtum,* or "border Germandom." Although official discussions about the institute dated back to 1917, it did not open until February 1919 with the geographer Leonhard Schultze-Jena as its director and Johann Wilhelm Mannhardt as its manager, or *Geschäftsleiter.*[118]

Schultze-Jena's role as director was largely a nominal and honorary one, whereas Mannhardt guided and ran the institute. Mannhardt had proposed the establishment of a research institute for the study of Germandom abroad while working and studying at the Colonial Institute in Hamburg before the war (where Obst had also lectured), he was responsible for the instructional activities of the institute and, in April 1926, he replaced Schultze-Jena as director in name as well as in fact.[119] Born in 1883 in Hamburg (where his father was the director of an eye clinic), Mannhardt studied jurisprudence and classical philology at Heidelberg and Freiburg, taught history at the Hamburg Colonial Institute and, when the war arrived, rose to the rank of captain in an artillery regiment. He earned a doctorate in political science, philosophy, and geography at Giessen and in 1925 received his *venia legendi,* or permission to teach, at Marburg.[120] As he himself made clear, Mannhardt brought to his activities at the institute the conviction that Auslandskunde, or foreign studies, was an endeavor that centered on Volkheit, or nationality, and that could only be analyzed by using political science, "political geography," and "the teachings of Kjellén."[121] For Mannhardt, as for many other ethnic studies advocates, geopolitics was a crucial analytical tool with close links to the ethnic cause. Political geography, he argued, demanded "just as much attention to the Volk as to the state," and he praised geographers who, like Robert Sieger, focused attention on "geopolitics and demopolitics [both terms were borrowings from Kjellén], indeed with contemporary sciences overall."[122]

At Marburg, he moved quickly and effectively to expand the institute. Initial funds were provided by the Prussian Ministry for Science, Art and Public Education, wealthy individuals such as Fritz André, *Geheimrat* (privy counciller) and member of the Marburg law faculty, and organizations like the Verein für das Deutschtum im Ausland (League for Germandom Abroad), which donated the considerable sum of ten thousand marks to help cover start-up costs. Beginning with no real facilities of its own, the institute within a decade acquired a substantial library collection and a building, the Deutsche Burse, which housed some of the institute's students. It also attracted respectable enrollments (up to forty-five) for its study groups although attendance at informal lectures declined somewhat over the decade.[123] The pedagogical philosophy of the institute was a synthetic one, fitting the interdisciplinary natures of both volkish and geopolitical studies in the era. Although officially affiliated with the philosophical faculty at Marburg, both the governing committee and the teaching personnel of the institute included members from all faculties.[124] And Mannhardt's efforts on behalf of Germandom at the institute were clearly well received by most of his colleagues. Members of the philosophical faculty had in 1918 themselves proposed the establishment of an institute for foreign German studies, and in 1926 the faculty urged that Mannhardt be offered a professorship to maintain the lead that Marburg had developed on other German universities in the field of Auslandsdeutschtum to which many other schools were now turning their attention.[125] Mannhardt was, accordingly, made an associate professor in the next year. In 1929 an actual chair (*Lehrstuhl*) was for the first time created in the study of border and foreign Germandom, and Mannhardt was made a full professor to fill it.[126]

The application of geopolitics to the study of border Germandom was a frequent topic among lecturers from a variety of fields who were attracted to Mannhardt's institute. The official mission of the institute was to study foreign Germandom "as a science" and to investigate "the entire intellectual and material culture of those Germans who, settled in the midst of non-Germanophone surroundings, have kept their mother tongue and with it their tribal consciousness (*Stammesbewußtsein*)."[127] The institute's courses, open to students from all fields, promoted the geopolitical agenda of the inherent weakness of postwar central European political geography and the imperative nature of German spatial expansion. These included The Geopolitics of Zwischeneuropa, The Demopolitics of Zwischeneuropa, Europe in Geopolitical Perspective, Volk ohne Raum and Foreign Germandom, Political Geography of Germany and Its Eastern Neighboring States, and Fundamentals of Racial Hygiene and its Significance for the Struggle for Existence of Border and Foreign Germandom.[128] As these titles suggest, the institute's offerings, emphasized the centrality of race and ethnicity to German renewal, to the cultural and political geography of the region, and to foreign policy, the latter of which was also treated in informal weekly discussions under Mannhardt's direction on Foreign Policy Questions of the Day.

Two facts are worth noting regarding the institute's lecture courses, both of which are revealing for the study of geopolitics and volkish questions in this period. First is the institute's effort to foster interdisciplinary integration. At the institute, as in the writings of the field's leading theorists, geopolitics was more than simply another academic discipline; it was a lens through which to reexamine all disciplines, almost a worldview in itself, used here in combination with volkish theories. This view was expressed in the conscious selection of the institute's governing board members from a variety of disciplines and in its use in teaching of *Sammelvorlesungen,* or combined lecture courses, in which faculty from different fields lectured on various aspects of a common theme in courses open to students from all the university's departments. This accorded with what Mannhardt called "the synthetic character" of study at the institute and produced courses like that offered in the winter of 1930-31 under the title Germandom Abroad to which lecturers and professors from Marburg's theological, legal, and philosophical faculties all contributed.[129] Second, a revealing minor detail, is the way the institute's courses appear in the Marburg lecture guide. Between 1922 and 1931 courses offered under the auspices of the institute appeared under three different general subject titles, beginning as The Science of Germandom Abroad in 1922, evolving into Borderland and Foreign Studies in 1927, and finally emerging in 1931 as *Volkstums- und Staatenkunde* (Ethnology and state studies).[130] No similar contortions in nomenclature were thought necessary for fields such as geography, law, and other established disciplines in the university's curriculum. The indecision about what to call those subjects taught at the IGAD is a concrete expression of the vexing dilemma of disciplinary identity that faced both geopolitical and volkish studies and that they never finally surmounted.

The influence of geopolitics at the institute is unsurprising, given that Mannhardt's own views on volkish questions contained a strong admixture of geopolitical geodeterminism. *Der Faschismus* (Fascism), a work published in 1925 that earned him his venia legendi at Marburg, presents a sympathetic critique of the roots and nature of the ideology that, as his committee noted with approval, synthesized historical, geographical, economic, and political theory, an approach espoused by many geopoliticians.[131] His study of ethnic Germans in the South Tyrol, a revanchist tract published in 1928 as *Südtirol. Ein Kampf um deutsche Volkheit* (South Tyrol: A struggle for German nationality), adopts an extremely geodeterministic view of character formation through geography. "Boden, as well as wind and climate, are to a certain degree the unchanging shapers of nationality. The Alps present a landscape all their own," Mannhardt wrote. "Only a sense of responsibility and strength of character permit resistance (to the weather). In the mountains the necessity to resist the harsh climate steels the body and makes the people resourceful."[132]

The government of Prussia fostered the development of volkish and geopolitical education at the Marburg Institute morally by its support for the founding of the institute and thereafter materially with a steady flow of state funds. The Prussian Ministry for Science, Art and Public Education supplied occasional funds to pay lecturers and buy books, paid expenses to enable Mannhardt to attend meetings outside Germany, and supplied an annual state subsidy that went as high as RM 8,250 for 1933.[133] The ministry also provided RM 10,000 in 1926 to the League of Friends of the Marburg Institute for Border and Foreign Germandom, which was used toward the construction of a dormitory for students at the IGAD.[134] Prussian financial aid continued into the Nazi era although Mannhardt himself was forced out of the institute in 1936 after hostile demonstrations by Marburg students.[135] This substantial support from the Prussian state government is at first glance surprising in light of the predominance of Socialists in Prussia, often described as "the bulwark of the Republic" for its strong commitment to Weimar democracy. It is less surprising, perhaps, when one considers Prussia's overt educational commitment to geopolitical education and its ongoing efforts to found similar volkish and area studies foundations at other universities.

These efforts were crowned with success in the form of several institutes with loose university affiliations, some of which have been mentioned, that received a powerful boost in Prussia from the advocacy of Albert Brackmann, a historian and director of the Prussian State Archives from 1929 to 1936. Brackmann, like Mannhardt, had argued for foreign studies rooted in a synthetic approach along lines suggested by Kjellén in 1917, and his ideas influenced the Prussian Ministry for Science, Art and Public Education in the following years.[136] Efforts to foster foreign studies were by no means confined to Prussia, however. Institutes like Mannhardt's were founded throughout Germany with the support of the federal government, of which one of the best examples was the Stiftung für deutsche Volks- und Kulturbodenforschung (Foundation for Research on German Ethnic and Cultural Soil [SDVK]) at Leipzig. The foundation opened in 1926 through the support of the national government as its leader, Wilhelm Volz, later reported: "In reality, [the SDVK] was a creation of the Reich Interior Ministry. It was the goal of the foundation to shape a uniform, overlapping method to investigate the consequences of the new borders in cultural, social, and economic areas and to bring this investigation closer to various scientific disciplines."[137]

Volz, Albrecht Penck, and the volkish political activist Karl Christian von Loesch had authored a proposal for the foundation in 1922, and once in operation it sponsored meetings and conferences of specialists on border issues over the next several years.[138] In addition, the foundation published a journal, *Deutsche Hefte für Volks- und Kulturbodenforschung* (German pamphlets for ethnic and cultural soil research), which, to judge by its contributors and editors, succeeded in the SDVK's goal of bringing together various disciplines.[139] Those who worked on it at various times included geopoliticians from various disciplines, geographers Otto Maull, Erich Obst, and Karl Haushofer, the historian Walther Vogel, and politicians and volkish scholars, including Otto Boelitz and Mannhardt, and its articles regularly expressed the influence of geopolitics in their consideration of volkish issues.[140] The foundation's raison d'être stemmed from Penck's volkish/geographical theories of the German Volksboden, which portrayed most of central and eastern European culture as a product of German settlement and ideas. As Penck argued, the emanations of Germanic culture overshadowed a broad penumbra of regions even where no actual German population centers existed. "The German Kulturboden is the greatest achievement of the German people," Penck wrote. "Wherever Germans live in company and use the earth's surface, it comes into existence, whether or not it leads thereafter to the development of Volksboden. . . . A small number of Germans can suffice to transform a great land into German Kulturboden."[141]

Despite the financial support of the government the Leipzig foundation reduced its activities in 1931, closing three years later because of a combination of financial mismanagement and local political opposition.[142] Nonetheless, as in the case of the Marburg institute, the Leipzig foundation's history illustrates the significant initiating and sustaining role governmental agencies played in fostering the dissemination of geopolitical and, in these cases, volkish thought. The same is true for academic institutions such as the state-funded and unequivocally republican Deutsche Hochschule für Politik (German University for Politics [DHP]) in Berlin, where Adolf Grabowsky, Otto Hoetzsch, Karl Christian von Loesch, and others combined support for democracy with a geopolitical perspective in courses aimed at journalists, political functionaries, and aspiring foreign service officials.[143] In its emphasis on interdisciplinary education and political activism the DHP resembled the foreign studies institutes springing up at German universities in the period. The first proposals for the DHP originated in the same period as the genesis of the foreign studies idea, in 1914. It first opened its doors after the war in October 1920. And, like the foreign studies institutes, it derived its funding from a combination of private donors (the Stuttgart industrialist Robert Bosch among them) and state funds.[144]

Unlike the foreign studies institutes, however, the DHP, opened in 1920 in the presence of President Ebert, was committed to support of the Republic and from its beginnings identified with the parties of the Weimar Coalition. The DHP's democratic affiliation makes the geopolitical influence there even more striking. Adolf Grabowsky's geopolitical seminars were a required part of the DHP's popular four-semester course of study in general politics, but Grabowsky was far from being the only representative of geopolitical theories in the university's classrooms in the Berlin Schinkelbau.[145] Ernst Jäckh, director and cofounder of the DHP, made his own geopolitical predilections clear in his book *Deutschland. Das Herz Europas* (Germany: The heart of Europe) in which he argued in good geopolitical fashion that Germany's lack of "geographically secure boundaries" had decisively shaped both the German character and German politics. Jäckh dedicated his book "to the German statesman, Gustav Stresemann" and declared that he would "diagnose Germany as the completely concrete and physical heart of Europe, site the German organ within the European organism, biologically establish its position, connections, links. That means, first, geographically and geopolitically. It cannot be repeated enough: the geographic foundation is determining for the national fate of a people, for its national as well as international politics, and it was and is for Germany as the heart of Europe more decisive than for any other country and people in world history."[146]

Interest in colonies and ethnic Germans abroad led other instructors at the DHP to adopt geopolitical theories. Karl Christian von Loesch of the Deutscher Schutzbund (German Protective League), Heinrich Schnee of the Deutscher Kolonialkongress (German Colonial Congress), and Martin Spahn of the Center Party all incorporated geopolitical themes in their teaching to promote their particular political goals at the university. Loesch lectured on the importance of the Auslandsdeutschtum as a key to the reassertion of German power in central Europe.[147] Schnee, as the Weimar era's most prominent spokesman for the recovery of the German colonial empire, urged the return of Germany's colonies as a geopolitical necessity. Karl Haushofer lectured at the university as well, but the most interesting of the teachers who brought geopolitics to this officially pro-government venue was Martin Spahn, a Catholic politician and enthusiast for a renewed greater Germany in central Europe who represented a link between the University for Politics and the radically conservative group of teachers, writers, and theorists at the University for National Politics.[148]

The founding of the Hochschule für nationale Politik (University for National Politics), later known as the Politisches Kolleg (PK) to distinguish it from its Republican rival, was reactionary in the most literal sense of the word. Members of the so-called Juniklub or June Club, around the romantic conservative Moeller van den Bruck, were apparently discussing the foundation of a center for political studies when the Republicans around Jäckh opened the DHP. Outraged, and claiming the liberals had stolen their idea, Spahn and other members of the Juniklub circle moved within a very short time to open their own "national" alternative institute, and the PK was formally opened on 11 November 1920 although actual instruction began early the following year.[149] Beginning in the Berlin Motzstrasse 22 (in the same building where the DSB and several other conservative organizations were headquartered), the PK eventually moved to Spandau to take up the work of educating Germans in how to deal politically with "the fearful destruction of the external power of our state, the constant threatening of its inner cohesion after the defeat and the collapse, the growing disappointment that bureaucraticism and parliamentarism bring on the nation."[150]

This disappointment was addressed—and fostered—over the next twelve years by a coterie of thinkers who used geopolitical concepts at the Politisches Kolleg. Spahn, for example, was an admirer and personal friend of Karl Haushofer (Spahn tried unsuccessfully to talk Haushofer into opening a branch of the PK in Munich in the early 1920s) and intimately familiar with geopolitical ideas.[151] He lectured at the PK on Weltpolitik, Mitteleuropa, and Grossdeutschland, among other topics.[152] There is no need to guess at Spahn's views on these topics, because his prolific writings are filled with discussions of them. "The historical development of every people," he wrote, "its growth, fulfills itself in the way it roots itself ever more firmly in its Boden, grows with its Boden and imbues it with its disposition. Likewise the Boden affects the people and helps form its character. The state creates law, oversees conditions, orders the relations under which the process of growth of Volk and Raum is played out." The war was lost, Spahn insisted, because Ratzel's ideas were ignored in

German war planning, and he advocated the restoration of Germany as *Führervolk* of Europe as the key to creating stable politics in central Europe.[153] Spahn promoted geopolitical revisionism with a vengeance, arguing that Germany could become healthy only through restoring the organic connection with its space that was destroyed by the war.[154]

Spahn's students were not forced to rely on their own resources in arriving at the conclusion that these teachings denied the legitimacy of Poland, Czechoslovakia, and the other new states of the region. Spahn made the point himself. Geography and race, he insisted, required that Bohemia be brought under German rule. "The position of Bohemia in the middle European space allows us to recognize its importance. It forms . . . the unity of the two corner fortresses that flank the mountain wall which cuts through Germany from Osnabrück to the middle Danube. . . . We must deal with them [the Czechs] in Bohemia as with the French on the Rhine. The struggle with weapons has become a contest of race against race. We cling to the soil, we claw ourselves into it. They seek to rip us from it."[155] Spahn was, furthermore, committed to active propagandizing of these views in the border areas, forming a Middle Europe Committee in 1928 with members of the PK, journalists, and industrialists to coordinate propagandizing efforts because "we Germans must set our sights more seriously and resolutely than before on the complementing of economic by cultural-political propaganda."[156]

Spahn's geopolitical fervor was mirrored by his colleagues at the Political College. Karl Hoffmann, Spahn's assistant in the Workshop for Foreign Policy at the PK until his death in the mid-1920s, approached postwar international politics with a heavy emphasis on the determining force of the earth-space for the development of state relations.[157] The most significant thinker among Spahn's colleagues, however, was the sociologist Max Hildebert Boehm, leader of the *Arbeitsstelle für Nationalitäten- und Stammesprobleme* (Workshop for Nationality and Ethnic Problems) at the PK. Boehm's section of the PK has since been evaluated as its most scientifically rigorous, but in his lectures in courses such as The *Grossdeutsch* Question and Mitteleuropa (including a section on The Middle-European Space and its Geopolitical Foundations) and in his voluminous publications Boehm merged a very subjective geopolitical sensibility with an inventive analysis of the relationship of the people and the state, always in the interest of revision of the peace settlement.[158]

Like Albrecht Penck and other geographers, Boehm believed in the existence of the Germanic Kulturboden, in his own case to lay claim to what he called the *Mischgebiete,* areas in east and west Europe where ethnic Germans played the dominant economic and cultural role among several nationalities. "If German was, for broad circles, not the mother tongue here," he wrote, "it was, nonetheless, the language of culture and every higher form of intellectual activity."[159] While sharply repudiating racialist approaches to determining who in the border regions belonged to the German people ("the border population is a race in itself"), he supported an aggressive effort to preserve popular identification with Germany in the border regions by promoting cultural and political autonomy for German groups in other states.[160] He also made it clear that German renewal could come only on the basis of sound geopolitical concepts. "As long as every form of the Elbe border question has not been resolved, and the connection between the watch on the Rhine, the Danube, and the Weichsel has not been placed in the center of our thought, the rebuilding of the east for a future German position of power is a pretty dream," he wrote. "The mental grasp of these connections already signifies the first step from utopia to realization."[161] This would solve the problems he felt geography and ethnicity had created on Germany's borders, but he was not entirely averse to rewriting those borders themselves. As early as 1924 Boehm advocated a German Anschluss with rump Austria, and he hoped to rebuild the internal peace of Europe primarily to be ready for what he saw as a coming global struggle of the continents.[162]

Boehm separated his institute from the PK in 1926, transforming it into the Institute for Border and Foreign Studies, or *Institut für Grenz- und Auslandstudien* (he cited Mannhardt's "older and considerably larger" institute as a model) and taking up new quarters at Grunewaldstrasse 15 in Steglitz.[163] Boehm's departure, after Spahn's reentry into the Reichstag two years earlier, corresponded with a decline in the fortunes of the PK. With Spahn's attentions directed elsewhere and with the loss of leading faculty members such as Boehm, enrollments and funding from private donors declined. It was forced to suspend courses briefly in 1927 and reopened in 1928, interestingly, in partnership with its rival the DHP as part of a fund-sharing Arbeitsgemeinschaft. The partnership was a troubled one, surviving only until 1930. The PK continued a rocky existence thereafter until 1933.[164] Boehm also took his independent institute into a working relationship with the DHP in 1930 when he took over the leadership of the Ethnopolitical Seminar at the republican university.[165] However close the two institutes may have been during Weimar, however, their respective true colors showed under the political litmus test of the Nazi era. Jächk, Otto Suhr, and others close to the DHP (with the exception of Otto Hoetzsch) lost their jobs and were hounded, in some cases, out of the country. Leaders of the PK, by contrast, had no quarrel with national socialism. Spahn, in fact, joined a faction of the DNVP in joining the Nazis in June of 1933, helping dissolve what remained of Hugenberg's party, and Boehm passed the Nazi era in a comfortable and prestigious academic position for "ethnic theory" at Jena.[166]

A variety of other institutions, the German Academy in Munich, for example, also worked to familiarize a broad academic audience with geopolitical ideas, but they were concerned less with reaching students directly than with propagandizing among their teachers in the hopes of exerting indirect influence.[167] How did the students themselves respond? To all appearances, they responded with marked enthusiasm. Scholars are generally agreed that the politics of German students as a whole moved sharply toward the Right during the Weimar period as did those of their teachers at both the secondary and university levels.[168] It would not be surprising to find that geopolitical ideas, particularly in combination with very popular volkish theories, were well received in such a student milieu, and there are indications that this was, in fact, the case. The students who gathered in 1929 at Hannover for the *Deutscher Studententag,* or German Students' Congress, for example, approved a resolution calling for the establishment of teaching positions for geopolitics and *Volkstumskunde* (ethnology), going so far as to recommend that all students be tested on their knowledge of geopolitics, Auslandsdeutschtum, and the history of the world war.[169] Their demands went unheeded, but it scarcely mattered. Whether standardized tests and formal chairs for geopolitics existed or not, by 1929 geopolitical geodeterminism was, in geography, foreign studies, and political science, an accepted part of German higher education.

CHAPTER 7

"The Suggestive Map"
Geopolitics and Cartography

> The suggestive map! German conscientiousness asks: Can there be any
> other kind of map than an image that strives to recreate the earth's
> surface or a portion of it on a page, so far as can be done with printer's
> ink and dye, according to the highest degree of accuracy?
>
> Karl Haushofer, "Die suggestive Karte," 1922

The gradual incorporation of geopolitical principles into German education between 1918 and 1933 took place because bureaucrats, scholars, and
teachers shared the conviction that Germany had been unjustly treated
in the settlement of World War I and that popular geopolitical awareness
was essential to reversing the verdict of Versailles. The same conviction
also transformed German cartography in these years. Spurred by the perceived need to mobilize the German people to meet its desperate international situation, geographers adopted the view that the task of German
maps was no longer to graphically portray the spatial relationship of the
features of the earth's surface but to impart to Germans a sense of their
own danger, to make visible those geographical and political forces that
could not be seen on traditionally "accurate" maps. The new, geopolitically informed cartography would awaken Germans to the dynamic
interaction of space with political power.

The postwar attitude toward maps represented a significant departure from German scientific traditions. In the early decades of the twentieth century German cartography enjoyed a worldwide reputation for
scientific precision and painstaking accuracy. Since the days of the path-
breaking Behaim globe more than four centuries earlier, the German
geographical profession had been renowned for its resourcefulness and
adherence to strict principles in representations of the earth's physical

features. A generation of nineteenth-century geographical giants, including Alexander von Humboldt, Justus Perthes, August Petermann, and others, had established world standards for the compilation of atlases and the concise presentation of large amounts of data in clear and easily read maps.[1] In the aftermath of World War I, however, many geopoliticians, geographers, and cartographers in Germany embraced a new philosophy of mapmaking, one that argued that the heretofore dominant concern with accuracy, now denounced as a "petty loyalty to details," ought to be sacrificed to create maps that were "accurate" in a more impressionistic sense.[2]

The geopolitical challenge to dominant German notions about the objectivity of mapmaking represented a recognition, healthy in itself, that no map is entirely "accurate," just as no history is accurate in an exhaustive sense. As modern critics of cartographic "texts" have excitedly rediscovered, cartographers (like historians) make decisions about how to represent their data. Consequently, all maps omit certain facts and include others, implicitly communicating to the viewer the mapmaker's priorities, such as they may be.[3] Frequently, political perspectives shape this cartographic editorial decision making. Although some contemporary adherents of cartographic deconstruction have discovered new significance in the hidden messages of maps, the fact that maps contain ideas, opinions, and perspectives besides the geographic data they convey is not, in itself, a particularly novel insight. More than two centuries ago, Jonathan Swift lampooned the often transparent intentions of creative British cartographers when he wrote

> Geographers in Afric maps
> With savage pictures fill their gaps
> And over inhabitable downs
> Place elephants, for want of towns

Despite the truth of the self-evident fact that all maps presume and convey a particular worldview, German geopolitical maps of the 1920s and 1930s nevertheless represented an important break with tradition in their enthusiastic affirmation of their political mission. These maps did not simply contain an implied message about political values; they set out above all to convey an often explicit political statement, which took precedence over any idealistic strivings to create "accurate" or "scientific" portrayals of the physical world. Over the decade, geopolitical cartographers cast aside early pretensions at objective cartography, still strong in Penck's map of the German cultural soil, as their maps degenerated into mere cartogrammes, not really maps at all but political cartoons in map-like forms.[4] The ideological and symbolic content of geopolitical maps, their graphic language of shapes, colors, and blank spaces, conveyed and reinforced the geopolitical worldview of eternal interstate struggle and legitimated the geopolitical brief for German hegemony in central Europe.

It should not be supposed that the reform of cartography was merely an incidental concern of the geopoliticians. Expressive maps were central to the geopolitical project of creating geopolitical awareness in the German people, and they devoted a considerable literature to the theoretical arguments for such cartographic "progress." Maps were taken very seriously, furthermore, by both professional geographers and the general public. When the Berlin publishing house of Ullstein produced a new *Weltatlas* in 1923 that replaced the old German names of towns and geographical features in central Europe with names in Czech, Polish, and the languages of the other successor states established after World War I, the rabid criticism of the step from defenders of the German *Volkstum* (nationality) resulted in a lawsuit. Franz Ullstein, head of the house, sued Hermann Ullmann, Karl Christian von Loesch, and the other editors of the volkish journal *Deutsche Arbeit* for their accusations, laden with veiled anti-Semitism, that the new geographic nomenclature was treasonous and motivated by Ullstein's business interests in Slavic lands. Although Ullstein eventually dropped the suit, geopoliticians and geographers united to provide "scientific" briefs on behalf of Ullstein's accusers: Wilhelm Volz, Walther Vogel, and other geopolitically influenced thinkers supplied expert opinions to the court, arguing that "a German atlas is intended in the first place for Germans and must, therefore, take account of German needs; that is the only scientifically defensible standpoint."[5] Prompted by this case, the German Geographic Congress in 1925 resolved, at the urging of Albrecht Penck, to employ German names of historically German towns regardless of the state in which they happened to be located.[6]

In the districts of the foreign and border Germandom countless good German names for geographic objects of all kinds (villages, regions, mountains, bodies of water), often holding valuable memories of a historical nature, are threatened with extinction. The German Geographic Congress recognizes a national duty to protect these names and calls on all concerned parties, authors and editors of maps, atlases, travel books, and geographic publications of all kinds and representatives of schools and the press, business and trade as well with the urgent plea to give preference to the German name in all cases where geographic double names exist and to put it in first place.[7]

In defiance of postwar political reality, therefore, German geographers decided that Lwow, Bratislava, and Sibiu were to remain, for Germans at least, Lemberg, Pressburg, and Hermannstadt. Some cartographers never needed prompting on the issue, of course, particularly those affiliated with conservative nationalist groups. In a famous map from 1924 put out by the Austro-German *Volksbund* and entitled "It Ought to Be the Entire Germany!" all the traditional German names are retained. (See fig. 3.) The *Volksbund* was quartered in the Schloss Bellevue in Berlin where Loesch's *Deutscher Schutzbund* had originally been located, and it is safe to assume there were links between the two groups.[8] This particular map is a good starting point for a consideration of geopolitical cartography because it presents a microcosm of the stylistic evolution of the field during the Weimar (and Nazi) years. Although the main map holds to fairly standard, "scientific" conventions of cartographic representation for linguistic and political maps and portrays the natural and human-made features outside as well as within the borders of Germany, it also contains a foreshadowing of the coming geopolitical cartographic style. Displayed in three panels in the lower right section of the sheet are three stark, black-on-white outlines entitled *Rumpfdeutschland, Grossdeutschland,* and *Gesamtdeutschland*. The last of these, including all regions where German was the language of the majority of the population, was, of course, the largest, embracing most of central Europe. Both the title of the entire map (a popular slogan of the German Democratic Party in these years) and of the inset captioned "Gesamtdeutschland" convey unmistakably the message that all the regions shown are, by rights, German.[9]

Geopolitical cartographers over the decade became highly skilled in the use of linguistic and cartographic symbols to convert seemingly scientific maps into sophisticated political messages. The most prominent geopolitical cartographer, Arnold Hillen Ziegfeld, argued that geopolitics could help German students to envision the world anew, and called

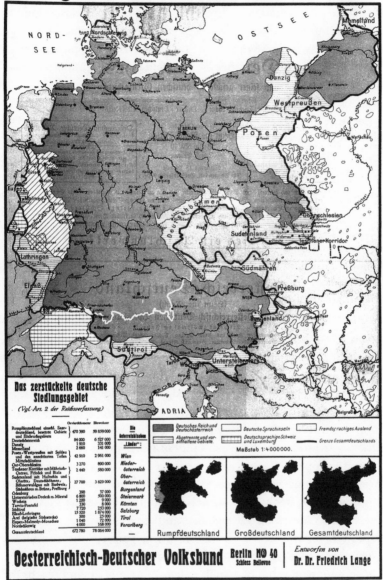

Fig. 3. *Das ganze Deutschland soll es sein!* (It shall be Germany entire!) Courtesy of Staatsbibliothek Preussischer Kulturbesitz, Kartenabteilung.

upon cartographers to meet their needs: "The desire to encompass the play of historical, political, economic, and cultural forces behind appearances has led to liberation and repudiation of the previously dominant fundamental guidelines to reproduce only the quantifiable, the *so-called reality*. . . . Today it is recognized that the desire to use maps as a means of creative representation is justified."[10] Ziegfeld played an important role in what he described as the "struggle for a new world image."[11] He was the cartographer who drew Penck's trendsetting map of the German cultural soil (see fig. 1), and his maps appeared frequently in geopolitical and volkish books and periodicals throughout the period.

Ziegfeld's maps made a graphic case for German expansion in central Europe on grounds of economics, culture, and security. His map entitled "German Culture and Its Effect," which appeared on the cover of *Volk und Reich* in 1928, typified his style. (See fig. 4.) The dense black mass of the coterminous German Reich and its appanage in East Prussia spills over into most of the regions outside the borders of Germany through the use of crosshatching and other shadings. The color scheme vividly emphasizes the subordinate relation of these areas to their German cultural center. The shaded areas strike the viewer as emanating from the solid Teutonic core, and in this way the map stakes out a vivid graphic German claim to most of central Europe. The map's silences are expressive as well. Only in German lands is there a detailed siting of rivers and urban centers; as distances from the German hub become greater, details become sparser, until at the far eastern edge, in the Soviet Union, the map trails off into a blank, featureless waste, containing neither cities nor borders nor even rivers. Again, as with the shading scheme, the map is here reinforcing the message of the centrality of Germany as the cultural heart of central Europe.

These techniques were repeated in countless geopolitical maps Ziegfeld produced for books and journals, including *Volk unter Völkern, Volk und Reich,* the *Grenzdeutsche Rundschau,* and others. His map, "The Middle European Economic Space" from 1925, also portrays the consolidated German settlement region in north central Europe as a sort of dark sun, the economic penumbra of which radiates east, north, and south, from the Adriatic to the Arctic Circle and from the mouths of the Rhine far into the Ukraine. (See fig. 5.) Nor did he neglect to highlight German claims to lands to the west through his maps. The maps of the Low Countries, which he produced for a propaganda pamphlet of the DSB in

1925 (entitled *Rhein und Reich*), use similar techniques to emphasize German claims to Luxembourg, Alsace, and Lorraine and considerable portions of Belgium and the Netherlands.[12] (See figs. 6, 7.)

The shading scheme in Ziegfeld's maps, interestingly, is always reversed when the point is to convey not German cultural or economic potency but the threatening and undeserved military vulnerability of the German state under the new European dispensation. The message of his map entitled "The Pressure on the German States" could scarcely be more overt. Here the regions of German settlement, now light-shaded, are menaced by the dark, dense masses depicting Slavic and Italian regions. To ensure that the text's message is absolutely unmistakable, arrows radiate outward from the Slavic lands, pincering and penetrating the exposed portions of the German-settled areas (see fig. 8). Even more indicative of his sensationalistic "Germany-at-risk" style is Ziegfeld's map, "Polish Club Activities within and outside of the East Prussian Border" (see fig. 9). The German area is now entirely devoid of shading. It is menaced from all sides by the threatening darkness of the Polish state, which is overlaid with a dense network of obscure and vaguely military-looking glyphs, providing an image as of camps or bases. From Warsaw, arrows, whose meaning is not explained in the map's legend, strike out in direct lines over the chief German settlements of the East Prussia. These German settlements, furthermore, are at the center of networks of concentric circles that have the effect of concentrating upon the German towns all the forces represented on the map. The innocuous subject of the map, the location of Polish presses, religious groups, and youth, women's and singing clubs, is, thus, graphically translated for the map's readers into a cryptic but decipherable diagram for air strikes or other forms of military aggression directed from Warsaw. And, given Ziegfeld's views on the purposes of cartography, this was undoubtedly its intent as a cultural text.

As these maps demonstrate, geopolitical cartography represented in practice a repudiation of the constraints imposed by "scientific" standards, a repudiation motivated by their political agenda. The best example of this geopolitical movement for liberation from the constraints of rational cartography was the attack on the linguistic map spearheaded in the middle 1920s by Ziegfeld and Albrecht Penck. Linguistic and ethnographic maps, Ziegfeld argued, had made "decisive progress" during the Weimar era on the "artistic side" through "liberation from faith in the infallibility of statistics and renunciation of conventional types of ethnographic representation."[13] In his own and Penck's portrayal of the extent of German culture this meant that they would no longer consider those regions where German was the dominant tongue but instead would darken all those portions of their maps where they detected any significant German cultural influence whatsoever. Relying on agricultural practices, forms of domestic architecture, road construction, and other indicators, Penck created a penumbra of German cultural influence that stretched far beyond the regions of actual German settlement. This radically extended the area of German influence, according to Penck, which now reached "half again as far as the German ethnic soil," all the way to the borders of Russia.

Penck's own description of the concept of the Kulturboden vividly illuminates the crucial role played by the experiences of the First World War in the east. "Here was the great cultural border, which the German soldiers felt only too sensibly as they marched toward the east," Penck wrote. "It is so striking that one can see it from the train. The neat stone houses in the villages cease. The construction becomes less careful, the forest is visibly poorly cultivated. . . . A small number of Germans can suffice to transform a great land into German cultural soil."[14] Penck's magnification of German claims was quickly adopted by political propagandists, some of whom had anticipated his arguments in their own maps, as in the case of Gottfried Fittbogen's propaganda map, "The German Volk in Middle Europe" of 1924 (see fig. 10).

German teaching reflected the influence of Penck's map even more rapidly than did German political journalism. Within one year maps in geography textbooks such as Johannes Wütschke, *Unsere Erde,* were relying on Penck to teach German students about the putative German *Kulturgrenze* that stretched through far eastern Europe on a rough line from the Crimea to St. Petersburg. This map, by an eerie coincidence, traces almost exactly the line where the furthest German and Finnish advances into Russian territory exhausted themselves seventeen years later. Wütschke's book enjoyed the official endorsement of the Prussian Ministry for Science, Art, and Popular Education, which included the book among the relatively few permitted for use in Prussian geography courses in 1927.[15] Similarly, one of the most widely used school atlases, the *Fischer-Geistbeck Stufenatlas* for high schools, had by its fourth expanded edition in 1927 found room for a map, explicitly based on Penck's, which showed the German cultural soil extending deep into the Ukraine.

The suggestive power of such maps exploited the cachet of "science" to convince German students of the injustice of eastern Europe's political geography.

Conservative revisionists and geopoliticians alike applauded the repudiation of constricting "scientific" cartographic conventions. Otto Maull, for example, called for the creation of a geopolitical cartography of "purely programmatic maps." Through the use of simple and vivid graphic images, this cartography would convey geopolitical messages ("How impressive is a map of Germany that establishes the effect of [Germany's] dynamic forces only with a pair of arrows!"), and he cited his own map of the European *Lebensgemeinschaften* (life communities) as an example of this programmatic cartography (see fig. 11).[16] While geopoliticians such as Maull and Josef März advocated the use of "the map as means of propaganda," and conservative political publicists extolled the value of geopolitical maps, Volkstum activists in the Verein für das Deutschtum im Ausland also gave their approval to the new approach, believing that it freed German mapmakers from the constraints of population statistics.[17] "[Maps of the cultural soil] show the extent of our Volkstum not only linguistically but also culturally, above all so far as the type of agriculture and the use of German as a language of trade are concerned. . . . It is not only a scientific achievement but also a *volkspolitische* [ethnopolitical] act."[18]

The standards and techniques promoted by Ziegfeld, Penck, Maull, and others soon came to dominate geopolitical cartography. Many of the maps in a work such as Franz Knieper, *Politische Geographie (Geopolitik) für den Unterricht,* published as a textbook in 1933, included maps which, like Ziegfeld's, showed exposed parts of the German state threatened by Slavic penetrations. His maps entitled "The Encirclement of East Prussia" and "The Dangerous Position of Upper Silesia," for example, can be considered traditional maps only in the broadest sense (see figs. 12, 13). They convey very little genuine information about geographic features: neither directions (none of them indicate compass points) nor distances (there are no scales or legends), drainage, settlement patterns nor any of the other data normally considered the concern of maps find a place in these maps. Instead, they present stylized images of parts of Germany being pinched and clamped by Poles, Czechs, and Lithuanians, whose modest and largely obsolete military establishments have become thick, arrow-headed bands of black directed at the heart of the German regions. Knieper's maps, "The German Borderland Inhabitants" and "The Armaments of

Our Neighbors," also recall Ziegfeld's map portraying the "pressure" exerted by Germany's neighbors (see figs. 14, 15). In both cases, the area of the German state is empty, or nearly so, and surrounded by threatening formations.

By the early 1930s geopolitical maps had forsaken nearly all objective geographic standards or values in order to cultivate alarmist and revisionist feeling among Germans. Maps such as "Power Groupings in Europe" from Haushofer's edited collection of essays entitled *Jenseits der Grossmächte* showed Germany barren and defenseless, hemmed in by blackened, shaded, and starred enemies (see fig. 16). Eventually, geopoliticians abandoned even the pretense of making maps. When Karl Springenschmid published a collection of geopolitical maps in 1933, he entitled the work not an atlas but a "geopolitical sketchbook."[19] In the foreword written by Karl Haushofer the word *map* was studiously avoided. "The following sketches show—in clear contradiction of a purely materialistic concept— that a strong will to statehood always and everywhere remains decisive and can raise itself over geographic factors. But it must always—and this is essential—keep them in view to be able to master them."[20] In a series of drawings under captions such as "The Land of the Center," "Germany's Security?" and "The Dangers of the Central Position," Springenschmid used symbols, lines, blank spaces, repetition, and other devices to emphasize Germany's vulnerability (see figs. 17 a, b, c). Here the combination of maps, all directed to evoking the same response, invited comparison between the several offerings and heightened the impact of the intended message through replication. The maps under "Germany's Security," for example, showed Germany yoked and enmeshed in an all-encompassing network of fine lines resembling the spokes of a bicycle wheel or the filaments of a spider's web. These matrices thus cast over the German state were, ostensibly, depictions of avenues of air attack. The entire nation was thus made vulnerable to attack from the capitals of all surrounding states. Conjoined with the other maps representing the threats to German security, these maps created a powerful image of engulfment and swift, enveloping technological warfare. Germans, they implied, could not escape. Only resistance or preemption offered safety.

Trends like these in geopolitical cartography only intensified under the Nazis, and maps that used some of the graphic devices of geopolitical cartography were an important part of Nazi propaganda both before and during the Second World War. As a Western critic during the war wrote, such mapping "borrows the prestige of science and at the same time violates its spirit."[21] The formulation is apt. If there is indeed no such thing as a purely "scientific" or "objective" map, as critics of cartographic texts argue, it remains true that most maps are, in intended purpose at least, aimed at conveying accurate scientific knowledge. Certainly, during the Weimar period, German road maps, topographical charts, and other kinds of practical cartographic tools never became "geopoliticized." Under the pressure of political and social upheaval, however, geographers and political activists joined geopoliticians in abandoning traditional "scientific" cartographic aims.[22] In so doing they lent the mantle of prestige worn by German geographical science to nonscientific purposes and used their knowledge and abilities to heighten the fears and hostilities of Germans. As time would show, their "magic geography" contributed to the realization of the most disastrous of consequences for the German people. The attempt to realize under German rule all the regions that geopoliticians depicted as the German cultural soil ended, at last, in the utter devastation of an overextended and exhausted imperial Germany.

Volk und Reich

Politische Monatshefte

Heft 9/10 / 1928

Die deutsche Kultur und ihre Auswirkung

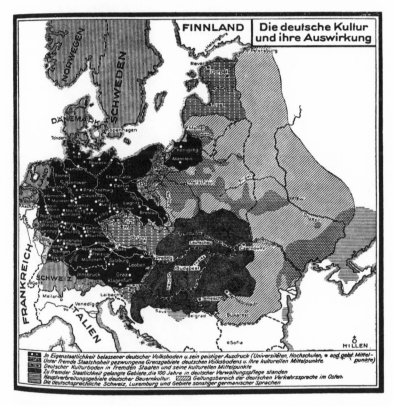

Fig. 4. *Die deutsche Kultur und ihre Auswirkung* (German culture and its effect), from the cover of *Volk und Reich*. Courtesy of Bildarchiv Preussischer Kulturbesitz, Kartenabteilung.

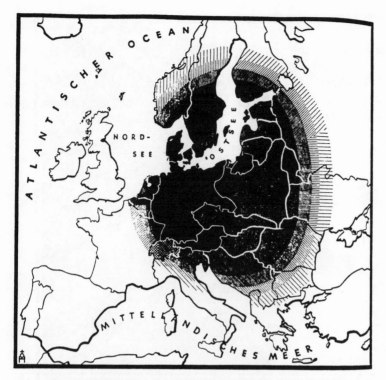

Fig. 5. *Der mitteleuropäische Wirtschaftsraum* (The Central European economic region), from *Volk und Reich*. Courtesy of Bildarchiv Preussischer Kulturbesitz, Karten-abteilung.

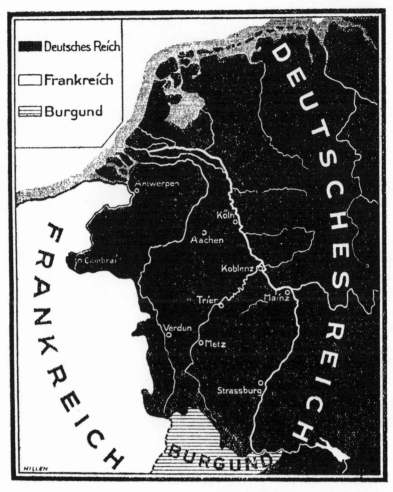

Fig. 6. *Westdeutschland im Deutschen Reiche vom 925* (Western Germany in the Germany reich of 925). Courtesy of Bundesarchiv Koblenz, NL 160 Pechel.

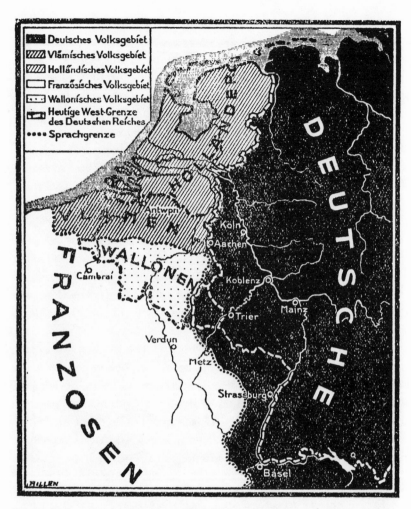

Fig. 7. *Volkspolitische Karte von 1925* (Ethnopolitical map of 1925). Courtesy of Bundesarchiv Koblenz, NL 160 Pechel.

Fig. 8. *Der Druck auf die deutschen Staaten* (The pressure on the German States), from *Volk und Reich*. Courtesy of Bildarchiv Preussischer Kulturbesitz.

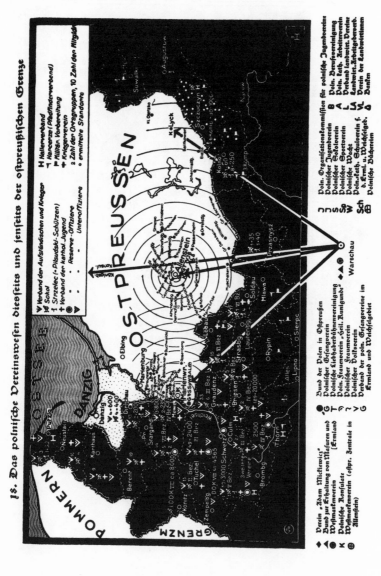

Fig. 9. *Das polnische Vereinswesen diesseits und jenseits der ostpreußischen Grenze* (Polish club activities within and beyond the East Prussian border), from *Volk und Reich*. Courtesy of Bildarchiv Preussischer Kulturbesitz.

Fig. 10. *Das deutsche Volk in Mitteleuropa* (The German volk in Central Europe). Courtesy of Geheimes Staatsarchiv Preussischer Kulturbesitz, HA XII.

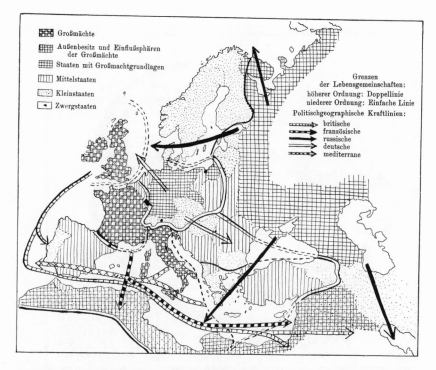

Fig. 11. *Die Machtgliederung und die Lebensgemeinschaften der Staaten Europas* (The power configuration and life communities of the states of Europe), from O. Maull, *Politische Geographie* (Berlin: Verlag von Gebrüder Borntraeger, 1925).

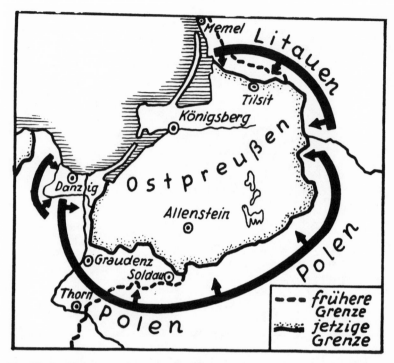

Fig. 12. *Die Einkreisung Ostpreussens* (The encirclement of East Prussia), from F. Knieper, *Politische Geographie (Geopolitik)* (Bochum: F. und F. Kamp Verlag, 1933).

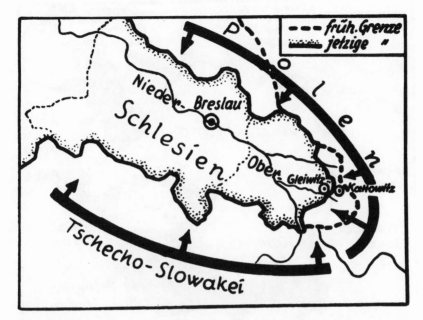

Fig. 13. *Die gefahrvolle Lage Oberschlesiens* (The endangered position of East Prussia), from F. Knieper, *Politische Geographie (Geopolitik)* (Bochum: F. und F. Kamp Verlag, 1933).

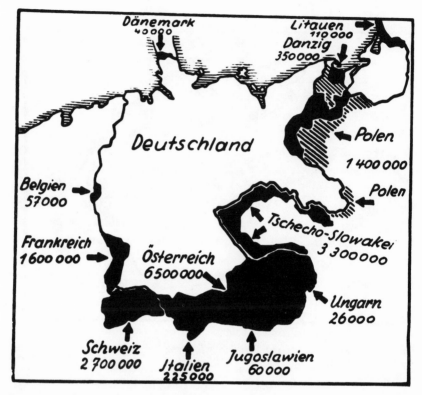

Fig. 14. *Die deutschen Grenzlandbewohner* (Inhabitants of the German borderlands), from F. Knieper, *Politische Geographie (Geopolitik)* (Bochum: F. und F. Kamp Verlag, 1933).

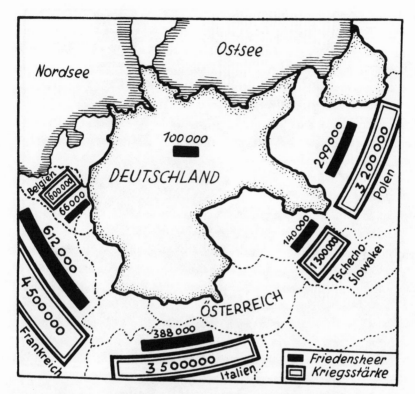

Fig. 15. *Die Rüstungen unserer Nachbarn* (The armaments of our neighbors) from
F. Knieper, *Politische Geographie (Geopolitik)* (Bochum: F. und F. Kamp Verlag, 1933).

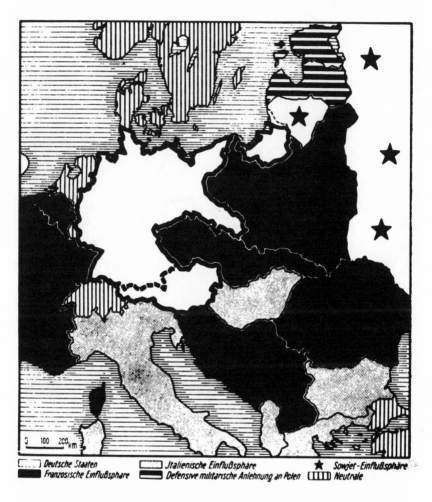

Fig. 16. *Abb. 38* Mächtegruppierung in Europa (Power groupings in Europe), from
Karl Haushofer, ed., *Jenseits der Grossmächte* (Leipzig: B. G. Teubner, 1932).

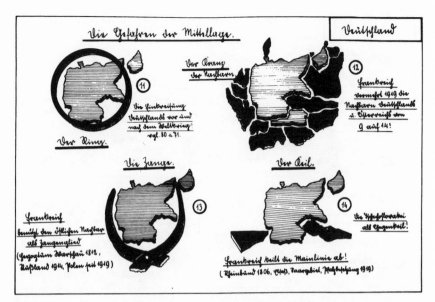

Fig. 17a. *Die Gefahren der Mittellage* (The dangers of the central position)

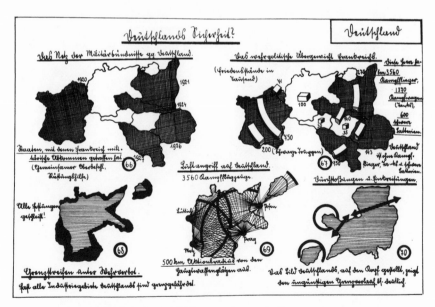

Fig. 17b. *Deutschlands Sicherheit?* (Germany's security?)

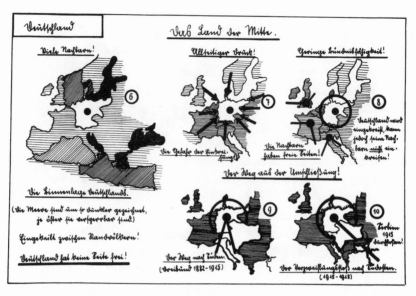

Fig. 17c. *Das Land der Mitte* (The land of the center)

Maps on these pages are from K. Springenschmid, *Die Staaten als Lebewesen. Geopolitisches Skizzenbuch* (Leipzig: Verlag Ernst Wunderlich, 1933).

CHAPTER 8

Space for the Third Man

Geopolitics and the Weimar Crusade for Colonies

In Germany today, every third man is one too many! . . . For the
German problem of the third man, and that means for the German
moral problem and it means for the German social problem, there is
only one solution, the procurement of space.

Hans Grimm, "Übervölkerung und Kolonialproblem," 1922

While geopolitical enthusiasts in German schools and the German media
were cultivating a new geographic sensibility among the German public,
some groups were already applying the implications of geopolitical ideas
in an effort to shape Weimar domestic and foreign politics. The geopolitical argument that Germany required additional Raum found a ready
audience during the Weimar years among the leaders of the crusade to
regain the lost German colonial empire. While most geopolitical thought
focused on border revisions and the establishment of a German Mitteleuropa, German colonialists demanded direct political control over vast
regions of Africa to solve the German space problem.[1] The urgent tone
of their writings on the topic now seems difficult to understand. Indeed,
a striking aspect of German colonial propaganda during the Weimar
era is the disparity between the actual significance the overseas empire
had held for German society, which was very small, and the enormous
amount of language, paper and ink, and futile energy expended on its
recovery after the Versailles peace settlement. Contrary to the fervent
declarations of revanchists such as Heinrich Schnee, former governor of
German East Africa and later president of the Deutsche Kolonialgesellschaft (German Colonial Society [DKG]), the colonies never assumed
more than a marginal role in German economic and social life during the

nearly four decades they were ruled by Germany. German emigration to the colonies in Africa and the South Pacific, for example, was insignificant. The most populous German colony, Southwest Africa, counted fewer than fifteen thousand German residents in 1914. The nations of North and South America were always much more popular as destinations for German emigrants than were Germany's own colonies. Nor did the colonies ever mean much economically, save, of course, to those small elites whose livelihoods derived directly from them. They had supplied small quantities of raw materials and tropical products but not at prices lower than were available from other sources, nor had they provided significant markets for German exports.[2] Only the German base at Tsing-Tao gave access to a potentially promising export market, but the "China market" remained for Germany, as for the other Western powers at the time, no more than an elusive mirage.

Perceptions, nonetheless, can be as important historically as realities, a truism that seems particularly relevant to relations between states. For the course of national politics popular opinions often assume greater importance than the objective benefit derived from influence in or possession of a particular area. The example of the American experience in Vietnam is one of many that comes to mind as a powerful confirmation of this principle. Bismarck's very establishment of a German colonial empire in the 1880s has been seen as an attempt to rally and unify popular opinion behind his government, and from that time to the collapse of the Kaiserreich in 1918 the colonial empire, despite its nugatory value for the nation, had been the object of extensive political agitation.[3] In the prewar era groups such as the Deutsche Kolonialgesellschaft and the Alldeutscher Verband (Pan-German League) had expended considerable effort to convince Germans that the empire was essential to the national welfare. During the war itself the demand for extensive African acquisitions became a regular part of the war aims propaganda of the Pan-Germans and other colonialist groups.[4]

Because it is clear that many Germans of the Weimar era shared Schnee's belief that the colonial empire was crucial to German well-being, the significant issue is not the objective importance of the empire but the nature and sources of the empire's public image.[5] Thomas Childers, writing in a slightly different context, has called for a thoughtful reconsideration of political language—"the terms and linguistic constructions used by individuals, interest organizations, and political parties"—as a key to enhancing understanding of Republican society and the fate of its political institutions.[6] The language of Weimar-era arguments for a German overseas colonial empire, which shaped German perceptions of the value of colonies, gained much of its political and public resonance from the gradual absorption into colonial rhetoric of geopolitically influenced theories linking Raum, Lebensraum, and the survival of the German race. The biologism and organic state theory acquired by the colonialists from the rhetoric of geopolitics represented a significant departure in colonialist revanchism from early legalistic and economic claims to the colonies.

This is not to suggest that colonial agitation of the period did not display a good deal of continuity with the economic colonialist propaganda of the Wilhelmine era. Colonialist novels such as *Peter Moors Fahrt nach Südwest,* for example, were popular even before the First World War, and prewar colonial propaganda urged Germans to look to Africa as a serious alternative destination for emigrants.[7] But postwar colonialist propaganda evolved in important ways as well. Over the 1920s and early 1930s the themes and tone of colonialist propaganda began to reflect a radicalized geopolitical awareness. Colonialists' arguments displayed a very geopolitical awareness that Germany had now entered a new global age, different from that of the nineteenth century in its confidence in the transforming influence of new technologies. For colonial propagandists, as for geopoliticians, air travel, wireless, and other technological advances were making the whole earth, the globe itself, into the ultimate Raum. A distinctively new pseudoscientific eugenic influence, which used geopolitical terms to convey the necessity of settlement space to the well-being of the German race, also reflected a new, geopolitical element in German colonialist propaganda. Whereas geopolitical ideas led some to argue that Germans ought to focus on eastern Europe and not Africa as a field of expansion, they were used by others to bolster overseas colonial demands. Colonialists increasingly exploited geodeterminist spatial arguments to convince Germans of the need for a revival of their erstwhile colonial empire. This geodeterminism forged conceptual links between colonialists and geopoliticians, providing a shared language to justify German colonial claims on the basis of racial survival, cultural superiority based in technological achievement, and ethnobiological paranoia.

"Drang nach Afrika": Geopolitics and the Lost Empire

Historians at one time supposed that Weimar geopoliticians were, in general, opposed to a renewal of German overseas colonialism. Both Lothar Gruchmann and Klaus Hildebrand, for example, advanced this view in important studies of German imperialism published in the 1960s.[8] Even at that time, however, some dissented from this view, which minimized the heterogeneity of geopolitical thought and identified "geopolitics" too narrowly with the views of Karl Haushofer.[9] No one familiar with the recent historiography of the topic would make such an argument.[10] The rubric of geopolitics concealed a good deal of heterodoxy on crucial political issues, and the colonial question was no exception. Although there certainly were cases, that of Haushofer most notably, to support the argument that geopoliticians were hostile to or uninterested in a reacquisition of the empire, many more were passionate colonialists, and colonial agitators saw no incongruity in borrowing geopolitical terms and ideas. Geopoliticians who opposed renewed German colonial activity usually did so because of pragmatic concerns about political practicality on one level and arguments about the geopolitical consequences to be drawn from Germany's position in central Europe on the other. Geopolitical anticolonialism revealed Weimar geopolitical insight into the postwar world state system, but it was countered by a large contingent of geopoliticians who were convinced that Germany's future without colonies would be a desperate one.

When Karl Haushofer, in one of his most famous statements on the colonial question, responded to a published poll on the colonial issue conducted by the Institute for Foreign Policy in Hamburg, he emphasized the divisiveness created by colonial demands, the impracticality of reacquiring colonies, and the disadvantages of rejoining the "oppressor front" of the colonial powers. The condition of the great world empires of the day was, he argued, "a colonial mess," and German participation would not be worth "the loss of our freedom of choice and our alignment in the oppressor front against the colored races and the degree of hate this would incur." Pragmatic considerations of Germany's international leverage also dissuaded Haushofer from pressing the colonial issue because German demands would be "out of the question given our present powerlessness."[11] Haushofer's analysis of the colonial situation displayed atypical clarity, but it was not, obviously, a resounding categorical repudiation of the prospect of colonies for Germany. As an old Asia hand himself, Haushofer retained strong romantic conceptions of overseas exploration and settlement, and he was amenable to arguments that only colonies could provide necessary bases and raw materials. In his 1924 book *Geopolitik des Pazifischen Ozeans,* for example, he still lamented the material losses represented by the confiscation of Germany's island territories, and he waxed poetic about the "endless blue waves, white foaming surf roaring round deep-green atolls . . . tropical jungles with treasures in gold and flowing jewels, as in New Guinea; educable people, children of bliss and sunny worlds."[12] But Haushofer's real interest, as he made clear in several articles and books, was the formation of a continental bloc consisting of Germany, Russia, and other revisionist powers to resist "Anglo-Saxon" colonialism and world hegemony.[13] For him, this goal always took precedence over any attempts to regain an overseas colonial empire.

Haushofer was not alone in concluding, however reluctantly, that geopolitical realities precluded the reacquisition of Germany's empire. The *Eiserne Blätter,* a volkish propaganda sheet put out by Gottlob Traub, minister and member of the German National People's Party, posed the question "Where Is the German Colonial Land," and used geopolitical arguments to cite "eastern Europe" as the correct answer. Prewar colonial policy was already, insisted the writer, an "unconsidered risk," and overseas colonies were an unaffordable luxury for a continental power that still faced a struggle for existence. "In Europe, where we now live—in the middle of envious peoples—we will always be either hammer or anvil of European history. Therefore, we cannot use colonies, even if we ignore entirely the great changes in the Ethiopian world, which today no longer make a colonial mandate a pleasure."[14] Like Haushofer, Traub and the writers of the *Eiserne Blätter* always favored an eastern orientation and cooperation with the Soviet Union, fearing that colonial adventures would distract attention from what they considered the more vital eastern task facing Germany.[15] German geography dictated a different direction for its expansionist needs, according to these thinkers. This was the essence of Alfred Etscheit's opposition to a renewal of colonialism in an exchange on the subject printed in the *Deutsche Rundschau* in 1928 when he argued that Germany, as a result of its central position in Europe, had "more pressing concerns" on the continent than in lands across the sea.[16]

These cases aside, however, geopoliticians who opposed colonial acquisitions during the Weimar era were the exception and not the rule. The
colonial cause was overwhelmingly popular within the geographic profession as a whole, and colonialist ranks boasted an impressive contingent of
geopoliticians.[17] Erich Obst, for example, from his position as chairman
of the Geographical Institute at the Technical University of Hannover
and as a longtime co-editor of the *Zeitschrift für Geopolitik,* represented
procolonial views in the academy and the press throughout the Weimar
era.[18] He was joined by a small army of distinguished geographers and
journalists who exploited geopolitical concepts to demand the return of
the colonies, including Arthur Dix, Richard Hennig, Josef März, Franz
Thorbecke, and Karl Sapper. All these geopolitical writers contributed to
a colonialist transformation of the term *Lebensraum.* The term had its origins, as has been seen, in the geopolitical concept of the German role in
central Europe, subsequently acquiring a broader and less-precise meaning for geopoliticians in the wake of German defeat in 1918. Gradually,
geopolitical use of the term was radicalized, so that it encompassed implications of autarchy for the German state in central Europe, and, in the
hands of colonialist geopoliticians, it acquired an entirely new meaning:
it came to symbolize the necessity of settlement areas in overseas colonies.[19] In keeping with the organic and often crudely Darwinist view of
the state that they promoted, these geopoliticians extended the eternal
struggle between states for Lebensraum to territories overseas.[20] They
cast the tendency for great powers to expand in colonial spaces, whether
to acquire additional living space, to enhance national security or gain
economic resources, as an instinctive inclination, a part of the "striving
toward the sea" that inhered, by nature, in advanced political organisms.[21]

The Weimar geopolitical colonialists were able to depict overseas
colonies as a necessary adjunct to and extension of the German Lebensraum. Before the war, as Woodruff Smith has observed, Lebensraum was
associated primarily with "easterners" whereas *Weltpolitik* was the rallying
cry of overseas colonialists. After the war, some geopoliticians began to
attempt a synthesis of the two approaches, arguing that the acquisition of
living space was an integral part of a successful Weltpolitik. In 1926, for
example, the *Zeitschrift für Geopolitik* published a special issue devoted to
the colonial question in which Obst wrote the keynote article under the
title "Wir fordern unsere Kolonien zurück!" (We demand our colonies
back!). Whereas many of the articles stressed traditional Weltpolitik argu-

ments depicting colonies as an economic and security necessity, Obst added a comparatively new spatial twist. Today, he wrote, "we lack the land to be able to settle the uprooted part of the ethnic community in spatial contiguity in German lands. . . . Without colonies suited to the settlement of whites Germany is forced every year to great sacrifice of blood to foreign lands and remains in consequence of its gigantic population pressure naturally the source of inundation of foreign ethnic soil."[22] In the same issue, another writer used similar arguments and applied the term "*Grossdeutschland* of the future" to the colonial empire, invoking a term (*Grossdeutschland*) normally associated in the German context with continental expansionism.[23] Other writers, conceding that German colonies in East Africa and the South Seas could not support many white settlers, presented German Southwest Africa as *Siedlungsraum,* or settlement space for the German "race" constricted in central Europe.[24] Leo Waibel, for example, made this argument and contended further that the presence of German settlers in *Südwest* had in fact already rendered it a part of the German Volks- und Kulturboden, pointing out that the colony had a mere 275,000 native inhabitants in any case (compared to perhaps 15,000 German settlers) and that these were of "low quality."[25]

Similar racial themes were used frequently by geopoliticians to depict overseas colonies as a segment of the German Raum or Lebensraum. Many, like Waibel, presumed that the presence of ethnic German settlers rendered colonial areas part of the German Volksboden. Other thinkers used updated versions of standard "white-man's-burden" racism, common to all the Western imperialist countries, arguing in this instance that Germany owed it to itself as a "white" nation and to the world as a moral duty to resume the task of lifting up the benighted natives of the colonies. Still others linked the survival of the German race with the acquisition of more space. This argument usually took the form of the cry of Volk ohne Raum! or people without space, the title of Hans Grimm's enormously popular novel of German colonists in Southwest Africa. The title of the book, which was published in 1926 and enjoyed resounding popular success, became a motto for both geopoliticians and colonialists alike. Grimm himself enjoyed broad connections among colonialist and journalistic circles, not least the result of his writings on behalf of the colonial cause throughout the 1920s.[26] Grimm reproved those on both right and left who opposed renewed colonialism, admonishing Haushofer specifically at times, insisting that they did not understand the geographical dimensions of Germany's spatial hunger, which rendered it capable of solution chiefly through expansion in Africa.[27] Since the beginning of the decade, in fact, Grimm had been arguing that Germany had room for only two of every three Germans within its borders, that this was contributing to the moral and spiritual decline of the Germans, and that new space had to be found in Africa. "For the German problem of the third man," Grimm declared, "and that means for the German moral problem, and that means for the German social problem, there is only one solution, the procurement of Raum, of workspace and playspace."[28]

A striking example of the melding of racial theory and geodeterminism to create a new geopolitical rhetoric of colonial expansion can be found in Hans Simmer's book, *Grundzüge der Geopolitik in Anwendung auf Deutschland,* which appeared in 1928. Defeated and "curtailed" nations such as Germany, Bulgaria, and Hungary, burdened with growing populations, naturally sought expansion. "All nations that possess a life will wish or strive for spatial expansion," Simmer wrote. "The life will alone often categorically demands an enlargement of the Lebensraum." His justification for expansion combined the destructive geodeterminism, organic state theory, and racial and spatial rhetoric that typified much of the geopolitical colonialist writing of the period.

> Here it is above all the colonies that should take up the excess population, whose runoff into foreign lands is thereby hindered or at least ameliorated, and so that the emigrants remain preserved to their own nationality and home economy. . . . We Germans are today especially the Volk ohne Raum, and we must sooner or later procure the lacking Raum if we do not wish to perish. No people of the world, therefore, has a morally founded claim to more Raum like that of the Germans. For our people and our economy an expansion of Lebensraum must remain the most important goal. Our very destiny is dependent upon maintaining the will to a greater Lebensraum, which may be won by economic penetration, or by revision of the borders and return of the colonies.[29]

As was the case with Obst's argument about the German colonial need, Simmer's writing expresses a veiled threat that Germany will, one way or another, procure the needed room. By combining race with space, or the survival of the German race with acquisition of new space either in the east or the colonies, Simmer and other geopoliticians began to focus on a new German destiny in Africa as the solution of the future to Germany's demographic/geographic dilemma. "The African expanses of *Raum ohne Volk* stand in immediate juxtaposition to the German Volk ohne Raum in overpopulated Europe," they insisted. "Africa lies before the gates of Europe and has for Europe the same significance that it already had during the *Imperium Romanum* and again acquired in the Age of Discovery: it was and is colonial land."[30] When they took cognizance of the birthrate decline, geopolitical colonialists such as Arthur Dix dealt with the problems it posed for their overcrowding arguments by falling back on the inversion of Lebensraum first detailed by Burgdörfer and cited by Dix in his *Weltkrise und Kolonialpolitik* (World crisis and colonial politics), arguing that Germany's population was declining precisely because of lack of space.[31]

Geopolitical theorists blended many other elements into their colonial apologetics. The need for colonies as training grounds to instruct young Germans in a broad view of world affairs was a recurrent theme as was the view that Africans were unfit to run a decent economy or administration except under European tutelage. Adolf Grabowsky, an ardent colonial advocate, combined these arguments with the consequences of the geopolitical view that all relations between states must be in the form of struggle to argue for the return of Germany's old colonies. Unlike Asia, which was no longer fit for colonizing because of the advances made by its peoples in recent times, Africa still needed Germans, and Germans needed Africa. Grabowsky emphasized the imperative of productivity for Germany as well as the world need to use all available resources, asking, "Capitalism is an unheard of unleashing of the earthly powers of productivity: Shall it draw up short at Africa because the Negro is not yet fit to be the subject of capitalism? That is neither possible nor would it be gratifying. It means leaving a part of the world unused." He stressed the specific German need for the broadened outlook that imperial responsibility conferred as well. "[Colonies] still lead to oceanic thought and thereby counteract the capitalistic mechanization of constricted Europe. They are still the schools of the young. . . . So long as the competition of states exists, every state must seek to breed such pioneers in its own colonies. That goes particularly for Germany with its narrow petty-bourgeois outlook in which we are driven deeper and deeper, the further distant we are from colonizing activity. We have no school outside; we are riveted in our narrow borders."[32]

Africa would expand the horizons of Germany's next generation of leaders and provide an outlet for the unfolding of Germanic energy, geopoliticians argued, whereas Africans needed Germans in order to make their lands productive and orderly. This was, in part, a Germanized version of older "white-man's-burden" arguments, which posited that because of the superiority of "white" cultures, European states were entitled to colonize, especially in Africa, in order that the natives might be lifted up to European standards of civilization.[33] At the same time this German mission was a part of the maximal utilization of the earth's geopolitical resource potential. Most of the geopoliticians dwelt upon German administrative proficiency and technological achievement to prove their point here. Africa, they argued, needed "European administration, European work toward the reorganization of its population, toward the struggle against water shortage and water surplus, toward the shortage of help against human and animal sickness, European commercial connections, European economic leadership."[34] Colonialism would persist, they argued, because of African need, and Germany ought to be part of it. "So long as there are in the tropical world lands that are simply not in the position to provide on their own the financial, technical, medical powers that are indispensable in the twentieth century, so long is the colonial age not yet at an end."[35]

Technological achievement provided proof of the continued cultural superiority of the white nations for Weimar geopoliticians. At the same time it functioned as the evident catalyst of a new global age from which Germany could not afford to be excluded and in which colonial possessions were a prerequisite to national success. Outside geopolitical and colonial circles technological themes helped popularize the geopolitical message by linking it to the enthusiasm for new technologies—zeppelins, airplanes, radio—characteristic of Weimar culture.[36] By incorporating the glamour of modern technology into their vision of Germany's colonial mission the geopolitical colonialists augmented the romantic appeal of overseas imperialism and lent a concrete, contemporary aspect to the attractiveness of colonies.[37] According to colonialist geopoliticians, for example, the development of new communications technologies, particularly radio but including modernized cable lines as well, intensified the liability represented by the loss of Germany's empire. The new media of communication enhanced national power both as instruments of national security and through the dissemination of political propaganda; without its own bases abroad for these purposes Germany was at a disadvantage.[38]

Worst of all, however, was the harm done by the loss of the colonies to Germany's future in the air. The postwar world stood "on the eve of the first world air network" in which aviation would act as a technological intensifier to "concentrate the political endeavors of the colonial lands."[39] Germany, stripped of overseas possessions, would be reduced to a minor player in the development of world air travel and be denied the powerful political benefits that aviation conferred upon colonial empires. Although geopoliticians generally felt that advances in aviation worked to great advantage for Germany in Europe, in global terms they felt that "the loss of the German colonies has had a catastrophic impact on aviation."[40] Aviation was a defining characteristic of the new world age, an age in which "not a speck of the earth's face can remain hidden" and in which the division of the earth's air zones would complete "the final form of power political spatial domination" and for which colonial possessions would prove essential.[41] Bad enough to be without overseas naval bases, which were both growth points for expansion and vital pillars of world political efficacy—even worse in the dawning age to be robbed of one's own network of air bases for the projection of global power.[42]

The colonial question presented an opportunity to apply geopolitical ideas to a current international question, and Weimar geographers and geopoliticians seized upon it with enthusiasm. Their diverging responses to it, however, betrayed the fundamentally political, rather than scientific, nature of the geopolitical endeavor. Both geopolitical easterners and geopolitical colonialists relied more on considerations of political expediency than upon "objective" geopolitical truth in determining their stands. It is impossible, when reviewing the extensive geopolitical literature of the period pertaining to the colonial question, to escape the feeling that geopoliticians generally decided how they felt about the issue and then set out to construct "scientific" geopolitical arguments to support their positions. Dix, for instance, had decided early in the 1920s that the colonial age was over, and although the international colonial system did nothing but deteriorate over the period (from the point of view of the colonizers), he reversed this verdict by the end of the decade, seemingly without a discernible geopolitical stimulus.[43] Dix's position, like Haushofer's, seems more readily explicable by subjective rather than scientific factors. That geopolitics could be a powerful tool to those committed to the empire, however, is evident from the use made of it by Weimar colonial organizations.

New Foundations for the Empire: Space in Colonialist Propaganda

While geopoliticians thus articulated a "scientific" case for Germany's colonial demands, their message was being received by colonialist activists, who eagerly adapted geopolitical rhetoric to their political needs. It is clear from many sources that the language of space and race characteristic of geopolitical colonial advocacy was absorbed into the colonialist movement proper as was the geopolitical treatment of the impact of technology on the colonial question. Like geopoliticians themselves, the colonialists felt the First World War had revealed certain fundamental truths about the German situation in central Europe, above all the German need for space. "Only gradually the consciousness dawned in the German people about the final causes of the war and the need of the postwar era," wrote Erich Duems of the German Colonial Society in 1932, "the German spatial need. The novelist Hans Grimm became the indicator of the German fate with his book *Volk ohne Raum* and the prophet of a new German future."[44] The solutions proposed by the colonialists to realize the new German future, however, were anything but novel, lacking both imagination and practicability. The empire had not benefited Germany greatly in the past and was not likely to do so now. In international terms it was more a liability than an asset because Germany never possessed the means to defend it. Furthermore, there was never the remotest chance that postwar France would cede to Germany a renewed colonial role in Africa. In retrospect, an air of the surreal clings to Weimar colonialism, the result, perhaps, of the patent futility of the colonial nostalgia fantasy. It is tempting to view all the journals and newspapers, colloquia, meetings, congresses, and resolutions as nothing but the frantic gestures of a dispossessed elite spinning elaborate fantasies. This view would be mistaken. The debate about colonies, for the participants and their audience, was a real and frequently passionate one, and it was the object of considerable energy in Weimar political life. Geopolitical ideas, which used technology and the so-called new globalism to infuse colonial propaganda with a sense of the "dynamic" aspects of space, were one of the most important sources of the resonance the colonial cause enjoyed.

Organizations dedicated to colonial propaganda proliferated during the Weimar era. Some of these groups, such as the German Colonial Society, dated back to the founding of the empire in the 1880s, but these were joined by a host of others, most of which had overlapping memberships: groups such as the Deutscher Kolonialkriegerbund (German Colonial Serviceman's League) the Bund für koloniale Erneuerung (League for Colonial Renewal) the Koloniale Frauenhilfe (Colonial Womens' Aid) and many others showed variations in emphasis throughout the era, but they remained unified by the common aim of nurturing the German colonial grievance.[45] All the colonial organizations were, after 1922, loosely united under the umbrella of the *Koloniale Reichsarbeitsgemeinschaft* (Reich Colonial Task Force or [KORAG]).[46] Usually relatively small (the DKG's membership peaked at just over twenty thousand in the Weimar era), these groups nonetheless disposed of a great deal of money and used it to bankroll a large and very active propaganda machine. Newspapers, journals, popular magazines, lecture services, colloquia, flyers, and even beer coasters in taverns kept the idea of colonies before the German people, maintained interest in the yearly colonialist congresses, and fomented support for the demands of the Interfraktionelle Koloniale Vereinigung (Interfractional Colonial Coalition) in the Reichstag.[47] Many of the leading colonialists had personal connections with geopoliticians, and groups such as the Colonial-Economic Committee brought together geographers and colonialists of all political stripes from writers and merchants to socialist politicians and right-wing members of the German National People's Party.[48] Geopolitical colonialist arguments appeared regularly in such revanchist organs as the *Koloniale Rundschau* and the *Übersee- und Kolonial-Zeitung*.

The absorption into colonialist propaganda of geopolitically influenced demands for space to maintain the German population, next to more traditional economic and cultural arguments, was part of a deliberate shift in the official colonial propaganda program. The yearly congresses of the KORAG were the high point of the German colonialist year, and at the 1925 meeting in Munich, a glittering social event attended by the would-be éminence grise of Bavarian politics, Crown Prince Ruprecht, they agreed upon "Richtlinien für koloniale Propaganda" (Guidelines for colonial propaganda), whose primary emphasis was still on legal claims to the old colonies.[49] "The colonial movement of our day," according to the guidelines, "is founded on two facts: one, on the illegal seizure of our colonies, carried out under violation of the Wilsonian promise and which is to be justified by the lie of our inability and unworthiness to colonize. After that, out of political, economic, and cultural grounds of irrefutable necessity."[50] Under the influence of Erich Duems, however, who became general secretary of the KORAG in 1928, a new "General German Colonial Program" was approved at the colonial congress in Cologne that year. Pragmatic claims to the colonies founded in demographic, economic, and cultural necessity were now accorded equal status with formal legalistic claims. This allowed greater tactical flexibility in popular propagandizing, according to the program, which went on to call expressly for settlement colonies overseas to receive excess population. "The timely procurement of our own large settlement areas in the still free earth-spaces [Erdräumen]," according to the guidelines, "is a duty of national self-preservation."[51]

This pragmatic approach, strengthened in new guidelines issued by the DKG in 1930, which included an emphasis on the need for settlement space plus raw materials, was not entirely new, of course.[52] The argument from economic necessity had been an integral part of the colonial revanchist movement from the beginning, and elements of the rhetoric of space, some geopolitical in tone, had been present before as well. Heinrich Schnee, who assumed leadership of the DKG in 1930 (and had been the last governor of German East Africa and a German People's Party deputy in the Reichstag), had argued in the mid-1920s that "overpopulated Germany needs not only overseas food and raw materials sources to complement the home economy, but it must also have colonies as an outlet for its population."[53] As the author of the book Die koloniale Schuldlüge (The colonial guilt-lie), which went through twelve editions and attained a popularity unrivaled by other colonialist tracts, Schnee was the best-known German colonial advocate of the era.[54] He enjoyed close connections with many geopolitical writers, including Dix, Obst, Hennig, and Hans Grimm, and a broad circle of academic connections overseas.[55] Like Grimm, he felt that Germany had space sufficient for only two of every three Germans and, like many geopoliticians, he saw colonies as schools for teaching Germans to think in world-political terms.[56] It is clear that geopolitical thought influenced Schnee because geopolitical

Raum and population arguments assumed a place of prominence in his work. "The German colonial problem is a part of the German space problem, which is older than the present crisis, and its solution reaches far into the German future," Schnee argued. "We are convinced that the constricted middle European space does not suffice for the economic maintenance, the social healing, the spiritual development, and the numerical expansion of the German ethnic community. We require for this the acquisition of new German living spaces overseas."[57]

Such echoes of geopolitics, with which Schnee was closely familiar, are found everywhere in his extensive writings on behalf of the colonial cause. Memorandums Schnee wrote in 1930, for example, reasoned that "Germany lacks space for its growing population . . . [and the colonies would] in reference to the settlement of Germans acquire an increasing importance. . . . That these areas offer space not simply for the current population but in gradual development for tens of thousands and later for hundreds of thousands of whites is clear from a comparison with the similar climatic and other conditions of parts of South Africa."[58] When, in the following year, Arthur Dix sought Schnee's advice on his manuscript for the book *Was geht uns Afrika an?* (What does Africa matter to us?), Schnee urged a greater emphasis on the African need for German technological leadership and of the fact that Germany's population required increased Raum, suggestions that Dix appears to have followed in the finished product.[59]

Although Schnee's own colonial propagandizing emphasized Germany's overpopulation and plight as Volk ohne Raum, he was ideologically and politically opportunistic. Like the geopoliticians, he was not troubled by the logical contradictions between the arguments for more space based on the birthrate decline and those based on purported overcrowding. In 1927, for instance, the colonialist journal *Weltwirtschaft,* put out by the German World Economic Society, of which Schnee was president, featured a lengthy article employing the geopolitical argument that the decline in the birthrate was a symptom of too little Raum and that there would continue to be fewer and fewer new Germans until new space was acquired. The author, Saenger, a demographer whose work often appeared in the *Zeitschrift für Geopolitik,* pointed out that German social harmony was endangered by lack of living space, and like Burgdörfer he argued that geography imposed demographic imperatives upon the German nation, which, in turn, created a need for settlement colonies.

"Germany requires a large, self-renewing population, precisely because of its position, or it will not be able to avoid inundation by foreign elements. . . . A contradiction exists between the national necessity to keep the population growing and young and the actual economic and political situation, which compels a slowing of population growth. . . . The most important task falls to foreign policy, which must try to effect an expansion of subsistence areas. Toward this end it must strive, for example, for the reacquisition of the colonies."[60] Here recurrent themes of geopolitical literature concerning birth trends were used to make colonial demands. The fear of German extinction through "inundation" by more fecund neighbors, the conviction that a healthy state organism required a young and growing population, these and other concepts were combined with references to Germany's precarious geographic position in Europe to make the demand for new colonial space overseas.

For the next several years, until the fall of the Weimar Republic, strains of both population arguments appeared regularly in colonial propaganda. Colonialists such as Richard Fehn, a lecturer at the German Academy in Munich, continued to argue that Germany suffered from *Raumnot,* or spatial need, because of overpopulation and overcrowding. This spatial plight could only be satisfied in the colonies. "The soil encompassed by the German people has become too confined," Fehn argued, "and will become ever more confined. . . . The German population surplus needs Raum. . . . The soil foundation must become greater for the German people; Germany's sphere of influence must extend itself upon settlement space that is large enough to offer the German people, one of the most capable and efficient, sufficient ground for free growth. But an expansion of the too-constricted space is only possible through colonization."[61] At the same time, the official organ of the KORAG, the *Übersee- und Koloniale Zeitung,* was proposing a reconciliation of the two views. In an article from 1930 entitled "Alles fängt mit dem Lande on" (Everything begins with the land) Paul Kupfer lamented the lack of Raum-consciousness among the German people and argued that colonial expansion was justified both by overcrowding *and* by the threat of German underpopulation: "The question of Lebensraum was the core question of the world war. Even today, this is recognized by only a few, even though Volk ohne Raum as a phrase and concept has long since entered the German vocabulary. . . . Since the loss of the colonies, a single square kilometer must provide living space for 133 Germans. . . . Where shall the

German population surplus, which is still there despite the birthrate decline, go to? Germany needs two things: a planned emigration and the preservation of the emigrants within Germandom."[62]

Many colonialists were persuaded by arguments like this to view space as the answer to both the birthrate decline and the German economic situation. The Deutscher Koloniale Verein (German Colonial League), for example, associated with the KORAG and numbering, by its own count, twenty thousand members, maintained ties to *Auslandsdeutsch*, or Germans abroad, both in Europe and particularly in former German colonies overseas.[63] Its leaders were convinced that, although emigration was not harmful in the old days of overpopulation, in these days of birthrate decline every one of the sixty thousand to seventy thousand Germans who emigrated each year represented an irreparable loss to German culture and the German economy. Intensified population loss through emigration also constituted a threat to survival for the German "race." This threat could be offset in one way alone, by maintaining the "Germanness" of the emigrants in "consolidated German settlements," meaning German-ruled colonies overseas. The supposed threat to the race posed by the birthrate decline and emigration was a frequently expressed concern of colonial enthusiasts, and their solution was German expansion. Only if the emigrants were kept "German in language and consciousness" could they be of aid in preserving Germany in its hour of crisis, and this required settlement colonies and a regularized plan of emigration.[64] "The solution of the future, therefore, is not space just anywhere for emigrating Germans, but German space for German emigrants!"[65] Furthermore, it was geography itself that lent German demographic trends their urgency. The "threat" of the Geburtenrückgang was a danger, according to colonialists, precisely because of the ethnic and population pressures that geography had placed at Germany's doorstep in the east. Such concerns played an important role even in the thinking of the most overtly "economic" colonial revisionists, such as Wilhelm Külz, the head of the Society for Colonial Renewal. Despite a conscious propaganda emphasis on the economic need for colonies Külz warned that unless German emigrants were kept where they could be "economic and cultural value factors for Germany" the birthrate decline must "one day be bitterly felt."[66]

The colonialist emphasis on race created a natural bond with geopolitics. German geography had close links with German physical anthropology from its beginnings, as illustrated in the *Völkerkunde,* or ethnology, of the geographer Karl Ritter, and these affinities were a part of the geographical bequest to geopolitical theories. In turn, the colonies themselves had served as laboratories for prewar racist anthropologists such as Eugen Fischer, racial ideologies had always played some role in colonial apologetics, and the interest of Germany's scientific elites in the former colonies remained strong after the war.[67] Almost as a matter of course, then, colonialists began to supplement the spatial argument for colonies with a racial hygiene twist that shared many terms and concepts with geopolitics. This version of colonial-geopolitical propaganda, in articles with titles such as "Schafft Raum zur Überwindung einer schweren Zukunft" (Procure space to overcome a bleak future), argued that Germany was still overcrowded and that the birthrate decline was simultaneously stimulating the production of a larger low-quality gene pool to be surmounted only by the acquisition of Raum. This colonialist argument linked concern not only for the survival of the race but for the maintenance of "racial quality" with demands for the acquisition of expanded geographical spaces overseas for German settlement. "The quality of the younger generation has decreased and will, according to the laws of racial hygiene, further deteriorate," argued one writer. Only the "inferior classes" were reproducing at a rate above that necessary for mere replacement, but they were doing so at an alarming rate. The scale of dislocation predicted from the German insufficiency of space now was amplified from a German to a European level through the threat of a desperate Germany compelled to seek relief for its spatial needs in conquest. "It gives rise to thoughts," argued the same writer, that in the absence of a peaceful allocation of augmented space, "the overburdened future generations, packed like sardines, will themselves conquer with the sword the Raum they require."[68]

The vision of colonial settlement as eugenic therapy that would promote the propagation of the best elements in the German ethnic body thus penetrated colonialist rhetoric piggybacked upon geopolitical concepts. Relying heavily on geopolitical terms and ideas cited from the works of Ratzel and Haushofer, Julius Lips, a teacher of anthropology and sociology at Cologne, argued in an essay called "Ethnopolitik und Kolonialpolitik" (Ethnopolitics and colonial policy) in the *Koloniale Rundschau* that colonial politics and the acquisition of new space would play a vital role in shaping, to use Lips's unsettling formulation, the relation of ethnicity to state life. This was, of course, a veiled reference to state-controlled eugenic policy. The use of the term *Ethnopolitik* itself is a measure of the colonialist debt to geopolitical thought since the term received its first extended treatment in German in the translation of Kjellén, *Der Staat als Lebensform* (The state as a life form).[69] "That portion of anthropology that transcends the purely methodological formulation of the cultural disciplines, which does not content itself with the mere cultural-historical working out of historically determinable cultural processes, I call ethnopolitics," Lips wrote, describing it further on as "dynamic anthropology" (just as some geopoliticians called their field "dynamic political geography").[70] Lips was no racist, but his ethnopolitical approach led him to believe that any future German colonial empire would, in the interest of the German nation, perforce be much more deliberately eugenicist. "A future German colonial policy," Lips wrote, "will not face the task of, in the first instance, maintaining a view of where the best sisal and coffee, where the best cotton grows, where the procurement of native forced labor can best be carried out, where the iron mining is most profitable; it will not follow in the footsteps of the imperialistic policy of other European powers. It will doubtlessly have to be ethnopolitically oriented."[71] Lips's definition of *ethnopolitics* was, incidentally, very similar to a definition of *biopolitics* offered in the *Zeitschrift für Geopolitik* one year later by Louis von Kohl, who described it as concerned with the "interaction of Volk and Raum" or people and space, and said it investigated "the development of a Volkskörper [ethnic body] and its Lebensraum over time."[72]

The resolution of the contradictions between the competing approaches to colonial ideology through insistence upon space as a solution to both problems foreshadowed a similar conflict and reconciliation in imperialist ideology during the Nazi era. At that time the conflict between the supporters of *Ostpolitik*, who favored expansion in eastern Europe, and the advocates of *Kolonialpolitik* would be resolved by arguing that the two forms of expansion were complementary rather than competitive or mutually exclusive.[73] The colonialists were always haunted by the fear that the desire for revanche in the east would draw attention from the demand for overseas colonies, and many of them had privately espoused a combination of the two forms of expansionism since at least the mid-1920s.[74] The argument that colonies served the needs of both those concerned abut the birthrate decline, many of whom also advocated eastern settlement, and those who feared overpopulation, a view typically associated in the German imperialist discourse with colonialism, was an early attempt to reconcile the two conflicting tendencies in German expansionism that anticipated the Nazi-era slogan of "Kolonialpolitik und Ostpolitik." This view envisioned *Mittelafrika* as a necessary complement to Mitteleuropa, characterizing the colonial empire as an adjunct to the eastern expansionism embodied in the radical agrarian "*Blut und Boden*" (Blood and soil) ideology of Walther Darré.

By casting colonies as a means to improve Germany's racial stock colonialists combined geopolitics and eugenics to lend an up-to-date tone to Weimar imperial dreams. Evoking a vision of a "closed world" without room for the maintenance of the German people, colonialists modernized the case for German colonies by insisting that old-fashioned economic concepts of imperialism no longer met the needs of the German people. Instead, they drew an explicit connection between the ending of the birthrate decline, improving the "quality" of the German population, and the acquisition of new colonies. This approach to colonialism was described as *social* rather than *imperial,* and the colonialists used it to insist, in terms clearly taken over from geopolitics, that the white race required colonies to keep growing. Colonies, once reacquired, would bridge divisions within the German state organism and restore "the unity of *Reich, Volk,* economy, society, and administration that characterizes the state as a life form (and which) we can already see realized in large part in the world empires." They would also furnish a demographic reservoir for Germany abroad. "The birth statistics of overseas lands prove that the whites in new land reproduce approximately twice as rapidly as in the homeland. The significance of settlement colonies for the regeneration of the motherlands has received till now too little attention."[75]

The use of the term *social* colonialism, in contrast with what was called *imperial* colonialism, raises a seemingly incongruous facet of the links between colonialist and geopolitical thinking. This is the presence within the colonialist movement of a cohort of socialist colonialists who made frequent use of geopolitical concepts and rhetoric to advance their colonial demands. Despite the fact that the Social Democrats were, as a party, more sympathetic to liberation movements than to imperialism, the circle of right-wing Social Democrats around Max Cohen-Reuss, including Ludwig Quessel and Herman Kranold, supported the Interfractional Colonial Coalition and published regular calls for renewed colonial activity in Joseph Bloch's *Socialist Monthly.* Cohen-Reuss, the most ardent of the colonialist socialists, later served as a member of the governing board of the Society for Colonial Renewal.[76] This was the same circle of Socialists who were attracted to geopolitical ideas, and there is more logic in their socialist colonialism than is at first evident. The surmounting of all divisions within the German body politic was always a primary goal of geopolitical thinkers, and they felt that the "science" of geopolitics was a useful tool for this internal unification. As Karl Haushofer argued, geopolitics was a social integrator through which even members of different parties (as long as they were sufficiently patriotic) could arrive at the same view of German foreign policy.

When Hermann Müller repudiated any colonial aspirations for the Social Democrats in a speech in 1928, he was taken to task by a fellow Socialist, Karl Valentin Müller, who called for "colonialism without imperialism."[77] How colonialism could be divorced from imperialism, precisely, was rarely made clear, but the procolonial arguments that appeared regularly in the *Sozialistische Monatshefte* often used terms and ideas with which conservative geopolitical colonialists would have felt entirely at home. As has already been noted, these Socialists were very favorably disposed not only to geopolitics but to eugenics as well, calling repeatedly for government efforts to prevent the reproduction of "inferior" people and those "unworthy of life."[78] In light of these views support for colonialism is entirely logical. They combined these interests with advocacy of colonialism as a way to help German workers, and they were quite friendly to the conservative colonial organizations, praising Schnee's work and sponsoring procolonial colloquia at the Deutsche Hochschule für Politik in Berlin.[79]

These conservative socialist colonialists argued, like Arthur Dix, that Africa was the "natural European colonial district," whose cultures were too primitive (with the possible exception of those developed in North Africa) to develop themselves, and, like Franz Thorbecke, that Germany was "by geographic position and economic need the predestined colonizer of Africa."[80] Because of the pressure generated by its "surplus" population, Germany was in a position to furnish the demographic (and technological) resources for further European development of Africa. Such a development would be thoroughly natural and organic because "Africa forms a unity of destiny with Europe not only because of its position (next to Europe and between Asia and America)," they argued, but because "it is also the only area of the earth where a large field of activity still awaits Europe. Europe is over-instrumentalized, Africa unexploited."[81] Because of geography, in other words, Africa was fated to be Europe's natural reservoir of land and resources. The willful misreading of geography that puts Africa "next to Europe and between Asia and America" is also typical of geopolitical arbitrariness with geography. Africa is no more next to Europe than it is to Asia: This is purely a matter of perception. As the historian of the *Sozialistische Monatshefte* has argued, the circle of Socialists around the journal always represented a minority point of view in the party, which, given this group's imperialist and eugenic tendencies, was surely to the party's credit.[82]

A final element of the geopolitical argument for the vital significance of the colonies that found its way into the colonial rhetoric of the time was that involving the needs created by new technology and the particular German contribution to technology. On the one hand, colonialist propaganda in many venues took the traditional line that German culture justified the German right to colonies, especially in Africa, through the superiority of its accomplishments. In article after article German colonialists in this period emphasized the German *Kulturleistung,* or cultural achievement, in the colonies, declaring that the natives had fared better under the Germans and still required German help.[83] As Schnee argued, the indigenous peoples of Africa, unlike the "old culture peoples" of Asia, were technologically and politically "too far behind in their development to be able to rule themselves."[84]

The optimistic geopolitical stress on the potential of technology for the realization of a better German future also found expression in the colonialist movement. The clearest example of the importance of German utilization of technological advance in colonialist propaganda is found in the activities of Arbeitsgemeinschaft für Auslands- und Kolonialtechnik (AKOTECH) or Task Force for Foreign and Colonial Technology, a colonialist organization affiliated with the KORAG. Beginning in 1925, the AKOTECH collaborated with the Technical University of Berlin in sponsoring lecture courses covering topics linking modern technology, colonialism, and the future survival of the German race. These lecture series continued through the early 1930s, addressing topics such as "Technology in Warm and Cold Lands." The speakers came from business and the professions and included engineers, geologists, and geographers and geopoliticians such as Arthur Dix and Paul Rohrbach, a Baltic German geographer and student of Ferdinand von Richthofen whose colonial activism dated back to Wilhelmine days.[85] The speakers, following guidelines set by the AKOTECH, pursued the theme that overpopulated Germany could not be excluded from the technological development of colonial lands: "The increasing overpopulation and industrialization of the earth must necessarily lead, on the one hand, to a shortage of space and raw materials and, on the other, to a constriction of export areas. . . . [therefore] the task falls particularly upon the European nations to open up the tropics and subtropics in the vicinity of Europe. Particularly the German people, which has been robbed of its colonies, as a people who chiefly finds its occupation in industry has the greatest interest in bringing a capability for quality to the technology of the means of this opening."[86] The topics covered by the AKOTECH/TH-Berlin lectures were strongly flavored by the geopolitical colonialist agenda. They included "Air Travel in Africa and Asia" sponsored by the Junkers aircraft factory at Dessau, "The Birth Rate Decline," "Colonies as Rejuvenation Sites for the Home Culture," "The Necessity of the Opening of Tropical Africa and of the Acquisition of Our Own Colonies," and "Technology in the Hot Lands," which covered "Aviation," "Railroads," and "The Inclination and Disinclination of the Races toward Work."

The geopolitical and colonialist movements assisted one another, to common advantage, in agitating against the terms of the Versailles peace settlement. For many adherents of geopolitical thinking the colonial question served as a whetstone for the refinement of their theories, and the abundance of colonial media organs provided a convenient platform for disseminating the truths of geopolitical "science" to a receptive audience. For the colonialists geopolitics lent a veneer of scientific respectability to the quest for a revived empire and supplied a useful armory of spatially grounded proofs of the dire demographic, political, economic and cultural consequences of German exclusion from colonial activity. They ensured that Bavarian and Prussian schools advocated the colonial cause in geography and history courses, and by 1928 more than two million German school children had viewed slide and lecture presentations sponsored by the youth committee of the DKG.[87] As a part of general German agitation for revision of the harsher aspects of the Versailles peace settlement, the colonial grievance provided a convenient tool to drum up sympathy abroad and indignant patriotism among Germans.

To the German woman or man on the street, however, the colonies seem rarely to have been a pressing concern, a fact frequently lamented by the colonialists but one scarcely surprising in light of the intensity of economic, social, and political turbulence during the Republic's short life.[88]

Although it has been argued that support among the parties for revision of the colonial settlement was purely pro forma, a case can nonetheless be made that the colonial cause had a political clout founded in genuine public resonance.[89] The colonial idea retained a passionate following of academics, government officials, journalists, and politicians throughout the era. All the political parties to the right of the Social Democrats felt a formal commitment to the reacquisition of the colonies was in their electoral interest. Many deputies of the Reichstag were committed to German colonial activism, and the subject came up for debate on a number of occasions in the Reichstag, at times to make demands, in terms explored here, for "expansion of the German living space."[90] The pressure exerted by the colonial movement also had a demonstrable influence on the conduct of German diplomacy by Stresemann and the other foreign ministers of the Republic, usually a deleterious one in that it further constricted their already limited freedom of maneuver, particularly in negotiation with the British and French.[91] Finally, most of the colonialists welcomed the Nazi regime when it took power in 1933, and it is probably true that the colonialist obsession with a genuine but not very important colonial grievance and much of the rhetoric with which they expressed it contributed to popular receptivity when these terms and the colonial grievance were exploited by the National Socialists. A geodeterminist rhetoric of culture, states, and politics linked to colonialism by geographers and geopoliticians in terms of space, race, and living space was easily exploited in the political arena to serve the illusion that Germany's crisis could be solved in the colonies.

CHAPTER 9

Geopolitics and Republican Foreign Policy

> Above all, geopolitics must create the instrument of a successful foreign
> policy and the necessary receptivity in the entire people to the elements
> that produce it. . . . If we do not succeed in this preparation, this
> propaedeutic, to call mass geopolitical understanding into life, then
> foreign policy with all its great dreams remains idea and never
> becomes reality.
>
> Karl Haushofer, "Geographische Grundzüge auswärtiger Politik"

Colonial revisionism was only one aspect of a very full geopolitical foreign policy agenda. The raison d'être for geopolitics was, after all, foreign
policy, and in its attention to the conduct of diplomacy geopolitics was
very much in step with Weimar German society in general. What Karl
Haushofer called the drive to create "mass geopolitical understanding"
of international relations in the Weimar Republic began with the significant advantage that the German public was already closely engaged with
questions of foreign policy. The conduct of official diplomacy served as
a lightning rod for the manifold currents of opposition to the Weimar
Republic. The nearly universal agreement on the ends of revising or ter-
minating the Versailles settlement was complemented by equally widespread disagreement on the most effective means of attaining that end.
Bitter public controversy accompanied every diplomatic undertaking.
Foreign policy initiatives of all kinds, from Gustav Stresemann's decision
to submit to French occupation of the Ruhr in 1923 through the Locarno
agreements of 1925 to the negotiation of revised reparations agreements
in 1929, were sure to provoke storms of outrage. Stresemann, as the chief
architect of German foreign policy for the better part of a decade, was

acutely conscious of the constrictions imposed upon his freedom of diplomatic action by this volatility of public opinion, which was always exploited by his enemies and sometimes stimulated by "grumbling" within his own party.[1]

The "power of public opinion formation and propaganda," as the leading historian of Weimar foreign policy has noted, influenced German diplomacy at the time as "a significant and frequently unpredictable factor of modern foreign policy, open to opinion manipulation and swelling occasionally to mass psychosis."[2] Other historians have also suggested that popular perceptions played an unusually prominent role in shaping Weimar foreign policy by restricting the range of options for which German statesmen could hope to find domestic approval.[3] Geopolitics shaped and stimulated this public discontent with official foreign policy. In increasingly strident tones geopoliticians attacked the foreign policy of Stresemann and his successors, charging that it failed to address the realities of Germany's geographic encirclement and its right to recover areas of German settlement in central and south-central Europe. Gradually, the imperialistic language and aggressive tenor of geopolitical language became impossible for German statesmen to ignore as it penetrated the foreign policy discussions of the major parties.

Germany, Geopolitics, and the Postwar State System

The Weimar public's preoccupation with diplomacy often had unfortunate consequences. The intense nationalism of the period tended to portray every compromise with Germany's neighbors, such as the very beneficial rescheduling of reparations arranged in 1929, as "betrayal." Yet from a Realpolitik perspective compromise and peace undoubtedly worked in the interests of German power. Ironically, the consequences of Germany's defeat had redounded in certain respects to the advantage of Germany's foreign policy position. The nation's political power base was diminished, it is true, through the loss of territory and population and by the military restrictions placed upon it in the Versailles treaty as well. Objectively, however, these losses were not as bad as they at first glance seemed. The return to France of Alsace-Lorraine, for example, whose people had largely remained French at heart, probably did little to hurt Germany's power position. And although much historically German territory had been forfeited in the east, it was also here where the greatest opportunities now awaited Germany. The situation in east central Europe, where the world war had crippled or removed Germany's ancient adversaries, is accurately described by Detlev Peukert:"The driving back of Russia and the division of middle Europe into a handful of small and medium states, whose actual long-term dependency on France was not promising, offered the German Reich the chance of informal hegemony in central, eastern and southern Europe, if it understood how to utilize its economic and cultural weight through a policy of understanding and cooperation with the young national states."[4]

German statesmen were often forced to play to a nationalistic German public opinion, however, rather than exploit opportunities for the peaceful unfolding of German power in the region. One excellent example of this dilemma was the harsh German rejection of plans advanced by Aristide Briand (a statesman possessed of sufficient political courage to face public displeasure) for greater European unity in 1929. This rejection, which has been depicted as an attempt "to attain a 'positive domestic political effect'," appealed to Germans of all political stripes who were frustrated with the slow progress German diplomacy was making toward revision, and it accorded with the geopolitical demand for a decisive and independent foreign policy.[5] In a similar case the German delegation's demands for revision of Germany's eastern borders in 1929 threatened to derail talks leading to the improvement of Germany's reparations payment schedule in the Young Plan. These demands, like the response to Briand's plan, had important domestic roots.[6] Opportunities for the peaceful expansion of German power in central Europe were missed, it has been suggested, because many Germans in influential positions in politics, education, and journalism adhered to a conflictual concept of state relations, which disdained peaceful revisionism as the ineffectual tool of the weak.[7] The universal goal of revision, furthermore, was cast in a wide variety of terms, which ranged from scaling down Germany's debt payments to drawing new borders. Not only was the precise meaning of revision interpreted in many ways, therefore, but economics and politics conditioned tactical approaches. German progressives and industrialists, in general, tended to favor revision through cooperation and internationalism, looking to political and economic partnership with Germany's neighbors to improve Germany's situation. This ethos, which was strong in Stresemann's German People's Party (DVP), was faithfully reflected in the foreign policy of its leader.[8] Conservatives and agrarians with influence in parties like the German National People's Party, by contrast, generally espoused German unilateralism with the aim of extending German economic hegemony in *Mitteleuropa*.[9]

The geopolitical approach to German foreign policy during these years depicted the revision of the peace settlement as justifiable, necessary, and inevitable. This view of the Versailles settlement was, in itself, not unreasonable. The treaty was seriously flawed in many respects (the provisions for German reparations to the Allied Powers, for example), and over time revision was naturally to be expected. The philosophy of revision advocated by geopoliticians, however, tended toward unilateralism, confrontation, and German expansionism. Haushofer, Grabowsky, Obst, Spahn, Dix, and others, whatever differences may have separated them, argued with Ranke for the *Primat der Aussenpolitik,* the primary importance of foreign policy supposedly dictated by Germany's geographical position in the "heart" of Europe.[10] Geopoliticians naturally applied to the specific case of German foreign policy the general image of state relations depicted in their works. Typically, this picture focused on the life-or-death struggle between peoples, a multinational, German-dominated Reich as the natural form of spatial organization of central Europe, and the destiny imposed upon Germany by its Mittellage in Europe. "Germany is the land without a back, the single great European state in a pronounced central position," Hermann Lautensach wrote. "The German people must never forget this continental foundation of its existence."[11] Europe as a whole, they argued, was bound sooner or later to erupt into its natural state of international conflict as a result of the collision of the geopolitical Kraftlinien of France, England, and Russia. For Germany the task of foreign policy was to decide where and when to deploy its resources to restructure Europe's state system to its best advantage, which for most geopoliticians meant using German power opportunistically to extend German power in the east.[12] Within this general framework, however, the geopolitical approach was sometimes surprisingly nuanced. Obst argued, for instance, that the Versailles treaty had robbed Germany of the tools of traditional power politics. The nation, therefore, had to steer a foreign political course between east and west, exploiting agreements with its neighbors when possible but retaining sufficient independence of action to effect the ultimate goal of creating a "greater political spatial organism" in central Europe.[13]

The necessity for treaty revisions designed to enlarge Germany's Raum was insisted upon by geopoliticians, who fostered an alarmist sensibility, warning that Germany's leaders ignored the dangerous geographic *Ein-kreisung,* or encirclement, of Germany. Lautensach argued that Germany's Mittellage was no longer simply continental, but had been transformed by the war and technological progress into a "planetary central position," which carried with it enhanced dangers but also "a certain freedom of movement."[14] Geopolitics, by promoting a new "spatial consciousness" and a "plastic spatial image" of central Europe, could show Germans that they were trapped in an iron ring of enemies and could also suggest strategies to help them escape this *Umklammerung* (pincering).[15] The image of encirclement recurrently evoked by German geopoliticians expressed a paranoid dimension of the geopolitical imagination. Haunted, as Bismarck had been, by a vision of hostile envelopment, they rejected any official recognition of the permanence of postwar borders, seeking instead to make Germany secure through expansion followed by closure; German diplomacy, many felt, should aim to establish an autarchic "national, enclosed economic space."[16] The conviction that new borders alone could guarantee German security led geopoliticians to attack revision based upon peaceful cooperation with the victor powers. Reconciliation or compromise, they feared, would legitimize existing political arrangements in Europe, and prevent boundary revision. They thus rejected initiatives such as Locarno or the Dawes and Young plans, concentrating instead on a constant demand for the extension of German power toward the east and the incorporation of German ethnic groups throughout central Europe into a single state.[17]

All these attitudes found expression in the geopolitical response to the Locarno agreements, one of the great diplomatic accomplishments of the Stresemann era. Geopoliticians condemned Locarno because the supposedly "Anglophile" policy pursued by Stresemann heightened the dangers of German geography while ignoring the opportunities it offered. "Our position in central Europe offers us the opportunity to escape the French pincers through a policy toward the east," wrote one. "Despite that, we went to Locarno. That was only possible because we had long since given up the possibility of pursuing independent policy."[18] The conservative geographer Wilhelm Volz, head of the Deutsche Stiftung für Volks- und Kulturbodenforschung (DSVK), echoed this argument, suggesting that foreign powers would interpret Germany's agreement to Locarno as proof that it was renouncing its claims in the east as well, which he felt would be disastrous. If the spirit of Locarno meant anything at all, he argued, it ought to mean that Germany could expand in the east, beginning with the reacquisition of upper Silesia.[19] In many ways, of course, these geopoliticians completely misunderstood the nature of the agreement, which did precisely what they criticized it for not doing. That is, Locarno tied France's hands in the west and left Germany a relatively free field in the east. It was Germany, not France, which gained security and breathing space at Locarno, but their commitment to unilateralism blinded geopoliticians to the power political gains won by Stresemann at the Locarno negotiating tables.

In the pages of the *Zeitschrift für Geopolitik* Locarno was greeted with suspicion from the first, developing quickly into outright hostility. "We have never made any bones about regarding the 'spirit of Locarno' with a certain skepticism," Obst wrote. The agreement would only intensify the weakness of fragmented Zwischeneuropa between a now secure western bloc and the looming Soviet menace in the east. "In the west, Great Britain solidifies its position in league with all its dominions and colonies; in the east Russia does the same. How will Zwischeneuropa continue to exist in the distant future, where will it nourish itself, where draw its raw materials, where export its finished products?"[20] Only the "supranational combination" of central Europe, Obst argued, could prevent its being ground to pieces between the eastern and western powers. Other writers suggested that now was the best opportunity to press more aggressively than ever for the return of the Saarland, but the typical geopolitical response to Locarno was to argue that now Germany had to act with resolution to strengthen itself in the east.[21] The Russian-German trade agreement of 26 April 1926 was greeted as a corrective to the one-sided Westernism of the Locarno agreements, offering an alternative bloc to that of the West, one to which the "spiritually related peoples of central Europe can adhere." The "lamentable Locarno-Pact" would lead to genuine improvement in Germany's relations with its western neighbors only in the extent to which it earned "the agreement of the Entente to the right of self-determination of all Germans."[22]

This was not a right, however, which the geopoliticians were eager to extend to non-German nationalities in the east. The unrelenting demand for an aggressive eastern policy was the dominant foreign policy motif of Weimar geopolitics. Building on theories of a German racial mission, geopoliticians argued that Germans were bound by geography to develop "the undersettled spaces of Eurasia" while maintaining racial separation from their neighbors in the east. This ominous racial and geographic foreign policy theme, foreshadowing Nazi views on German policy in Eastern Europe, was expounded by Spahn, Haushofer, and others in the early 1920s.[23] Germans, Haushofer argued, had to expand in the east, but avoid "racial mingling" in the "cultural mish-mash" of the area: "The racial idea implies above all a strict duty to abstemiousness in regard to the lures of foreign cultures and vague distant spaces."[24] Germany's leaders were urged to fulfill "the German mission in the central European space" by cementing "a district determined for unity by nature, a living whole, Mitteleuropa."[25] Germans, "the greatest and most powerful of the peoples of central Europe," were called upon to lead the other peoples of the region in building their lands: "It is a soil capable of development, but inflexible."[26] Here, too, the concept of the Kulturboden was crucial, allowing German geopoliticians to argue that even eastern lands that were not populated with Germans lay within the German cultural penumbra.[27] Where culture would not justify their claims, they relied on geography, arguing that because of geography and culture "the maintenance of a Czechoslovakian state in its present form is, out of the most natural geopolitical grounds, impossible."[28]

What did such views mean when translated into prescriptions for Republican foreign policy? They meant that Germany must aggressively pursue its "natural" leadership role in eastern Europe, that it must recognize its own essential "easternness" and liquidate the Polish "problem." A few geopoliticians, accordingly, actually praised Locarno for leaving the situation in the east fluid and advocated the use of this opening to pressure the League of Nations for recognition of German claims in the region. Weimar political parties agreed almost unanimously on the impossibility of an "eastern Locarno" guaranteeing Poland's borders in part because they felt it violated German self-determination but also because this would perpetuate what was viewed, in accord with geopolitical parlance, as the "fragmentation" of eastern Europe.[29] The League could be of help here by securing the rights of German settlers throughout eastern Europe. "In Transylvania, in the Caucasus, in the Urals, and on the Volga there are the premature advance posts of a coming age, there Germany under guarantee of the League can accomplish useful work in the east for itself and for the world."[30] Germany would then fulfill its mission to develop "Kultur instead of the 'Civilization' of the West: Whether this takes place sooner or later, voluntarily or reluctantly, is the fateful question of our time."[31] German interests and the self-interest of Germany's neighbors, particularly Poland, demanded that all comply with the geo-graphically determined destiny of the German people. "The historical task that destiny places before a people arises essentially from the peculiar-ities of its geographical position." Czechoslovakia, according to this view, was not a viable political construct, and the demise of Poland was immi-nent: Poland's turbulent politics were the expression of "the fevered con-vulsions of a state body wrestling with death. . . . Poland, as it now stands, is a diplomatic abortion. It can be revived only if it is cut back to its natu-ral borders and financially purged."[32] Germany had to bring the Poles to their senses, by force if necessary. "If it is not possible to bring the peoples of central Europe to a consciousness of the historical unity of their cul-ture, and in some way to lay to rest the outstanding conflicts between them—which by no means must occur through peaceful means—Poland will be the first victim if Russia again turns toward the west."[33]

For geopolitics, the "German east" furnished the site where theories of geodeterminism and racialism could be merged in praxis through ex-pansion. The geopolitical belief that imperialistic expansion was a natural manifestation of organic state life was here complemented with the view that the German race was the only one capable of bringing order to the area and by arguments like Haushofer's justifying racial discrimination.[34] The mingled fear, contempt, and racist hostility toward the Slavic peoples expressed in geopolitical texts, population tracts, and other writings, the assault on the political organization of the Slavic states (expressed in terms such as *Zwischeneuropa*) and the incessant demands for more space in the east undoubtedly complicated the conduct of a peaceful diplomacy of revision. The manifest shortcomings of the peace settlement in the east, reflected in the unsettled politics of all the successor states, increased public receptivity to extreme revisionist propaganda, of which geopoli-tics was often a part.[35] In the hands of its least-sophisticated advocates, the geopolitical critique of Germany's postwar foreign policy position de-scended to the viscerally racist. "The earth-given relations do not change, just as little the character of the people," wrote one. "European culture re-mains foreign and antagonistic to the Asian steppe peoples, and these will always find their way toward the European plain. . . . Squeezed between a niggerized France and the Mongolian wave, our descendants will find themselves in a desperate situation."[36] Others found a ray of hope in Ger-many's postwar position. "Geopolitically, we Germans derive advantages as well as disadvantages from our central position," Karl Christian von Loesch told the *Deutsches Herrenklub* in 1929, pointing out that the eighty million Germans in central Europe had the power to obstruct any settlement of the region's borders of which they did not approve.[37] Despite their exaltation of the new in the form of modern technology, furthermore, most of the geopoliticians clung to an old-fashioned Wilhelmine concept of international relations as a fundamentally unmediated power struggle, a view that was scarcely conducive to the goals of peaceful, multilateral revision pursued by Stresemann.[38]

Geopolitical hostility often focused on Poland, particularly because of the "unnatural" separation of Danzig from the rest of Germany by the Polish corridor to the sea. The existence of the corridor violated all laws of political geography, argued Albrecht Haushofer, Friedrich Heiss, and others. It guaranteed Poland nothing in terms of access to the sea; its existence was based only on hatred for Germany and, some geopoliticians argued, the borders of Poland weakened Germany's ability to stand as a bulwark against Soviet aggression.[39] The state of Poland itself was "a horrifying example of how states were made at Versailles." Only by revising the status of Poland and the other lands between Germany and Russia could the Germans avoid being crushed between western "high capitalism" on the one side and eastern Bolshevism on the other.[40] Poland, it was argued, hindered Germany in performing this valuable function because its "contemporary extent reaches in the east as in the west far too much into other lands," with the result that space needed for German settlement and population expansion was in the hands of the Poles.[41] The Polish "population surplus," furthermore, constituted a geopolitical "threat and danger for its neighbors, particularly in the border regions where the Polish surplus confronts a numerically inferior population as is the case above all on the German border."[42] Poland, as they saw it, was the vanguard of Slavic aggression. Whereas Locarno had created an "Iron Curtain" to the west of Germany, the east was open: "The thinly-peopled districts east of the Elbe are bled white, and create space for the fertile, westward-pushing Slavs. . . . In the east, on the open, lonely border is the great danger. . . . In the east, all is in flux."[43] The unremarked contradiction between a supposedly overcrowded Germany's need for Lebensraum and the threat of the Slavic flood inundating a sparsely populated German east, which was treated in the works of Dix, Burgdörfer, and others, was characteristic of geopolitical writing.

The economic dislocation caused by the creation of the Polish state only intensified its intolerable racial threat to the German nation, which required the building of a human "peasant wall" of resistance against

Slavic advance. Volz, in his position as head of the DSVK, argued that, economically, "space is absolute" and that each region had a "naturally given structure of the economy of the space."[44] This geopolitical reality, coupled with racial competition, made German economic reform in the east essential. "And when once again all goes well with the peasants in the east—but only then—will we acquire the indispensable peasant and settlement wall."[45] Germany's eastern problem, others wrote, had two sides, "one economic, one geopolitical," caused by the Treaty of Versailles' destruction of the natural territorial economy of the east. The recognition that "Volk and Raum belong to an indivisible unity has led to the definition of the state as a spatial organism, an idea which was of course first adopted in geopolitics . . . but which is recommended above all to the practical politician." All of Germany's border with Poland had been drawn in geopolitical error "because the unity of the economic space was ignored."[46]

Other factors strengthened the geopolitical brief for eastern expansion. Adopting a Mackinderesque geopolitical model of Russia as the invulnerable heartland in struggle with the peripheral states of Europe (Randstaaten), writers such as the explorer Sven Hedin joined their voices to the geopolitical call for Germany's eastern mission, including rearmament.[47] Even many advocates of a peaceful and economically oriented policy in the east felt geography dictated German expansion there. Hans Zehrer in Die Tat, for example, argued that "the Danube will take the place in the coming German Reich that the Rhine has played politically heretofore," and writers for the Sozialistische Monatshefte made the argument that the lands between the Rhine and the Vistula formed a unity of trade and politics that Versailles had destroyed and that it was the task of German diplomats to restore.[48] From the Zeitschrift für Geopolitik to the Sozialistische Monatshefte, furthermore, geopolitics and the vision of the organic state united Germans who called for German unification with Austria from the early 1920s onward. "Austria must be taken up spiritually, economically, geographically in a new German state organism whose form has been programmatically demanded here since 1918."[49]

Germany's dismal economic situation through most of this period also played an important role in the popularity of visions of a German-dominated Mitteleuropa, which many saw as a means of resuscitating struggling German industries. Although Mitteleuropa acquired a "scientific" justification and political/racial overtones in geopolitical theory, it always retained an economic component. The disruption of the "natural" economic unity of eastern Germany by the arrangement of borders and the separation of Danzig was always a key component of geopolitical hostility toward Poland. Geopolitically influenced concepts of the German role in Mitteleuropa played an influential role in the formation of a series of Mitteleuropa institutes founded in Vienna, Budapest, and other central European cities in the 1920s, which were supported by contributions from German steel, electrical, and other heavy industrial interests.[50]

There is also good reason to believe that the attitude of the German diplomatic establishment toward the lands to the east of Germany was influenced by geopolitical Mitteleuropa theorizing. The German envoy to Rumania, for example, echoed geopolitical arguments in a memorandum in 1928 in which he argued that the southeast of Europe formed "a space dominated intellectually and economically by Germany, which one can call Mitteleuropa." "Here lie regions of colonization before our gates, here are tasks and goals for the Germandom gathered in the Reich, which may be more certainly attained the less they are accompanied by noisy publicity and politics, the more they serve as guiding lights for what may be called an unpolitical politics of economic and cultural expansion."[51] Like the geopoliticians, he argued that proximity, ethnicity, and German efficiency dictated a hegemonic German eastern policy. The Foreign Office, furthermore, played an active part in the 1920s in disseminating geopolitical theories. *Deutschtumspolitik*, according to one historian, was always "an integrated tendency of official German foreign policy."[52] Propagandistic organizations such as the Deutscher Schutzbund (German Protective League [DSB]) enjoyed the financial support of the Foreign Office and the Reich Finance Ministry throughout the Weimar period in the hope that they would serve the recovery of "all the losses that Germandom has suffered in the struggle for the soil and other economic positions."[53] The Cultural Section of the Foreign Office, which originated in the reform of the diplomatic service in 1919, worked in the words of its head in 1929 as a "focal point" for the Auslandsdeutsch movement.[54] Generous subventions were channeled through the Cultural Section to groups such as the Verein für das Deutschtum im Ausland and the German Protective League to support propaganda work among ethnic Germans living abroad, propaganda which often included geopolitical justifications for German predominance in central Europe. Loesch, the head of the Protective League and a prominent adherent of geopolitical ideas, was considered at the Foreign Office to be a "man of extraordinary expertise, good international connections, and strong initiative."[55]

Stresemann himself, in his treatment of the borders with Poland and especially of the status of German minorities there, tried to appease popular opinion about the German role in central Europe while avoiding antagonizing the Allies. It was he who helped make revision of these borders "an axiom of German politics" in these years, and his attitude toward Poland, although not bent on war, was clearly aggressive.[56] He greeted civil unrest in Poland with glee and told the Arbeitsgemeinschaft deutscher Landsmannschaften in 1925 that "what I imagine is that once conditions arise that appear to threaten European peace or the economic consolidation of Europe by developments in the east, and one begins to consider whether the entire nonconsolidation of Europe might not have its sources in the impossible border drawing in the east, that Germany then [will have] the possibility to achieve success with its demands."[57] Stresemann's manipulation of the question of the rights of German minorities in his conduct of relations with Poland and in the League of Nations was also largely dictated by hopes to build internal support for his policies rather than by commitment to the abstract rights of minorities. As historians have pointed out, however, this was a dangerous policy because it alienated Germany's neighbors and isolated Germany internationally when pursued by Stresemann's less-dexterous successors.[58] It also helped alienate Germans from the League.[59]

The Foreign Office worked in many ways to promote the influential concept of a large but vaguely defined German cultural area in east central Europe. Its officers played an active role in the formation of the Protective League in 1919 as a coordinator of the activity of German groups in the states to Germany's east, clearly believing that this would promote German interests in the region. "Because of the Treaty of Versailles, the national borders coincide with cultural borders even less than before the war," wrote Ministerial Director Heilbron of the Cultural Section. "It is for us a task of decades to support, maintain, and promote German culture beyond the momentary borders."[60] Support for the Deutschtumspolitik was deliberately concealed from the entente and from Germany's neighbors, and its goal was the creation not of irredentism itself but of a "useful apparatus" to forward official foreign policy.[61] Funds for German groups in the separated districts were funneled through the Protective League by the Foreign Office to keep "the German ethnic group as strong as possible."[62] The attempt of the Foreign Office to promote *überparteilichkeit,* or nonpartisanship, in the movement failed, however: From start to end it remained dominated by the Right, particularly members of the German National People's Party, with the result that what began as the Foreign Office's tool became its nemesis.

The geopolitically influenced propagandizing of the Germandom-groups supported by the Foreign Office began to haunt German diplomats in the mid-1920s as this rhetoric was employed to complicate the conduct of German foreign policy. The DNVP, usually a bitter opponent of Stresemann's *Erfüllungspolitik* (fulfillment policy), exploited geopolitics to denounce the policy. Gerhard Raab used geopolitical terms to explain the goals of German diplomacy to the party's convention in December 1926 and, in explicitly geopolitical fashion, located the sources of Germany's political and historical development in its geography.

> The primacy of foreign policy means, first, that foreign policy must acquire Lebensraum, space to maneuver. . . . [This means, in consequence], the greater the pressure from without, the smaller the degree of freedom within. It is in the nature of rules that they are broken. Our entire German history from the fall of the Hohenstaufen to the foundation of the new empire is nothing but a disturbing chain of violations against this rule. And yet precisely we Germans—positioned in the center of Europe, with eternally fluid, wavering borders, which are almost nowhere secured and strengthened by natural topography, frequently awash in overpowering influences of a partially power-political, partially cultural sort from east and west, north and south—we German people in this situation require more than any other people on earth an authoritarian embodiment of our national political structure, a strict internal order, consolidating all our powers.[63]

Raab's picture of a vulnerable Germany, "awash in overpowering influences," corresponds precisely with geopolitical imagery of the threatening Slavic "inundation" from the east and of a Germany left open to all enemies by its geography. The fulfillment policy typified by the Dawes Plan ("which unbearably burdens our economy!") was a sign of the nation's internal weakness, of its failure to attain the strict and authoritarian internal cohesiveness that geography mandated as its only permissible political structure.[64] Stresemann's successors in the early 1930s were subjected to similar criticism from the DNVP, which continued to use geopolitical language to emphasize its objections. "We need a final break with the fulfillment policy," the party's Freedom Program of 1932 argued. "The German people cannot live in its present space. It needs expanded Lebensraum. Furthermore, the border formation in the east is of a sort to make the coexistence of Germany and Poland completely impossible."[65]

The geopolitical penetration of the domestic political debate about foreign policy was by no means confined to the far Right. Many of the relatively moderate members of the DNVP who seceded from the party in protest against their leader Alfred Hugenberg's opposition to the Young Plan in 1929, including Hans-Erdmann von Lindeiner-Wildau, incorporated geopolitical language in their critique of German foreign policy.[66] More moderate parties also exploited geopolitics. The annual consideration of the Foreign Office budget in the Reichstag was a perennial source of domestic debate about the proper aims and methods of German foreign policy, and many delegates resorted to geopolitical terms and concepts to support their arguments. One of the "grumblers" within Stresemann's own party, Freiherr von Rheinbaben, argued in the 1926 debate that Locarno had settled the west for the time being and that "now the eastern question must stand in the forefront of Germany's entire foreign policy. There is, unfortunately, nothing more important than support for the struggle of Germandom against the oppressors there on the eastern boundary."[67] Another deputy echoed these views, "We are of the opinion that Germany's future lies in the east."[68] By 1931, again in the debate over the foreign office budget, a deputy like Sachsenberg of the relatively moderate Economic Party (Wirtschaftspartei) could argue in overtly geopolitical terms for an "active" German foreign policy in the east.

> Germany lies wedged between this powerful Asian economic bloc and the Western powers under the leadership of America. . . . Wedged between the two groups, Germany is also in a hugely dangerous position that can be overcome only if our people recognize the connections and if the state's leadership can, on the basis of such a recognition, rely on the support of the majority of the German people . . . whether Germany will be in the position, under these circumstances, to take up the mediator role that falls to it by virtue of geography and psychology, is impossible to say

as is the answer to the question of which side Germany ought to join if this mediator role becomes impossible to assume.[69]

Geopolitical rhetoric was particularly strong in the Deutsche Demo-kratische Partei (German Democratic Party [DDP]) the result in consid-erable part of the active membership of Obst, who passed a strong geo-political flavor to the DDP's successor, the German State Party (Deutsche Staatspartei), after the elections of September 1930. From its inception in the wake of the revolution the DDP supported the formation of a vaguely defined Grossdeutschland based upon the consolidation of all ethnic Germans in central Europe.[70] Both Obst and Berhnard Dernburg, who had been state secretary in the Reich Colonial Office before the war, pushed the party toward an unequivocal demand for return of the colonies through most of the 1920s.[71] By 1930, when the party evolved into the German State Party in the face of the German peoples' manifest lack of interest in the moderate liberalism of the DDP, the colonial inter-est of the party's members had become focused much more upon the east of Europe than upon Africa, and the DSP argument for expansion was couched in overtly geopolitical terms. Although Obst, for example, was sufficiently clear-sighted to recognize that it was impossible to unite all the German settlements scattered through central and eastern Europe, he demanded the unification of Germany and Austria. "Grossdeutschland, the object of our heartfelt longing, will be called under the guiding par-ticipation of German-Austria to build by means of peaceful understand-ing a bridge between industrial Mitteleuropa and agricultural eastern Europe."[72] This new Grossdeutschland would eliminate the Polish corri-dor and redraw Germany's other eastern boundaries.

Geopolitics, then, contributed to a complication of Germany's foreign relations, particularly with its eastern neighbors, by propagating geodeter-minist ideas that penetrated both the foreign policy and party political establishments. Both Poland and Czechoslovakia, for example, were or-dinarily presented as temporary and politically illegitimate political constructs, which were sooner or later doomed to collapse. Geopolitical language played a particularly important role in the instruments of the Foreign Office's Deutschtumspolitik, and the *Deutschtum* organizations, influenced by geopolitical ideas of the German eastern mission and incor-porating them in its propaganda, rendered "foreign policy compromises—at least with Poland—practically impossible."[73] For Stresemann, whose own views on the meaning of German geography convinced him that peaceful methods were the only possible course to revision, popular, geopolitically influenced ideas of a German-dominated Mitteleuropa proved an insurmountable obstacle, even among members of the Foreign Office itself, to a new foreign policy for Germany in central Europe.[74]

Against Internationalism:
Geopolitics, Paneuropa, and the League of Nations

Geopolitical engagement with German foreign policy during the Weimar era went beyond its criticism of official foreign policy to penetrate the German public debate about even more theoretical aspects of international relations. Every move made by German statesmen was, of course, scrutinized by geopoliticians, who interpreted for Germans the degree to which their diplomats' actions conformed to sound geopolitical principles. In their efforts to mediate popular perceptions of official policy, however, geopoliticians were also concerned with what Germans thought of new ideas about foreign policy and relations between states. Many proposals to reorder interstate relations according to cooperative principles, for example, emerged from the carnage of World War I. Most notable of these, of course, was the League of Nations, but the League was far from being the only such multilateral diplomatic device to demand the attention of Germans in the postwar years. Other schemes for world or European political integration were also proposed, but most never got beyond the academic environment in which they were born, lived a short life, and died. One of the few exceptions, however, was the proposal for European federalism known as "Pan-Europe," which became the focus of considerable public attention and scholarly debate as well in the years before Nazism silenced most public discussion of alternative diplomacies.

Both the League of Nations and Pan-Europe engaged the attention of geopolitical thinkers very closely. These two subjects became sounding boards for the geopolitical exploration of theories of international cooperation, and the geopolitical dialogue with both the League and the Pan-European idea reveals the extent and the limits of the geopolitical understanding of the postwar international system. While recognizing the theoretical utility of international organizations in the resolution of interstate conflict, geopoliticians in general attacked both the League and the Pan-European idea as tools for the extension of English or French hegemony and urged Germans to hold to unilateralism in foreign policy. Although the Pan-European idea remained an ignis fatuus, the League held genuine promise for remodeling international relations, promise that, for a variety of reasons, was never realized. German public hostility to the League, which grew steadily after German entry in 1926 and culminated in withdrawal from the League under Hitler, was fostered and promoted by a steady geopolitical campaign against internationalism. This geopolitical unilateralism urged Germans to reject not only extant international institutions, such as the League, but even to distance themselves from multilateral theoretical constructs, such as the idea of Pan-Europe.

In the spring of 1924, just a few months after the first issue of the *Zeitschrift für Geopolitik* appeared, another magazine devoted largely to issues of international relations began publication in Germany. Entitled *Paneuropa,* it was the organ of the Pan-European movement. Pan-Europeanism, which envisioned a federalized, supranationally governed Europe, was the dream of Austrian Count Richard N. Coudenhove-Kalergi. The magazine, like the programmatic book of the same name published the year before by Coudenhove-Kalergi, expressed a view of international relations quite different from that found in geopolitics. Dedicated to uniting all Europe between the Channel and the Soviet Union, Pan-Europeanism, as Coudenhove-Kalergi developed the idea from 1924 to 1933, lacked the Germanocentrism of Weimar geopolitical thought. Surprisingly, however, the Pan-European view of the state and of the future of Europe also had a good deal in common with the theories of geopoliticians on these topics.

The program that Coudenhove-Kalergi set forth in 1923 was directed toward rebuilding Europe to resist what he saw as the imminent danger looming on both flanks: domination by either Soviet military power or American financial might.[75] The chief obstacle that Europeans had to surmount to be able to face down these threats was the political fragmentation of the continent.[76] This disunity Coudenhove-Kalergi proposed to overcome by the political and economic unification of Europe. His was a strangely distorted "Europe" geographically, however, one that omitted both Russia and England but which included Greenland and France's enormous empire in Africa (see fig. 18). Although he charged that England and Russia had grown out of Europe through their imperial expansion, he did not apply the same judgment to France. Pan-Europeanism was skeptical of theories of race and emphasized that the unification of

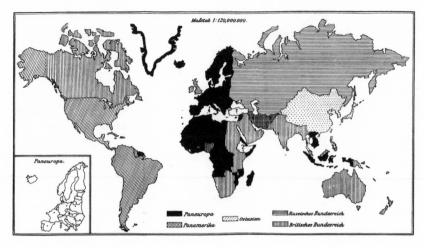

Fig. 18. *Tafel III: Weltkarte* (Diagram 3: World map), from R. N. Coudenhove-Kalergi, *Paneuropa* (Vienna, 1923).

Europe would be based neither in race nor ethnicity but in the shared cultural heritage of the many peoples of the continent.[77] Coudenhove-Kalergi's conviction of the urgency of this unification was driven by a perceptive analysis of the changes in the world state system since the war. He recognized that the growth of Soviet, American, and East Asian power had ended the age of European world hegemony, and he was convinced that the "dogma of European nationalism" was a pernicious "myth."[78] Borders drawn on the basis of "national self-determination," he argued, would always be a cause of war. The overlapping of linguistic, economic, historical, and cultural borders in Europe precluded the possibility of creating stable, ethnically homogeneous nations.[79]

Coudenhove-Kalergi's Pan-European ideology was separated from the main currents of Weimar geopolitical thought, therefore, by its internationalism, its skepticism about race, and its Francophile leanings. Moreover, by locating the dynamic element in state relations not in geography but in politics and culture, it acquired a theoretical sophistication and flexibility that always eluded geopolitics. Still, the language of Pan-Europeanism intersected with that of geopolitics at many points. There can be no doubt that the two were part of a shared discourse about politics and state relations, and their joint use of organic and geocentric theoretical frameworks illustrates the extent to which such notions had become the common property of Germanophone intellectuals across the political spectrum. Like the German geopoliticians, Coudenhove-Kalergi was a citizen of an empire that had been toppled by the war, and like them, he looked to organic state theories as a guide to a new political stability for central Europe. Pan-Europeanism emphasized, for example, that only "organic" political organizations could endure, insisting that states ought to be organized according to their "historic, economic, cultural, and geographic connections."[80] His Pan-European plan, Coudenhove-Kalergi argued, met these criteria and could, thus, be expected to produce a successful and enduring political structure. Like Dix and other geopoliticians, Coudenhove-Kalergi embraced the powerful political effects of new technology:"The world becomes smaller every day. . . . Paris and Berlin have become neighboring towns through air travel."[81] And, in common with many geopoliticians Pan-Europeanism was unwilling to concede that the colonial age of Europe was past. Like the geopolitically influenced circle of foreign policy theorists at the *Sozialistische Monatshefte,* for example, Pan-European enthusiasts viewed Africa as the natural complement to Europe, "in qualitative terms, the most productive human reservoir of the world."[82] Like Haushofer and others, Coudenhove-Kalergi emphasized the importance of will in international relations, and he even borrowed specifically geopolitical terms, *Kraftfelder* for instance, to describe the spatial component of international conflict of interests.[83] Pan-Europeanism and geopolitics, although different significantly in important ways, clearly inhabited the same conceptual frame of reference concerning international relations. The effects of the war in central Europe exercised a decisive influence in convincing both geopoliticians and Pan-Europeans that future stability had to have a basis in something deeper and presumably more organic than their prewar empires.

Geopoliticians were quite conscious of the links between Geopolitik and Paneuropa and it prompted them to give close attention to elucidating the differences between the two views of the future of the European state system. Geopoliticians took Pan-Europeanism very seriously, and their responses to its challenging proposals for the German future ranged from grudging admission of the validity of some Pan-European ideas to complete rejection of the entire notion of supranational organization. Pan-Europe was most commonly attacked by geopoliticians, ironically, for the very reason Coudenhove-Kalergi argued it was practicable, that is, its relationship to organic political structures. He insisted that, culturally and politically, the gradual unification of Europe represented an organic and natural process. The important omission here from the geopolitical point of view, of course, is the ethnic or racial connection with the soil, which they would have argued was an essential ingredient of any organic political construct and which would be missing from a united Europe. The "Pan-European perversity" was a "practical impossibility," they argued, because of its failure to accord with the "deeper will of world development."[84] This conviction of Pan-European impracticality was in part the result of the raw revanchism of geopolitics. From the mid-1920s on geopoliticians generally anticipated the course of Nazi foreign policy, preferring what they saw as "natural" alliances with other revisionist powers like Italy or Japan to the multilateral cooperation of Pan-Europe.[85] The positive value of struggle in the geopolitical worldview, furthermore, contributed to their skepticism about Pan-Europe, which they argued would lead to the atrophy of European peoples by eliminating productive competition between states.[86]

Pan-Europe elicited a particularly hostile response from geopolitical thinkers who were committed to consolidating all the scattered elements of the German Volk in a united Mitteleuropa. The advocates of Pan-Europe, they charged, possessed an underdeveloped sense of racial consciousness, and they lacked appreciation for the importance of the organic nature of Mitteleuropa, which Pan-Europe could never hope to rival. Racially, Pan-Europe would produce a mongrelized ethnicity like that found in the United States of America. "Only mongrels and people not firmly anchored in a Volkstum wish to create a corresponding European nation, a goal which is neither attainable nor worthwhile," wrote Loesch. "'The Eurasian-Negro race of the future, outwardly perhaps similar to the ancient Egyptians, will replace the multiplicity of peoples with a multiplicity of personalities.' . . . There [Coudenhove-Kalergi] shows his vision of the future."[87] The Pan-Europeanists also ignored the geopolitical reality of Europe, namely that the peripheral states with their free outlets to the sea could never interest themselves in central Europe as much as in the outside world. In keeping with the geopolitical analysis of the "dynamism" of their field they argued that Pan-Europe presented a "static solution" to the problems of Mitteleuropa, whereas a dynamic and "evolutionary" solution was the only one with hopes of success. Instead, "the problem of European unification is in large part that of the unification of central and east-central Europe. Here one meets the greatest obstacles through the entanglement of peoples, falsely drawn boundaries, traditional hostilities, and the lack of natural state and ethnic borders."[88] Solve this problem, and the rest of the continent would take care of itself, geopoliticians argued: "The only path to Paneuropa leads through Mitteleuropa."[89]

Even more important to many geopoliticians was their perception that Pan-Europe was a French plot, or, at least, that those Germans who supported it were unwitting dupes of the French. Nationalist hostility to the French here combined with the geopolitical anticipation of greater opportunities available to the east to cement their opposition to Pan-Europe.[90] Coudenhove-Kalergi was accused of sacrificing the threatened German Volkstum in eastern Europe by succumbing to the blandishments of French offers of security and peace.[91] "Only limitless ignorance of history allows Coudenhove-Kalergi to ignore the French-German confrontation."[92] Germany, in fact, had to beware of Pan-Europeanism because "France's Pan-European goal is the stabilization of the current situation," which would end any hope for German revision of borders in the east of Europe.[93] Coudenhove-Kalergi's response to geopolitical support for Mitteleuropa over Paneuropa and attacks on his proposal was telling; he argued that the resurrection of Mitteleuropa presaged a new German politics of hegemony in central Europe, that it distracted Germany from the real threat of the Soviet Union, and that it would be the death rather than a key to the realization of a harmonious Europe.[94]

Coudenhove-Kalergi's warnings of the dangers of Mitteleuropa made little impression on geopoliticians, who found in it a useful conceptual justification for the extension of German hegemony toward the east. Despite their overall rejection of Pan-Europe, however, some geopoliticians regarded its attempt to hold off the extra-European powers sympathetically, viewing Coudenhove-Kalergi's plan as "premature" rather than essentially misguided.[95] The same cannot be said for the German geopolitical response to the League of Nations, which unlike Pan-Europe was a genuine factor in German foreign policy in these years and which the geopoliticians unanimously denounced as a tool of the victor powers for the exploitation of Germany and other oppressed states. The nexus of nationalism and geopolitical organic state theory produced a vehement repudiation of the League that developed in geopolitical literature even before the Locarno agreements of October 1925 prepared the way for the reception of a German delegation at Geneva.

In the *Zeitschrift für Geopolitik,* for example, the League was treated with scorn as a clumsy facade for British and French manipulation of Europe and the world. The true League of Nations was the British empire, whereas the organization at Geneva was only a *Schein-Völkerbund* (imaginary League of Nations). "It is no wonder that it was considered entirely in order that the central powers be excluded from the society of 'free nations of the world,' after the English had by systematic propaganda produced the conviction that the 'Huns' were a direct threat to 'fair play'."[96] One could find in the same pages bitter denunciations of the inactivity of "the French-directed League of Nations" in resolving the position of the Saar and of German minorities in eastern Europe.[97] This critique of League policy as an expression of the wishes of the English and French had a great deal of accuracy. Japan's distancing of itself from the league, the League's exclusion of the Soviet Union and the repudiation of the League itself by the United States had the result that "all that occurs in the League of Nations does so under the direct or secret influence of the two exclusively European world powers, England and France."[98]

The geopolitical commitment to "organic" political structures and to the revision of Germany's borders to incorporate ethnic Germans in neighboring states provided a comfortable theoretical foundation for years of steady denunciations of the League. The question of the rights of German minorities, in particular, spurred hostility to the League among geopolitically engaged adherents of German Volkstum theory such as Martin Spahn. Rather than seeing in the League a means of addressing the issue, they tended to argue against the League as an intolerable hindrance to unilateral German action to resolve the minorities question.[99] "Should [Germany] yet find an opportunity to do something for its minorities, it sees itself, since its entry into the League of Nations, exposed to the common objections of France and Poland."[100] While professing acceptance of Stresemann's goals of peaceful revision, geopoliticians argued that rather than jump into a world organization German foreign policy ought to concentrate on developing a regional league in central Europe, which would be more "organic" and in which, obviously, German influence would be paramount.

In terms of goals, therefore, we agree entirely with the League of Nations policy pursued energetically by Stresemann. What divides us is much more the means of reaching this goal. We hold it impossible to make the spring from a single state to a world league; we would rather develop a series of continental leagues, which could, perhaps, one day unite and meld into a world league of peoples. . . . In short, we are for an organic development of communities of peoples, for a slow, steady growth from small to large, and we expect little from more or less arbitrary, unnatural political constructions.[101]

The tacit approval of Stresemann's policy of using the League as a means of attaining German revisionist goals did not last long. This was the result not only of political rivalry (Obst, for example, the author of the statement above, belonged not to Stresemann's DVP but to the DDP at this time) but also to the incredible lack of realism many geopoliticians displayed in their understanding of the nature of diplomacy. For example, Obst argued that the entry into the League could be judged a success if Stresemann succeeded in attaining the following wish list of foreign policy concessions to Germany: the elimination of the German war guilt clause; French evacuation from German territory on the Rhine; the return of Danzig, Upper Silesia, the Polish Corridor, and all German colonies overseas; Anschluss with Austria, the annexation of other German-settled regions in central Europe; and the elimination of reparations payments.[102] It scarcely needs to be said that serious hopes of attaining such a program were sheer fantasy. The fact that the many educated Germans involved in geopolitics (and in politics as well) subscribed to it as a serious strategic framework for German foreign policy reflects the extremely radical nature of what they expected German foreign policy to achieve and makes it clear that they were practically bound to be disappointed.

One of the most surprising aspects of official German policy upon entry into the League was Stresemann's own fostering of grandiose illusions, similar to those of the geopoliticians, about what German participation in the League could be expected to attain. This only contributed to the intense public disillusionment later when the very real but less-dramatic gains of German diplomacy in the League went unrecognized. To overcome conservative hostility to the Locarno treaty and its provisions for German entry into the League, particularly in the DNVP where geopolitical thinkers such as Spahn played an important role, Stresemann himself held out great hopes to the German public. The League, he promised critics, would aid the minorities, end reparations, gain Austria, win armaments parity, and regain for Germany, as Stresemann put it, "the moral right to the allocation of colonial mandates."[103] This domestic rallying tactic was ill-considered. When, for example, Stresemann won through the League the dissolution of the Interallied Control Commission, gained a seat on the League's Mandate Committee for the governance of colonies, and helped influence the decision of the general assembly to take up the disarmament question in 1927, all within the first eighteen months of Germany's entry, these important and very real gains for Germany were minimized in public eyes and barely noted by geopolitical commentators hungry for more spectacular results.

Stresemann's efforts to appease his domestic opponents by reassurances of the revisionist value of the Locarno League provisions were wasted. Geopoliticians, for example, constantly denounced the geographic ignorance displayed by his policies. "It is not as if we believed that we could succeed in gaining recognition for the value of political geography in the circles of official or parliamentary representatives of German policy," Haushofer complained, "we have long since abandoned this hope."[104] German conservatives were, of course, committed, like Stresemann, to the dismantling of Versailles, but unlike him they saw the League as an obstacle rather than an aid.[105] The attacks on the agreements in the DNVP, for example, were relentless and steeped in geopolitical rhetoric. By agreeing to renounce the use of force in the east, members argued, Stresemann, Locarno, and the League had "cut off the last escape remaining for the German Volk."[106] Graf Westarp of the DNVP relied on a geopolitical analysis of the true determinants of state relations, which were not to be found in artificial organizations or agreements, to denounce the treaty and argue that Germany had to keep the east route open. The fundamental "consideration for us is that Germany as the land of the middle of Europe must preserve its freedom of maneuver," he argued in the Reichstag. "But Russia and Bolshevism are not identical for us, above all not for all time, not in the long run, for which these agreements have been concluded, and the connections of peoples to each other work themselves out not only—perhaps not at all—according to the opposition of state forms, but according to the geographically, ethnically, historically developed requirements and relations of the peoples."[107] Geopoliticians also resented the League for its role as enforcer of German military weakness. Scarcely more than one year after Germany's entry into the League, in fact, geopoliticians were already urging German withdrawal so that the process of rebuilding German military power without hindrance might begin. "The German foreign minister will very soon be pressed by German public opinion, quite properly, to offer an unequivocal declaration at Geneva: either immediate general disarmament, or Germany will withdraw from the League."[108]

The most sophisticated geopolitical critique of the League of Nations, as of many other topics, was penned by Adolf Grabowsky. He had already in the late 1920s expressed the view that the League was inadequate as a tool for restructuring the "unhinged world dynamic," and in 1932 he contributed a substantial appraisal of the League to Haushofer's collection of essays, *Jenseits der Grossmächte,* which illuminated that body's shortcomings at length.[109] Like other geopoliticians, he argued that the League was controlled by England and France and that these nations were "antidemocratic and static as far as overall foreign policy is concerned, and with them the League is as well."[110] He argued that the League's static view of peace, that is, peace as stability, was obsolete and had to be replaced by a dynamic and preemptively revisionist view of peace and peace maintenance, which would, of course, include instituting changes that would address German grievances.[111] By pressing its border concerns and the need for revision and change, Germany in the League represented dynamism, democracy, and progress. It even represented, implicitly, a form of anticapitalism because the League was an expression of the values of "high capitalism" that were challenged by German revisionism.[112] This is a moderate geopolitical critique of the League because Grabowsky did not call for Germany to exit the organization but only to reform it to better meet German needs. His revisionist concepts of "dynamic peace" and his attack on what he saw as the immobility of the League, however, suggest the extent to which time was running out for peaceful diplomacy in Germany. Even German moderates were by 1932 becoming frustrated with the gradual pace of revision and calling for a more "dynamic" approach to foreign policy.

Criticism of the League incorporating the supposed Realpolitik of geopolitical analysis and generally lacking Grabowsky's moderation and insight gradually had its effect on Germany's position in the League and its ability to use the opportunities offered by League membership. From

1928 onward Stresemann and his successors abandoned the original discreet and successful German League diplomacy, instead using the League not as a genuine avenue of diplomacy but as a mere device to placate and gain the support of rightists at home. Hermann Müller, speaking to the League as chancellor in September of 1928, used his pulpit to attack the League's passivity, especially on the minorities question, a tactic chosen not out of diplomatic grounds but to pacify conservative critics of the government in Germany. Müller continued his attacks on the League later in the year, again to satisfy critics on the right, led by Kuno von Westarp of the DNVP, among others.[113] At the same time Stresemann responded with extreme sharpness to a speech at the League's meeting in Lugano by the Polish foreign minister, Zaleski, who had delivered a speech threatening the German minorities.[114] The domestic political effects of Stresemann's fiery rhetorical response were very good, and they did not pass unnoticed, but the entire affair culminated the following year in a defeat for the German minority rights offensive in the League when the London Report of May 1929 rejected German proposals for increased international responsibility for the oversight of minority rights.[115] Thereafter, beginning with Stresemann's successor Julius Curtius and continuing into the Nazi period, the German approach to the League was calculated almost entirely for its domestic political effect, although this failed to silence domestic complaints about the reserve of the German delegation at the League.[116] By the end of 1929, then, Germans saw that both the evacuation of the Rhineland and the reduction of reparation payments had been accomplished outside the League, whereas neither the border revision nor the minority rights they had been led to expect had been achieved within the League.[117] All this tended to bear out criticisms, like those made by geopoliticians, of the "static" and "inorganic" nature of the League and to prepare Germans to welcome the abandonment of such internationalist devices when the Nazis took that fateful step in 1933.

CHAPTER 10

The Legacy of Weimar Geopolitics

The Volk ohne Raum nonsense . . . an epoch-making mental illness of epidemic proportion.

Rolf Hochhuth, *Eine Liebe in Deutschland*

Karl Haushofer, the foremost German geopolitician of the Weimar and Nazi eras, committed suicide after the Second World War. This desperate act, the expression of mingled grief, remorse, and despondency may have been prompted by reflection upon the enormity of Nazi barbarism and the appalling scale of the German (and European) catastrophe. For Haushofer, as for historians ever since, their contribution to the Nazi reign of terror has been the most important historical aspect of geopolitical ideas. The historiographical focus on geopolitics under the Nazis, however, has obscured its role in the Weimar Republic. This work has attempted to restore geopolitics to its position in the political and academic culture of Weimar Germany. It has also tried to modify and expand historical understandings of geopolitics by reexamining the content and rhetoric of geopolitical theories, the sources of the appeal of geopolitical ideas, the venues of geopolitical discourse and the means by which geopolitical thought was disseminated. It has tried to show that Germans were learning to think like geopoliticians long before the Nazis rose to power, and to demonstrate how the vitality and widespread acceptance of geopolitical ideas in the Weimar Republic played a crucial role in preparing Germans to reject the Republic as a political form unsuited to Germany's "organic" needs.

Just as the history of geopolitics antedated Weimar, however, so it continued after the fall of the Republic in 1933. Certain questions about

the place of geopolitical ideas in national socialist Germany follow naturally and logically from the course of this study, and it seems appropriate
to conclude by addressing these. How, for example, did geopolitical ideas
introduced into German education under Weimar democracy evolve
in German textbooks, schools, and universities under Hitler's dictator-
ship? What became under the Nazis of Haushofer, Grabowsky, Dix,
Banse, Burgdörfer, Vogel, and the numerous other ideologues and theorists who promoted geopolitics during the Weimar era? Most important,
perhaps, are the central questions of how geopolitical thought may have
contributed to the racial and foreign policies of the German state under
Nazi rule.

There can be no question that geopolitical ideas under national socialism retained the strong presence they had acquired in German
education during the Weimar years. Geography and history textbooks for
students, and handbooks for teachers as well, frequently used geopolitical
ideas and terms, citing Haushofer and Ratzel with Hitler to tell students,
for example, that "the meaning and the iron will of national socialist
statesmanship are the securing of our Lebensraum and a sensible organization of space. . . . To create a spatial organization suitable to Germany
means to undo the damage caused by an unavailing population policy."[1]
First-hand accounts of German elementary and middle-school level education during the Nazi years are filled with recollections of lessons on the
coming *Germanisches Weltreich* (German world empire), Germany's just
claim to additional Lebensraum and topics such as "Germany's Geopolitical Situation in the World."[2] These and other staples of the geopolitical
rhetoric of the 1920s were taken up under the Hitler regime as integral
parts of what one former student recalls as the "indoctrination of children
and teenagers with plans for global conquest."[3]

The situation of geopolitics in German academic life at higher levels
during the Nazi years was similar. German intellectuals throughout
the Nazi era continued to insist upon the necessity of instruction in geopolitical principles at all levels of German education, including the highest, and the conservative, nationalistic German professoriate of the day,
quickly adjusting to life under Hitler, appears in general to have gone
along.[4] Individual geographers, including Obst, Banse, Hugo Hassinger
at Vienna, Norbert Krebs at Berlin, and many others, continued to represent a geopolitically influenced voice in the academic life of national
socialist Germany, and geopolitical ideas acquired new and influential institutional voices in a variety of settings. A good example of the almost

irresistible momentum propelling geopolitics in German academic life by the mid-1930s was the attention paid to geopolitical theories at the Institut für Völkerrecht, or Institute for International Law, at the University of Göttingen. Led until the summer of 1937 by the jurist Herbert Kraus, a political moderate who was denounced by local Nazis as a "democrat, liberal, typically internationalist" product of the Weimar "system-regime," the Institut between 1933 and 1937 built up an extensive collection of geopolitical literature, organized a *geopolitische Arbeitsgemeinschaft* (geopolitical workgroup), and was cited within university circles as a prime example of the successful introduction of a "geopolitical mentality" into a variety of disciplines.[5]

As with the geopolitical presence in German schools, so for most individual geopoliticians the advent of the Nazi era signified the attainment of a new level of legitimacy and public acceptance. There are to this, as to all historical generalizations, a few important exceptions. Adolf Grabowsky, for example, well known for his democratic sympathies and affiliation with the republican Deutsche Hochschule für Politik, fled to Switzerland in 1934. Neither Arthur Dix nor Walther Vogel lived to see Germany's final descent into the maelstrom created by Nazism, Dix dying in 1935 and Vogel in 1938. Socialist geopolitics, of course, like all things socialist in Germany, vanished after 1933. Many more geopoliticians, however, found the national socialist regime thoroughly congenial. The controversial Ewald Banse retained a professorship at Hannover until he was ousted after the Second World War. Johann Wilhelm Mannhardt of the Institut für Grenz- und Auslandsdeutschtum at Marburg proved insufficiently zealous in his commitment to the new order in Germany to satisfy his students and was forced to leave, being compensated by the regime in 1937 with a professorship at Breslau for *Soziologie, Weltpolitik, und Hochschulwesen* (Sociology, World Politics, and University Affairs).[6]

Many of those individuals who went from a Weimar-era association with geopolitical ideas and publications to positions of importance in the Nazi regime were, naturally enough, those whose ideas on volkish and racial questions coincided most closely with Nazi racial attitudes. The demographer Hans Harmsen, for example, an academic collaborator of Friedrich Burgdörfer, used the pages of the *Zeitschrift für Geopolitik* in 1933 to call for "racial offices" (*Rasseämter*) to carry out a "racial accounting" of the German people, the issuing of passes certifying genetic health, and government-enforced measures to lessen the numbers of those suffering from hereditary illnesses.[7] Harmsen's writings earned sufficient prominence under the Nazis to enable him to participate in the organization (and editing of the published papers) of the International Congress on Population Science held at Berlin in 1935.[8] Burgdörfer himself proceeded from membership on the parliamentary Reich Committee on Population Questions, formed by the Ministry of the Interior in 1929, to the Nazi version of the same, the Committee of Experts for Population Policy, likewise formed by the Ministry of the Interior in June 1933 after Hitler came to power. Here he helped draft compulsory sterilization laws and measures treating the so-called Rhineland bastards, joining the Nazi party in 1937 and continuing to serve as director of the Reich Statistical Office, where he remained an influential public apologist for Nazi racial policies to the very last days of Hitler's rule.[9] Another volkish enthusiast, Karl Christian von Loesch of the *Deutscher Schutzbund,* also a contributor to the *Zeitschrift für Geopolitik* and adherent of geopolitical ideas, became director of the Institut für Grenz- und Auslandsdeutschtum in Berlin-Steglitz, where he enjoyed close connections with the influential office of the Reichskommissariat für die Festigung Deutsches Volkstums (RKFDV) and took part in the discussions leading to the Nazi resettlement plan for eastern Europe, the Generalplan Ost.[10]

Karl Haushofer's fate, however, suggests that those intellectuals with links to geopolitics who "made it" during the Nazi years probably owed their success to the congruence of their racial views with those of the Nazis rather than to their theoretical commitments to geocentric geopolitics. Identified both before and since the Nazi era as the moving force behind the popularity of geopolitical ideas, Haushofer's career under the Nazis moved from early influence and academic prominence to eventual political disillusionment, harrowing personal loss, and irrelevance to the course of policy and public affairs.[11] Haushofer served as president of the German Academy, an interdisciplinary league of German academics interested in volkish issues and in promoting ties with ethnic Germans abroad, from 1934 to 1937.[12] The aging general (he was seventy in 1939) continued to lecture and broadcast, and up to 1940 or so he publicly applauded national socialist foreign policy as the realization of his theories. The centerpiece of Hitler's foreign policy, however, the invasion of the Soviet Union, directly violated Haushofer's longtime insistence on the necessity for a German-Japanese-Russian bloc. In the wake of the invasion and of the bizarre flight of Haushofer's student Rudolf Hess to Scotland in 1941, Haushofer faded from public life and influence.[13] When his son, Albrecht, was arrested, incarcerated, and eventually murdered for his connection with the attempt on Hitler's life in July 1944, Haushofer was helpless to intervene on his behalf.[14]

The course of Haushofer's career under the Nazis might well be taken as an allegory for the fate of geopolitical ideas in general between 1933 and 1945. Widely known and seriously regarded during the early years of the Nazi regime, geopolitical ideas faded quickly into irrelevance as the pressures arising from diplomatic crises, war, and the execution of Nazi racial plans forced the pace of Hitler's decision making. There is no question, for instance, that Hitler's ideas about the proper conduct of foreign policy and the necessity for expanding the German Lebensraum show a good deal of continuity with Weimar and Wilhelmine currents of imperialist thought.[15] The term *Lebensraum* itself was frequently employed by Hitler in his private and public statements on policy, and his fundamental understanding, such as it was, of the nature of international relations corresponded completely to geopolitical notions of interstate politics as an arena of unending struggle for survival. The power of states, as conceived by Hitler and by geopoliticians, consisted not in economic, cultural, or diplomatic influence in a region but in "dominance over clearly defined spaces."[16]

As many critics have pointed out, however, the precise meaning of the term *Lebensraum* had always been vague from the time of Ratzel through Haushofer to Hitler. For Ratzel, as has already been seen, it had denoted space sufficient to provide a decent standard of living, but not necessarily autarky, for Germany. Haushofer's idea of the meaning of *Lebensraum* and his ideas on how to best attain it evolved constantly throughout the last two decades of his life.[17] Geopolitical concepts and terms, *Lebensraum* among them, clearly were central to Hitler's sense of his mission as Germany's leader. Nonetheless, it would be erroneous to suppose, as has often been done in the Allied countries both in the heat of wartime passion and for decades after the Second World War, that geopolitics or geopoliticians provided some sort of blueprint for Hitler's war. Hitler was influenced by geopolitical ideas and the even older prewar tradition of Wilhelmine German imperialist thought, and he gladly used the pseudo-scientific rhetorical trappings of geopolitics to legitimate his conduct.[18] But his ultimate goals and especially the means by which he attained them were of his own devising. This is particularly clear upon examination of Nazi conduct regarding two issues of central concern for geopoliticians during the Weimar years: German participation in Western colonization of the non-European world and German relations with the Soviet Union.

The reacquisition of African and other overseas colonies was an important part of the geopolitical program for German recovery during the Weimar years.[19] For the Nazis in general, however, and for Adolf Hitler in particular, this aspect of the German geopolitical agenda had very little resonance. The dream of a colonial empire for Germany never remotely rivaled Hitler's obsession with German expansion in the east. Certainly, he paid occasional lip service to the demand for colonies arising among those of his followers afflicted with colonial nostalgia, but the issue was never seriously pursued by the foreign policy apparatus of Hitler's Germany, significantly, until the end of May 1940 with German fortunes at their zenith in the wake of the French collapse and all things seemingly possible.[20] Although he clearly felt that colonies might have some value in the distant future for Germany, events conspired to divert Hitler from serious pursuit of the colonial dream.

From the seizure of power until the outbreak of war Hitler's frequently expressed (and ultimately illusory) conviction of the necessity for a German alliance with England mandated that Germany tread lightly on the touchy and potentially divisive issue of a redistribution of imperial possessions in favor of Germany.[21] At the end of August 1939, on the very eve of the war, in fact, Hitler was still hoping to buy British acquiescence in his European plans by offering to guarantee the position of the British world empire in return for a free hand in the east.[22] And, once war broke out in the autumn of 1939, more pressing concerns and the patent unsuitability of the German navy for the seizure of distant colonies overshadowed the colonial issue. Although Hitler held to vague long-range plans for a return to German overseas colonization, therefore, his views and policies on the question followed paths quite different from those advocated by most Weimar geopoliticians.[23]

The gap between geopolitical doctrine and national socialist practice regarding German foreign policy widens still further when one examines the conduct of German relations with the Soviet Union under Hitler. For Haushofer and many other geopolitical theorists Germany's real enemy lay not in the east (if one overlooked Poland and the successor states of east-central Europe) but in the global maritime predominance of the two allied and culturally related Anglo-Saxon societies of the United States

and the United Kingdom. England, the object of Hitler's sporadic diplomatic courtship, was for the geopoliticians the spider "that has spun a
net of fine political threads over the world."[24] Accordingly, geopoliticians
throughout the 1920s and 1930s pinned their hopes for a successful revanchist German foreign policy to a dream of a continental bloc, embracing
the Soviet Union and Japan, as a counterweight against the British and
American flank powers.[25] For Adolf Hitler, by contrast, the Soviet Union
remained Germany's chief adversary from his days of imprisonment at
Landsberg through the string of triumphs of the late 1930s to the time
the Red Army battered its way into his Berlin bunker in 1945. "A war of
conquest against Russia," as one historian has put it, "was for Hitler the
main means of fulfilling his desire for more Lebensraum."[26]

The key to this, the greatest discordance between geopolitical thought
and Nazi policy, lies in the role of race in the two respective worldviews.
For geopoliticians race was important, but it always remained subordinated to space. The external influences emanating from space, in fact,
did a great deal to shape those characteristics typical of the various races,
according to the geopolitical analysis. Raum, not *Rasse,* was at the core of
their understanding of the world. For Hitler and his closest followers, on
the contrary, race eclipsed all other considerations, including space. The
racial restructuring of German society was at the heart of Nazi domestic policies, and race was equally central to their foreign policy. Operation Barbarossa, the great centerpiece of German foreign policy under
Hitler's leadership, targeted the Soviet Union as the victim of Wehrmacht ferocity out of considerations that were heavily racial in nature.
It was the racial inferiority of the Slavic "subhumans" who populated
Russia's vast agricultural spaces that justified Nazi aggression in the name
of a higher order of humanity, and it was Hitler's perception of the Soviet
Union as the heart of the supposed Jewish Bolshevik conspiracy (and
its position as a center of Jewish population) that made it the target of his
anti-Semitic state policy as well.[27] The deviation of Nazi foreign policy
from geopolitical percepts and the decline in the fortunes of geopolitics under the Nazis, culminating in the late 1930s with open attacks on
geopolitical doctrines by Nazi theorists, originated in conflicting understandings of the significance of race.[28]

To absolve geopolitics of responsibility for the Nazi catastrophe because historians have exaggerated the importance of geopolitics under

Hitler, however, merely replaces one distortion of the past with another. Hans-Adolf Jacobsen, author of a comprehensive and magisterial biography of Karl Haushofer, rightly places Haushofer and the ideas he represented among those elements that did most to justify and legitimate national socialist rule in the popular mind.[29] This judgment is fitting. It is clear, as has been indicated, that those ordinary Germans who fought in the Nazi cause made frequent use of geopolitical terms and ideas to frame to themselves a justification for the state policy in which they were participants. As German troops marched east, they were told again and again, and many seem to have accepted, that this was a justifiable struggle for Lebensraum.[30] The ideas internalized by soldiers at the front played an important role as well in the justification of the war for those at home, be they schoolchildren, radio listeners, or newspaper readers.

If geopolitics under the Nazis became a sort of epidemic mental illness, therefore, as Rolf Hochhuth has suggested, it was something significantly different during the Weimar Republic. In the Weimar era the flowering of geopolitical thought is better described as a misguided but perfectly understandable response to the shattering upheaval of war, defeat, and revolution. The new ideas provided Germans with a way to understand what had happened and, just as importantly, with hope that the results of the war need not be permanent. The message of geopolitics was a hopeful one. The geodeterminism implicit in Adolf Grabowsky's concept of the "heroic earth," of a geocentric approach to history, was mediated by cultural factors such as technology and organizational skill. The German defeat and its devastating results were not implicit in German geography but were the result of mistakes German leaders had made in reading that geography. By reinterpreting the German space not as a passive setting but as an active force shaping the world according to its own laws, geopolitical thinkers offered an optimistic confidence that the world would become better for Germans if only they could decode those laws and act in accordance with them. While lending urgency to their message by warning that Germany was extraordinarily vulnerable, geopoliticians yet insisted that natural geopolitical law presaged a return of German power in central Europe. "In the long run," as Albrecht Penck told Germans, "land and nature are stronger than man."[31] This geodeterministic optimism was as important in promoting the popularity of geopolitics as was its apparent ability to provide a "scientific" explanation for Germany's foreign policy and military disasters during the world war.

This work has also argued that the appeal of geopolitical thought was considerably more widespread in these years than is generally acknowledged. It was precisely the effectiveness of the geopolitical pose as a scientific guide to understanding Germany's troubles and as a Wegweiser to better times that explains this attractive power and that allowed geopolitical ideas to transcend the right. Socialist journalists, liberal democratic academics, romantic novelists, conservative students, and reactionary bureaucrats all looked to the geodeterminist historical and political rhetoric of geopolitics to support their proposals for German recovery. Factors of gender and class do little to explain this broadly based appeal; the geopoliticians were indeed men, and most were educated members of the middle or upper classes, but the ability to meet certain gender and educational criteria was simply a prerequisite, in most cases, for being an active participant in the German public discourse of the day. Instead, the key to the popularity of geopolitics is the shared disaster of war and its aftermath. All had suffered together through German defeat and social chaos. Despite their political differences the need to find an explanation for Germany's problems and hope for the future provided a nexus, a point of intersection where the geodeterminism of politically neutral geopolitical "science" was able to enter the rhetoric of groups that were otherwise widely separated by domestic political differences.

The same dynamic allowed geopolitics not only to bridge the gaps between differing political philosophies but also to surmount barriers between academic disciplines and to link them. Geopolitical ideas were most widely accepted among the geographic and historical professions, but politically engaged academics in many other fields as well found them useful. Jurists, doctors, political scientists, demographers, and sociologists were attracted by the apparent explanatory utility of geopolitics and its ability to add political relevance and currency to their work.[32] Just as the impartiality of geopolitical science eased the way for its acceptance by a variety of political groups, so it functioned to heighten geopolitical appeal to thinkers far beyond the geographic profession. The vagueness and imprecision of key geopolitical concepts may have helped its dissemination between academic disciplines as well. The opaque language of some geopoliticians and the haziness of many geopolitical ideas (Just how binding were geopolitical "laws"? How could the relationship between the environmental influence of geography and culture be systematized?) gave it a superficial compatibility with several fields. Geopolitical insights, many felt, could complement rather than replace existing fields of humanistic investigation.

The governments of the Reich and several of the German states promoted the dissemination of geopolitics. The presence of geopolitics in German schools, from the lower levels through the universities, was the result in part of the pressure of crusading academics. They expected geopolitics to rebuild national harmony, to hone a national determination to obtain revision of the war's outcome through whatever means were necessary, and to shape the way Germans talked and thought about politics and the German state. But the success of geopolitics in reaching Germans owed just as much to the active intervention of educational bureaucrats as to proselytizing academics. The texts that state agencies pushed the schools to adopt and their guidelines for geographical and historical instruction reflected a conviction that geopolitics belonged in the schools in order that young Germans might understand the very influential "earth-dependent" factors that had shaped their state and its history. The national government, through its support for Deutschtum groups that made extensive use of geopolitical terms and ideas, also played a crucial role in helping geopolitics to shape the popular debate about German politics and foreign policy.

This work has also tried to reposition geopolitics in the Weimar context by showing how it incorporated many elements of Weimar modernism. Geopolitical thought was long associated with what was characterized as the "utopian antimodernism" of the Nazi movement, the effort to legitimate and recreate an idealized past German society.[33] But geopoliticians were far from rejecting modernity wholesale. Rather, they exercised a fine eclecticism, blending modern ideas and attitudes with some models from the past. Geopoliticians and thinkers engaged with geopolitics; Haushofer and Martin Spahn, for example, often idealized medieval corporatist political models. And geopolitics was, on the whole, distinctly antiurban, thus distancing itself from what is, perhaps, the central defining feature of modernity. At the same time, however, they hailed the achievements of German technology with marked enthusiasm, embracing them, as did wholehearted modernists, because they promised to transform the world. Geopolitical rhetoric also absorbed many ideas and concepts that were characteristic of the contradictory qualities of Weimar modernism: its antirationalism coupled with a glorification of science, mysticism joined with materialism, and especially the popularity of Darwinist ideas, environmentalism, and racial concepts all helped it make connections with segments of the public outside the historical or geographical professions.

In its Weimar context, geopolitics was a destructive and misleading attempt to give a nomothetic structure to that which cannot be reduced to law, the relationship between geography and politics. The frequently illogical, self-contradictory, and inconsistent quality of geopolitics in the era resulted from the fundamentally misguided attempt to make a science of what is not scientific. Instead of clarifying the manifest possibility of improving Germany's international position through peaceful and economic means, geopolitics dwelt on apocalyptic visions of racial and political conflict and promoted a juvenile, primitive, and ultimately barbaric understanding of international relations. Geopoliticians worked diligently to convince Germans of the inevitability of conflict in central Europe for Germans, and to a large extent they succeeded, helping to make their own dire prophecies self-fulfilling. Ironically, the success of the geopolitical endeavor meant disaster for Germany. Although geopoliticians helped awaken the spatial and power-political awareness that Germans supposedly lacked, Germany then proceeded not to renewed world power but to its most disastrous defeat.

Is geopolitics any more useful today? The term, which was thoroughly discredited by its association with the Nazis, has regained its popularity in recent years.[34] Contemporary geopolitical analysis is certainly less superficial than that practiced in Weimar Germany. Geopolitical studies of international relations today are likely to feature systems analysis, game theory, and sophisticated discussions of linkages or global policy orientations. None of the modern scholars who have dusted off geopolitics and given it a glossy new coat of varnish accept the "organic" concept of the state without qualification, a crucial and healthy departure from the Weimar variant of geopolitics. Despite its updated trappings, however, contemporary geopolitical discourse at times falls into patterns reminiscent of earlier geopolitical thinking. The argument that the borders of states in postcolonial Africa are arbitrary and, thus, bound to be sources of instability and conflict, for example, rests on the subtext that they do not conform to an ethnically or geographically determined "natural" (even "organic") border pattern. This approach to understanding borders is similar to that of early twentieth-century geopoliticians. Prominent German historians, furthermore, have begun to argue once more that

Germany's role in beginning the two world wars depended less upon its political leadership than upon the challenge posed by its central European geographic position.[35] This is a return to geodeterminist principles of historical development with which Weimar geopoliticians were entirely comfortable.

The danger in this revival of geopolitical thinking is that the structure of the word itself is taken too literally, and geography is placed before politics. It is neither incorrect to insist that geography affects politics nor to study the interaction between the two. The fact that Great Britain is an island state has, of course, had a profound impact on the ways in which its economy and political system have developed. In similar fashion America's geographical separation from other world powers in its early years gave it certain opportunities it might not otherwise have enjoyed. In both cases, however, and in many others it has been and will continue to be politics that determines the significance of geography and not the reverse. The politics of France and Germany, for example, have determined the meaning of their geographical interface at their common border. Although the geography of the region has not changed since the Franco-Prussian War or since June of 1940, the politics that infuse that geography with meaning are transformed, and therein lies the change in the significance of that once fateful and currently innocuous juxtaposition of states.

Geopolitics introduced a corrosive and reductivist determinism into the popular and academic understanding of the Weimar-era state system. It threatens today to inject vagueness and a muted determinism into the understanding of interstate relations. This critique of geopolitics, which reduces the role of geography to that of a secondary player in shaping interstate relations, might seem to imply an extreme liberal American position on the relationship between geography and politics, a quasi-Wilsonian view that the world can be remade politically as peoples and nations see fit. Such a position would be as naive and destructive as geopolitical thought has been. Human nature being what it is, plans to remake the world system from the ground up are unlikely to succeed any time in the near future. That system can be improved incrementally, however, as Stresemann and some other European statesmen of his era understood, as long as its failures are recognized as the result of human errors in responding to geography, politics, and culture. The case of Weimar, by contrast, suggests that there is scant hope as long as conflict is attributed to geography rather than to humanity.

Notes

Preface

1. S. D. Brunn and K. A. Mingst, "Geopolitics," in *Progress in Political Geography,* ed. Michael Pacione (London, 1985), 43. For references to the "Institute für Geopolitics" (*sic*) and other various forms of this supposed institute see Brunn and Mingst, "Geopolitics"; Geoffrey Parker, *Western Geopolitical Thought in the Twentieth Century* (London, 1985), 57; Derwent Whittlesey, "Haushofer, The Geopoliticians," in *Makers of Modern Strategy: Military Thought from Machiavelli to Hitler,* ed. Edward Mead Merle (Princeton, N.J., 1944), 388–414; and Hans W. Weigert, *Generals and Geographers: The Twilight of Geopolitics* (New York, 1942). For a brief but better informed general consideration see Peter Slowe, *Geography and Political Power* (London, 1990), 21–23.

2. Hans-Adolf Jacobsen, *Karl Haushofer: Leben und Werk* 1: 248–49, and *Ausgewählter Schriftwechsel, 1917–1946* (Boppard am Rhein, 1979) 2: 152–54.

3. Franz Schoenberner, *Confessions of a European Intellectual* (New York, 1946), 303.

4. As Schoenberner says, although exaggerating Hitler's ignorance, "But nothing is more amusing than the idea that the illiterate Hitler embarked on his career of world conquest after having studied Haushofer's highly abstract and complicated scientific theories about the 'Heartland Europe,' etc." Ibid., 304.

5. Rudolf Kjellén, "Studier öfver Sveriges politiska gränser, "*Ymer* 9 (1899): 283. For a good example of the use of the term in his writings for a German audience before the end of the First World War see Rudolf Kjellén, *Der Staat als Lebensform,* trans. Margarethe Langfeldt (Leipzig, 1917), 46–93.

6. For the position of geopolitics before the war see Ulrich Ante, *Zur Grundlegung des Gegenstandsbereiches der politischen Geographie: Über das 'Politische' in der Geographie* (Stuttgart, 1985), 36–37; Karl-Heinz Harbeck, "Die 'Zeitschrift für Geopolitik' 1924–1944" (Ph.D. diss., Kiel University, 1963), 1. For a contemporary characterization of geopolitics as a product of the war see GStA: NL Vogel; HA I, Rep. 92, no. 21, piece 6 (A. R., "Akademische Auslands- und aussenpolitische Studien," *Frankfurter Zeitung,* 4 February 1926).

7. For Grabowsky's view of political history and its grounding in geopolitics see Adolf Grabowsky, *Staat und Raum. Grundlagen räumlichen Denkens in der Weltpolitik* (Berlin, 1928), 63 ff.; Alfred Hettner, "Methodische Zeit- und Streitfragen. Teil V; Die Geopolitik und die politische Geographie," *GZ* 35 (1929): 332. The same view is found in Richard Hennig,

"Geopolitische Einflüsse auf Deutschland als Wirtschaftsgebiet und als Staat," *GA* 33 (1932): 82.

8. On the founding and circulation, see Harbeck, 1–15, 257–64.

9. Haushofer had monthly broadcasts on Bayerischer Rundfunk between 1924 and 1931 when they were cancelled for a short time. Jacobsen, *Haushofer* 1: 183, 2: 121. On the Dix and Grabowsky broadcasts see BAP: NL Dix; 90 Di 2, folder 7, pieces 44–47 ("Deutsche Stunde in Bayern an Dix," 10. 02. 27, and "Volkswirtschaftsfunk; Vorträge").

10. For analysis of the content of some academic geography journals showing an irregular increase in the frequency of geopolitical articles beginning in the early 1930s see Henning Heske, "German Geographical Research in the Nazi Period: A Content Analysis of the Major Geography Journals, 1925–1945," *PGQ* 5 (1986): 267–81. See also M. Schmidt and H. Haack, *Geopolitischer Typen-Atlas. Zur Einführung in die Grundbegriffe der Geopolitik* (Gotha, 1929); Manfred Langhans-Ratzeburg, *Begriff und Aufgaben der geopolitischen Rechtswissenschaft* (Berlin, 1928); Hugo Hassinger, *Geographische Grundlagen der Geschichte* (Freiburg im Breisgau, 1931).

11. Pechel cited in Volker Mauersberger, *Rudolf Pechel und die 'Deutsche Rundschau' 1919–1933. Eine Studie zur konservativ-revolutionären Publizistik in der Weimarer Republik* (Bremen, 1971), 262; GStA, NL Vogel; HA I, Rep. 92, no. 21, piece 6 (A. R., "Akademische").

12. Otto Maull, review of *Geopolitik*, by Richard Hennig, *ZGEB* (1929): 61.

Chapter 1. Rethinking Geography: The Genesis of German Geopolitics, 1890–1914

1. The term is Mary Louise Pratt's, cited in Anne Godlewska and Neil Smith, eds., *Geography and Empire* (Oxford, 1994), 7.

2. Geert Bakker, *Duitse Geopolitiek, 1919–1945: een imperialistische ideologie* (Utrecht, 1967), 170 ff. For brief accounts of international developments see G. Parker, *Geopolitical Thought*, and W. H. Parker, *Mackinder: Geography as an Aid to Statecraft* (Oxford, 1982).

3. The literature on Mahan and his influence is considerable. For an insightful discussion of his doctrines see William E. Livezey, *Mahan on Sea Power* (Norman, Okla., 1981). For discussion of his impact, and the New Navalism generally, in various settings see Roger Dingman, "Japan and Mahan," 49–66, and Holger H. Herwig, "The Influence of A. T. Mahan upon German Sea Power," 67–84, both in *The Influence of History upon Mahan*, ed. John B. Hattendorf (Newport, R.I., 1991); and Keiichi Takeuchi, "The Japanese Imperial Tradition, Western Imperialism and Modern Japanese Geography," in *Geography and Empire*, ed. Godlewska and Smith, 188–206.

4. Cited in Herwig, 67.

5. Christian Graf von Krockow, *Die Deutschen in ihrem Jahrhundert 1890–1990* (Reinbek bei Hamburg, 1992), 399n.

6. Both within and outside of Germany Mahan has been considered since the Second World War a founder of geopolitics. See, for example, Heinz Gollwitzer, *Geschichte des weltpolitischen Denkens* (Göttingen, 1982), 63; and Margaret Tuttle Sprout, "Mahan: Evangelist of Sea Power," in *Makers of Modern Strategy: Military Thought from Machiavelli to Hitler*, ed. Edward Mead Merle (Princeton, N.J., 1944), 415–45.

7. A. T. Mahan, *The Influence of Sea Power upon History* (1890; reprint, Boston, 1941), 29–35.

8. Ibid.

NOTES TO PAGES 4–7 / 255

9. Mahan put his own political geographical philosophy in the following words in a work published in 1900: "The empire of the sea is doubtless the empire of the world." See A. T. Mahan, *The Problem of Asia* (Boston, 1900), 7.

10. Halford J. Mackinder, "The Geographical Pivot of History," in *Democratic Ideals and Reality* (New York, 1962), 242. This chapter was originally presented as a lecture to the Royal Geographical Society in 1904.

11. *Heartland*, the term for an expanded version of the *pivot*, was used in Mackinder's *Democratic Ideals and Reality*, which first appeared in 1919.

12. Ibid., 109, 260. Mackinder's theory is analogous, although on a global rather than national or continental scale, to the famous "frontier theory" of the American historian Frederick Jackson Turner.

13. As one of his biographers puts it, "Mackinder became one of the most influential thinkers of modern times, helping to determine the course of history through his impact on the external policies of Germany before the war and the United States after it." This is an inflated assessment found in Parker, *Mackinder*, 147. A more recent biographer concedes Mackinder's influence but reaches more judicious conclusions: "However, Mackinder did not contribute in an original way to German ideas of geopolitik [*sic*]. . . . He was the prestigious outsider quoted to buttress established orthodoxy." Brian W. Blouet, *Halford Mackinder: A Biography* (College Station, Tex., 1987), 178.

14. See the account of this in James Trapier Lowe, *Geopolitics and War: Mackinder's Philosophy of Power* (Washington, D.C., 1981), 86–87.

15. Mackinder felt such conflict was inevitable; Haushofer and many of his disciples fervently hoped and believed otherwise. See Blouet, 167.

16. Kjellén, *Der Staat*, v. He also includes *Herrschaftspolitik*, or the science of government and administration; *Ethno-, oder Demopolitik*, the study of ethnicity, population and *Volk; Wirtschaftspolitik*, the science of economics and the state; and *Soziopolitik*, the study of the state as "a society in the specific sense"; ibid., 43 ff. Karl Haushofer would later call Kjellén's book, "The work . . . in which the theory of geopolitics is most clearly developed." Karl Haushofer, "Politische Erdkunde und Geopolitik" in Karl Haushofer, ed., *Bausteine zur Geopolitik* (Berlin, 1928), 59.

17. Kjellén, *Der Staat*, 46.

18. For useful accounts of Ratzel's life and work, see Mark Bassin, "Friedrich Ratzel, 1844–1904," in *Geographers: Biobibliographical Studies* 11 (1987), 123–32; G. Buttmann, *Friedrich Ratzel. Leben und Werk eines deutschen Geographen, 1844–1904* (Stuttgart, 1977); and Woodruff D. Smith, *Politics and the Sciences of Culture in Germany, 1840–1920* (New York, 1991), 142–44, 223–27.

19. For modern assessments of Ratzel's influence see Michel Korinman, *Quand l'Allemagne pensait le monde: Grandeur et décadence d'une géopolitique* (Paris, 1990); Mechtild Rössler, *"Wissenschaft und Lebensraum," Geographische Ostforschung im Nationalsozialismus* (Berlin, 1990), 2; Ante, 32–36; Josef Matznetter, ed. *Politische Geographie* (Darmstadt, 1977), 6–7; Bakker, 170–71; Günter Heyden, *Kritik der deutschen Geopolitik. Wesen und soziale Funktion einer reaktionären soziologischen Schule* (Berlin, 1958), 105–6. For the views of some Weimar geopoliticians on Ratzel's contribution see Otto Maull, *Politische Geographie* (Berlin, 1925), v; and Hennig, "Einflüsse," 82.

20. For an insightful chronicle of theories on natural borders that developed on the other side of the Rhine see Peter Sahlins, "Natural Frontiers Revisited: France's Boundaries since the Seventeenth Century," *AHR* 95 (1990): 1423–51.

21. Ante, 33-34, for example, argues that later writers oversimplified Ratzel's view of the state as an organism.

22. For a discussion of this and other themes in Ratzel's political geography see Mark Bassin, "Imperialism and the nation state in Friedrich Ratzel's political geography," *Progress in Human Geography* (1987): 477-78.

23. Ratzel cited in Karl-Georg Faber, "Zur Vorgeschichte der Geopolitik. Staat, Nation und Lebensraum im Denken deutscher Geographen vor 1914," in *Weltpolitik, Europagedanke, Regionalismus. Festschrift für Heinz Gollwitzer*, ed. Heinz Dollinger and Horst Grunder (Münster, 1982), 396. On the Pan-Germanist view see Roger Chickering, *We Men Who Feel Most German: A Cultural Study of the Pan-German League, 1886-1914* (Boston, 1984), 77-83; and Alfred Kruck, *Geschichte des Alldeutschen Verbandes* (Wiesbaden, 1954), 181-82.

24. Henry Cord Meyer, "Der 'Drang nach Osten' in den Jahren 1860-1914," *Die Welt als Geschichte* 17 (1957): 1-8.

25. Friedrich Ratzel, *Politische Geographie*, 3d ed. (Munich, 1923), 1, 2.

26. Ibid., 3.

27. Ratzel cited in Bassin, "Imperialism," 473.

28. Ratzel, *Politische*, 4. The geodeterminist strain of Ratzel's thinking about the relationship between a state and its geography was recognized clearly by his contemporaries. See, for example, a review of Fredrich Ratzel, *Die Erde und ihr Leben*, by Wilhelm Bölsche, "Eine vergleichende Erdkunde," *DR* 113 (1902): 312-15.

29. Ratzel, *Politische*, 89.

30. For example, Ratzel argued that it was Europe's expanding population and its concomitant flourishing culture that explained European predominance in world politics in his era: "This population-generating power of Europe is the basis of its leading position in the history of humanity for two thousand years. Europe occupies, by virtue of its population power, the position of a superior, culturally powerful homeland toward a great part of the earth. It is in the larger scale what once Rome was as it founded its world empire in the narrower framework of the Mediterranean lands. If one speaks of the victorious dissemination of the white race over the earth, one ought to say more precisely: of the European branch of the white race, since Persians and Indians have not participated in this growth, this expansion, which is actually a symptom and a consequence of the high level of European culture." Ibid., 107.

31. Ratzel introduced the word in 1901 in *Der Lebensraum. Eine biogeographische Studie.* (Munich, 1901). For some discussions of the term, its introduction and impact see Bakker, 170-71; K. Lange, "Der Terminus 'Lebensraum' in Hitlers 'Mein Kampf,'" *VJHZ* 13 (1965): 425-37; Matznetter, *Politische*, 6-8; and Woodruff D. Smith, *The Ideological Origins of Nazi Imperialism* (New York, 1986), 83-86.

32. Friedrich Ratzel, *Anthropo-Geographie oder Grundzüge der Anwendung der Erdkunde auf die Geschichte* (Stuttgart, 1882), 1:116.

33. Ratzel, *Politische*, 155.

34. Kjellén, *Der Staat*, 60.

35. Ratzel, *Politische*, 3: "I therefore call a nation a group of politically joined groups or individuals who need be neither ethnically nor linguistically related but are spatially bound by common ground."

36. Kjellén, *Der Staat*, 22.

37. Alfred Hettner, *Das europäische Rußland. Eine Studie zur Geographie des Menschen* (Leipzig, 1905), 7, 87, 57. Hettner would later become critical of the pretensions of geopolitics although not necessarily of its aims or premises.

38. An interesting account of the Pan-German League's view of the relationship between geography and state power is found in Gerd Fesser, "Die Mutterlauge der Nazis," *Die Zeit*, 8 July 1994, 54. The article is more scholarly than its sensationalistic title suggests.

39. Friedrich Ratzel, *Das Meer als Quelle der Völkergröße. Eine politisch-geographische Studie* (Munich, 1900). For a good example of the key role of oceans in later geopolitical thought see Karl Haushofer, *Geopolitik des Pazifischen Ozeans. Studien über die Wechselbeziehungen zwischen Geographie und Geschichte* (Berlin, 1924).

40. Otto Maull, "Friedrich Ratzel zum Gedächtnis," *ZfG* 5 (1928): 617. Ratzel's prewar influence upon German geography was just as enormous although in different ways. He was cited in a wide variety of settings: for example, he was an influential supporter of German polar exploration and is credited with coining the term *Antarktis* in J. Löwenberg, *Die Entdeckungs- und Forschungsreisen in den beiden Polarzonen* (Leipzig, 1886), 142.

Chapter 2. "The Product and Requirement of a New Age": The Great War and the Transformation of German Geopolitics

1. On the prewar roots of many manifestations of Weimar German culture the best treatment in English is still Peter Gay, *Weimar Culture: The Outsider as Insider* (New York, 1970), 16.

2. Chickering, 74; Jost Hermand, *Der alte Traum vom neuen Reich. Völkische Utopien und Nationalsozialismus* (Frankfurt am Main, 1988), 97.

3. Bassin, "Imperialism," 481.

4. See chapter 4 for Grabowsky. For a discussion of Naumann and the history and definitions of *Mitteleuropa* and some judicious insights into its use by geopoliticians as well see Henry Cord Meyer, *Mitteleuropa in German Thought and Action, 1815–1945* (The Hague, 1955).

5. On Brest-Litovsk and its results the most thorough study is J. W. Wheeler-Bennett, *Brest-Litovsk: The Forgotten Peace, March 1918* (New York, 1936). Rainer Matern, *Karl Haushofer und seine Geopolitik in den Jahren der Weimarer Republik und des Dritten Reiches. Ein Beitrag zum Verständnis seiner Ideen und seines Wirkens* (Ph.D. diss., Karlsruhe, 1978), 53, also addresses the view of the east in German geopolitics but is far too respectful of Haushofer's ideas.

6. Karl Rathjens, "Das Hamburgische Weltwirtschaftsarchiv und seine Bedeutung für die Geographie," *PM* 73 (1927): 161.

7. Albert von Hofmann, *Das deutsche Land und die deutsche Geschichte* (Stuttgart, 1930), 9.

8. Louis von Kohl, *Ursprung und Wandlung Deutschlands. Grundlagen zu einer deutschen Geopolitik* (Berlin, 1932), 5.

9. Arthur Dix, *Geopolitik. Lehrkurse über die geographischen Grundlagen der Weltpolitik und Weltwirtschaft* (Füssen a. Lech, n.d. [1926 ?], 17–18. Emphasis in original.

10. Hennig, "Einflüße," 82.

11. W. Classen, "Die Geopolitik auf der Höheren Schule," *GA* 32 (1931): 17.

12. Karl Haushofer, "Geographische Grundzüge auswärtiger Politik," *SM* 24 (1927): 260.

13. K. Haushofer, "Politische Erdkunde," 60.

14. See for example Karl Haushofer, "Bevölkerungsdruck und Verstädterung im Lichte west-pazifischer Erfahrung," *ZGEB* (1930): 287–300, where he writes of the

"neglected duty" to consider geographical factors, which crippled Staatswissenschaft before the war.

15. On the role of the war in the rise of the new "science" see also Matern, 53-57; Henry Cord Meyer, *Mitteleuropa*, 309; Bakker, 172. A good treatment of the general effect of the war in shaping approaches to German foreign policy can be found in Peter Krüger, *Versailles. Deutsche Aussenpolitik zwischen Revisionismus und Friedenssicherung* (Munich, 1986), 51-59. For another contemporary appraisal of the war as a catalyst to geopolitics see W. Ule, review of *Bausteine zur Geopolitik,* ed. Karl Haushofer, *PM* 75 (1929): 41. Ule writes, "After the war there developed under the influence of political events a wholly new area of knowledge within anthropogeography that is characterized as geopolitics and that has called forth an extensive literature in a short period." See also the essay by Erich von Drygalski, "Die Entwicklung der Geographie seit Gründung des Reiches," *MGGH* 43 (1933): 1-11, in which he notes the postwar emphasis on political geography.

16. Wilhelm Huber, *Politische Geographie. Eine Auswahl, zusammengestellt zur Einführung in geopolitisches Denken* (Munich, 1927), 5, 6.

17. Hettner, though expressing sympathy for geopolitical concerns, argued that it was "a curious error, however, that the geopolitical viewpoint is considered something new and that geography is supposed to have neglected to place itself at the service of politics until now. . . . Only the word 'geopolitics' for these efforts is new, it is a new label for an old thing." Hettner, "Methodische," 335-36. Hettner's annoyance at geopolitical claims to novelty may have been spurred in part by resentment at the neglect of his own earlier work in political geography that these claims reflected.

18. Criticisms of Haushofer's literary style and of the general vagueness of geopolitics are legion. Matern, 42, for example, in an extremely sympathetic assessment still conceded Haushofer's lack of clarity. Alfred Hettner, review of *Deutschland und das Weltbild der Gegenwart,* by Adolf Grabowsky, *GZ* 34 (1928): 308, praises the geopolitical content of the book while decrying the "frequently more obscuring than clarifying expressions" of geopolitics. Walther Vogel, a historian committed to a geopolitical exposition of history, scored Haushofer in 1932, arguing his "baroque, often barely intelligible literary style, (does) not appear to conceal a particular wealth of thought." Walther Vogel, review of *Jenseits der Grossmächte,* ed. Karl Haushofer, *PM* 78 (1932): 150-51. In a review of Haushofer in 1928 J. Sölch wrote that the work was difficult because of the "peculiarity" of the style and concluded devastatingly that "I must fear, unfortunately, that the rapid exhaustion that his lessons produce will hinder their penetration into broader classes of our population." J. Sölch, reivew of *Grenzen in ihrer geographischen und politischen Bedeutung,* by Karl Haushofer, *GZ* 34 (1928): 626.

19. Klaus Kost, *Die Einflüsse der Geopolitik auf Forschung und Theorie der Politischen Geographie von ihren Anfängen bis 1945. Ein Beitrag zur Wissenschaftsgeschichte der Politischen Geographie und ihrer Terminologie unter besonderer Berücksichtigung von Militär- und Kolonialgeographie* (Bonn, 1988), 110.

20. The judgment is Walter Laqueur's made in reference to the writings of the Frankfurt School. It could be applied with equal justice to geopolitics. Walter Laqueur, *Weimar: A Cultural History 1918–1933* (New York, 1974), 63.

21. Dix, *Geopolitik,* 8.

22. Friedrich Leyden, review of *Politische Geographie,* by Otto Maull, *ZGEB* (1926): 364-66.

23. Maull cited in Ante, 44. The effort to separate the fields has, perhaps, been of more interest to geographers since the Second World War than it was at the time. Modern

historians of geography who concede that the two terms were used "more or less synonymously" for some time after Kjellén still hope to salvage the legitimacy of the political geography tradition in Germany by separating it from geopolitics, which they accordingly depict as an unfortunate deviation in the development of an otherwise useful discipline. In the period immediately after the Second World War the German geographer Carl Troll attempted to free academic political geography from the stigma attached to geopolitics by arguing that geopolitics had always been "expressly differentiated from political geography" and that it was never accepted as a part of the academic discipline. As has just been demonstrated, Troll's argument cannot be accepted as a general rule, a fact elucidated at exhaustive length in the recent works of Klaus Kost, who points out that many of the key concepts of geopolitical thought were already present in political geography before the late 1920s. Troll's argument that geopolitics was always suspect among German academic geographers, an argument echoed by Geert Bakker and other later historians of the field, also fails to hold up as a general judgment. See Bakker, 178; Brunn and Mingst, 60; Kost, *Einflüsse*, 280–83; Matznetter, *Politischei*, 2–9; C. Troll, "Die geographische Wissenschaft in Deutschland in den Jahren 1933 bis 1945. Eine Kritik und eine Rechtfertigung, "*Erdkunde* 1 (1947): 18.

24. Lautensach cited in Troll, 333. See also the attempt to distinguish between the two offered in Ernst Tiessen, "Die Eingrenzung der Geographie," *PM* 73 (1927): 8. "Political geography and geopolitics are not the same. The latter is founded upon the conditioning of state relations by nature, the latter more upon mental combinations. Geopolitics is therefore no part of geography."

25. Hennig and Korholz, *Geopolitik*, 1. For Hennig's political associations see BDC, Hennig personnel file, S.II "Antrag zur Bearbeitung der Aufnahme, 17.12.40."

26. Dix to the Twenty-first German Geographical Congress, Breslau, 1–4 June 1925. Reprinted in *VDG* (Berlin, 1926), 222–23.

27. Maull, *Politische Geographie*, 53, 56.

28. Norbert Krebs, review of *Geopolitik*, by Richard Hennig, *GZ* 37 (1931): 557.

29. Ante, for instance, argues that Hugo Hassinger and a few others were writing genuine political geography in the 1920s free of the reductivism and determinism of geopolitics. Books like Hassinger's *Geographische Grundlagen der Geschichte* (Freiburg im Breisgau, 1931), although admittedly no simplistically determinist work, show a reliance on the works of Haushofer, Maull, Ratzel, Kjellén, and others clearly a part of the geopolitical mainstream and use a refined form of geographical determinism reflected in statements such as "The state and its economy are and remain chained to the soil." Hassinger, 7.

30. Cited in Ante, 43.

31. This ironic state of affairs is expressed in the subtitle of Hans Weigert's wartime study of geopolitical ideas, *Generals and Geographers: The Twilight of Geopolitics.*

Chapter 3. Struggle, Survival, Space: The Language of Weimar Geopolitics

1. Smith, *Ideological*, 17.

2. The term *ideology* is treated here in the sense in which it is used by Smith as "a set of ideas employed to facilitate the accomplishment of political action and to justify particular social orders." Smith, *Ideological*, 12.

3. As the observant conservative journalist Paul Fechter noted in the *Deutsche Rundschau*, "*Raum* has become current to a heightened degree in the last few years. . . . One

finds discussions of Raum problems, Raum formation, Raum systems. . . . One begins to sense that it is more than the divinely ordained residing place of our small life, that in the one word *Raum* a sum of the most wonderful things and concepts has been summarized." Paul Fechter, "Der amerikanische Raum," *DR* 55 (1929): 47.

4. Maull, *Politische Geographie*, vi. Emphasis added.

5. Wilhelm Volz, "Lebensraum und Lebensrecht des deutschen Volkes," *DA* 24 (1925): 174.

6. For a discussion of this German view of the war see Modris Eksteins, *Rites of Spring: The Great War and the Birth of the Modern Age* (New York, 1989), 92–94.

7. Unsigned article, "Wir wollen Grossdeutschland," *GB* 1 (1924): 3.

8. Volz, "Lebensraum," 169.

9. Louis von Kohl, *Ursprung und Wandlung*, 565.

10. Karl Haushofer, "Politische Geographie," 53.

11. GStA, HA XII: Zeitgeschichtliche Sammlung, 2, no. 287 ("Ringendes Deutschtum 3. Der Deutsche Osten").

12. "Aufruf des 'Stahlhelm'-Landesverbandes Brandenburg, 2.9.1928," in *Die ungeliebte Republik: Dokumente zur Innen- und Aussenpolitik Weimars 1918–1933*, ed. Wolfgang Michalka and Gottfried Niedhart (Munich, 1980), 251–52.

13. See the discussion of Schmitt's *Grossraum* theory and its relations to geopolitics in Joseph W. Bendersky, *Carl Schmitt: Theorist for the Reich* (Princeton, N.J., 1983), 250–63. For Langhans-Ratzeburg, see below, chapter 4.

14. Maull, *Politische Geographie*, 87.

15. *Lebensraum*, like all geopolitical terms, had a variety of definitions. In addition to the original offered by Ratzel (whose debt to Darwin has been discussed), Haushofer developed a definition focusing on space sufficient for "the maintenance of the life forms (human, animal, plant) that exist therein," related to such factors as the ability to provide food and alleviate "excessive" population density. See Jacobsen, *Haushofer*, 2: 247.

16. Richard Hennig and Leo Korholz, *Einführung in die Geopolitik* (Leipzig, 1934), 1. The book first appeared in 1933 and went through three printings within one year. For similar views see Wütschke, *Erdball*, 9.

17. Hennig argued that geopolitics had created a "science of boundaries." Hennig and Korholz *Geopolitik*, 107.

18. Hans Golcher, "Grenzstruktur und Staatlicher Organismus," *ZfG* 4 (1927): 811.

19. Karl Haushofer, *Grenzen in ihrer geographischen und politischen Bedeutung* (Berlin, 1927), 98.

20. "There are books that distinguish themselves through an objective usefulness, usually grounded in an elementary clarity of concept," wrote Otto Maull. "These are books for which the highest praise culminates in the fact that they fill that well-known 'gap in the literature.' Haushofer's *Grenzen* most decidedly does not belong among them. The gap in which it might have fit was there. . . . But . . . it was in itself far too small to have absorbed what Haushofer has made, creating strongly, indeed powerfully, from an astonishing inner wealth." Otto Maull, review of *Grenzen in ihrer geographischen und politischen Bedeutung*, by Karl Haushofer, *ZGEB* (1929): 62.

21. The terms *Volk* and *volkish* require clarification, especially because their relationship to geopolitics is discussed at some length below. Their use here follows that of George Mosse who described *Volk*, as used in the Weimar era, as referring to "the union of a group of people with a transcendental 'essence'. . . . The essential element here is the linking of

the human soul with its natural surroundings, with the 'essence' of nature." George Mosse, *The Crisis of German Ideology: Intellectual Origins of the Third Reich* (New York, 1964), 4.

22. Karl Haushofer, "Die Bedeutung der südlichen Grenzzone für die volksdeutsche Arbeit," *GR* 6 (1929): 155. Albrecht Haushofer devoted an entire book to the subject in *Pass-Staaten in den Alpen* (Berlin, 1928).

23. Sieger was at this time deputy chairman of the German Geographic Congress. See his address reprinted in "Die geographische Lehre von den Grenzen und ihre praktische Bedeutung," *VDG* (Berlin, 1926): 200-203. On his role in geographical research in the volkish movement see Rössler, 53, and below.

24. Johann Sölch, *Die Auffassung der 'natürlichen Grenzen' in den wissenschaftlichen Geographie* (Innsbruck, 1924), 49-50.

25. Albrecht Haushofer, *Pass-Staaten,* 7.

26. See the discussion of this belief in David L. Sills, ed., *The International Encyclopedia of the Social Sciences* (New York, 1968), s.v. "Environmentalism," by O. H. K. Spate; and R. Peet, "The Social Origins of Environmental Determinism," *AAAG* 75 (1985): 309-33.

27. Hassinger, 20.

28. See Otto Maull, "Die Umwertung des menschlichen Lebensraumes in näher und ferner Zukunft," *ZfG* 5 (1928): 87. A similar argument is made in C. Ittameier, "Geopolitische Einflüsse auf die Erhaltung und Vermehrung der Eingeborenen Bevölkerung Ostafrika in Alter und Neuer Zeit," *ZfG* 1 (1924): 497-509.

29. The term is from David N. Livingstone (Queen's University, Belfast), "Climate's Moral Economy: Science, Race, and Place in Post-Darwinian British and American Geography" (paper presented to an International Conference on Geography and Empire, Queen's University, Kingston, Ontario, 8-10 April 1991). See idem, in *Geography and Empire,* ed. Godlewska and Smith, 132-54.

30. The phrase is from the title of Hans Grimm's novel of 1926, which had enormous impact and sold hundreds of thousands of copies. For discussions of its geopolitical aspects and role in geopolitical thought see, respectively, Smith, *Ideological,* 218-22, and Peter Zimmermann, "Kampf um Lebensraum. Ein Mythos der Kolonial- und der Blut-und-Boden-Literatur," in Horst Denkler and Karl Prümm, eds., *Die deutsche Literatur im Dritten Reich* (Stuttgart, 1976), 165-82.

31. Dietmar Petzina, Werner Abelshauser, and Anselm Faust, eds., *Sozialgeschichtliches Arbeitsbuch* (Munich, 1978), 3: 22, 27. In 1910 the population density per square kilometer had been 120 persons; in 1925 it was 133 persons.

32. For a discussion of the effect of demographic changes on the economic prospects of the age cohort of 1900 see Detlev Peukert, *Die Weimarer Republik. Krisenjahre des klassischen Moderne* (Frankfurt am Main, 1987), 20. For some examples of geopolitically oriented uses of the argument that Germany had insufficient space for the needs of its people see the anonymous article "Die Ukraine und Deutschlands Zukunft," *SM* 21 (1924): 153 ff.; Alois Fischer, "Zur Frage der Tragfähigkeit des Lebensraumes," *ZfG* 2 (1925): 842-58; Albrecht Haushofer, "Bemerkungen zum Problem der Bevölkerungsdichte auf der Erde," *ZfG* 3 (1926): 789-97; Herbert Martens, review of *Volk ohne Raum,* by Hans Grimm, *DR* 53 (1926): 294-97; and Hermann Ullmann, review of *Volk ohne Raum,* by Hans Grimm, *DA* 26 (1927): 176-78.

33. Gerhard von Janson, "Raumwirtschaft," *GB* 4 (1927): 29.

34. On his positions in the Reich Statistical Office see BDC, Burgdörfer personal file, "Vorschlag zur Ernennung"; on his position in the Reich Committee on Population

Questions, see BAP, RMdI 15.01/26233/1, Bl. 11-12; "Der Präsident des Reichsgesundheitsamts an den Reichsministerium des Innern," 13 December, 1929; and below, chapter 3.

35. Friedrich Burgdörfer, *Volk ohne Jugend. Gerburtenschwund und Überalterung des deutschen Volkskörpers* (Berlin, 1932), xiii-xiv.

36. There were exceptions, however, such as Karl Haushofer, who felt Germany was overpopulated but was much more enthusiastic about expanding eastward rather than in colonies.

37. Burgdörfer, *Volk ohne Jugend*, 38.

38. Ibid., 84, 419. For a good brief treatment of official approaches to fertility and womanhood under the Nazis see Robert Proctor, *Racial Hygiene: Medicine under the Nazis* (Cambridge, Mass., 1988), 118-30.

39. Fischer, 858.

40. See below, chapter 3.

41. This misperception is common in works that identify geopolitical thought in the period too narrowly with the work of Karl Haushofer. Lothar Gruchmann's statement that "die geopolitische Schule Karl Haushofers sah eine Neuaufteilung der Erde in mehrere regionale Kontinentalsysteme voraus, die das Zeitalter der überseeischen Reiche und das freien Welthandels beenden würde" is accurate as far as it goes, but Haushofer's was clearly not the only variant of geopolitical thought. The same is true of Klaus Hildebrand's consideration of geopolitical thought, which concentrates on a later period (the mid- to late-1930s when geopolitics was, in fact, generally opposed to overseas colonies) and relies heavily on Haushofer. Heide Gerstenberger takes a broader view of geopolitics and recognizes both strains of imperialist thinking in geopolitical propaganda. See Lothar Gruchmann, *Nationalsozialistische Grossraumordnung. Die Konstruktion einer 'deutschen Monroe Doktrin'* (Stuttgart, 1962), 20-21; Klaus Hildebrand, *Vom Reich zum Weltreich. Hitler, NSDAP und koloniale Frage 1919-1945* (Munich, 1969), 375; and Heide Gerstenberger, *Der revolutionäre Konservatismus. Ein Beitrag zur Analyse des Liberalismus* (Berlin, 1969), 27.

42. This approach helped link geopolitics to the wave of romantic nostalgia centered on the old empire during the Weimar years. Nostalgic colonialist sentiment made the decade of the 1920s the golden age of the German colonial novel, a point noted by Horst Grunder in *Geschichte der Deutschen Kolonien* (Paderborn, 1985), 218.

43. Erich Obst, "Wir fordern unsere Kolonien zuruck!" *ZfG* 3 (1926): 153-55. For similar arguments see this entire issue, particularly the articles by Walter Behrmann, "Die geopolitische Stellung Neuguinea vor und nach dem Weltkriege," 207-13, and Karl Haushofer, "Das deutsche Volk und sein Südsee-Inselreich," 201-6, both in *ZfG* 3 (1926), written at a time when Haushofer was still clearly in favor of overseas colonies, or any of the following: Arthur Dix, *Weltkrise und Kolonialpolitik. Die Zukunft zweier Erdteile* (Berlin, 1932), 28-29; Kurt Godav, "Die Notwendigkeit der Kolonien," *DA* 28 (1929): 233-35; Hans Grimm, "Die neue Furcht vor Kolonien," *GB* 4 (1928): 262-65.

44. Friedrich Burgdörfer, *Der Geburtenrückgang und seine Bekämpfung. Die Lebensfrage des deutschen Volkes,* Veröffentlichungen aus dem Gebiete der Medizinalverwaltung. 27 Vols. (Berlin, 1929), 2: 141, 160.

45. Johann Sölch, "Raum und Zahl. Die Zukunftsfrage des deutschen Volkes," *GZ* 39 (1933): 40-42. Other geographers shared the view that the geographical establishment had to take cognizance of Burgdörfer's writings. See the effusive review of Burgdörfer's book by Friedrich Tamss, "Die Lebensaussichten des deutschen Volkes," *PM* 79 (1933): 60-62.

46. Haushofer's close familiarity with Anglo-Saxon geopolitical theories is beyond question. His wife, for example, translated the Englishman James Fairgrieve's book *Geography and World Power* into German in 1925, and Haushofer wrote the introduction for the German edition. See James Fairgrieve, *Geographie und Weltmacht*, trans. Martha Haushofer, (Berlin, 1925).

47. Josef März, "Das Schicksal überseeischer Wachstumsspitzen (Die Stützpunkte der grossen Mächte. Grundlagen und Entwicklung)," in *Zur Geopolitik der Selbstbestimmung*, ed. Karl Haushofer (Munich, 1923), 266, 454.

48. Ibid., 294-95.

49. Karl Haushofer, *Geopolitik des Pazifischen*, 124.

50. Josef März, *Landmächte und Seemächte* (Berlin, 1928), 35.

51. See chapters 4 and 8 for discussions of these issues.

52. Von Kohl, *Ursprung und Wandlung*, 5.

Chapter 4. The New Weapon: Geopolitics in Weimar Culture and Politics

1. Jacobsen, *Haushofer*, 2: 132; "Karl Haushofer to Dr. Klesse," 6 February 1933.

2. Mark Bassin notes that the affinity between Marxist determinism and some strands of geopolitical thought in the period "deserves further research." Mark Bassin, "Race contra Space: The Conflict between German *Geopolitik* and National Socialism," *PGQ* (1987): 132.

3. For recent discussions of these and other characteristics of Weimar modernism see Alexander von Bormann and Horst Albert Glaser, eds., *Deutsche Literatur. Eine Sozialgeschichte, Vol. 9, Weimarer Republik-Drittes Reich* (Reinbek bei Hamburg, 1983); Jost Hermand and Frank Trommler, *Die Kultur der Weimarer Republik* (Frankfurt am Main, 1988); Peter Reichel, *Der schöne Schein des Dritten Reiches. Faszination und Gewalt des Faschismus* (Frankfurt am Main, 1993), 48-78; Stephen Lamb and Anthony Phelan, "Weimar Culture: The Birth of Modernism," in *German Cultural Studies: An Introduction,* ed. Rob Burns (Oxford, 1995), 53-99.

4. Peukert, 166.

5. Peukert writes, "Aber die Einstellungen zur Modernisierung lassen sich nicht so einfach in die Kategorien: hie 'Fortschritt' und hie 'Reaktion' einteilen, schon weil die Modernisierungsprozesse selber sich widersprüchlich auswirkten" [But attitudes toward modernization are not so easily divided into categories, here 'Progress' and here 'Reaction,' since the process of modernization took effect inconsistently]. Peukert, 23. Laqueur makes a similar point: "The attempt to classify the intelligentsia on political lines is fraught with danger. Cultural life is not parliamentary; most of the issues debated are not political, and votes are not usually given according to party affiliation. The cultural avant-garde, to give but one example, is by no means identical in composition with the advocates of political revolution." Laqueur, 41.

6. Eksteins, xv-xvi: "Introspection, primitivism, abstraction, and myth making in the arts, and introspection, primitivism, abstraction and myth making in politics, may be related manifestations. Nazi kitsch may bear a blood relationship to the highbrow religion of art proclaimed by many moderns."

7. On Versailles as an integrating factor see, among others, Sebastian Haffner, *Von Bismarck zu Hitler. Ein Rückblick* (Munich, 1987), 183; Andreas Hillgruber, "Kontinuität und Diskontinuität in der deutschen Aussenpolitik von Bismarck bis Hitler," in

Grossmachtpolitik und Militarismus im 20. Jahrhundert (Düsseldorf, 1974), 24; and Krüger, *Versailles,* 30. The debate over the real and perceived failings of the treaty has produced an extensive historiography over the past seventy years, beginning with John Maynard Keynes's attack on the provisions of the treaty in 1919. The best representation of Versailles as a social-psychological burden for the Republic is in Karl Dietrich Bracher, *Die Auflösung der Weimarer Republik* 2d ed. (Stuttgart, 1957); for the argument that the real, rather than the psychological, burdens of the treaty were unbearable for the Republic see Ludwig Zimmerman, *Studien zur Geschichte der Weimarer Republik* (Erlangen, 1957).

8. Popular resentment of the treaty was fanned by officially subsidized propaganda campaigns in which committees of lawyers, historians, and others (including the geopolitically influenced historian Paul Herre) produced learned briefs condemning the Versailles settlement. See Ulrich Heinemann, *Die verdrängte Niederlage. Politische Öffentlichkeit und Kriegsschuldfrage in der Weimarer Republik* (Göttingen, 1983), 13-14, 122-23, and 152-54. For a good example of geopolitics in Herre's history see Paul Herre, *Spanien und Portugal* (Berlin, 1929), the twelfth volume in the Weltpolitische Bücherei series edited by Adolf Grabowsky.

9. For an example of the geopolitical attack on Versailles see Ernst Tiessen, "Der Friedensvertrag von Versailes und die Politische Geographie," *ZfG* 1 (1924): 203-20.

10. Bernhard Kellermann, *Der Tunnel* (Berlin, 1913).

11. See Peter S. Fisher, *Fantasy and Politics: Visions of the Future in the Weimar Republic* (Madison, Wis., 1991), particularly p. 56 and his description of the plots of the films "Die neue Kolonie" and "Der Kampf ums Gold" on p. 107. See also the discussion in Hermand and Trommler, 58-64.

12. The quotation from Graf Coudenhove-Kalergi is in Hermand and Trommler, 59. See also Reichel, 53-56.

13. See Laqueur, 32-34, for a good treatment of the German obsession with technological progress in this period and of the heroic view of science and scientists.

14. Max Krahmann, "Kapital, Technik und Geopolitik," *ZfG* 4 (1927): 859. The subject of the article is the necessity of improved agricultural technology for German farmers.

15. Bruno Krüger, "Von Deutschlands Weltpolitischer Aufgabe," *ZfG* 3 (1926): 808.

16. Ibid., 813.

17. Ibid., 816.

18. Josef März, *Die Ozeane in der Politik und Staatenbildung* (Breslau, 1931), 9, argues that technology changed the geopolitics of maritime competition. Karl Haushofer, *Geopolitik des Pazifischen,* 216, argues that states will use radio to push claims out over empty oceans and that one result may be "the gigantic stretch Manila-Seattle-Panama-New York, more than half the earth's surface, shall be considered American coastal trade and remain closed to rivals."

19. Erich Maschke, "Der geopolitische Film," *ZfG* 5 (1928): 275, 277.

20. Arthur Dix, "Wirtschaftsstruktur und Geopolitik," *Volkswirtschaftliche Blätter* 28 (1929): 467. (Found in BAP: NL Dix, 90 Di 1, folder 63, pp. 240-49).

21. Dix cited in Paul Langhans, "Die 21. Tagung des Deutschen Geographentages zu Breslau in der Pfingstwoche 1925," *PM* 71 (1925): 150.

22. Johannes Wütschke, "Geopolitik und europäischer Luftverkehr," *ZfG* 1 (1924): 221.

23. Hans Hochholzer, "Zur Geopolitik des Flugwesens," *ZfG* 7 (1930): 248, 242.

24. Stephen Kern, *The Culture of Time and Space, 1880-1918* (Cambridge, Mass., 1983), 317.

25. Dix, "Wirtschaftsstruktur," 467; Hochholzer, "Flugwesens," 245.

26. For the emphasis on location see, in addition to Hochholzer, Wütschke, "Luft-verkehr," 221; Walther Vogel, *Das neue Europa, und seine historisch-geographischen Grundlagen,* 3d ed. (Bonn, 1925), 91; "Home harbor" from Heinz Schmalz, "Politik im Luftraum," *ZfP* 19 (1929-30): 786, 789.

27. See the map depicting Germany's vulnerability to air attack, for example, in Karl Springenschmid, *Die Staaten als Lebewesen. Geopolitisches Skizzenbuch* (Leipzig, 1933), 3.

28. Eksteins, 322.

29. The analogy to the "scramble for Africa" at the end of the nineteenth century was drawn in Gustav Fester, "Polarpolitik," *ZfG* 7 (1930): 802.

30. Richard Hennig, "Geopolitische Wirkungen des beginnenden Weltluftverkehrs," *GZ* 34 (1928): 586.

31. Fester, "Polarpolitik," 803, 805.

32. Ludwig Quessel, "Kurze Chronik," *SoM* 61 (1924): 315. For the role of technology in creating a German interest in the poles see also K. Lampe, "Versuch eine Politischen Geographie der Polargebiete," *GA* 31 (1930): 105-110. The geopolitical reading of the future of polar politics was less than clairvoyant. The poles have remained devoid of political significance and have, in fact, been distinguished in the twentieth century as regions of exemplary international cooperation. This applies even to disagreements between the United States and the Soviet Union in the darkest days of the cold war. Presumably, this is the result of the absence of practical value of the Arctic and Antarctic in the eyes of the parties involved. The predictions of geopoliticians tell us more about their own preoccupations than about the political geographic reality of the poles. Their Darwinian obsession with the role of struggle in state relations precluded the geopoliticians from envisioning the harmonious future of polar politics.

33. Geopolitical writers saw urbanization as a source of immorality, infertility, and crime. See, for some examples, Friedrich Burgdörfer, "Stadt oder Land? Berechnungen und Betrachtungen zum Problem der deutschen Verstädterung," *ZfG* 10 (1933): 105-13; Karl Haushofer, "Bevölkerungsdruck und Verstädterung"; Elisabeth Pfeil "Die deutschen Juden als Beispiel für das Aussterben bei Verstädterung," *ZfG* 10 (1933): 113-18.

34. Klaus Bergmann, *Agrarromantik und Grossstadtfeindschaft,* Marburger Abhandlungen zur Politischen Wissenschaft (Meisenheim am Glan, 1970), 20: 179.

35. Ibid., 182-85.

36. Louis von Kohl, *Ursprung und Wandlung,* 572-73.

37. From its inception as a modern discipline German geography was linked with German anthropological racial theorizing through the geographic subdiscipline of *Völkerkunde* practiced by Karl Ritter, among others. See Robert Proctor, "From *Anthropologie* to *Rassenkunde* in the German Anthropological Tradition," in *Bones, Bodies, Behavior: Essays on Biological Anthropology,* ed. George W. Stocking, Jr. (Madison, 1988), 140.

38. Hassinger, *Geographische,* 24, 29.

39. Hennig and Korholz, *Geopolitik,* 292.

40. Von Hofmann, *Das deutsche Land,* 9.

41. Albrecht Haushofer, review of *The Revolt against Civilization,* by Lothrop Stoddard, *DR* 51 (1925): 54.

42. Bakker, 173, 177; Heyden, 119 ("Die Geopolitik ist ein eklektisches Sammelsurium von einzelnen Leitsätzen der dekadenten irrationalen Philosophie, gestützte auf den geographischen Determinismus und den sozialen Darwinismus.")

43. On this issue, incidentally, geopoliticians parted ways with Spengler. They were critical of what they considered Spengler's insufficient attention to racial factors in German destiny and his imprecision in discussing racial categories. See Otto Mayr, "Die räumliche Ausdehnung des abendländischen Kulturkreises in Oswald Spenglers 'Unter-gang des Abendlandes'," *ZfG* 1 (1924): 807-10. On Spengler's misgivings about the utility of race see Laqueur, 93.

44. H. Kotthaus, "Die Grossmächte nach den Weltkrieg (Nach Kjellén Haushofer)," *RF,* 16 May 1931, 5.

45. See, for example, the reprint in the *Zeitschrift für Geopolitik* of the speech by Hans von Lindeiner-Wildau, a member of the German National People's Party, to the Reichs-tag, entitled "Zur Führerfrage," *ZfG* 3 (1926): 196-99.

46. Haushofer cited in Kotthaus, pt. 6, 18 June 1931, 4.

47. Walter Benjamin, "Das Kunstwerk im Zeitalter seiner technischen Reproduzier-barkeit," in *Schriften,* ed. T. Adorno (Frankfurt am Main, 1955), 1: 396-97.

48. See the maps and analysis in chapter 7 below on geopolitical cartography.

49. Robert Fox, "Die Forderungen des Verbandes deutscher Hochschullehrer der Geographie, "*GA* 29 (1928): 70.

50. Hans Mühlestein, "Deutschland in der Ost-West-Spannung," *ZfG* 3 (1926): 6-7.

51. Colin Ross, "Die Einschaltung des Irrationalen in die Rationalisierung," *ZfG* 7 (1930): 860.

52. Heinrich Block, "Eurasien," *ZfG* 3 (1926): 8.

53. See the sketch of Banse and his work in chapter 4 below.

54. Erich Günther, "Künstlerische Geographie," *Die Tat* 16 (1925): 824. For a good ex-amination of *Die Tat,* its publicistic activities and the role of organic thinking in its view of states and peoples see Hans-Paul Brunzel, '*Die Tat' 1918–1933. Ein publizistischer Angriff auf die Verfasung von Weimar innerhalb der 'konservativen Revolution'"* (Ph.D. diss., Bonn, 1952), 47-50.

55. Günther, "Künstlerische Geographie," 824.

56. Hermann Lautensach, "Geopolitik und Schule," *GA* 28 (1927): 342.

57. Karl Haushofer, *Geopolitik des Pazifischen,* 1.

58. For the intriguing background of the magazine and the institute see Michael Huhn, "'Europäische Gespräche'—Eine aussenpolitische Zeitschrift der Weimarer Zeit," in *Wissenschaftliche Verantwortung und Politische Macht,* ed. Klaus Jürgen Gantzel (Berlin, 1986), 65-185.

59. Otto Forst de Battaglia, "Geopolitik," *EG* 10 (1932): 24-25.

60. Mark Bassin has argued persuasively that racial and geopolitical ideas clashed with one another: This may be true for the Nazi period, and certainly they were not easy to harmonize with one another in terms of formal logic, but such an analysis is certainly inaccurate for the Weimar era. As has been seen, geopolitical and racial ideas coexisted peacefully in the works of many Weimar intellectuals. Bassin's focus is on the roots of German geopolitics in scientific materialism and determinism, a valid approach but one that overlooks the roots of geopolitics in nineteenth-century romantic concepts of the interaction of geography and humanity. In this sense geopolitics shared important antira-tionalist elements with the racial ideology of the Nazis that developed out of the volkish movement. Battaglia clearly recognized the romantic element in the ancestry of geopoli-tics, and a similar point has been made recently in Faber, 389-406. See Bassin, "Race," 115-34.

61. Battaglia, "Geopolitik," 31.

62. Ibid., 34.

63. Cited in Hennig and Korholz, *Geopolitik*, 98.

64. Karl Haushofer et al., eds., *Bausteine*, 48.

65. Otto Maull, *Politische Geographie*, 46.

66. Karl Haushofer, "Das erwachende Asien," *SM* 24 (1926): 121.

67. Ibid.

68. As Jeffrey Herf has written, "The reactionary modernists combined political reaction with technological advance. Where German conservatives had spoken of technology or culture, the reactionary modernists taught the German Right to speak of technology and culture." Jeffrey Herf, "Comments on Reactionary Modernist Components of Nazi Ideology," in *The Rise of the Nazi Regime: Historical Reassessments*, ed. Charles S. Maier, Stanley Hoffmann, and Andrew Gould (Boulder, 1986), 38. See also the treatment of this question in Jeffrey Herf, *Reactionary Modernism: Technology, Culture and Politics in Weimar and the Third Reich* (Cambridge, Eng., 1984).

69. Gruchmann, 9.

70. According to George Mosse, Nazi racialists repudiated Darwinian evolutionism for just this reason while Darwin's focus on struggle was retained. Mosse, 103.

71. That this was so is acknowledged in Bassin, 132. An excellent example is Hennig and Korholz, *Geopolitik*, which makes extensive use of a combination of racial and geopolitical ideas.

72. Theodor Dorn, "Vom deutschen Sterben," *GB* 1 (1924): 103. See also Friedrich Ebeling, "Bevölkerungspolitische Gefahren für die deutschen Minderheiten," *GR* 5 (1928): 174–76; Karl Christian von Loesch, "Schutzarbeit und Schutzbundtagung 1927," *GR* 4 (1927): 2–3; and Hans Harmsen, "Das deutsche Volk hat aufgehört ein wachsendes Volk zu sein!" *VR* 4 (1928): 385–87.

73. Klaus Ebhardt, "Bevölkerungspolitik und Raumnot," *GB* 4 (1928): 224.

74. Ibid., 244. Ebhardt also addressed the societal position of women in an atypically straightforward manner, arguing that legalized abortion in the Weimar Republic would serve a useful selective purpose in helping to eliminate low-grade human life. Abortion, he wrote, "possesses for the moment a not-unfavorable selective role primarily through prevention of the birth of the inferior" (223).

75. Joachim Petzold, *Wegbereiter des deutschen Faschismus. Die Jungkonservativen in der Weimarer Republik* (Cologne, 1978), 188.

76. Max Hildebert Boehm, cited, ibid., 188.

77. Adolf Helbok, "Unterbauung der grenz- und auslandsdeutschen Geschichtswissenschaft durch Landesgeschichte auf Grund gesamtdeutscher Siedlungsforschung," *DR* 52 (1926): 249; Kurt Trampler, "Der Lebensausgleich zwischen Staat und Volk," *DR* 58 (1932): 165.

78. Rudolf Pechel, "Karl Haushofer. Zu seinem 60. Geburtstag," *DR* 55 (1929): 167–68.

79. Ewald Banse, "Landschaft und Volkheit als Kernbegriffe der Geographie," *GA* 34 (1933): 215. *Volkheit* Banse defined as "a destiny-community of people of the same or related blood within a distinct landscape style" (217).

80. Gordon Craig, *Germany 1866–1945* (New York, 1978), 563.

81. W. Freiherr von Gayl, "Die Bedeutung des Ostens in der deutschen Volkspolitik," *VR* 4 (1928): 568.

82. See, for example, Edgar Julius Jung, *Die Herrschaft der Minderwertigen. Ihr Zerfall und ihre Ablösung durch ein neues Reich* 1929; reprint, 30 (Berlin, 1930), 91.

83. See the criticism of Naumann in Martin Spahn, "Mitteleuropa," *VR* 1 (1925): 36-37.

84. Martin Spahn, "Grossdeutsch," *GB* 2 (1925): 177-78. On the role of geopolitical ideas in Spahn's volkish writings see Gabriele Clemens, *Martin Spahn und der Rechtskatholizismus in der Weimarer Republik* (Mainz, 1983), 104-17.

85. Spahn, "Mitteleuropa," 4.

86. See the discussion of the origins of this idea in Hans-Dietrich Schultz, "Deutschlands 'natürliche' Grenzen. 'Mittellage' und 'Mitteleuropa' in der Diskussion der Geographen seit dem Beginn des 19. Jahrhunderts," *GG* 15 (1989): 248-81. Schultz points to a new variant of Mitteleuropa theorizing that began with Joseph Partsch's 1903 book *Central Europe*, which appeared in German in 1904 under the title *Mitteleuropa*. With this work, as with Naumann's, the term drew more upon a combination of geography with political power and economics than upon ethnicity or race, and demographic change as such played no role as a legitimating factor.

87. M. Friedrichsen, "'Deutschland' als 'natürliche' Grosslandschaft Mittel-Europas," *ZfG* 4 (1927): 429.

88. Theodor Dorn, "Der Weg nach dem Osten," *GB* 4 (1927): 34.

89. Johann Thies, *Die Staaten als völkische Lebensräume. Für den Erdkunde- und Geschichtsunterricht bearbeitet* (Dresden, 1933), 17.

90. For a discussion of the revival of the theory of the Mittellage see Jürgen Kocka, "Kritik und Identität. Nationalsozialismus, Alltag und Geographie," *NG* 33 (1986): 890-97.

91. Karl Haushofer, "Grundlagen, Wesen und Ziele der Geopolitik," in *Bausteine zur Geopolitik*, ed. Karl Haushofer (Berlin, 1928), 34. The same observation has been made recently in Willi Oberkrome, *Volksgeschichte. Methodische Innovation und völkische Ideologisierung in der deutschen Geschichtswissenschaft 1918-1945* (Göttingen, 1993), 24.

92. For an account of the founding see *PM* 70 (1924): 37.

93. For an account of the role of geopolitics in the VDA see Hans-Adolf Jacobsen, ed., *Hans Steinacher. Bundesleiter des VDA 1933-37* (Boppard am Rhein, 1970), especially the introduction and 1-43. See also Barbara Vogel, "Der Verein für das Deutschtum im Ausland (VDA) an der Hamburger Universität in der Weimarer Republik," *Zeitgeschichte* 16 (1988): 12-21.

94. For information on the Deutscher Schutzbund (DSB) and similar groups, see Karl-Heinz Grundmann, *Deutschtumspolitik zur Zeit der Weimarer Republik,* Beiträge zur baltischen Geschichte (Hannover-Dohren, 1977), 7: 123-88; Petzold, 98-103; Hans-Joachim Schwierskott, "Arthur Moeller van den Bruck und die Anfänge des Jungkonservativismus in der Weimarer Republik. Eine Studie über Geschichte und Ideologie des revolutionären Nationalismus" (Ph.D. diss., Erlangen, 1960), 92-103; and Kurt Sontheimer, *Antidemokratisches Denken in der Weimarer Republik. Die politischen Ideen des deutschen Nationalismus zwischen 1918 und 1933* (Munich, 1968), 247-48.

95. Grundmann, 123.

96. Ibid., 131-33, 185.

97. Karl Christian von Loesch and A. Hillen Ziegfeld, eds., *Volk unter Völkern. Bücher des Deutschtums* (Breslau, 1925). See the brief but enthusiastic assessment of the work by the geopolitician Albrecht Haushofer, review of *Volk unter Völkern,* ed. Karl Christian von Loesch and A. Hillen Ziegfeld, *ZGEB* (1926): 206.

98. Albrecht Penck, "Deutscher Volks- und Kulturboden," in *Volk unter Völk-ern. Bücher des Deutschtums*, ed. Karl Christian Loesch and A. Hillen Ziegfeld (Breslau, 1925) 63.

99. Ibid., 70. See the use of the map in the section "Karten zur Geopolitik" in one of the Weimar era's most popular geography texts; Albert Scheer, ed., *Fischer-Geistbeck Stufenatlas für höhere Lehranstalten* (Bielefeld, 1927), II.

100. See the correspondence between Boehm and Karl Haushofer in Jacobsen, *Haushofer*, 2: 104, which expresses Haushofer's personal misgivings about the uses of volk-ish theory.

101. See BAP: 61 Schu 1, folder 4, pieces 21-22, "Jahresbericht des Deutschen Schutzbundes, 1 May 1926 to 1 May 1927."

102. Ibid., piece 27: "zone of ethnic mixture," translated here from *Völkermischgebiet*, was used by geopoliticians as well. See the discussion of the term, for example, in Johannes Wütschke, *Unsere Erde. Erdkundliches Lehrbuch für höhere Schulen auf der Grundlage des Arbeitsunterrichts* (Leipzig, n.d.), 133-34.

103. Ibid., pieces 31, 28.

104. See BAP: 61 Schu 1, folder 5, piece 9, "Jahresbericht, 1929", p. 76.

105. See BAK: NL 160 (Pechel), folder 121, "Vorläufige Tagesordnung, 10. Bundes-tagung, 14-16 Mai 1929, Salzburg." According to his biographer, Rainer Matern, Haus-hofer wanted a "*volksnahe Geopolitik.*" Matern, 122.

106. Mauersberger, 42.

107. "The workgroup pursues the goal of handling in common action the burning questions of border and foreign Germandom as simultaneously as possible (but) with di-vided roles," Pechel said, "so that the impression is given that the excitement over these issues is so strong among the German public that the journals treat the issue sponta-neously." Pechel cited, ibid., 161-62.

108. Pechel cited, ibid., 178; ibid., 70 n.

109. BAK: NL 160 (Pechel), folder 126, "Bericht über die 10. Tagung der 'Arbeits-gemeinschaft deutscher Zeitschriften für die Interesse des Grenz- und Auslands-deutschtums,' 2. Dez. 1930," and "Liste der Teilnehmer der Tagung," and folder 124, "An-wesenheitsliste." Many of the journals represented, including *Simplizissimus* and the *Vierteljahrsschrift für Politik und Geschichte* were by no means affiliated with the far Right. Martin Spahn had suggested the formation of such a consortium of journals on behalf of German cultural research and publication before the First World War. See Rüdiger vom Bruch, *Weltpolitik als Kulturmission: Auswärtige Kulturpolitik und Bildungsbürgertum in Deutschland am Vorabend des Ersten Weltkrieges* (Paderborn, 1982), 54, and especially 78.

110. BAK: NL 160 (Pechel), folder 126, "Addressenliste."

111. Charles Bloch, "Der Kampf Joseph Blochs und der 'Sozialistischen Monatshefte' in der Weimarer Republik," *Jahrbuch des Instituts für Deutsche Geschichte* 3 (1974): 257-58.

112. Max Hodann, "Anthropogeographie," *SoM* 32 (1926): 333.

113. Max Cohen, "Kolonialwirtschaft ist Notwendig," *SoM* 34 (1928): 1044, 1046. "The right of self-determination of the African peoples is, apart from certain regions of north Africa, practically without significance," Cohen wrote, "so long as the resources dor-mant in African soil are not utilized." A call for Euro-African economic unity appeared in Herman Sörgel, "Europa-Afrika. Ein Weltteil," *SoM* 37 (1931): 983-87. These views are strikingly similar to those of the conservative geopolitical colonialist Arthur Dix. See the treatment of Dix in chapter 5.

114. See the two articles by Ludwig Quessel, "Die Aussenpolitik des Reichstags," *SoM* 33 (1927): 265–70, and "Die Bilanz unserer Aussenpolitik," *SoM* 35 (1929): 11–17.

115. Ludwig Quessel, "Youngplan und Reichsschuld," *SoM* 35 (1929): 482, and Herman Kranold, "Nach dem Youngplan," *SoM* 36 (1930): 9–17.

116. See, for example, Bernhard Dernburg, "Deutschland und der Dawesplan," *ZfG* 4 (1927): 6–14.

117. Max Klesse, "Mehr sozialistische Bevölkerungspolitik," *SoM* 34 (1928): 314–19; Max Hodann, "Bevölkerungspolitik," *SoM* 34 (1928): 529–30; Georg Wolff, "Das Qualitätsproblem in der Bevölkerungspolitik," *SoM* 37 (1931): 145–49; Herman Kranold, "Aussenkolonisation," *SoM* 38 (1932): 196. Klesse, for example, wrote: "The purely quantitative process of the birth collapse becomes considerably more dangerous for our self-maintenance as a people in general and for the liberation struggle of the working class in particular in that it is bound up with a qualitative worsening of the offspring, which is based in three essential causes: (1) The childlessness or relatively few children of the high-value parent couples, (2) the wealth of children of the lumpenproletariat, (3) the debilitating effects of the large city on our offspring." Klesse, 314–15. His solution is settlement in new spaces. Robert Proctor points out that eugenicist ideas enjoyed a considerable following among a circle of SPD thinkers led by Karl Valentin Müller in the Weimar years. See Proctor, *Racial Hygiene*, 22.

118. Georg Engelbert Graf, "Geographie und materialistische Geschichtsauffassung," in *Der lebendige Marxismus. Festgabe zum 70. Geburtstage von Karl Kautsky*, ed. O Jenssen (Jena, 1924), 587.

119. Ibid., 569.

120. Ibid., 586.

121. Peter J. Perry, "Thirty Years On: Or, Whatever Happened to Wittfogel?" *PGQ* 7 (1988): 76.

122. Karl Wittfogel, "Geopolitik, geographischer Materialismus und Marxismus," *Unter dem Banner des Marxismus* 3 (1929): 734.

123. Ibid., 735.

124. Ibid., 699.

125. Ibid., 727. This view also prefigures Wittfogel's own postwar theories, detailed in *Oriental Despotism*, about the effects of geography on political organization.

126. G. L. Ulmen, *The Science of Society: Towards an Understanding of the Life and Work of Karl August Wittfogel* (The Hague, 1978), 89.

127. See the comments on St. Petersburg, for example, in Marshall Berman, *All That is Solid Melts into Air: The Experience of Modernity* (New York, 1982), 173–76; Peukert, 181.

128. The contradictory combination of hostility to modern social and economic arrangements with admiration for the technological efficiency and achievements of the modern era that characterized much German conservative thought during the Weimar period has produced contortions over nomenclature. Herman Lebovics, in *Social Conservatism and the Middle Classes in Germany, 1914–1933* (Princeton, 1969) uses the term *social conservatism* to describe "the rejection of many of the features of the twentieth-century industrial market economy, and the desire to modernize many of the social and economic values of the pre-industrial era" (ix). Heinrich Kessler points out that the terms *new conservative, young conservative, conservative-revolutionary,* and *new nationalist* are used interchangeably in German historiography to describe the political dimensions of the movement. See Kessler, *Wilhelm Stapel als politischer Publizist. Ein Beitrag zur Geschichte des konservativen Na-*

tionalismus zwischen den beiden Weltkriegen (Nuremberg, 1967), 3. Other terms to explain the phenomenon, or similar ideologies, have included *reactionary modernism* (Jeffrey Herf), *German anticapitalism* (Werner Sombart) *national bolshevism* (Ernst Niekisch) and *revolutionary conservatism* (Heide Gerstenberger). Modris Eksteins has argued, persuasively, that in fact movements motivated by these ideas, especially the National Socialist movement, were trying not to impose a vision of the past but a vision of the future. Neither the Nazis nor the geopoliticians, however, were very interested in what Eksteins calls "the quest for liberation," which with "the act of rebellion" was supposedly an identifying characteristic of modernism (Eksteins, xv-xvi). *Reactionary modernism* seems a perfectly good term for these ideas as long as it is clear that no paradox is intended, but that reaction and irrationalism are simply viewed as components of a broader modernist framework.

Chapter 5. The Geopolitical Minimum: Seven Case Studies

1. The attempt to integrate many fields of social science was also evident in the writings of Weimar's volkish movement. See Oberkrome, 28.

2. Geoffrey Parker, for instance, mentions him only in passing in his *Geopolitical Thought,* 57. Heide Gerstenberger, 25, and Rössler, 33-34, also give only incidental treatment to Banse's work in the Weimar era. He is treated in Kost, *Einflüsse,* at some length, but for his *Wehrgeopolitik,* not "expressionist geography." See 154-56 and 190-91.

3. Dietmar Henze, *Ewald Banse und seine Stellung in der Geographie auf Grund seiner Schriften, Tagebücher und Briefe* (Ph.D. diss., Frankfurt am Main, 1968), 1-10. Much of the biographical information in what follows is from Henze's informative work. His treatment of Banse's ideas and professional behavior amounts to a whitewash, however, which dismisses Banse's *Wehrwissenschaft* as a harmless deviation and ignores the vindictive anti-Semitism Banse displayed toward academic rivals during the Nazi period. See Rössler, 34 n.2.

4. Henze, 15-26.

5. Banse cited, ibid., 19.

6. Ewald Banse, *Expressionismus und Geographie* (Braunschweig, 1920), 21.

7. Ewald Banse, *Landschaft und Seele. Neue Wege der Untersuchung und Gestaltung* (Berlin, 1928), vii.

8. Ibid., 50.

9. Ibid., 44.

10. Ibid., 45.

11. Ibid., 53. Incredibly, Banse's ideas about the impact of cloud formations upon human character were prefigured in the writings of Friedrich Ratzel, who made many similar observations decades earlier in Friedrich Ratzel, "Die Wolken in der Landschaft," *DR* 112 (1902), 22-50.

12. Ibid., 60, 66-67.

13. Ibid., 62-63.

14. Ibid., 80.

15. Ibid., 83.

16. Banse's efforts to redefine the geographical boundaries of "the Orient," an effort that preceded the First World War, were sometimes sharply attacked by professional geographers. See Rüdiger Beyer, "Ewald Banse 1883-1953," *Geographers: Biobibliographical Studies* 8 (1984): 2.

17. Ewald Banse, *Das Buch vom Morgenlande* (Leipzig, 1926), 6-7.

18. Ibid., 10-11. Note the similarities with the view of the role of climate in cultural development expressed above in Hassinger, 60 n.88.

19. Banse, *Morgenlande*, 33.

20. Ibid., 33.

21. Ibid., 34.

22. Banse cited in Henze, 42.

23. Banse, *Morgenlande*, 121.

24. Ewald Banse, "Über den Zusammenhang von Landschaft und Mensch," *VRa*, 7 (1932): 8-9.

25. Banse, "Landschaft und Volkheit," 217.

26. Ewald Banse, "See und Gebirge," *Die Tat* 20 (1928): 265.

27. Banse, "Landschaft und Volkheit," 217.

28. Beyer, 2; Henze, 52, 59.

29. Hassinger to Banse, cited in Henze, 124.

30. Hermann Lautensach, "Landschaft und Seele. Gedanken zu Ewald Banses gleichbenanntem Buch," *ZGEB* (1930): 301-2. See also the criticisms in reviews by Alfred Hettner, *GZ* 34 (1928): 626-28, and Heinrich Schmitthenner, *GZ* 36 (1930): 100-103.

31. Drygalski cited in Henze, 124, and Max Eckert, "Banses Geographische Landschaftskunde," *GA* 33 (1932): 243-44.

32. Oswald Muris, "Banses Buch der Länder," *GA* 30 (1929): 130-31.

33. Günther, "Künstlerische Geographie," 824 and 828. Banse cited, 827.

34. The field was first developed by Haushofer in the early 1920s. See Hans-Adolf Jacobsen, "Auswärtige Kulturpolitik als 'geistige Waffe.' Karl Haushofer und die Deutsche Akademie (1923-1927)," in *Deutsche Auswärtige Kulturpolitik seit 1871,* ed. Kurt Düwell and Werner Link (Vienna, 1981), 225.

35. The sources of the decline are a subject of some debate. For a detailed examination of the issue, see John E. Knodel, *The Decline of Fertility in Germany, 1871–1939* (Princeton, 1974). Knodel (4-5) points out that the crude birthrate declined in these years by more than 50 percent and was, on the eve of World War II, below the replacement rate despite the sharp contemporary decline in the mortality rate.

36. For examples of their writings see the volume that they edited jointly, Hans Harmsen and Karl Christian von Loesch, eds., *Die Deutsche Bevölkerungsfrage im europäischen Raum* (Berlin, 1929).

37. See the passage on Burgdörfer in Götz Aly and Karl Heinz Roth, *Die restlose Erfassung. Volkszählen, Identifizieren, Aussondern im Nationalsozialismus* (Berlin, 1984), 29-32.

38. See BDC, Burgdörfer personnel file, S.II. "Vorschlag zur Ernennung," and a copy of an article from *Münchener Neuesten Nachrichten,* 8 February 1939, contained in this file.

39. Burgdörfer, *Der Geburtenrückgang und seine Bekämpfung.*

40. Ibid., 7.

41. Ibid., 102-3, 46, 63.

42. Ibid., 122. Burgdörfer's warnings of the Slavic demographic danger found a ready reception among volkish-geographic circles. He was cited as the authority on the "problem," for example, in Kurt Krause, "Zwischeneuropa," *GA* 33 (1932), 383.

43. Burgdörfer, *Geburtenrückgang,* 160.

44. Paul Weindling, *Health, Race and German Politics between National Unification and Nazism, 1870–1945* (Cambridge, Eng., 1989), 422-23. Harmsen, like Burgdörfer a demographer, argued that only a growing, agricultural peasant population could defend German

land in the east in the geopolitical struggle. See Hans Harmsen, "Die deutsche Bevölkerungsfrage als Problem der völkischen Schutzarbeit," in *Die Deutsche Bevölkerungsfrage,* ed. Harmsen and Loesch, 4. Saenger published regular statistical essays in the *Zeitschrift für Geopolitik* in these years, providing statistical "proof" of the geopolitical threat posed by the birth decline. See, for example, K. Saenger, "Die Statistik im Rahmen der Geopolitik," *ZfG* 7 (1930): 255.

45. Friedrich Burgdörfer, "Die Gefährdung des ostdeutschen Volkstums," *SM* 28 (1930), 12. This essay appeared as part of a special issue entitled "The Plight of the German East" (Die Not des deutschen Ostens). The term *Ethnopolitik* was introduced by Kjellén and was frequently used by geopoliticians.

46. Friedrich Burgdörfer, "Die schwindende Wachstumsenergie des deutschen Volkes im europäischen Raum," in *Die deutsche Bevölkerungsfrage,* ed. Harmsen and Loesch, 10-31.

47. BAP: 61 Re 1, Reichslandbund 57 (Burgdörfer), Bl. 24; "Gespräch mit Mussolini über die Bevölkerungspolitik," *Völkischer Beobachter,* 8 March 1938.

48. Burgdörfer, *Volk ohne Jugend,* 399-401.

49. Ibid., xiv, 417.

50. Ibid., 400-401.

51. Ibid., 419, 423.

52. Ibid., 38.

53. See his article, Bürgdörfer, "Stadt oder Land?" 110, in which he argues that the chief goals of national policy must be to strengthen rural population as the best "regeneration source" for the population and to reduce the size of German cities. A good treatment of the role of antiurban thought in Weimar, which, however, mentions Burgdörfer only in passing, is Bergmann.

54. See the special issue entitled "Geburtenrückgang," in *SM* 25 (1927): 155-90.

55. Johann Sölch, "Raum und Zahl," 42. See the account of Sölch's career in Josef Matznetter, "Johann Sölch 1883-1951," *Geographers: Biobibliographical Studies* 2 (1978): 117-25.

56. Friedrich Tamss, "Die Lebensaussichten," 61.

57. Herbert Barthel, "Der Geburtenüberschuss in Polen," *PM,* 79 (1933): 63.

58. BAP: 61 Schu 1, 5, *Jahresbericht,* 1929, Bl. 76.

59. BAP: RMdI 15.01: 26233, "Der Präsident des Reichsgesundheitsamts an den Reichminister des Innern," 13 December 1929, Bl. 11-12, and "Der Reichsminister des Innern an den Reichsarbeitsminister" 2 January 1930, Bl. 24-25. The fact that Grotjahn, a prominent adovcate of eugenics, was also a member of the SPD was used politically by other eugenicists to claim that the appeal of their ideas went far beyond the Right; see Heide Gerstenberger, 23 n, and Weindling, 333-36, 446. Grotjahn had occupied himself with the birth decline since the mid-1920s as well and attributed its sources as did his nonsocialist colleague Burgdörfer, to disruptions caused by the war and the intensified urbanization of the German population. See his article, "Geburtenhäufigkeit," in *Berliner Tageblatt,* 13 December 1927, 12. See also Michael Burleigh and Wolfgang Wippermann, *The Racial State: Germany 1933-1945* (Cambridge, Eng., 1991), 32-33, and, on Social Democratic eugenics and racial hygiene theories in the 1920s, Loren R. Graham, "Science and Values: The Eugenics Movement in Germany and Russia in the 1920s," *AHR* 82 (1977): 1133-64.

60. BAP: RMdI 15.01: 26233, "Denkschrift über den Geburtenrückgang und seine Bekämpfung," 10 February 1927, Bl. 95, 96, 91. The authorship of the *Denkschrift* is not given. It originated in the *Reichsgesundheitsamt* and cites at many points figures, reports,

and publications from Burgdörfer's Reich Statistical Office. The title, arguments, and even many of the terms used (e.g., *Spielraum*) point to Burgdörfer's influence.

61. BAP: RmDI 15.01: 26233/1, "Der Geburtenrückgang in Deutschland, seine Folgen und seine Bekämpfung," Bl. 52, 51, 53.

62. "Übersicht der Entschließungen des Reichstags nebst Beantwortungen der Reichsregierung," *VDR*, 434; 49.

63. *VDR* 18 June 1930, 428: 5582-83. The deputy, Joos, described the *Reichsausschuss* as "a committee of medical specialists, social hygienists, national economists, sociologists, statisticians, and practical women and men."

64. *VDR* 12 June 1929, 425; 2322-23. The speaker was the DBP deputy Gandorfer.

65. On his radio broadcasts, see BAP: 61 Re 1 Reichslandbund 57 (Burgdörfer), the pamphlet "Kinderreichtum-Volksreichtum: Nach einem Vortrag über den Deutschlandsender."

66. Dix cited in Paul Langhans, "Die 21." 150. See also the complete text of Dix's speech reprinted in *VDG* (Berlin, 1926): 220-28. His attempt to create a new field of "geoeconomics," promoted in his 1925 book, *Geoökonomie. Einführung in erdhafte Wirtschaftsbetrachtung*, did not meet with a positive reception from the profession. See, for example, the skeptical review by E. Fels in *MGGM* 18 (1925): 528-29.

67. Arthur Dix, *Politische Geographie. Weltpolitisches Handbuch,* 2d ed. (Munich, 1923), iii.

68. In 1930, for example, the editor of the journal *Weltwirtschaftliches Archiv* wrote Dix, rejecting an article for publication: "Presumably this result will bother you less than me, since all the journals of Germany stand open to you, and many editors will be happy at my obduracy, from which they may now profit." See BAP: NL Dix: 90 Di 2; Mappe 8, Bl. 65 ("Inst. für Weltwirtwschaftlich Seeverkehr an der Universität Kiel an Dix," 31 December 1930).

69. BAP: NL Dix: 90 Di 2; Mappe 7, Bl. 12 ("ADV to Dix, 16 June 1925, signed Duems"), and Bl. 55 ("ADV to Dix, 23 September 1927").

70. See the introductory note to *ZfG* 4 (1927).

71. He addressed members of the *Reichswehrministerium* (Defense Ministry) in 1924, and the Colonial University at Witzenhausen in 1931. See Reichswehrministerium to Dix, 3 August 1925, and the *Tagesordnung* of 8-13 April 1931 for the meeting of the Deutsche Studentenschaft and the Deutsche Kolonialgesellschaft at Witzenhausen (BAP: NL Dix: 90 Di 2; Mappe 7, Bl. 13, and Mappe 8, Bl. 67-68). His radio lectures on colonies were carried on Ostmarken-Rundfunk, Deutsche Stunde in Bayern, Deutsche Welle, and Volkswirtschaftfunk. See *Ostmarken-Rundfunk* to Dix, 22 November 1926; *Deutsche Stunde in Bayern* to Dix, 10 February 1927; *Volkswirtschaftsfunk, Vorträge*; and Dix to *Deutsche Welle,* 6 December 1927 (copy) (BAP: NL Dix: 90 Di 2; Mappe 7, Bl. 30, 44-47, 59).

72. See "Staatswissenschaftliche Vereinigung in Berlin (Stand vom April, 1928)" and "Gesellschaft für Erdkunde zu Berlin (1928)," (BAP: NL Dix: 90 Di 2; Mappe 262, Bl. 12-13, and Bl. 72). See also "Vorstand," *Verhandlungen des Vorstandes des Kolonial-Wirtschaftlichen Komitees* 1 (1932): 1-3.

73. Dix, *Geopolitik,* 4.

74. "Geopolitics is politics conducted with particular reference to the earth-spatial. . . . Like politics in general, geopolitics is, therefore, to be conceived simultaneously as science and as guide." Ibid., 20-21. For a contemporary example of similar confusion see

Gearóid O Tuathail, "The Language and Nature of the 'New Geopolitics': The Case of U.S.-El Salvador Relations," *PGO*, 5 (1986): 73-85. O Tuathail uses the term to denote both U.S. policy itself ("contemporary U.S. geopolitics in Central America") and to refer to a general analytical approach to understanding state relations without bothering to define or distinguish between the two.

75. Dix, "Wirtschaftsstruktur," 467.

76. Dix, *Geopolitik*, 22.

77. Dix, "Wirtschaftsstruktur," 473. The term here translated as "the Global Village" is *"Das Dörfchen Erde."*

78. Ibid., 479.

79. Ibid., 480.

80. Arthur Dix, "Weltgeschichte—Kolonialgeschichte," *UKZ* 41 (1929): 214.

81. Dix, *Weltkrise*, 11.

82. Ibid., 224-25.

83. Arthur Dix, *Was geht uns Afrika an?* (Berlin, 1931), 94. It may be that the natives found German governance less benevolent than Dix imagined. Evelyn Waugh reported meeting many nostalgic Germans returning to their old farms and plantations during his travels in East Africa in the postwar decade and quotes an Austrian farmer who pined for the good old days under the Germans: "'Before the War,' he said, 'every native had to salute every European or he knew the reason why. Now, with all this education . . . .'" Evelyn Waugh, *When the Going Was Good* (London, 1946), 181-82.

84. See his analysis of the links between population structure and national economy in Arthur Dix, "Die Abhängigkeit der Wirtschaftsstruktur von der Bevölkerungsstruktur in Deutschland," *VB* 26 (1927): 31-37.

85. Dix, *Weltkrise*, 25, 28.

86. Dix, *Politische Geographie*, 87, 38-40.

87. Ibid., 173, 151.

88. Ibid., 528.

89. Ibid., 40.

90. Ibid., 115.

91. Dix, "Wirtschaftsstruktur," 467.

92. Grabowsky attacked Haushofer's attempt to attribute a specific percentage of the source of world historical changes to geography and added that it was peculiar "that a man like Haushofer knows fundamentally only two history-making forces, space and the hero, whereby racial factors and moral forces are placed in the heroic worldview with profuse lack of clarity." Adolf Grabowsky, "Das Problem der Geopolitik," *ZfP* 22 (1932-33): 778. He does, however, praise the "vigorous and leaderlike personality" of Haushofer.

93. He published a collection of poems, entitled simply *Gedichte*, in 1912, for example, and published a play, *Der Neger. Tragische Komödie in 3 Akten*, in 1926. His efforts in the field of belles-lettres attracted little notice.

94. Laqueur, 208.

95. Grabowsky cited in Detlev Lehnert, "'Politik als Wissenschaft': Beiträge zur Institutionalisierung einer Fachdisziplin in Forschung und Lehre der Deutschen Hochschule für Politik (1920-1933)," *Politische Vierteljahresschrift* 30 (1989): 454.

96. The Brockhaus encyclopedia, for example, in its brief entry on Grabowsky characterizes him as an advocate of a Verständigungsfrieden. See *Enzyklopedie Brockhaus*, 1969, 540.

97. Adolf Grabowsky, *Die polnische Frage* (Berlin, 1916), 89.

98. He praised the "Hanseatic spirit" that the Polish middle classes had absorbed from their neighbors and enthused that Warsaw presented "image after image as of German cities from a pleasanter era," Ibid., 12–13.

99. Ibid., 67.

100. Other books in the series included Otto Maull, *Politische Grenzen,* Walther Pahl, *Der Kampf um die Rohstoffe,* Josef März, *Landmächte und Seemächte,* and Paul Herre, *Spanien und Portugal.* Alfred Hettner praised the series in the *Geographische Zeitschrift* for its geopolitical approach: "This collection is intended in one series to instruct the German people, whose understanding for external politics and especially world politics is still very small indeed. We can all be thankful to the deserving editor, therefore, and we geographers in particular must consider it as a considerable advance over so many other political writings that it clearly recognizes the rooting of politics in the nature of the earth's surface and particularly emphasizes this side of world politics." Alfred Hettner, review of *Weltpolitische Bücherei,* ed. Adolf Grabowsky *GZ* 35 (1929): 299–300.

101. Grabowsky, *Staat und Raum,* 6.

102. Ibid., 10–11. Walther Vogel echoed these words almost exactly in his book *Das Neue Europa.* See below.

103. Grabowsky, *Staat und Raum,* 12.

104. Ibid., 23–25.

105. Ibid., 53.

106. Ibid., 90, 46–48.

107. Ibid., 43.

108. Grabowsky, *Der Neger,* 74.

109. Klaus Kost has characterized Grabowsky's commitment to geopolitics as a subsidiary part of his general interest in political theory, and this seems fair in light of Grabowsky's writings on geopolitics as a method. Kost, *Einflüsse,* 60.

110. Grabowsky, "Das Problem," 784.

111. Ibid., 783.

112. Ibid., 771, 770, 777.

113. Adolf Grabowsky, "Der Primat der Aussenpolitik," *ZfP* 17 (1928): 527–42, and Eckart Kehr, "Englandhass und Weltpolitik," *ZfP* 17 (1928): 500–526.

114. Grabowsky, "Primat," 529.

115. Ibid., 530–31.

116. Ibid., 530.

117. See Adolf Grabowsky, "Völkerbund, Weltorganisation und Pazifismus," in *Jenseits der Grossmächte,* ed. Karl Haushofer (Berlin, 1932), 448–77; "Genf und Wir," *Die Tat* 20 (1928): 696–701, (in which he writes, "No reasonable man among us wishes for war, but the best means to avoid it is precisely to endeavor by all means to again bring in order the world dynamic that has gone off its hinges."); and idem, "Remarque und Russland," *RF* 11 July 1929, 1. For his articles in more popular venues, see "Ein Bund der Neutralen," *Berliner Tageblatt,* 16 August 1923, and the wartime "Das Deutsche Volk der Zukunft," *Das Neue Deutschland,* 21 January 1915, both in BAP: 61 Re 1 Reichslandbund 162 (Grabowsky), Bl. 14 and Bl. 17.

118. Grabowsky, "Primat," 800, 801.

119. Grabowsky, *Staat und Raum,* 5.

120. He spoke, for example, to the Greater Berlin section of the League of German School Geographers on "the significance of geopolitics for education" in 1927. See *GA* 32 (1931): 308.

121. See chapter 6 below for a treatment of the university and the role of geopolitical ideas there.

122. For a view of the university as staunch defender of republican democracy see Ernst Jäckh and Otto Suhr, *Geschichte der deutschen Hochschule für Politik* (Berlin, 1952), 15. For a reappraisal see Lehnert.

123. *VVDH,* summer semester 1926, 18.

124. For enrollments see Jäckh and Suhr, 77; on the political science degree, Lehnert, 445.

125. The others were "domestic policy," "legal foundations of politics," and "economics," and a short-lived journalism course. *VVDH,* summer semester 1925, 5-6. See also Jäckh and Suhr, 78-79.

126. Ernst Jäckh, *Deutschland. Das Herz Europas* (Stuttgart, 1928), 14-15.

127. Grabowsky, "Das Problem," 801. Ironically, for all his criticisms of Haushofer, this emphasis on prognosis echoed Haushofer's. "Geopolitics begins with the prognosis, with the prediction of the political weather situation, unlike more static, purely descriptive political geography," Haushofer told an audience to one of his radio addresses. See BAK: NL 122, Haushofer, Band 834, Haushofer radio address, "Wie wendet man geopolitische Prinzipien praktisch an?" February 1931.

128. Heinz-Werner Hübner, "Vom Feldzug zum Krieg," *Die Zeit,* 14 June 1991, 12.

129. Hellmut Harke, "Die Legende vom mangelnden Lebensraum," in *Auf den Spuren der Ostforschung,* ed. Claus Remer (Leipzig, 1962), 59.

130. A partial bibliography of his writings may be found in the appendix to Jacobsen, *Haushofer,* vol. 2.

131. These and many more are listed in Mauersberger, 262. See also Jacobsen, "Auswärtige Kulturpolitik," 218.

132. Erhard Schütz, *Romane der Weimarer Republik* (Munich, 1986), 37. As Schütz points out by way of comparison, in the latter year one hundred thousand copies of Mann's *Der Zauberberg* were sold. The Nazis, of course, immediately grasped the potential of the new medium.

133. Jacobsen, *Haushofer,* 1: 183.

134. "Unrat" was, of course, the nickname given by his students to the corrupt and despotic Professor Rat, protagonist of Henrich Mann's prewar novel, *Professor Unrat.* He was later sentimentalized in Josef von Sternberg's interwar film, *Der blau Engel,* starring Marlene Dietrich.

135. Jacobsen, *Haushofer,* 162.

136. Matern claims that Haushofer told a friend in 1934 that he had known Hitler personally since 1919. After the war, Haushofer claimed it was not until 1922 that he first met Hitler. Bakker says they met in 1920. Jacobsen suggests a first meeting in July 1921, and Rudolf Pechel wrote in 1947 that Haushofer was acquainted with Hitler by 1922, when he arranged a meeting with Hitler for the journalist. See Bakker, n. 49; Jacobsen, *Haushofer,* 2: 470; Matern, 110; Rudolf Pechel, *Deutscher Widerstand* (Zurich, 1947), 277. Haushofer's academic reputation in the 1920s was by no means negligible. He was sought as a reference, for example, by the city of Frankfurt when it prepared to undertake the

funding of the Institut für Kulturmorphologie in 1925; see Wolfgang Schivelbusch, *Intellektuellendämmerung. Zur Lage der Frankfurter Intelligenz in den zwanziger Jahren* (Frankfurt am Main, 1982), 21.

137. Early in 1933, for example, Westdeutsche Rundfunk carried as part of its "Aus dem Leben der höheren Schule" series broadcasts by Banse ("Landschaft und Mensch: die seelische Verflechtung beider geographischer Faktoren") and Lautensach ("Politische Geographie und Geopolitik in Wissenschaft und Unterricht"), *GA* 34 (1933): 26.

138. BAK: NL 122, Karl Haushofer; 834, "Was ist Geopolitik?" 28.05.29, II.

139. BAK: NL 122, Karl Haushofer; 834, "Was ist Geopolitik?" p. 2, X.

140. Ibid., XII.

141. BAK: NL 122, Karl Haushofer, 834, "Wie wendet man geopolitische Prinzipien praktisch an?" February 1931, I.

142. Ibid., II.

143. Ibid., V.

144. Ibid., VII.

145. The definitive treatment of his ideas and life is Jacobsen's exhaustive two-volume work.

146. Karl Haushofer, *Der Nationalsozialistische Gedanke in der Welt* (Munich, 1933), 14, 6.

147. Lion Feuchtwanger, *Erfolg. Drei Jahre Geschichte einer Provinz* (Munich, 1955), 155.

148. Manfred Langhans [-Ratzeburg], "Rechtliche und tatsächliche Machtbereiche der Grossmächte," *PM* 70 (1924): 1.

149. Manfred Langhans [-Ratzeburg], "Karte des Selbstbestimmungsrechtes der Völker," *PM* 72 (1926): 1.

150. Ibid., 2–3.

151. Ibid., 9.

152. On Schmitt's theories see Bendersky and Peter Gowan, "The Return of Carl Schmitt," *Debatte* 2 (1994): 82–127.

153. Otto Köllreuter, review of *Politische Geographie*, by Otto Maull, *Archiv des öffentlichen Rechts* 48 (1925): 111. Walther Merk pursued a similar approach in *Wege und Ziele der geschichtlichen Rechtsgeographie* (Berlin, 1926). Max Georg Schmidt, coauthor of the *Geopolitische Typen-Atlas,* also praised Langhans-Ratzeburg's cartographic principles. See his article, "Eine geopolitische Weltkarte," *GA* 34 (1933): 141–44. Geojurisprudence had its critics as well, however. E. Posse wrote in 1931, "Is the need really so pressing, then, after geopolitics has just found acceptance among the other disciplines as a separate science, to lay it now on the vivisection table and to fragment it so that in the end only the dead skeleton remains? A few years ago, Arthur Dix discovered geoeconomics; there has also been talk of geomedicine, and now Langhans-Ratzeburg comes along with geojurisprudence." See E. Posse, review of *Die grossen Mächte, geojuristisch betrachtet*, by Manfred Langhans-Ratzeburg, *Kölnische Zeitung,* Beilage, 10 May 1931.

154. Karl Haushofer, "Geopolitik und Geojurisprudenz," *Zeitschrift für Völkerrecht* 14 (1928): 564.

155. Ibid., 568. On a similar abandonment during the Weimar period of "purely legal," meaning absolute, standards, in the law of debt rather than the law of states, see Michael L. Hughes, *Paying for the German Inflation* (Chapel Hill, N.C., 1988), 20–21.

156. Langhans-Ratzeburg, *Begriff und Aufgaben der Geographischen Rechtswissenschaft* (Berlin, 1928), 9.

157. Ibid., 11-12. The same conclusion was reached in A. Kästner, *Das Problem einer Geo- und Ethnojurisprudenz* (Ph.D. diss., Leipzig, 1931).

158. Ibid., 10.

159. Ibid., 56, 61.

160. Ibid., 34-35.

161. Ibid., 46-47.

162. Ibid., 64.

163. Ibid., 65.

164. Manfred Langhans-Ratzeburg, "Die strittigen Gebiete der Erde," *PM* 75 (1929): 10-11.

165. Manfred Langhans-Ratzeburg, *Die Volgadeutschen. Ihr Staats- und Verwaltungsrecht in Vergangenheit und Gegenwart* (Berlin, 1929), 139.

166. Manfred Langhans-Ratzeburg, *Die grossen Mächte geojuristische betrachet* (Munich, 1931), 214.

167. Ibid., 227.

168. Manfred Langhans-Ratzeburg, "Das japanische Reich geojuristisch betrachtet," *ZfG* 7 (1930): 71-72.

169. For example, Karl Haushofer argued that geopolitics was intended, in part, as a means of explaining to Germans those historical failures that had led to defeat; "Grundlagen, Wesen und Ziele der Geopolitik," in *Bausteine zur Geopolitik,* ed. Karl Haushofer, (Berlin, 1928), 29. Some examples of geopolitical case studies that are historical in their orientation are von Hofmann, *Das deutsche Land*; Georg Wegener, *Die geographischen Ursachen des Weltkrieges* (Berlin, 1920); A. Haushofer, *Pass-Staaten.*

170. On Penck's role in the creation of the professorship in historical geography see Kost, *Einflüsse,* 53. On the Council for Foreign Studies (Beirat für Auslandstudie) and Vogel's role in it see the account in GStA, Rep. 92; NL Vogel, no. 21, piece 6 (*Frankfurter Zeitung,* 4 February 1926). See also H. Wätjen, "Nachruf auf Walther Vogel," *Historische Zeitschrift* 158 (1938); 673-74.

171. GStA, Rep. 92; NL Vogel, no. 21, piece 3; "Zur Befolgung der Seminarordung."

172. He lectured in May 1926 on "Economics and Geopolitics" at the Handels-Hochschule of Leipzig. See "Redner des Weltwirtschafts-Institut," in *Weltwirtschaftsdämmerung. Festschrift zum 10jährigen Bestehen des Weltwirtschafts-Instituts der Handels-Hochschule Leipzig,* eds. Karl Haushofer and Walther Vogel (Stuttgart, 1934), 128-32.

173. The best example of Hassinger's historical geopolitics is his *Geographische Grundlagen der Geschichte* (Freiburg im Breisgau, 1931). In 1932 Otto Forst de Battaglia cited Vogel, along with Paul Herre (whose works appeared in Grabowsky, "World-political Library") and Albert von Hofmann as the leading representatives of geopolitical thought among contemporary German historians. See Battaglia, "Geopolitik," 31.

174. Vogel, *Das Neue Europa,* v.

175. Ibid., v.

176. Ibid., 2, 4.

177. Ibid., 5.

178. Ibid., 6.

179. Ibid., 91.

180. Ibid., 87.

181. Walther Vogel, "Die Bilanz des staatlich-völkischen Lebensraumes," in *Weltwirtschaftsdämmerung,* ed. Haushofer and Vogel, 88-89. In this article (87) Vogel offered the

following definition of *Lebensraum*: "'Lebensraum' is the space necessarily belonging to a living being, therefore, also a people, within which it may satisfy in adequate measure its necessary living requirements."

182. Vogel, *Das Neue Europa,* 99.

183. Ibid., 100–101.

184. Ibid., 414–22.

185. Elements of this analysis can be found in such recent works as E. L. Jones's *The European Miracle: Environments, Economies and Geopolitics in the Histories of Europe and Asia,* 2d ed. (Cambridge, Eng., 1987).

186. For the role of general hostility to the postwar redrawing of borders in the revitalization of historical geography see Oberkrome, 24–25.

187. Walther Vogel, "Rhein und Donau als Staatenbildner," *ZfG* 1 (1924): 63–73, 135–47.

188. Ibid., 144.

189. Vogel, review of *Jenseits der Grossmächte,* 150.

190. Vogel, *Das Neue Europa,* 102.

191. See Wätjen, 674, and GStA, I HA, Rep. 92, NL Brackmann, "Protokoll, 3 April 1930," Bestand 77, Bl. 761–69.

192. GStA, Rep. 92; NL Vogel, 21, "Landeskunde von Europa: Seminar"; 22, "Historische Geographie, WS 1927-28"; 20, "Grundzüge der allgemeinen Politische Geographie, SS 1927."

193. Walther Vogel, "Ziele und Wege der Auslandstudien," *Koloniale Rundschau* (1925): 81.

194. Ibid., 81, 82.

Chapter 6. A Text for Imperialism: Geopolitics and the German Student

1. For an interesting firsthand account of how geopolitics was used in Nazi schoolrooms see Erika Mann, *School for Barbarians,* trans. Muriel Rukeyser (New York, 1938), 62–63. An overview of geographic education in Germany in the later years of Weimar and under the Nazis is to be found in Henning Heske, . . . *und morgen die ganze Welt. Erdkundeunterricht im Nationalsozialismus* (Giessen, 1988).

2. J. H. Paterson, "German geopolitics reassessed," *PGQ* 6 (April 1987): 109.

3. Heske, *Morgen,* 37–39.

4. For contemporary evaluations of the field by several professional geographers see Hans Dietrich Schultz, "Die Situation der Geographie nach dem Ersten Weltkrieg. Eine unbekannte Umfrage aus dem Jahre 1919, historisch kommentiert," *Die Erde* 108 (1977): 75–102.

5. H. Harms, *Fünf Thesen zur Reform des geographischen Unterrichts. Ein Vortrag,* 7th ed. (Leipzig, 1921), 5.

6. Ibid., 7, 6.

7. Ibid., 31.

8. See the treatment of this aspect of Meinecke's historical theory in Georg G. Iggers, *The German Conception of History: The National Tradition of Historical Thought from Herder to the Present,* rev. ed. (Middletown, 1983), 195–225.

9. A. Geistbeck, "Die Beduetung der Erdkunde und erdkundlicher Bildung für das deutsche Volk in der Gegenwart," in *Reformvorschläge des deutschen Geographentages für den*

erdkundlichen Unterricht an den höheren Schulen, ed. Deutscher Geographentag (Lübeck, 1909), 7, 2. A similar emphasis on contemporary political utility as the proper goal of geographical education is expressed in R. Langenbeck, "Die Lehrziele, die Lehrmethode und die Lehrpläne des erdkundlichen Unterrichts," *Reformvorschläge* (Lübeck, 1909), 12–32.

10. Heske, . . . *und morgen,* 35.

11. Erich Obst, "Die Krisis in der geographischen Wissenschaft," *PJ* 192 (April–June 1923): 22.

12. Ibid., 21.

13. Ibid., 19. This call for geopolitics as a "science of the present" remained popular into the Nazi era. See Erich Scheil, "Politische Geographie im Rahmen eines gegenwarts-betonten Unterrichts," *Neue Bahnen* 44 (1933): 220–25. Scheil argued that geopolitical teaching in the schools should center on geographical explication of newspaper stories.

14. Ibid., 24.

15. Karl Haushofer, *Geopolitik des Pazifischen,* 341; Hermann Lautensach, "Geopolitik und Schule," in *Bausteine,* ed. Karl Haushofer et al, 307. Lautensach's essay was reprinted in the *Geographischer Anzeiger.* See Hermann Lautensach, "Geopolitik und Schule," *GA* 28 (1927): 341–48.

16. Karl Haushofer, "Geopolitik und Kaufmann," in *Bausteine,* ed. Karl Haushofer et al., 274.

17. Hermann Lautensach, "Geopolitik und Staatsbürgerliche Bildung," in Karl Haushofer *Bausteine,* ed. Karl Haushofer et al., 287.

18. Johann Thies, *Geopolitik in der Volksschule. Eine methodische Einführung zur national-politischen Erziehung der deutschen Jugend* (Berlin, 1932), 17.

19. Lautensach, "Staatsbürgerliche," 289–90. For an example of a similar call for concentration on contemporary political issues as a means of focusing and revitalizing the teaching of geography see Karl Heck, "Wo stehen wir heute in der Schulgeographie?" *GA* 34 (1933): 242–48.

20. Albert Schaefer, "Zur Behandlung geopolitischer Fragen im Erdkundeunterricht der Primen," *GA* 34 (1933): 145, 149.

21. Karl Haushofer, "Grundlagen," 30.

22. Lautensach, "Geopolitik und Schule," *GA,* 322.

23. Hermann Haack, review of *Der Rhein,* by Karl Haushofer, in *GA* 29 (1928): 348.

24. Hans Osse, "Geopolitik und Volkserziehung," *DR* 58 (1932): 36.

25. Ibid., 35. On the necessity of developing "geomedicine" see Heinz Zeiss, "Die Notwendigkeit einer deutschen Geomedizin," *ZfG* 9 (1932): 474–84.

26. Obst, "Krisis," 24. Obst praised Ewald Banse as the most sophisticated practitioner of this new geography.

27. Theodor Langenmaier, "Die Reform des Geographie-Unterrichts im Sinne der Willensbildung," in *Freie Wege vergleichender Erdkunde* ed. Erich von Drygalski (Munich, 1925), 371.

28. Fox, "Die Forderungen," 70.

29. Jorgen Hansen, "Sinn und Methode des erdkundlichen Unterrichts auf der Grundlage der Heimatkunde," in *Die Neue Geographie in der Schule. Ausgewählte Aufsätze zur gestaltenden Erdkunde,* ed. Jorgen Hansen (Braunschweig, 1931), 16.

30. Georg A. Lukas, "Geopolitische Fragen im Geographie-Unterricht: 7. Die Südtiroler Frage," *GA* 29 (1928): 187–92; idem, "Geopolitische Fragen im Geographie-

Unterricht: 11. Die Einheit der deutschen Ostfront," *GA* 34 (1933): 346-50; idem, "Geopolitische Fragen im Geographie-Unterricht: 10. Mitteleuropas geopolitische Achse," *GA* 32 (1931): 302-5.

31. Arbeitsgemeinschaft für Geopolitik, "Denkschrift: Geopolitik als nationale Staatswissenschaft," *ZfG* 10 (1933): 301, 303. The memorandum also called for the teaching of subjects such as geomedicine, geojurisprudence, and "art geography." The AfG was founded in February 1932 with several hundred members to advance the use of geopolitics as a foreign-political propaganda tool. See the following for accounts of the AfG: Henning Heske, "Karl Haushofer: His Role in German Geopolitics and in Nazi Politics," *PGQ* 6 (1987): 135-44: Jacobsen, *Haushofer,* 1: 278-80.

32. On the *Gleichschaltung* of the profession see Rössler, 30-36.

33. See the following articles in *Neue Bahnen*: Artur Dumke, "Geopolitik in der Volksschule," ibid. 45 (1934): 155-58; Johann Thies, "Die Geopolitik als nationale Staatswissenschaft und ihre Eingliederung in die deutsche Volksschule," ibid. 45 (1934): 208-14.

34. Cited in Heske, . . . *und morgen,* 35.

35. Ibid., 35-36.

36. R. H. Samuel and R. Hinton Thomas, *Education and Society in Modern Germany* (London, 1949), 12. A more recent and insightful examination of the German education system may be found in Fritz K. Ringer, *Education and Society in Modern Europe* (Bloomington, Ind., 1979), 32-69.

37. Ministerium für Wissenschaft, Kunst und Volksbildung, "Erdkundlicher Unterricht in den höheren Lehranstalten," *ZgU* 66 (5 May 1924): 134.

38. Ministerium für Wissenschaft, Kunst und Volksbildung, "Richtlinien für einen Lehrplan der Deutschen Oberschulen und Aufbauschulen" (Beilage, 1924) 66:12, 28.

39. Ministerium für Wissenschaft, Kunst und Volksbildung, *Richtlinien für die Lehrpläne der höheren Schulen Preussens: Amtliche Ausgabe* (Berlin, 1925), 19.

40. Ibid., 22.

41. Ibid., 61.

42. Instruction in Hansen, "Heimatkunde," was characterized as an "obvious duty" of geographic instruction. Ibid., 20.

43. Ibid., 62.

44. See the support for the guidelines in Karl Heck, "Preussische Schulreform und Erdkunde," *GA* 27 (1928): 20-21. Walter Behrmann criticized their apparent trendiness in Behrmann, "Über die Berücksichtigung der Lehrpläne der Höheren Schulen im Hochschulunterricht," *GA* 28 (1927): 356. "Anyone who doesn't know the origins of the Prussian guidelines can certainly not escape the impression that the authors of the guidelines wanted to prove that they would be 'up to date.'"

45. Ministerium für Wissenschaft, Kunst und Volksbildung, *Richtlinien für die Lehrpläne,* 20.

46. Ibid., 19.

47. Ibid.

48. Ibid.

49. Otto Boelitz, "Die Behandlung der Fragen des Grenz- und Auslanddeutschtums auf unseren höheren Schulen," *DR* 53 (1927): 192.

50. Ministerium für Wissenschaft, Kunst und Volksbildung, "Bestimmungen über die Mittelschulen in Preussen," *ZgU* 67 (Beilage, 1925): 13-14.

51. Ministerium für Wissenschaft, Kunst und Volksbildung, "Richtlinien zur Aufstellung von Lehrplänen für die Grundschule," *ZgU* 63 (1921): 185–88.

52. Franz Thorbecke, "Die Stellung der Hochschullehrer zum geographischer Unterricht," *GA* 28 (1927): 294, 295.

53. Behrmann, Hochschulunterricht, 256. Fritz Klute also warned that geopolitics ought by rights to be handled at the university level alone because at the lower levels it too easily devolved into "politics and phrases." See Fritz Klute, "Die Lehrpläne der Geographie an den höheren Schulen," *GA* 28 (1927): 356.

54. W. Classen tells of his experience teaching a one-year study group in geopolitics in Duisberg and claims that the student body was enthusiastic in its response. Classen, "Geopolitik" 14–27.

55. Lautensach, for example, praised the geopolitical acumen displayed by the Bavarian educational authorities in their treatment of geographic instruction. See Lautensach, "Geopolitik und Schule," *Bausteine,* 309. For a tabular comparison of the geographic guidelines used in several of the German states see Klute, 351–59.

56. Paul Wagner, "Sächsische Schulreform und Erdkunde," *GA* 28 (1927): 22–23.

57. E. Oppermann, "Neue Lehrpläne in Braunschweig," *GA* 29 (1928): 160.

58. The first well-known use of these terms was in Theodor Waitz, *Anthropologie der Naturvölker,* published in 1859. See Smith, *Politics,* 49–50.

59. Ministerium für Wissenschaft, Kunst und Volksbildung, "Erkundlicher Unterricht," 12.

60. Obst was Supan's son-in-law: Hanno Beck, *Hermann Lautensach—führender Geograph in zwei Epochen. Ein Weg zur Länderkunde* (Stuttgart, 1974), 10.

61. Lautensach, "Geopolitik und Schule," *Bausteine,* 312.

62. Alexander Supan, *Leitlinien der allgemeinen politischen Geographie: Naturlehre des Staates,* 2d ed. (Berlin, 1922), 5.

63. Ibid., 1.

64. Ibid., 37.

65. Ibid., 23.

66. Ibid., 13–14.

67. Ibid., 12.

68. Ibid., 14.

69. Rudolf Reinhard, *Weltwirtschaftliche und politische Erdkunde,* 5th ed. (Breslau, 1925), 146–47.

70. Ibid., 147–48.

71. See, for example, the map by the geopolitical cartographer Hermann Haack, *Zwischeneuropa, physikalishce Karte* (Gotha, 1932); Giselher Wiesing, *Zwischeneuropa und die deutsche Zukunft* (Jena, 1932).

72. Kurt Krause, "Zwischeneuropa," *GA* 33 (1932): 380.

73. Ibid., 380. "Interim-Europe is thus becoming a region of ethnic fragmentation, a tremor zone of the first rank in Europe. . . . Interim-Europe is still unfinished state territory."

74. Wütschke, *Unsere Erde,* 117.

75. Ibid., 138.

76. Ibid., 134.

77. Samuel and Thomas, *Education and Society,* 80.

78. Paul Wagner, *Erdkunde für höhere Lehranstalten. Nach der Erdkunde von Fischer-Geistbeck untern Anlehnung an die neuen Lehrpläne* (Munich, 1926), 41.

79. Ibid., 43.

80. Richard Bitterling and Theodor Otto, *Fischer-Geistbeck Erdkunde für höhere Lehranstalten: Ausgewählte Abschnitte der Allgemeinen Erdkunde* (Munich, 1925), 98.

81. Ibid., 116.

82. Ibid., 116.

83. Friedrich Littig and Hermann Vogel, *Geographie für höhere Lehranstalten. Die geographischen Grundlagen der Staatenbildung und weltpolitischer Fragen mit besonderer Beziehung auf Deutschland,* 3d ed. (Munich, 1923), 1.

84. Ibid., 11.

85. Ibid., 26, 27, 28.

86. Ibid., 51.

87. Ibid., 56.

88. Ibid., 57.

89. "Geopolitics as a science has to do with both of the elementary basic forms of reality: with the given space of the earth and with the time unfolding therein . . . but only in connection with a third: the humanity, which fill this earth-space as a state-forming essence and which experiences time in it." Hans Linhardt and Gottfried Vogenauer, *Die Strukturskizze im geographischen und historisch-geopolitischen Unterricht* (Munich, 1925), 13.

90. Walther Gehl, *Geschichte für Mittelschulen. 5. Heft* (Breslau, 1927), 52.

91. Ibid., 62.

92. Walther Gehl, *Geschichte für höhere Schulen, 4. Heft* (Breslau, 1925–26), 149; Kurt Gerstenberg and Ernst Krüger, *Geschichtswerk für höheren Schulen* (Munich, 1933), 9: 273.

93. E. Anders, *Erdkundliche Grundlagen geschichtlicher Entwicklung* (Breslau, 1924), 55–56.

94. Otto Boelitz, *Das Grenz- und Auslanddeutschtum, seine Geschichte und seine Bedeutung* (Munich, 1926), iii–iv.

95. Thies, *Die Staaten,* 9.

96. Ibid., 22.

97. Franz Knieper, *Politische Geographie (Geopolitik) für den Unterricht* (Bachum, 1933), 5–6.

98. Ibid., 18–20.

99. Ibid., 22–23.

100. An analysis of geopolitical and political geographical content in leading geographic journals of the same period also reveals an irregular increase in the attention devoted to these topics. See Henning Heske, "Political Geographers of the Past III: German Geographical Research in the Nazi Period: A Content Analysis of the Major Geography Journals, 1925–1945," *PGQ* 5 (1986): 267–81.

101. Robert E. Dickinson, *Makers of Modern Geography* (London, 1969), 51–53.

102. Hermann Guthe, for instance, who taught at the TH Hannover from 1863 to 1873, was a mathematician and mineralogist who occasionally lectured on geographic topics in the pre-Obst era.

103. Beck, 10.

104. Rita Seidel, Horst Gerken, Oskar Mahrenholtz, Karl-Heinz Manegold, Cord Meckseper, Gerhard Schlitt, *Catalogus Professorum 1831–1981. Festschrift zum 150jährigen Bestehen der Universität Hannover* 2: 219.

105. Obst's two lecturers, Kurt Brüning and Hans Spreitzer, both assumed important academic positions in the Nazi era. Brüning in 1944 and 1945 led the Reichsarbeits-gemeinschaft für Raumforschung (Reich Work Group for Spatial Research) and Spreitzer from 1940 to 1945 was deputy leader of the Hochschularbeitsgemeinschaft für Raum-forschung (University Work Group for Spatial Research) at the German University in Prague. See Erich Obst, "Geographie," in *100 Jahre Technische Hochschule Hannover. Festschrift zur Hundertjarhfeier am 15. Juni 1931,* ed. University Rector and Senate (Hannover, 1931), 108-9: and Rössler, 267, 274.

106. For the political goals of Obst at this time in his affiliation with the journal see Harbeck, "*Zeitschrift,*" 80-84.

107. *Programm der Technischen Hochschule zu Hannover: Studienjahr 1925/26* (Hannover, 1925), 67; *Programm Hannover, 1926/27,* 23.

108. *Programm Hannover, 1925/26, 67.* The book was reviewed positively and at con-siderable length in Hermann Lautensach, "Erich Obsts 'England, Europa und die Welt'," *GA* 28 (1927): 320-28. Lautensach noted the book's geopolitical approach, and predicted that its analysis would make it "a standard work for decades to come." Ibid., 328.

109. *Programm Hannover, 1929/30,* 78. The reissuing of the work, a geopolitical stan-dard, was undertaken by Obst, Otto Maull, and Hugo Hassinger, edited by Karl Haus-hofer. See Rudolf Kjellén, *Die Grossmächte vor und nach dem Weltkriege,* 2d ed., ed. Karl Haushofer (Leipzig, 1932).

110. Obst, "Geographie," 108-9.

111. See Dix's reference to *Bonitierung* of the earth by regions in his speech to the German Geographic Congress of 1926, in *VDG* (1926): 220-28.

112. Unquestionably, the best source on Raumforschung is Rössler.

113. Obst, "Geographie," 108.

114. Seidel, *Festschrift zum 150jährigen Bestehen,* 1: 283.

115. From the lecture notes in GStA, HA I, Rep 92: NL Vogel, 20 "Grundzüge der allegemeine Politische Geographie" Bl. 5. Vogel's notes for several other courses in po-litical and historical geography are contained here as well.

116. Some course titles are "Geography of Germandom" (Sieger), "Geopolitical Chief Problems of World Aviation" (Ernst), "Fate of the German Eastern Border" (J. Stulz, at Cologne), and so on. For complete listings see "Geographische, ethnographische und verwandte Vorlesungen in deutscher Sprache an den Hochschulen Mitteleuropas im Som-merhalbjahr 1924," *PM* 70 (1924): 81-83, and the listings under the same title for the winter semester of 1928/29 in *PM* 74 (1928): 296-97.

117. Gerd Voigt, "Aufgaben und Funktion der Osteuropa-Studien in der Weimarer Republik," in *Studien über die deutsche Geschichtswissenschaft,* vol. 2; *Die bürgerliche deutsche Geschichtsschreibung von der Reichseinigung von oben bis zur Befreiung Deutschlands vom Faschismus,* ed. Joachim Streisand (Berlin, 1965), 370.

118. Hessisches Staatsarchiv Marburg (HSM): 307d, Nr. 383; Acc. 1967/11, pieces 3-8, "Lebenslauf, Johann Wilhelm Mannhardt," n.d.

119. Schultze-Jena's departure was motivated in part by disagreements with the administration over the ordinances governing the institute. See HSM: 307 d, Nr. 384; Acc. 1967/11, "Der Kurator an die Philosophische Fakultät, 12.4.26." For Mannhardt's functions see Johann Wilhelm Mannhardt, *Hochschule, Deutschtum und Ausland. Neue Wege deutscher politischen Wissenschaft und Erziehung* (Marburg an der Lahn, 1927), 13-14, 56-57.

120. Inge Auerbach, ed., *Catalogus Professorum academiae Marburgensis. Die akademischen Lehrer der Philipps-Universität Marburg* (Marburg, 1979), 2:563-64.

121. Mannhardt, *Hochschule,* 14, 51.

122. Johann Wilhelm Mannhardt, "Zum Tode Robert Siegers," *DW* 4 (1927): 96-97.

123. Ibid., 18-21.

124. Ibid., 11-13.

125. Ibid., 11. HSM: 307 d, Nr. 383; Acc 1967/11, piece 44, "Antrag der Fakultät, 22.2.26." The faculty document argued on Mannhardt's behalf as follows: "The wish to establish this subject as a topic of instruction also at other universities is being conveyed in growing strength in petitions and public demands to the governments of the federal states. It seems to us appropriate to officially strengthen the lead that the philosophical faculty of our university has in this regard . . . by communicating an offer of a professorship . . . to Dr. Mannhardt."

126. HSM: 307d, Nr. 383; Acc 1967/11, piece 64, "Ministerium für Wissenschaft, Kunst, und Volksbildung an die Philosophische Fakultät, 11.08.29" and pieces 61 and 62, "Protokoll über die Kommissionssitzung Mannhardt, 11.07.29" (copy). This document records the misgivings of some members of the faculty who questioned the legitimacy of "Auslandskunde" as an academic discipline.

127. Mannhardt, *Hochschule,* 11.

128. See *Verzeichnis der Vorlesungen. Philipps-Universität Marburg* (Marburg), (hereafter *VVM*) at the following semesters and pages: winter, 1931-32, 39-40; winter, 1930-31, 30; winter, 1929-30, 35; winter, 1932-33, 36; summer, 1926, 18.

129. The course included "Volk ohne Raum and Foreign Germandom," taught by Dr. Wiskemann, "Catholic Church and Foreign Germandom," taught by Professor Hermelink, and "Influence of German Legal Thought Abroad," taught by Professor Merk. *VVM*, winter, 1929-30, 35.

130. *VVM*, winter 1922-23, 27; winter 1927-28, 19; summer, 1931, 33.

131. HSM: 307 d, Nr. 383; Acc. 1967/11, piece 29, "Gutachten der Kommission."

132. Johann Wilhelm Mannhardt, *Südtirol. Ein Kampf um deutsche Volkheit* (Jena, 1928), 6-7.

133. In 1925, for example, the ministry supplied RM 2,000 for lecture fees, books, and other costs. The following year Mannhardt was paid to travel as an observer to the second congress of European minorities. HSM: 310, Nr. 4387, Acc. 1983/15, piece 7, "Preussiches Ministerium für Wissenschaft, Kunst und Volksbildung an den Universitätskurator, 29.4.25"; "Ausgabeanweisung, Preussisches Ministerium für Wissenschaft, Kunst und Volksbildung an den Kurator, 18.08.26"; pieces 146, 147, "Antrag auf Genehmigung von Überschreitung des Etats, 09.03.33," and piece 148, "Der Kurator der Universität an die Universitätskasse, 10.03.33".

134. Ibid., piece 43, "Preussisches Ministerium für Wissenschaft Kunst und Volksbildung an den Kurator des Universität Marburg, 14.09.26."

135. Otthein Rammstedt, *Deutsche Soziologie, 1933–1945. Die Normalität einer Anpassung* (Frankfurt am Main, 1986), 78 n.

136. Voigt, "Osteuropa-Studien," 373. Michael Burleigh, *Germany Turns Eastward: A Study of Ostforschung in the Third Reich* (Cambridge, Eng., 1988), passim, also deals at length with Brackmann.

137. Volz cited in Voigt, "Osteuropa-Studien," 378.

138. Ibid., 378.

139. For another account that emphasizes the interdisciplinary approach of the Stiftung see Burleigh, *Germany Turns Eastward,* 25–26.

140. See, for example, Hermann Wopfner, "Entstehung und Eigenart des tirolischen Volkstums," *DHVK* 1 (Heft 5, 1930–31), 290–96. Wopfner argues (290) that "one of the most important conditions of historical life is the space in which it is played out. For the Tyrolians it is significant that its living space is exclusively alpine." Later (295), he combines volk and geography: "In my opinion, the peculiarity of the living space, the ethnic composition and the legal standing of the peasant class count among the circumstances that account for the sharp differentiation of the Tyrolean population from that of the eastern Austrian alpine lands, and these are still today perceptible in their effects."

141. Penck, "Deutscher Volks- und Kulturboden," 69.

142. Voigt, "Osteuropa-Studien," 380. For an exchange of letters between Albrecht Penck and Albert Brackmann over the acrimonious last days of the Stiftung, which were plagued by internal dissension and attacks by the Leipzig press, see GSTA: Rep. 92, NL Brackmann; 64 Mappe 25, Bl. 86–98. See also Oberkrome, 80–81.

143. For a statement of the Hochschule's mission see "Zusammenfassender Bericht," *BDHP* 4 (1926), 9. The *Berichte* were published as supplements to Grabowsky, *Zeitschrift für Politik.* For a sample of Hoffmann's use of geopolitical themes and ideas in his approach to politics see Karl Hoffmann, "Zwischen zwei Zeitaltern," in *Die neue Front,* ed. Moeller van den Bruck, Heinrich von Gleichen, and Max Hildebert Boehm (Berlin, 1922), 359–77, especially 371–73.

144. Ernst Jäckh and Otto Suhr, *Geschichte der deutschen Hochschule für Politik* (Berlin, 1952), 11, 14, 15.

145. BAP: 61 Ko 1: 376, piece 25 *VVDH* (Berlin, 1926), 17. Seminars within this course of study sometimes enrolled as many as two hundred students per semester in the middle 1920s. *BDHP* 4 (1926): 11.

146. Jäckh, *Deutschland,* 14.

147. BAP: 61 Ko 1: 376, piece 18 *VVDH* (Berlin, 1926).

148. BAP: 61 Ko 1: 376, pieces 29–30 (*Dozenten-Verzeichnis,* 1926).

149. Clemens, 153–54: Sontheimer, 32: Schwierskott, 105.

150. BAP: 61 Ko 1: 375, piece 13 (*Hochschule für Nationale Politik, Vorlesungsverzeichnis,* winter 1924–25 [Berlin, 1924], 3).

151. Clemens, 152, 104. Spahn was essential to the funding of the PK because he enjoyed close connections to major donors such as Arthur Hugenberg, with whom he sat in the Reichstag for the Deutschnationale Volkspartei (DNVP) later in the 1920s, and Hugo Stinnes. Clemens, 162, and for his political relations with Hugenberg, see John A. Leopold, *Alfred Hugenberg: The Radical Nationalist Campaign against the Weimar Republic* (New Haven, Conn., 1977), 155, and 180 n.

152. BAP: 61 Ko 1; 375, piece 15, 16 (*Vorlesungsverzeichnis,* winter 1924–25, 6, 8, 9).

153. Spahn, "Mitteleuropa," 4, 38.

154. Spahn, "Grossdeutsch," 177–78.

155. Martin Spahn, "Böhmen und das deutsche Volk," *GB* 3 (1926): 64–65.

156. BAK: R 118/17, Hochschule für Nationale Politik ("Niederschrift der Besprechung vom 23. June 1928 im Politischen Kolleg, Berlin," 1, 4).

157. See, for example, Hoffmann, "Zwischen zwei Zeitaltern," 359–77.

158. Schwierskott, *Arthur Moeller van den Bruck,* 107: ZSTA Potsdam, 61 Ko 1: 375, piece 15 (*Vorlesungsverzeichnis,* winter 1924–25, 7).

159. Max Hildebert Boehm, *Die deutschen Grenzlande* (Berlin, 1925), 12.

160. Ibid., 15: Max Hildebert Boehm, "Staatsallgewalt und Nationalitätenproblem" in *Volk unter Völkern,* ed. Karl Christian von Loesch, (Breslau, 1925), 1: 205.

161. Max Hildebert Boehm, "Mitteleuropa und der Osten," *VR* 1 (1925): 71.

162. Max Hildebert Boehm, "Grossdeutsche Vorarbeit—An uns selber," *GB* 1 (1924), 4; Boehm, *Grenzlande,* 277. The concept of continental power groupings in the new world order that Boehm adopts here was central to geopolitical thought. See Gruchmann, 20-21. Boehm's application of geographic perspectives to questions of ethnicity and political autonomy was praised by Hermann Rüdiger before the German Geographic Congress in 1934. See Rüdiger, "Geographie und Deutschtumskunde," *VDG* 25 (1934): 88.

163. BAK: R 43 II/948, Reichskanzlei, frames 10-11 (Max Hildebert Boehm, "Das Institut für Grenz- und Auslandstudien, Berlin").

164. Clemens, 167-68. The leaders of the DHP complained that the PK violated the agreement between the two institutions by refusing to allow any but conservative scholars to teach its students. BAK: R 118/28, Hochschule für Nationale Politik ("Reichsministerium des Innern Wirth an Kuratorium des DHP, 5 May 1930," pieces 73-74).

165. BAK: R 43 II/948, Reichskanzlei, Frame 12 (Boehm, "Das Institut")

166. Leopold, 155: Rammstedt, 78: Christoph Klessmann, "Osteuropaforschung und Lebensraumpolitik im Dritten Reich," in *Wissenschaft im Dritten Reich,* ed. Peter Lundgreen (Frankfurt am Main, 1985), 357.

167. See Donald H. Norton, "Karl Haushofer and the German Academy, 1925-1945," *CEH* 1 (1968): 80-98.

168. For a treatment of this, especially of the Nazi accession to power in the Deutsche Studentenschaft in 1931, see Konrad Jarausch, *Deutsche Studenten 1800–1970* (Frankfurt am Main, 1984), 152-62. See also, for insight into the attitudes of members of the teaching profession, Jarausch, *The Unfree Professions: German Lawyers, Teachers and Engineers, 1900–1950* (New York, 1990), 54-77, 217-19. An insightful account of the politics of university students in the early years of the Republic is found in Uwe Lohalm, *Völkischer Radikalismus. Die Geschichte des Deutschvölkischen Schutz- und Trutz-bundes 1919–1923* (Hamburg, 1970), 164-67.

169. Sontheimer, 248.

Chapter 7. "The Suggestive Map": Geopolitics and Cartography

1. For an account in English of the German cartographers, see G. R. Crone, *Maps and Their Makers: An Introduction to the History of Cartography,* 4th ed. (London, 1968), 157-59. See also, Leo Bagrow, *Die Geschichte der Kartographie* (Berlin, 1951), 167-70; Oswald Muris, *Der Globus im Wandel der Zeiten* (Berlin, 1961), 47-62.

2. Karl Haushofer, "Die suggestive Karte," in *Bausteine,* ed. Karl Haushofer, et al. 343. This essay originally appeared in the periodical *Grenzboten* in 1922. See *Grenzboten,* 1 (1922): 17-18.

3. J. B. Harley was the most prominent of the cartographic deconstructionists to reveal the "hidden agenda" of maps. See J. B. Harley, "Silences and Secrecy: The Hidden Agenda of Cartography in Early Modern Europe," *Imago Mundi* 40 (1988): 57-76; idem, "Deconstructing the Map," *Cartographica* 26 (1982): 1-19; and idem, "Maps, Knowledge

and Power," in *The Iconography of Landscape,* ed. D. Cosgrove and S. Daniels (Cambridge, Eng., 1988), 277–312.

4. On geopolitical cartography see Harke, 59.

5. Wilhelm Volz, "Gutachten über den Ullsteinatlas," *DA* 24 (1925): 241. See also the reference to the case in Ullmann's memoirs. Hermann Ullmann, *Hermann Ullmann. Publizist in der Zeitenwende* (Munich, 1965), 63.

6. For the criticism and accounts of the case see "Ein 'deutscher' Weltatlas," *DA* 24 (1924): 21, and "Das Ende des Prozesses um den Ullsteinschen Weltatlas," *DA* 24 (1925): 339–40. On the Deutscher Geographentag see '+' [pseud], "Die Aufgaben eines deutschen Atlasses," *ZGEB* 7–8 (1925): 311. See also Gottfried Fittbogen's critique of the case and agenda for German maps, "Deutsche Atlanten und neue Geographie," *DA* 24 (1925): 141–44: "A German atlas that meets contemporary needs must observe three requirements: (1) it must show the old Reichsgrenzen, (2) it must show the settlement maps of ethnic Germans, and (3) it must use everywhere the German names (if not alone, at least on first reference).

7. GStA: Rep. 90, 1756 S. II. 3. 8, "Zentralausschuss des deutschen Geographentages an Reichsministerium des Innern," 30 June 1925 (copy).

8. Schwierskott, 100. On the *Volksbund* see also Ullmann, *Hermann Ullmann,* 75.

9. J. C. Hess, *"Das ganze Deutschland soll es sein." Demokratischer Nationalismus in der Weimarer Republik am Beispiel der Deutschen Demokratischen Partei* (Stuttgart, 1978), 15.

10. Arnold Hillen Ziegfeld, "Karte und Schule," in *Staat und Volkstum. Bücher des Deutschtums,* ed. Karl Christian von Loesch and Arnold Hillen Ziegfeld (Berlin, 1926), 2: 707–8. Emphasis in the original.

11. Ibid., 706. See his similar arguments in A. Hillen Ziegfeld, "Neue Atlanten— Neue Wege!" *GR* 7 (1930): 51–54.

12. The pamphlet is preserved in BAK: NL 160, Pechel, 121.

13. A. Hillen Ziegfeld, "Die deutsche Kartographie nach dem Weltkriege," in *Volk unter Völkern,* ed. Karl Christian von Loesch, 445.

14. Penck, "Deutscher Volks- und Kulturboden," 68–69.

15. *ZgU,* "Nachtrag zum Verzeichnis der genehmigten Lehrbücher," 5 June 1925, 186.

16. Otto Maull, "Über politischgeographisch-geopolitische Karten," in *Bausteine,* ed. Karl Haushofer et al., 339–40, 332.

17. Atlases with geopolitical maps were "political propaganda aids of outstanding value," according to Hermann Raschhofer, "Ein Ostpreussen-Atlas," *DA* 30 (1931): 112.

18. Dr. E., "Los von der Sprachenkarte," *DW* 3 (1926): 367. Another explication of the shortcomings of linguistic maps to determine boundaries appeared in Walter Geisler, "Politik und Sprachen-Karten: Ein Beitrag zur Frage des 'polnischen' Korridors," *ZfG* 3 (1926): 701–13.

19. Springenschmid.

20. Ibid., vi.

21. Hans Speier, "Magic Geography," *Social Research* 8 (1941): 330.

22. Kurt Tucholsky, the acid-tongued liberal journalist, noted in 1928 "that a great number of the larger atlases for school and home now falsify is well known. . . . Here (Germans) are systematically incited to annexation and revanchism." In Kurt Tucholsky,

"Sieg im Atlas," in Mary Gerold-Tucholsky and Fritz J. Raddatz, eds., *Gesammelte Werke, Bd. II, 1925–1928* (Reinbek bei Hamburg, 1960), 1258.

Chapter 8. Space for the Third Man: Geopolitics and the Weimar Crusade for Colonies

1. Hans Grimm, "Übervölkerung und Kolonialproblem," in *Die neue Front*, ed. Moeller van den Bruck, Heinrich von Gleichen, and Max Hildebert Boehm (Berlin, 1922), 345, argued that Germany had space for only two of every three Germans, hence, the plight of the so-called third man.

2. For statistics on population see Erich Duems, ed., *Das Buch der deutschen Kolonien* (Leipzig, 1937), i; on trade and population see Petzina, 3: 24-25. Werner Conze has pointed out that the loss of the colonies brought advantages as well as disadvantages: "The loss of the colonies was, indeed, not of great importance economically, (and) although Germany was excluded from any future colonial expansion, it also remained obviously outside the thenceforth ever-intensifying confrontation between the white man and the colored over sovereignty in the colonial territories." Werner Conze, *Die Zeit Wilhelms II. und der Weimarer Republik. Deutsche Geschichte 1890–1930* (Stuttgart, 1964), 157-58.

3. Hans-Ulrich Wehler, *Bismarck und der Imperialismus* (Cologne, 1969) (data) is the most famous exposition of this argument.

4. Fesser, 54.

5. The extent of German efforts to revise the colonial settlement becomes apparent later in this volume, but one proof of the widespread resentment of the loss of the empire can be found in the nearly unanimous approval of a vote of protest against the seizure of the colonies held in the National Assembly on 1 March 1919. The measure was approved in a rare example of Weimar political unity by a vote of 414 to 7, with the support of many members of the leftist (Unabhängige Sozialdemokratische Partei Deutschlands (USPD, or Independent Social Democratic Party). See Grunder, 217. Grunder also points out that colonial literature attained its peak popularity in the 1920s and 1930s rather than in the era when the Germans were in actual possession of colonies.

6. Thomas Childers, "The Social Language of Politics in Germany: The Sociology of Political Discourse in the Weimar Republic," *AHR* 95 (1990): 358.

7. See the discussion of colonial novels, Wolfgang Reif, "Exotismus und Okkultismus," in *Deutsche Literatur. Eine Sozialgeschichte*, ed. Alexander von Bormann and Horst Albert Glaser (Hamburg, 1983), 155-67. See also Joachim Warmbold, *"Ein Stückchen neudeutsch Erd' . . . " Deutsche Kolonial-Literatur. Aspekte ihrer Geschichte, Eigenart und Wirkung, dargestellt am Beispiel Afrikas* (Frankfurt am Main, 1989).

8. Gruchmann, 375.

9. A different view is expressed in Gerstenberger, *Der revolutionäre Konservatismus*, 27.

10. See the extensive discussion of geopolitical colonialist ideas in Kost, *Einflüsse*, 193-233.

11. Karl Haushofer, "Soll Deutschland Kolonialpolitik treiben? Eine Umfrage," *EG* 5 (1927): 638-39. Haushofer was genuinely farsighted on this issue, at least, and recognized the legitimacy of demands for local governance made by the colonized peoples. See "Karl Haushofer to N. N.," 10 September 1927, in Jacobsen, *Haushofer*, 2:82.

12. Karl Haushofer, *Geopolitik des Pazifischen*, 8, 128, and idem, "Das deutsche Volk," 202.

13. See Karl Haushofer, "Der Ost-Eurasiatische Zukunftsblock," *ZfG* 2 (1925): 81-87; "Karl Haushofer to Kurt von Boeckmann," 22 December 1925, in Jacobsen, *Haushofer,* 2:64, reveals that this was the key to Haushofer's repudiation of Locarno, which he said "spoils our eastern future possibilities" by aligning Germany with the West instead.

14. G. W. Schiele, "Wo liegt das deutsche Kolonialland?" *EB,* 16 May 1926, 335-36.

15. See E. von Tzedtwitz, "Deutschland und Russland. Sowjetrussland, Sicherheitspakt und Völkerbund," *EB,* 13 September 1925, 188-91.

16. Alfred Etscheit, "Braucht Deutschland Kolonien?," *DR* 54 (1928): 118.

17. The German Geographic Congress, for example, the most prestigious organization of German academic geographers, adopted a resolution demanding the return of the colonies in 1931. The resolution argued, among other things, that German science and German youth both required broader fields for their activities. See the account of the meeting in Paul Langhans, "Die 24. Tagung des Deutschen Geographentages zu Danzig," *PM* 77 (1931): 195-99. The resolution was sponsored by Franz Thorbecke of Cologne, Carl Troll of Berlin, and Heinrich Schmitthenner of Leipzig.

18. Seidel, *Festschrift zum 150jährigen Bestehen,* 1: 283, 2: 219.

19. See the discussion of the term in Smith, *Ideological,* 83-93.

20. Maull, *Politische Geographie,* 87-88; Hennig and Korholz, *Geopolitik,* 98. The world war was, as early as 1919, being analyzed by German geographers as a manifestation of the permanent interstate struggle for Raum. See Wegener, 20-27.

21. März, *Die Ozeane,* 61-62.

22. Erich Obst, "Wir fordern unsere Kolonien zurück!" 155. This article was reprinted under the title "Warum brauchen wir Kolonien? (Why do we need colonies?) in the company magazine of the Continental Caoutchouc- und Gutta-Percha Kompagnie BAP: 61 Ko 1; 1106, piece 44, 3-6.

23. Hans Meyer, "Geopolitische Betrachtungen."

24. Leo Waibel, "Südwestafrika," *ZfG* 3 (1926): 187.

25. Ibid., 191. ("Besides the remoteness and shortage of water, the small number of natives and above all their low quality give the land its special position within the German protectorates.") Waibel was a geographer at Kiel and later Bonn. A conservative member of the DNVP, he later fled Nazi Germany for the United States.

26. He was on friendly terms with, among others, Heinrich Schnee and Rudolf Pechel, the influential editor of the heavily geopolitical *Deutsche Rundschau.* See GStA: NL Schnee, 38/114, "Grimm to Schnee," 14 July 1931 and 38/115, "Grimm to Schnee," 18 September 1931, and BAK: NL 160, Pechel; 67, "Pechel to Grimm (copy)," 26 August 1932.

27. Grimm, "Die neue Furcht," 262-65.

28. Grimm, "Übervölkerung und Kolonialproblem" 338, 345. See the treatment of this aspect of Grimm's novel in Rolf Geissler, *Dekadenz und Heroismus. Zeitroman und völkisch-nationalsozialistische Literaturkritik* (Stuttgart, 1964), 148-49.

29. Hans Simmer, *Grundzüge der Geopolitik in Anwendung auf Deutschland* (Munich, 1928), 83-84. The same argument appears regularly in other geopolitical writings of the period. See the comments on "overpopulated" Germany's need for settlement colonies in Schmidt and Haack, *Geopoliticsher Typen-Atlas,* 47-48; and H. Key, "Die Folgen der amerikanischen Einwanderungspolitik," *ZfG* 2 (1925): 261-71. Key argues that Europe as a whole is overpopulated and overindustrialized and requires additional land in Africa and in the Americas.

30. Franz Thorbecke, "Warum Kolonien?" *Kölnischen Zeitung,* 24 April 1934.

31. Dix, *Weltkrise,* 25, 28.

32. Adolf Grabowsky, "Soll Deutschland Kolonialpolitik treiben? Eine Umfrage," *EG* 5 (1927): 638. This argument was popular with geographers such as H. Hertzberg, who makes it in "Die Deutschen, ein Kolonialvolk," *GA* 16 (1925): 68-71. This entire issue of the *Geographischer Anzeiger* was devoted to articles on colonial topics. The same argument is prominent in Meyer, who calls the colonies schools "for world-political understanding and will." Hans Grimm, although generally concerned with other aspects of the presumed German need for colonies, also argued that they taught world-political thinking to Germans. See his introduction, 3, to Frauenbund der Deutschen Kolonialgesellschaft, ed., *Deutsche Jugend und Deutsche Kolonien. Was unsere Jugend über deutsche Arbeit in unseren Kolonien wissen muss* (Aachen, 1932). See also his correspondence with the former colonial secretary Solf, which alludes to the "moral and *volkspädagogische*" function of colonies in BAK: NL 53, Solf; 81, "Solf to Hans Grimm, Colonies," 22 March 1930, and "Grimm to Solf, Colonies," 23 March 1930.

33. Wilhelm Külz, *Reichskommissar* of Southwest Africa before the world war and an extremely procolonialist official of the German Democratic Party during the Weimar era, argued after the war that "German colonial labor will, as in the past, so also in the future serve the cultural and economic welfare of the natives, . . . and (provide) settlement regions for the homeland's human surplus." Külz cited in Armin Behrendt, *Wilhelm Külz. Aus dem Leben eines Suchenden* (Berlin, 1968), 120.

34. Dix, *Weltkrise,* 224-25.

35. Hennig and Korholz, *Geopolitik,* 292.

36. See Laqueur, 32-33, for an assessment of the Weimar German obsession with technological progress and of the heroic view of science and scientists. A good brief discussion of the role of the new technology of radio in popular culture can be found in Peukert, 172-73. Peter Fritzsche, *A Nation of Fliers: German Aviation and the Popular Imagination* (Cambridge, Mass., 1991), treats the role of aviation and images of aviation in German culture of the period.

37. For a discussion of this modernizing function of technology for German nationalism generally see Herf, "Comments," 35-39.

38. Karl Haushofer, *Geopolitik des Pazifischen,* 39, 216. Otto Riedel, "Die deutschen Kolonien der Südsee," *ZfG* 1 (1924): 634. Otto Maull, by contrast, argued that it was precisely radio that could help Germany overcome the loss of political power produced by the loss of its cable and naval stations in the colonies. Maull, *Politische Geographie,* 515.

39. Hochholzer, "Flugwesens," 250, 254.

40. Rudolf Pommrich, "Geopolitische Ziele in der Luftpolitik," *ZfG* 4 (1927): 558-59. For optimistic geopolitical assessments of the impact of air travel on Germany's position in central Europe see the following: Richard Hennig, *Weltluftverkehr und Weltluftpolitik* (Berlin, 1930), 49; Hochholzer, "Flugwesens," 249; Wütschke, Luftverkehr, 221.

41. Dix, *Geopolitik,* 4, and Maull, *Politische Geographie,* 516. Technological advances in aviation would even extend the colonial competition to the polar regions, according to Lampe, "Versuch," 105-10.

42. The most prolific geopolitical exponent of the importance of naval bases abroad was Josef März. He treated the topic in many publications, most notably, "Schicksal," 165-468; idem, *Landmächte und Seemächte* idem, *Die Ozeane.*

43. Dix, *Politische Geographie,* 560.

44. Erich Duems and Willibald von Stuemer, eds. *Fünfzig Jahre deutsche Kolonial-gesellschaft 1882–1932* (n.p., n.d.), 100.

45. A complete overview of the various organizations allied under the umbrella of the Koloniale Reichsarbeits gemeinschaft (KORAG) can be found in BAP: 61 Ko 1; 1108, Bl. 55–59, "Übersicht über die kolonialen Organisationen," 11 January 1930. See also Hildebrand, *Vom Reich,* 57–63, Grunder, 219–21, and Wolfe W. Schmokel, *Dream of Empire: German Colonialism 1919–1945* (New Haven, Conn., 1964), 1–2.

46. Jürgen Kuczynski, *Studien zur Geschichte des deutschen Imperialismus. Vol. 2. Propaganda-organisationen des Monopolkapitals* (Berlin, 1950), 149.

47. Hildebrand, 102–3, provides a socioeconomic analysis of colonial enthusiasts and concludes they were predominantly male and members of the former colonial bureaucracy, academia, or the military along with a sprinkling of exporters, importers, and planters. An order of beer coasters for the DKG in 1927 carried the following inscription:

Ohne Kolonien
keine Sicherheit im Bezug von Rohstoffen!
Ohne Rohstoffe
keine Industrie!
Ohne Industrie
kein ausreichender Wohlstand!

Flyers included in the order carried the message, "Bemühe Dich, mehr wie bisher über die Grenzen Deines Vaterlandes hinauszudenken, so, wie es die Engländer, Franzosen und andere Völker Europas tun! Deutschlands Selbständigkeit und Existenz hängt von eigenem Kolonialbesitz ab!" See BAP: 61 Ko 1; 1106, Bl. 3–5, "Überseeische Industrie- und Handelsgesellschaft an die DKG," 27 May 1927 (copy).

48. The governing board, or *Vorstand,* of the colonial-economic committee was an extremely mixed bag, including Arthur Dix, Friedrich Burgdörfer, Hans Grimm, DNVP deputy Laverrenz, Socialist Max Cohen-Reuß, the geographer Paul Rohrbach, representatives of exporting industries, and many others. See the list of members in "Vorstand," *Verhandlungen des Vorstandes des Kolonial-Wirtschaftlichen Komitees,* 1 (1932): 1–3.

49. See the account of the congress in "Grosse Koloniale Kundgebung," in *RF* 11 June 1925, 4.

50. BAK: R 43 I; Reichskanzlei, Kolonien; 625, frame 178, "Richtlinien für koloniale Propaganda."

51. See the reprint of the program in Koloniale Reichsarbeitsgemeinschaft, ed., *Wesen und Ziele der deutschen Kolonialbewegung. Verkündigung eines Allgemeinen Deutschen Kolonialprogramms der Kolonialen Reichsarbeitsgemeinschaft am 22. Juni 1928 in Köln a. Rh.* (Berlin, 1928), 13–18. This and other evidence of enthusiasm for settlement colonies call for a reevaluation of Wolfe Schmokel's assertion that the colonialists did not take seriously the acquisition of overseas settlement space. See Schmokel, 49. For instance, see the resolution of the main assembly of the DKG in Königsberg, 12 June 1927, which precedes an argument for internal settlement by noting its commitment to the acquisition of "overseas German settlements . . . for our *Volk ohne Raum.*" BAK: R 43 I; Reichskanzlei, Kolonien; 626, frame 27, "Entschliessung gefasst auf der Hauptversammlung."

52. BAP: 61 Ko 1; 553, Bl. 51-53, "Richtlinien für die Behandlung der deutschen Kolonialfrage, 1930."

53. Heinrich Schnee, "Braucht Deutschland Kolonien? in *Deutschland in den Kolonien. Ein Buch deutscher Tat und deutschen Rechtes,* ed. DKG and Interfraktionelle Koloniale Vereinigung (Berlin, n.d.), 156.

54. The book, published in 1924, sold more than 150,000 copies; Grunder, 220.

55. See, for example, the correspondence with Grimm about colonial affairs in GStA: NL Schnee; HA I, Rep. 92, 38/114; Grimm to Schnee, 14 July 1931 and 38/115, Schnee to Grimm (copy), 18 September 1931; 57/4, Obst to Schnee, 29 January 1924 and 57/5 Obst to Schnee, 26 April 1928; 40/16, Hennig to Schnee, 21 June 1934 and 40/17, Schnee to Hennig, 30 June 1934. See as well his speech delivered to the Interparliamentary Conference of October 1925 in New York City, which emphasized space for population and economic necessity, in NL Schnee; 24/40. As president of the Arbeitsausschuss Deutscher Verbände (ADV) from 1924, Schnee also had links to approximately two thousand German organizations ranging from the *Deutscher Stadtetag* (German Civic Congress) to the Deutscher Schutzbund. See Heinemann, *Die verdrängte Niederlage,* 120-54, for a treatment of the ADV and Schnee's role in it.

56. Heinrich Schnee "Braucht Deutschland Kolonien?" 155, 157.

57. Schnee cited in Duems and Von Stuemer, 112. Jürgen Kuczynski has argued that this statement was inspired by the Nazis. In fact, Schnee's inspiration probably owed more to geopolitical rhetoric, with which he was intimately familiar (see below), than to the Nazis, who were already much less interested in colonies overseas than in eastern Europe. See Kuczynski, 2: 153.

58. GStA: NL Schnee; HA I, Rep. 92, 24/61, "Warum Deutschland Kolonien haben muss," dated 1930.

59. GStA: NL Schnee; HA I, Rep. 92, 37/131, Dix to Schnee, 11 April 1931, and Schnee to Dix (copy) 18 April 1931. The same argument is made by Dr. H. S., presumably Schnee in "Kolonialpolitischer Jahresrückblick," in Hermann Ullmann's conservative *Deutsche Arbeit,* 31 (1932): 194-97.

60. Dr. Saenger, "Das Bevölkerungsproblem," *Weltwirtschaft. Monatsschrift für Weltwirtschaft und Weltverkehr,* in BAK: NL Külz, 25, Bl. 17-18. See also the Saenger article on the relationship of geopolitics and statistics, in Saenger, 255-60. During the war, Otto Hoetzsch had also warned of the threat of "inundation" of the Germans although to argue on behalf of eastern rather than colonial expansion. Michael Burleigh, *Germany Turns Eastwards: A Study of Ostforschung in the Third Reich* (Cambridge, Eng., 1988), 20.

61. Richard Fehn, "Raumnot-Kolonien," *Bayerische Industrie. Organ des Bayerische Industriellen-Verbandes E.V.* 24 (1930): 14-15. This was a special "colonial issue," which also featured articles by Külz.

62. Paul Kupfer, "Alles fängt mit dem Lande an," *UKZ* 42 (1930): 325.

63. BAP: 61 Kol; 1108, Bl. 57, "Übersicht über die kolonialen Organisationen," 11.1.1930.

64. BAP: R 43 I, 626, Reichskanzlei—Kolonien, frames 135-38, "Denkschrift über deutsche Auslandssiedlung."

65. BAK: R 57 (DAI), 1006-13, pamphlet, "Was weisst du vom Kolonialdeutschtum?" (n.d.).

66. BAK: NL 42 (Külz); 25, piece 108, essay for "Der Auslandsdeutsche."

67. Fischer conducted research in Southwest Africa. See Proctor, "From *Anthropologie* to *Rassenkunde*," 145. See also the attitudes of the medical scientists studied in Stefan Wulf, *Das Hamburger Tropeninstitut 1919 bis 1945. Auswärtige Kulturpolitik und Kolonialrevisionismus nach Versailles* (Berlin, 1994), especially 5-12.

68. Friedrich Ebeling, "Schafft Raum zur Überwindung einer schweren Zukunft," *UKZ* 42 (1930): 407-8. Peter Zimmermann has pointed out that the colonialists also viewed colonies as an antidote to social dislocation, which they claimed arose from overcrowding. See P. Zimmermann, "Kampf um den Lebensraum," 166.

69. The term, like *Ethnopolitik* was a part of Kjellén's "empirical" system of political science. See Kjelén, *Der Staat,* 43 ff.

70. See the treatment and criticism of the concept of geopolitics as "dynamic" political geography in Hettner, "Methodische," 332-36.

71. Julius Lips, "Ethnopolitik und Kolonialpolitik," *Koloniale Rundschau* (1932): 532, 538. Lips was, in fact, a cultural relativist who was forced to resign his professorship at Cologne during the Nazi era because of his beliefs. See the account in Thomas Hauschild, "Völkerkunde im Dritten Reich," in *Volkskunde und Nationalsozialismus. Referate und Diskussionen einer Tagung,* ed. Helge Gerndt (Munich, 1987), 247-48.

72. Louis von Kohl, "Biopolitik und Geopolitik als Grundlagen einer Naturwissenschaften vom Staate," *ZfG* 10 (1933): 308.

73. Schmokel, 50-51.

74. See the letter on this topic from Schnee to Theodor Seitz, former governor of Cameroon and guiding spirit behind the founding of KORAG. BAP: 61 Ko 1 (Deutsche Kolonialgesellschaft), 1106, Bl. 22, Schnee to Seitz (copy), 15 June 1926.

75. Freidrich Müller-Ross, "Verschlossene Welt," *UKZ* 44 (1932): 134.

76. BAK: R 57 (DAI): 1004-37, "Arbeitsprogramm der Gesellschaft für Koloniale Erneuerung," n.d. The best study of the prewar history of Bloch's circle is Roger Fletcher, *Revisionism and Empire: Socialist Imperialism in Germany 1897–1914* (London, 1984).

77. BAK, R 43 I: Reichskanzlei, 626, frames 119-20, "Kann ein Sozialist Kolonialfreund sein?"

78. See the very positive review of R. Hennig's book *Geopolitik* by Adolf Reichwein, *SoM* 35 (1929): 449, and the enthusiastic review by Walther Maas of Haushofer's reissue of the Kjellén work, *Die Grossmächte vor und nach dem Weltkriege, SoM* 37 (1931): 267. On eugenics see Klesse, "Mehr sozialistische Bevölkerungspolitik," 314-19; Georg Wolff, "Das Qualitäts-problem in der Bevölkerungspolitik," *SoM* 37 (1931): 145-49, and Hodann, "Bevölkerungspolitik," 529-30. Hodann uses the phrase *lebensunwerten Lebens.*

79. Schnee inspired the colonial movement with "a progressive conception" of the colonial problem, according to Hermann Kranold, "Aussenkolonisation," *SoM* 38 (1932): 196. The Society of Friends of the Socialist Monthly sponsored an evening on 3 March 1930 in which they posed the question, "Does Europe Need Colonies?" The speakers were Schnee, Cohen-Reuss, former governor of East Africa, Albrecht von Rechenberg, and Julius Kaliski. It is difficult to imagine any of these speakers answering in the negative.

80. Max Cohen, "Für eine deutsche Kolonial-Zukunft," *SoM* 32 (1926): 687, 689; and idem, "Kolonialwirtschaft ist Notwendig," *SoM* 34 (1928): 1042-46.

81. Hermann Kranold, "Frankreich und die koloniale Aufgabe Europas," *SoM* 37 (1931): 983.

82. Bloch, "Der Kampf Joseph Blochs," 280.

296 / NOTES TO PAGES 212-216

83. See Heinrich Schnee, "Die Koloniale Schuldlüge," *SM* 21 (1924): 93-125; H. Hertzberg, "Die Deutschen, ein Kolonialvolk, *GA* 16 (1925) 68-71. Rudolf Böhmer, "Kolonialpolitik oder Proletarisierung," *DR* 55 (1929): 65-68; Dix, "Weltgeschichte-Kolonial geschichte," 213-14. Europeans also needed to teach Africans to respect European achievements, argued Erich Obst, who lamented to the Women's League of the DKG in 1934 that "an unconditional respect for the white man no longer exists among the coloreds." BAK: NL 122, Haushofer, 767 h, Obst speech manuscript, "Das Deutschtum in Afrika und seine Wünsche an die reichsdeutsche Heimat."

84. GStA: Rep 92, NL Schnee, 24/66, "Aufzeichnung betreffend koloniale Fragen," dated 1930. This is nearly identical to Dix's argument in *Weltkrise und Kolonialpolitik* where he argues that the problems of the Africans can be solved "only with the aid of European science." Dix, *Weltkrise,* 32.

85. BAK: R 57 (DAI), 1002-5, Ausseninstitut der TH-Berlin, Vorträge der AKO-TECH, 1925, and Plan für die ADOTECH Hochschulvorträge, 1929-1930. Rohrbach was generally perceived as an "easterner" although he lent his talents to the overseas colonialist cause here as he had also done before the war. Burleigh, *Germany Turns Eastward,* 22 and Rüdiger vom Bruch, *Weltpolitik,* 56-57.

86. BAK: R 57, (DAI); 1002-5, Plan für die AKOTECH, 1930, 2.

87. Whereas the Prussian Ministry for Science, Culture, and Public Education ordered that the colonial question be discussed in general terms, while taking consideration of Germany's special position on the question, the Bavarian State Ministry for Instruction and Culture declared in March 1930 that historical and geographical instruction had to give an opportunity to recall the German colonial past and the fact that "for a great people a colonial possession is necessary on political, economic, and cultural grounds." For the Prussian statement see GStA: Rep. 90, 2400, piece 386, *Erlass,* 3 June 1930, signed Grimme. On the Bavarian proclamation see *UKZ* 42 (1930): 329. On the lectures in schools see Kuczynski, 156.

88. The colonialists remained puzzled about what they saw as an insufficiency of passion in the German public's commitment to colonial revision. In 1932 Erich Duems wrote that "The negligible popularity of colonial thought is in itself a surprising fact. One would have supposed that a people like the German, which disposes of too little space, would have seized the possibility of winning great new spaces with passion and resolution." See Duems and Von Stuemer, 99.

89. Hildebrand, 59.

90. Both Schnee, of the Deutsche Volkspartei (DVP) and Wilhelm Külz, of the Deutsche Demokratische Partei (DDP), addressed the topic on a number of occasions, usually to stress the economic need for the colonies. See *Verhandlungen des Reichstages* (hereafter *VDR*) 425: 2839, 428: 5913, for Schnee's comments, and 428: 5921 for Külz. Laverrenz of the DNVP spoke of the need for more living space. See his speech of 27 June 1930, *VDR* 428: 5920.

91. See Schmokel, 76 ff.; and Adolf Rüger, "Der Kolonialrevisionismus in der Weimarer Republik," in *Drang nach Afrika,* ed. Helmuth Stoecker (Berlin, 1977), 243-72.

Chapter 9. Geopolitics and Republican Foreign Policy

1. Stresemann complained repeatedly about the difficulty of conducting a rational policy in view of the volatile response his diplomacy evoked outside and within his party.

See his chiding of the Reichstag for its lack of the "courage to be responsible" in 1923, Hagen Schulze, *Weimar. Deutschland 1917–1933* (Berlin, 1982), Schulze, 260, and his complaints about his own party in "Dr. Stresemann to Geheimrat Prof. Dr. Kahl, 13.03.29," *UF* 7: 343-44.

2. Peter Krüger, *Die Aussenpolitik der Republik von Weimar* (Darmstadt, 1985), 13.

3. Andreas Hillgruber, "Unter dem Schatten von Versailles—Die aussenpolitische Belastung der Weimarer Republik: Realität und Perzeption bei den Deutschen," in *Weimar. Selbstpreisgabe einer Demokratie,* ed. Karl Dietrich Erdmann and Hagen Schulze (Düsseldorf, 1980), 56.

4. Peukert, 55-56. This existence of peaceful opportunities was perceived as well by members of the German military in the mid-1920s in the period of their so-called new course on foreign policy. See Michael Geyer, *Aufrüstung oder Sicherheit. Die Reichswehr in die Krise der Machtpolitik 1924-1936* (Wiesbaden, 1980), 58-62. See also Hillgruber, "Kontinuität," 24.

5. Walter Lipgens, "Europäische Einigungsidee 1923-1930 und Briands Europa-Plan im Urteil der Deutschen Akten," *HZ* 203 (1966): 350.

6. Conze, 227.

7. Krüger, *Versailles,* 10.

8. One example of their focus was the strong support from industrialists for the loan and reparations agreements Stresemann helped negotiate in the Dawes Plan. See Henry Ashby Turner, Jr., *Stresemann and the Politics of the Weimar Republic* (Princeton, N.J., 1972), 172.

9. Leopold, 55-68.

10. Grabowsky, "Primat," 531-32; Karl Haushofer, "Geographische Grundzüge," 262.

11. Hermann Lautensach, "Deutschland und Frankreich," *ZfG* 2 (1925): 154-55.

12. Hans F. Zeck, "Europäische Aussenpolitik," *ZfG* 3 (1926): 577-78. "The world war has barely ended, and a new line of development is beginning that somehow and somewhere will lead to military conflict."

13. Erich Obst, "Berichterstattung aus Europa and Afrika," *ZfG* 3 (1926): 412.

14. Lautensach, "Deutschland," 154.

15. Mitarbeiter, "Deutschlands Weg aus der Einkreisung," *Die Tat* 22 (1931): 933-34. This article was based explicitly on an article written by Hans Zehrer, editor of *Die Tat,* for the *Zeitschrift für Geopolitik.*

16. Ibid., 941.

17. For geopolitical or geopolitically influenced criticisms of the reparations agreements see the following: Dernburg, 6-14; 'Pertinacior' [pseud.], "Politische Rundschau," *DR* 51 (1925): 95; G. Traub, "Der Young-Plan," *EB* 11 (1929): 490-92.

18. Harald Lauen, "Das entschlusslose Mitteleuropa," *GB* 3 (1926): 7. Others argued that Locarno would hem Germany in because now all the eastern states would want a similar border guarantee. See F. Schillmann, "Deutschland und die Welt," *GB* 2 (1925): 235-38.

19. Wilhelm Volz, "Locarno und Oberschlesien," *RF* 10 December 1925, 7.

20. Obst, "Berichterstattung," 58, 63.

21. Georg Krause-Wichmann, "Saargebiet und Locarno," *ZfG* 3 (1926): 227-33.

22. Obst, "Berichterstattung," 412, 414.

23. Karl Haushofer, "Eurasien?" *SM* 21 (1924): 192.

24. Ibid., 192.

25. Martin Spahn, "Die deutsche Sendung im mitteleuropäischen Raum," *SM* 21 (1924): 160.

26. Ibid., 164.

27. Ernst Ritter, *Das Deutsche Ausland-Institut in Stuttgart 1917–1945. Ein Beispiel deutscher Volkstumarbeit zwischen den Weltkriegen* (Wiesbaden, 1976), 14.

28. Kleo Pleyer, "Sudetenraum und Deutsch-Österreich," *ZfG* 5 (1928): 401.

29. Christian Höltje, *Die Weimarer Republik und das OstLocarno-Problem 1919–1934. Revision oder Garantie der deutschen Ostgrenze von 1919* (Würzburg, 1958), 118-19.

30. Ernst Barthel, "Deutschlands und Europas Schicksalsfrage," *ZfG* 3 (1926): 306.

31. Ibid., 308, 309.

32. 'Martellus' [pseud.], "Politische Rundschau," *DR* 52 (1926): 261.

33. Lothar Mischke, "Der polnische Staat als europäisches Problem," *ZfG* 2 (1925): 303, 310.

34. For insightful comments on this issue, see Harke, 60-61.

35. Krüger, *Aussenpolitik*, 12-13.

36. Dr. Buttersack, "Geopolitische Stümpereien und ihre Folgen," *EB* 8 (1926): 402-3.

37. Loesch speech reprinted in "Der Kampf für das Recht im Osten," *ZfG*, 7 (1930): 30.

38. Ibid., 218.

39. Albrecht Haushofer makes all these arguments in A. Haushofer, "Was ist ein Korridor," in *Deutschland und der Korridor*, ed. Friedrich Heiss and A. Hillen Zeigfeld (Berlin, 1933), 202-20; and idem, "Der Staat Danzig," *ZGEB* 7-8 (1926): 335-50.

40. K. C. von Loesch, "Polen," *DR* 51 (1925): 206; Erich Obst, "Sowjetische Aussenpolitik," *ZfG* 2 (1925): 9.

41. Erich Wunderlich, "Das heutige Polen. Eine geographischauslandkundliche Skizze," *Osteuropa. Auslandkundliche Vorträge der Technischen Hochschule Stuttgart* 5 (1933): 31.

42. Erich Wunderlich, *Das moderne Polen in politischgeograpischer Betrachtung*, 2d ed. (Stuttgart, 1933), 38.

43. Von Loesch, "Schutzarbeit und Schutzbundtagung," 2. The term here rendered as *Iron Curtain* is *eiserne(r) Vorhang*.

44. Wilhelm Volz, *Die Ostdeutsche Wirtschaft. Eine wirtschaftsgeographische Untersuchung über die natürlichen Grundlagen des deutschen Ostens und seine Stellung in der gesamtdeutschen Wirtschaft* (Berlin, 1930), 1, 5.

45. Ibid., 101.

46. Walter Geisler, *Schlesien als Raumorganismus* (Breslau, 1932), 1, 39.

47. Sven Hedin, "Die russische Gefahr," *RF* 16 April 1925, 3.

48. Ludwig Quessel, "Rhein und Weichsel," *SoM* 62 (1925): 264-69. Compare with Friedrichsen, 423-30.

49. Felix Stössinger, "Für den Anschluss Deutsch-Österreichs," *SoM* 62 (1925): 339. See similar arguments in Rudolf Cefarin, "Kärnten und seine geopolitische Bedeutung für das Deutschtum," *ZfG* 3 (1926): 338-40; Karl Haushofer, "Zur Geopolitik der Donau," *VR* 1 (1925): 161-73; Friedrich Papenhausen, "Geopolitische Erwagungen zum Deutsch-Osterreichischen Anschlussgedanken," *ZfG* 4 (1927): 319-25.

50. Roswitha Berndt, "Wirtschaftliche Mitteleuropapläne des deutschen Imperialismus (1926-1931)," in *Grundfragen der deutschen Aussenpolitik seit 1871*, ed. Gilbert Ziebura (Darmstadt, 1975), 320. German industrial leaders also founded a Mitteleuropäischer

Wirtschaftstag (Central European Economic Congress) in Vienna in 1925 to promote German economic penetration in the region. Ibid., 322. On the role of economic considerations in views of the German mission in central Europe see Krüger, *Aussenpolitik*, 306.

51. Cited in Reinhard Frommelt, *Paneuropa oder Mitteleuropa. Einigungsbestrebungen im Kalkül deutscher Wirtschaft und Politik 1925–1933* (Stuttgart, 1977), 70.

52. Grundmann, 7.

53. *ADAP*, Ser. B, I/1, 178; "Denkschrift betreffend die Bereitstellung von 30 Millionen RM für die Gewährung von Krediten an das Bodenständige Deutschtum im europäischen Ausland," 431.

54. The man who used this term was Hans Freytag. Cited in Kurt Düwell, *Deutschlands Auswärtige Kulturpolitik 1918–1932. Grundlagen und Dokumente* (Cologne, 1976), 103.

55. Cited, ibid., 106.

56. Martin Broszat, *Zweihundert Jahre deutsche Polenpolitik* (Frankfurt, 1972), 214.

57. Cited, ibid., 172.

58. "It thus seems likely that Stresemann used the minorities problem during the Locarno period, 1925-26, largely to convince his domestic critics that he planned to enter the League not simply to acquiesce to French wishes but to assert 'burning national interests.' By staking his claim to the minorities cause, Stresemann acquired an instrument which, when wielded skillfully and with restraint, united the Reich, proclaimed Germany an adherent of Wilsonianism, and provided a useful accompaniment to his western policies." Carole Fink, "Defender of Minorities: Germany in the League of Nations, 1926-1933," *CEH* 5 (1972): 338-39, and see 351-58.

59. Ibid., 355.

60. Cited in Norbert Krekeler, *Revisionsanspruch und geheime Ostpolitik der Weimarer Republik. Die Subventionierung der deutschen Minderheit in Polen* (Stuttgart, 1973), 34.

61. Ibid., 35. See also Harald von Riekhoff, *German-Polish Relations, 1918–1933* (Baltimore, Md., 1971), 194-225.

62. Krekeler, 67. In 1924, for example, the Auswärtiges Amt (AA) distributed more than two hundred thousand RM to banks in Posen, Bromberg, and Danzig through the German Protective League.

63. BAK: ZSg. 1-44/6(g), "Was wir wollen!" 2-3.

64. Ibid., 5.

65. BAK: ZSg. 1-44/12, "Das Freiheitsprogramm der DNVP," 23-24.

66. On the secession see Jonas, 168-69. See, too, Lindeiner-Wildau, 198.

67. *VDR*, 22.03.26, vol. 389, 6473.

68. Ibid., 6501.

69. Ibid., 17. 03. 31, vol. 445, 1643-44.

70. Hess, 113.

71. Ibid., 248-51.

72. BAK: NL 122, Haushofer/896; "Dr. Erich Obst, Aufsatz über Aussenpolitik," September 1930, 15a.

73. Krekeler, 37.

74. As Stresemann said when defending the Berlin Treaty in 1926, "The tasks of our policy are determined by the geographic position of Germany and by all that fate has decreed for the German people in a completely different way from the policy of the other great European nations. German foreign policy must in the first degree be peaceful policy

toward all sides." Cited in Höltje, 116. On attitudes within the foreign policy elite see Krüger, *Versailles*, 33, 132.

75. Richard N. Coudenhove-Kalergi, *Pan-Europa* (Vienna, 1923), ix, xi.

76. Ibid., 24-25.

77. Ibid., 135.

78. Ibid., 14-17, 135.

79. Ibid., 144.

80. Ibid., 83.

81. Ibid., 18-19.

82. Ibid., viii. Compare with Dix, *Weltkrise*, 11; Kranold, "Frankreich und die koloniale Aufgabe," 985; Max Cohen, "Die aussenpolitische Forderung," *SOM* 30 (1924): 288.

83. Coudenhove-Kalergi, *Pan-Europa*, 144, 22. Compare this, for example, with März, "Schicksal," 266, 454.

84. Ernst Barthel, "Deutschlands," 305; Hans Ludwig Krug, "Was bestimmt Europas Grenzen?" *ZfG* 9 (1932): 9.

85. See Richard Hennig, "Italien am geopolitischen Scheidewege," *ZfG* 4 (1927): 241-46; and Paul Ostwald, "Deutschland und Japan," *ZfG* 3 (1926): 620-24.

86. Grabowsky, "Soll Deutschland," 636.

87. Karl Christian von Loesch, "Die grösseren Zusammenschlüsse. Paneuropa," in *Jenseits der Grossmächte*, ed. Karl Haushofer (Leipzig, 1932), 393 n.

88. Ibid., 402-3.

89. Ibid., 415.

90. See the comments on this in Berndt, 318. See, also, Karl Haushofer, *Geopolitik der Pan-Idee* (Berlin, 1931), 27.

91. Rolf Wolkan, "Grossdeutschland und Paneuropa," *DA* 26 (1926): 33; Julius Paul Köhler, "Pan-Europa," *DA* 24 (1925): 229.

92. Ewald Weisemann, "Vereinigte Staaten von Europa?" *RF* 10 February 1927, 1.

93. Von Loesch, "Paneuropa," 404-5.

94. Richard N. Coudenhove-Kalergi, "Mitteleuropa," *Pan-Europa* 6 (1930): 87. The resurgence of Mitteleuropa ideology in central and eastern Europe in the late 1980s had a great deal in common with Coudenhove-Kalergi's *Pan-Europa*, particularly its attempt to resist the hegemony of the flank powers of the Soviet Union, now no longer a serious threat, and the United States. Peter Bender has written "The renaissance of Mitteleuropa is first of all a protest against the division of the continent, against the hegemony of the Americans and the Russians, against the totalitarianism of the ideologies." With the collapse of Soviet dominance it remains to be seen if the idea's positive message of unity is as strong as was its negative message of defense against outside aggressors. For an illuminating essay on the nontotalizing, postmodern elements of the modern Mitteleuropa idea see Hans-Georg Betz, "Mitteleuropa and Post-Modern European Identity," *New German Critique* 43 (1990): 173-92.

95. Von Loesch, "Paneuropa," 389.

96. Carl Hanns Pollog, "Wahrer Völkerbund und Schein-Völkerbund," *ZfG* 2 (1925): 467.

97. Ernst Sarre, "Das Saargebiet und der 10. Januar 1925," *ZfG* 2 (1925): 12. Sarre also claimed that the *Zeitschrift für Geopolitik* enjoyed international influence: "I am much obliged to the *Zeitschrift für Geopolitik* for inviting me to report to Germans in the Reich on the Saarland and its crisis. I recently became acquainted with this journal in England and

learned that various members of Parliament followed it closely. Under these circumstances I can take it as self-evident that the *Zeitschrift für Geopolitik* is widely disseminated among German political, business, and scholarly circles, and also that the deputies [of the Reichstag] and the diplomats in the Wilhelmstrasse are among its circle of friends." Sarre, 11.

98. Hermann Lautensach, "Berichterstattung über erdumspannende Vorgänge," *ZfG* 2 (1925): 596.

99. Karl Haushofer was critical of the League on these grounds. Matern, 37.

100. Martin Spahn, "Völkerbund und Sicherheitsfrage," *SM* 24 (1927): 285.

101. Obst, "Berichterstattung," 741.

102. Ibid., 742.

103. M.M. Lee, "Gustav Stresemann und die deutsche Völkerbundspolitik 1925-1930," in *Gustav Stresemann,* ed. M. M. Lee and Wolfgang Michalka (Darmstadt, 1982), 351; "Aus der Rundfunkrede Dr. Stresemanns über den Vertrag Locarno, 03.11.25," *UF* 6: 402.

104. Karl Haushofer, "Ausstrahlungen politischer Geographie," 71.

105. On Stresemann's goals in the League see Christoph Kimmich, *Germany and the League of Nations* (Chicago, 1976), 194-95.

106. "Geh. Regierungsrat Dr. Quaatz (DNVP) über Locarno und die deutsche Wirtschaft, 14.11.25," *UF* 6: 397-98.

107. "Aus der Rede des Abg. Graf Westarp (DNVP), 24.11.25," *UF* 6: 419-20.

108. Obst, "Berichterstattung," 922.

109. Grabowsky, "Genf und Wir," 701.

110. Grabowsky, "Völkerbund," 461.

111. Ibid., 449.

112. Ibid., 459, 450-51.

113. Lee, 357-58.

114. Krüger, *Aussenpolitik,* 471.

115. Lee, 361-62.

116. "Politische Rundschau," *DR* 57 (1930): 89.

117. Ibid., 365. See, also, Kimmich, 194.

Chapter 10. The Legacy of Weimar Geopolitics

1. Christoph Herfurth, *Geschichte und Geographie (Geopolitik)* (Langensalza, 1938), 8-9. Or see the guidelines for teachers from Theodor Müller, *Erdkunde, Heimatkunde und Geopolitik als völkisches Bildungsgut,* reprinted in part in Arbeitsgruppe Pädagogisches Museum, ed., *Heil Hitler, Herr Lehrer. Volksschule 1933-1945—Das Beispiel Berlin* (Reinbek bei Hamburg, 1983), 185.

2. See, for example, Willy Schumann, *Being Present: Growing Up in Hitler's Germany* (Kent, Ohio, 1991), 88-89, 110-11; Bernt Engelmann, *Im Gleichschritt marsch: Wie Wir die Nazizeit erlebten 1933-1939* (Cologne, 1982), 1: 43-51; Arbeitsgruppe Pädagogisches Museum, 100-114.

3. Schumann, 26.

4. See the demands in Kurt Wiedenfeld, "Von der Geopolitik," *DR* 259 (1939): 151, and for a telling assessment of the transition of the Weimar professoriate to its new conditions after 1933 see Wolfgang Abendroth, "Die deutschen Professoren und der Weimarer Republik," in *Hochschule und Wissenschaft im Dritten Reich,* ed. Jorg Tröger (Frankfurt am Main, 1986), 23-25.

5. For the assessment of Kraus's character as a scholar see BDC: Kraus personal file, Res., "Personalamt. an die Gauleitung der NSDAP Süd-Hannover-Braunschweig," 14 March 1934, Bl. I and II. On the development of a geopolitical presence at the Institut see Universitätsarchiv Göttingen, XVI. II. C. c. 1., Mappe II, Bl. 21, "*Deutsche Studentenschaft an den Kurator,*" 19 January 1934, and the resolution entitled "*Geopolitik und Wissenschaft*" from the *Tagung des Institus für Erziehung und Unterricht und der Arbeitsgemeinschaft für Geopolitik in Bad Saarow am 11. und 12. Mai 1935,* in XVI. II. C. c. 1., Bd. II, Allgemeines, Bl. 129-31. The resolution reads, in part, "Ausgehend von der Tatsache, dass die Geopolitik kein Sonderfach neben den bisherigen Fächern sein, sondern dass sie vielmehr, aufbauend auf bereits geleisteter Vorarbeit, alle in Frage kommenden Fächer mit der geopolitischen Geisteshaltung: Der Erkenntnis und dem Wissen einer organischen Staatsauffassung aus Blut und Boden durchdringen soll. . . . An einigen der genannten Universitäten bestehen bereits Ansätze im Sinne der hier vorgeschlagenen Massnahmen." (Proceeding from the fact that geopolitics is no special discipline beside the other disciplines, but that it ought far more to permeate all relevant disciplines with the geopolitical conceptual posture, the recognition and knowledge of an organic concept of the state on the basis of blood and soil. . . . Initiatives in the sense of the suggested measures already exist at some of the named universities.) Pencilled marginalia beside the statement read, "z.B., im Sem f. Völkerrecht!" (for example, in the seminar for international law!). See also Kraus's geopolitical teaching listed in *Georg-August-Universität zu Göttingen, Verzeichnis der Vorlesungen, Winterhalbjahr 1933/34* (Göttingen, 1933), 12.

6. For Banse see Beyer, 2. For Mannhardt see Rammstedt, 78.

7. Hans Harmsen, "Ziele und Möglichkeiten deutscher Bevölkerungspolitik. Die Familie ist Grundlage aller Bevölkerungspolitik," *ZfG* 10 (1933): 207-13. See also his essay from 1929, "Die deutsche Bevölkerungsfrage als Problem der völkischen Schutzarbeit," in Harmsen and Loesch, 1-9.

8. See Hans Harmsen and Franz Lohse, eds., *Bevölkerungsfragen. Bericht des Internationalen Kongresses für Bevölkerungswissenschaft, Berlin, 21 August-1 September 1935* (Munich, 1936).

9. On the "committee of experts" and its activities see Burleigh and Wippermann, 57-58. See Burgdörfer's article from January 1944, for example, "Die Lebensfrage des deutschen Volkes," *Nationalsozialistische Landespost,* 7 January 1944, in BAP: 61 Re 1; Reichslandbund 57 (Burgdörfer), Bl. 17.

10. See Karl Christian von Loesch, "Der Kampf für das Recht im Osten," *ZfG* 7 (1930): 29-41. See, also, Götz Aly and Susanne Heim, *Vordenker der Vernichtung. Auschwitz und die deutschen Pläne für eine neue europäische Ordnung* (Frankfurt am Main, 1993), 121-22, 424. On the RKFDV, the very best source is Robert Lewis Koehl, *RKFDV: German Resettlement and Population Policy, 1939-1945* (Cambridge, Mass., 1957).

11. For examples of his reputation before and since see the entry on Haushofer in Hugo Eckener, *Der Weg Voran!* (Leipzig, 1931), 107, and the positively outlandish account of Haushofer's supposed influence over Hitler in Trevor Ravenscroft's popular *The Spear of Destiny: The Occult Power behind the Spear which Pierced the Side of Christ* (New York, 1973), especially 202-9 and 218-21.

12. Norton, 80-98.

13. Jacobsen, *Haushofer,* 1: 257-58.

14. As Albrecht wrote in one of the moving sonnets he penned while awaiting death in Berlin's Moabit Prison, "Mein Vater war noch blind vom Traum der Macht" [My father was still blinded by the dream of power]. Cited in Norton, 98.

15. See the comments of Smith, *Ideological,* 238–58.

16. Andreas Hillgruber, *Hitlers Strategie. Politik und Kriegführung 1940–1941* (Frankfurt am Main, 1965), 592. For examples of Hitler's use of Lebensraum and similar geopolitical language, see Max Domarus, *Hitler, Reden und Proklamationen 1932–1945 Bd. I: Triumph, 1932–1934* (Munich, 1965), 1726–32, and Rainer Zitelmann, *Adolf Hitler. Eine politische Biographie* (Göttingen, 1989), 93–94.

17. For comments on this issue see Jacobsen, *Haushofer,* 1: 245–46.

18. Norman Rich, *Hitler's War Aims: Ideology, the Nazi State and the Course of Expansion* (New York, 1973), 1: 3–10; Gerhard L. Weinberg, *The Foreign Policy of Hitler's Germany: Diplomatic Revolution in Europe, 1933–36* (Chicago, 1970), 1–24.

19. See the discussion of geopolitical colonialism in chapter 8 above.

20. Hillgruber, *Hitlers Strategie,* 242–43.

21. On Hitler's hope, right into the actual outbreak of fighting, for a rapprochement and alliance with England see Domarus, 1: 39.

22. Zitelmann, 112.

23. Smith, for example, argues that after consolidating his position on the continent, Hitler still hoped "in the *very* long run" to be able to reestablish a German world empire. Smith, *Ideological,* 250–51. Italics in original.

24. Adolf Rein, "Grundzüge der Weltpolitik der letzten hundert Jahre. Eine raumpolitische Betrachtung," *ZFG* 1 (1924): 612.

25. Hillgruber, *Hitlers Strategie,* 241. See the expressions of support for such a policy in Heinrich Block, "Eurasien," *ZfG* 3 (1926): 15–16; "Berichterstattung," 131–36; and idem, "Sowjetrussische Aussenpolitik," 1–9 (which includes the remarkably prescient observation that "sooner or later, a new world war is likely, with a confrontation between Japan on the one side, and the east Asian colonial powers, above all the Anglo-Saxons, on the other."); Ostwald, 620–24; and Hans Ueberschaar, "Die japanische Staatskultur und ihr neues Verhaltnis zur Union der Sozialistischen Sowjet-Republiken," *ZfG* 3 (1926): 17–32.

26. Barry A. Leach, *German Strategy against Russia 1939–1941* (Oxford, Eng., 1973), 12; Weinberg, 12–14; Rich, 7–10; Zitelmann, 97.

27. Aly and Heim, 368–69; Leach, 12; Leni Yahil, *The Holocaust: The Fate of European Jewry, 1932–1945* (New York, 1990), 243–44.

28. On the Nazi attacks on geopolitics see Bassin, "Race," 126–29.

29. Jacobsen, 1: 258.

30. See, for example, Omer Bartov, *Hitler's Army: Soldiers, Nazis and War in the Third Reich* (New York, 1992), 124–25.

31. Penck cited in Albert von Hofmann, *Das deutsche Land,* 11.

32. Günter Heyden even characterizes geopolitics as a school of sociology, not geography or history.

33. The term is from Henry Ashby Turner, Jr., "Fascism and Modernization," *World Politics* 24 (1971–72): 547–64.

34. Both Paul Kennedy and E. L. Jones have used the term at some length in widely cited recent works: see E. L. Jones, *The European Miracle: Environments, Economies, and Geopolitics in the Histories of Europe and Asia,* 2d ed. (Cambridge, Eng., 1987), passim, and

Paul Kennedy, *The Rise and Fall of the Great Powers* (New York, 1987), 86–99. Both use *geopolitics* in a much more sophisticated and restricted sense than it was generally used in Weimar. For an account of the renewed legitimacy of geopolitics that set in from the early 1980s, see Leslie W. Hepple, "The Revival of Geopolitics," *PGQ*, supplement, 5 (1986): 521–36.

35. Both Hagen Schulze and Michael Stürmer have revived the theory of the impact of the Mittellage in recent years. See Kocka, "Kritik und Identität," 894–97.

Glossary

ANSCHLUSS-Union, especially the union of Austria with Germany in 1938.

ARBEITSGEMEINSCHAFT-Study or work group.

AUSLANDDEUTSCHTUM-Sometimes "Auslandsdeutschtum." Foreign Germandom, used to refer to ethnic Germans outside the borders of Germany, particularly those who had retained German as their primary language.

AUSLANDSKUNDE-Foreign studies.

BLUT UND BODEN-Blood and soil. A slogan of conservative nationalists associated with "volkish" political ideologies, later an important term in Nazi propaganda.

DEUTSCHTUM-Germandom, normally employed in reference to persons of German extraction living outside the borders of Germany.

DIKTAT-Dictate, usually used in the term "Versailler Diktat," or Dictate of Versailles, a derisive appellation used by conservative revisionists to describe the postwar settlement.

DRANG NACH AFRIKA-Drive toward Africa.

ERDGEBUNDENHEIT-Earth dependency. A geopolitical term used to describe the determining impact of geography upon politics, society, and culture.

ERFÜLLUNGSPOLITIK-Fulfillment policy, used to describe the foreign policy of Gustav Stresemann and its aim of proving the impractical nature of the Versailles peace settlement by strict fulfillment of its terms.

ETHNOPOLITIK-Sometimes "Demopolitik." Ethnopolitics, a term devised by Rudolf Kjellen to characterize the role of ethnicity in politics and the policies of states concerning ethnic questions.

FLURBEREINIGUNG-Literally, enclosure of land, often employed by nationalists to connote a redrawing and "rationalization" of central European borders in the interest of unifying ethnic groups, particularly ethnic Germans.

GEBURTENRÜCKGANG-Decline in the birth rate.

GESETZ DER GENESUNG-Law of recovery, used by geopolitical writers to denote the alleged tendency of states to seek new lands after loss of other territories through warfare.

GESETZ DER WACHSENDEN RÄUME-Law of expanding spaces, used by geopolitical writers to denote the alleged tendency of states to expand into "underpopulated" neighboring regions.

GESTALTENDE GEOGRAPHIE-Formative or developmental geography.

GLEICHSCHALTUNG-Unification or coordination, referring to the Nazi elimination of opposition in all public and professional institutions.

GRENZDEUTSCHTUM-Border Germandom.

GRENZE-Border, or frontier.

GROSSDEUTSCHLAND-Greater Germany, including the unification of all ethnic Germans in central Europe within one political entity.

HEIMATKUNDE-Local history and topography.

JUNKER-Aristocratic landowning class of east Prussia.

KAISERREICH-Imperial Germany under the Hohenzollerns.

KAMPF UM RAUM-Struggle for space, analogous to the Darwinian struggle for existence.

KRAFTFELDER, KRAFTLINIE-Fields of force, and lines of force.

KULTURBODEN-Cultural soil, the region subject to predominant German cultural influence.

KULTURVÖLKER-Peoples of advanced civilization.

LÄNDERKUNDE-Regional geography.

LEBENSRAUM-Living space.

MISCHGEBIETE-Regions of mingled ethnic populations.

MITTELEUROPA-Central Europe. The term was used in the early twentieth century in reference to proposals for greater economic and political unity in the region under German leadership.

MITTELLAGE-Central position.

NATURVÖLKER-Primitive peoples.

PRIMAT DER AUSSENPOLITIK-Primacy of foreign policy in determining the political policy agenda of a state.

RAUM-Space, or area.

RAUMFORSCHUNG-Area or spatial research, used to refer to regional planning.

STAATLICHE SPLITTERZONE-National fragmentation zone.

STAATSWISSENSCHAFT-Political science, denoting in nineteenth- and early twentieth-century Germany a discipline which combined elements of law, history and several fields.

VENIA LEGENDI-Permission to teach at a German university.

VOLK-People, or nation, often having racial connotations.

VOLK OHNE RAUM-People without space, an expansionist slogan taken from the title of an influential colonialist novel of the 1920s.

VÖLKERKUNDE-Ethnology.

VÖLKERMISCHGEBIETE-Region of ethnic mixture.

VOLKSBODEN-Ethnic soil, used to refer to regions of significant ethnic German population.

VOLKSSTERBEN-The dying out of the people or race.

VOLKSTUM-Nationality, or nationhood.

WELTPOLITIK-World policy, used to describe an aggressive foreign policy having global aspirations.

WISSENSCHAFT-Science.

ZWISCHENEUROPA-Between-Europe, or interim-Europe, used to describe the allegedly artificial states created from the remnants of the Russian, Habsburg, and German empires in central Europe after World War I.

Documentary Sources

Unpublished

Berlin Document Center (BDC)

Personal Documents:
   Friedrich Burgdörfer
   Richard Hennig
   Herbert Kraus

Bundesarchiv Koblenz (BAK)

R 43I	Reichskanzlei-Kolonien, Schulwesen (625, 626, 773)
R 43II	Reichskanzlei-Hochschule für Politik (948)
R 118	Politisches Kolleg (17, 28, 42, 53, 54)
R 45II	Deutsche Volkspartei (6, 7, 9)
R 45III	Deutsche Demokratische Partei (5, 7, 55)
R 57	Deutsches Auslandinstitut (1002–4, 1005, 1006)
ZSg.1–44	Deutschnationae Volkspartei (DNVP) (15)
NL 42	Külz (25, 30)
NL 53	Solf (81)
NL 122	Haushofer (767, 834, 896, 898, 940b)
NL 160	Pechel (67, 71, 103, 121, 125, 126)

Geheimes Staatsarchiv Preussischer Kulturbesitz, Berlin-Dahlem (GStA)

Rep 76	Ministerium für Wissenschaft, Kunst und Volksbildung (702, 1095, 1413)
Rep 90	Staatsministerium (2400, 1756)
Rep 303	Hochschule für Politik (284)
Rep 92	Nachlass Vogel
	14 Politische Geographie
	18 Vorlesung, Allgemeine Wirtschaft
	19 Geographische Bedingungen des Staates (SS 1921)

20 Grundzüge der allgemeinen Politischen Geographie
21 Landeskunde von Europa
22 Historische Geographie (WS 1927-28)
34 Politische Geographie (SS 1929)
Nachlass Brackmann
64 Stiftung für Volksforschung
77 Notgemeinschaft der deutschen Wissenschaften
Nachlass Schnee
24 Korrespondenz: Arbeitsausschuss Deutsch
Verbände
30 Korrespondenz: Draeger
31 Korrespondenz: Auswärtiges Amt, Stresemann
37 Korrespondenz: Loesch
38 Korrespondenz: Grimm
40 Korrespondenz: Henrig
57 Korrespondenz: Obst
HA XII: Zeitgeschichtliche Sammung

Bundesarchiv Potsdam

61 Ko 1	Deutsche Kolonialgesellschaft (67, 71, 74, 81, 149, 347, 375, 376, 382, 383, 553, 1106, 1108, 1109)
61 Schu 1	Deutscher Schutzbund (4, 5, 37)
60 Vo 1	Deutsche Volkspartei (53173, 53169, 45126)
RMdI 15.01	Reichsministerium des Innern (26233/1, 26233/2)
90 Di 2	NL Arthur Dix (7, 8, 63, 72, 262, 275)
61 Re 1	Reichslandbund
	57 Burgdörfer
	162 Grabowsky

Hessisches Staatsarchiv Marburg (HSM)

307 d, 383, Acc. 1967/11 Institut für Grenz- und
Auslandsdeutschtum
307 d, 384, Acc. 1967/11
310, 4387, Acc. 1983/15

Universitätsarchiv Göttingen

XVI.II.C.c.1. Die Entwicklung des Instituts für Völkerrecht an der Universität Göttingen

Published Sources

Document Collections

Akten zur deutschen auswärtigen Politik 1918–1945. Aus dem Archiv des Auswärtigen Amts.
Ser. B, 1925-33, vols. 1-21. Göttingen, 1966-83.
Domarus, Max. *Hitler. Reden und Proklamationen, 1932–1945,* vols. 1-2. Munich, 1965.

Michalka, Wolfgang, and Gottfried Niedhart, eds. *Die ungeliebte Republik. Dokumente zur Innen- und Aussenpolitik Weimars 1918–1933*. Munich, 1980.

Ursachen und Folgen. Vom deutschen Zusammenbruch 1918 und 1945 bis zur staatlichen Neuordnung Deutschlands in der Gegenwart. Eine Urkunde- und Dokumentensammlung zur Zeitgeschichte. Vol. 6, *Die Weimarer Republik. Die Wende der Nachkriegspolitik, 1924–1928. Rapallo-Dawesplan-Genf.* Berlin, 1961.

Verhandlungen des Deutschen Geographentages.

    21. Deutschen Geographentag, Breslau, 1–4 June 1925. Berlin, 1926.

    24. Deutschen Geographentag, Danzig, 26–28 May 1931. Breslau, 1932.

Verhandlungen des Reichstages. Stenographische Berichte und Anlagen. Berlin, 1924 ff.

Geopolitical and Related Literature to 1939

Anders, E. *Erdkundliche Grundlagen geschichtlicher Entwicklung*. Breslau, 1924.

Arbeitsgemeinschaft für Geopolitik. "Denkschrift: Geopolitik als nationale Stattswissenschaft." *Zeitschrift für Geopolitik* 10 (1933): 301–3.

"Die Aufgaben eines deutschen Atlasses," *Zeitschrift der Gesellschaft für Erdkunde zu Berlin* 7–8 (1925): 311.

Banse, Ewald. *Das Buch vom Morgenlande*. Leipzig, 1926.

———. *Expressionismus und Geographie*. Braunschweig, 1920.

———. *Landschaft und Seele. Neue Wege der Untersuchung und Gestaltung*. Berlin and Munich, 1928.

———. "Landschaft und Volkheit als Kernbegriffe der Geographie." *Geographischer Anzeiger* 34 (1933): 213–18.

———. "See und Gebirge." *Die Tat* 20 (1928): 262–67.

———. "Über den Zusammenhang von Landschaft und Mensch." *Volk und Rasse* 7 (1932): 8–18.

Barthel, Ernst. "Deutschlands und Europas Schicksalsfrage." *Zeitschrift für Geopolitik* 3 (1926): 309–9.

Barthel, Herbert. "Der Geburtenüberschuss in Polen." *Petermanns Mitteilungen* 79 (1933): 62–63.

Battaglia, Otto Forst de. "Geopolitik." *Europäische Gespräche* 10 (1932): 24–38.

Behrmann, Walter. "Die geopolitische Stellung Neuguinea vor und nach dem Weltkriege." *Zeitschrift für Geopolitik* 3 (1926): 207–13.

———. "Über die Berücksichtigung der Lehrpläne der Höheren Schulen im Hochschulunterricht." *Geographischer Anzeiger* 28 (1927): 349–56.

Bitterling, Richard, and Theodor Otto. *Fischer-Geistbeck Erdkunde für höhere Lehranstalten. Ausgewählte Abschnitte der Allgemeinen Erdkunde*. Munich, 1925.

Block, Heinrich. "Eurasien." *Zeitschrift für Geopolitik* 3 (1926): 8–16.

Boehm, Max Hildebert. *Die deutschen Grenzlande*. Berlin, 1925.

———. "Grossdeutsche Vorarbeit—An uns selber." *Grossdeutsche Blätter* 1 (1924): 4–8.

———. "Mitteleuropa und der Osten." *Volk und Reich* 1 (1925): 65–72.

———. "Staatsallgewalt und Nationalitätenproblem." In *Volk unter Völkern*, ed. Karl Christian von Loesch, 192–208. Breslau, 1925.

Boelitz, Otto. "Die Behandlung der Fragen des Grenz- und Auslandsdeutschtums auf unseren höheren Schulen." *Deutsche Rundschau* 53 (1927): 190–93.

———. *Das Grenz- und Auslanddeutschtum, seine Geschichte und seine Bedeutung*. Munich, 1926.

Böhmer, Rudolf. "Kolonialpolitik oder Proletarisierung." *Deutsche Rundschau* 55 (1929): 65-68.

Bölsche, Wilhelm. "Eine vergleichende Erdkunde." *Deutsche Rundschau* 113 (1902): 312-15.

Burgdörfer, Friedrich. *Der Geburtenrückgang und seine Bekämpfung. Die Lebensfrage des deutschen Volkes. Veröffentlichungen aus dem Gebiete der Medizinalverwaltung.* Berlin, 1929.

———. "Die Gefährdung des Ostdeutschen Volkstums." *Süddeutsche Monatshefte* 28 (1930): 6-12.

———. "Die Lebensfrage des deutschen Volkes." *Naionalsozialistische Landespost,* 7 January 1944.

———. "Die schwindende Wachstumsenergie des deutschen Volkes im europäischen Raum." In *Die deutsche Bevölkerungsfrage,* eds Harmsen and Loesch, 10-31.

———. "Stadt oder Land? Berechnungen und Betrachtungen zum Problem der deutschen Verstadterung." *Zeitschrift für Geopolitik* 10 (1933): 105-13.

———. *Volk ohne Jugend. Geburtenschwund und Überalterung des deutschen Volkskörpers.* Berlin, 1932.

Buttersack, Dr. "Geopolitische Stümpereien und ihre Folgen." *Eiserne Blätter* 8 (1926): 399-403.

Cefarin, Rudolf. "Kärnten und seine geopolitische Bedeutung für das Deutschtum." *Zeitschrift für Geopolitik* 3 (1926): 338-40.

Classen, W. "Die Geopolitik auf der Höheren Schule." *Geographischer Anzeiger* 32 (1931): 14-27.

Cohen, Max. "Die aussenpolitische Forderung." *Sozialistische Monatshefte* 30 (1924): 286-90.

———. "Für eine deutsche Kolonial-Zukunft." *Sozialistische Monatshefte* 32 (1926): 687-89.

———. "Kolonialwirtschaft ist Notwendig." *Sozialistische Monatshefte* 34 (1928): 1042-46.

Coudenhove-Kalergi, Richard N. "Mitteleuropa." *Pan-Europa* 6 (1930): 87-97.

———. *Pan-Europa.* Vienna, 1923.

Dernburg, Berhnard. "Deutschland und der Dawesplan." *Zeitschrift für Geopolitik* 4 (1927): 6-14.

"Die Aufgaben eines deutschen Weltatlasses." *Zeitschrift der Gesellschaft für Erdkunde zu Berlin* 7/8 (1925): 311-12.

Deutsche Hochschule für Politik, ed. "Zusamenfassender Bericht." *Berichte der Deutschen Hochschule für Politik* 4 (1926): 9.

"Ein 'deutscher' Weltatlas." *Deutsche Arbeit* 24 (1924): 21.

Dix, Arthur. "Die Abhängigkeit der Wirtschaftsstruktur von der Bevölkerungsstruktur in Deutschland." *Volkswirtschaftliche Blätter* 26 (1927): 31-37.

———. *Geopolitik. Lehrkurse über die geographischen Grundlagen der Weltpolitik und Weltwirtschaft.* Füssen am Lech, n.d. [1926?].

———. *Politische Geographie. Weltpolitisches Handbuch.* 2d ed. Munich, 1923.

———. *Was geht uns Afrika an?* Berlin, 1931.

———. "Weltgeschichte-Kolonialgeschichte." *Übersee und Kolonial-Zeitung* 41 (1929): 214.

———. *Weltkrise und Kolonialpolitik. Die Zukunft zweier Erdteile.* Berlin, 1932.

———. "Wirtschaftsstruktur und Geopolitik." *Volkswirtschaftliche Blätter* 28 (1929): 465-84.

Dorn, Theodor. "Vom deutschen Sterben." *Grossdeutsche Blätter* 1 (1924): 100-105.

———. "Der Weg nach dem Osten." *Grossdeutsche Blätter* 4 (1927): 32-36.

Dorpalen, Andreas. *The World of General Haushofer: Geopolitics in Action.* New York, 1942.

Dr. E. [pseud.]. "Los von der Sprachenkarte." *Deutsche Welt* 3 (1926): 366-67.

Drygalski, Erich von. "Die Entwicklung der Geographie seit Gründung des Reiches." *Mitteilungen der Geographischen Gesellschaft in Hamburg* 43 (1933): 1-11.

Duems, Erich, ed. *Das Buch der deutschen Kolonien.* Leipzig, 1937.

Duems, Erich, and Willibald von Stuemer, eds. *Fünfzig Jahre Deutsche Kolonialgesellschaft 1882-1932.* N.p., n.d.

Dumke, Artur. "Geopolitik in der Volksschule." *Neue Bahnen* 45 (1934): 155-58.

Ebeling, Friedrich. "Bevölkerungspolitische Gefahren für die deutschen Minderheiten." *Grenzdeutsche Rundschau* 5 (1928): 174-76.

————. "Schafft Raum zur Überwindung einer schweren Zukunft." *Übersee und Kolonial-Zeitung* 42 (1930): 407-8.

Ebhardt, Klaus. "Bevölkerungspolitik und Raumnot." *Grossdeutsche Blätter* 4 (1928): 218-25.

Eckener, Hugo. *Der Weg Voran!* Leipzig, 1931.

Eckert, Max. "Banses Geographische Landschaftskunde." *Geographischer Anzeiger* 33 (1932): 243-44.

Eichler, Adolf. *Das Deutschtum in Kongresspolen.* Stuttgart, 1921.

"Das Ende des Prozesses um den Ullsteinschen Weltatlas." *Deutsche Arbeit* 24 (1925): 339-40.

Etscheit, Alfred. "Braucht Deutschland Kolonien?" *Deutsche Rundschau* 54 (1928): 111-18.

Fairgrieve, James. *Geographie und Weltmacht.* Trans. Martha Haushofer. Berlin, 1925.

Fechter, Paul. "Der amerikanische Raum." *Deutsche Rundschau* 55 (1929): 47-59.

Fehn, Richard. "Raumnot-Kolonien." *Bayerische Industrie. Organ des Bayerische Industriellen-Verbandes E. V.* 24 (1930): 14-15.

Fels, E. Review of *Geoökonomie,* by Arthur Dix. *Mitteilungen der Geographischen Gesellschaft in München* 18 (1925): 528-29.

Fester, Gustav. "Polarpolitik." *Zeitschrift für Geopolitik* 7 (1930): 800-805.

Fischer, Alois. "Zur Frage der Tragfähigkeit des Lebensraumes." *Zeitschrift für Geopolitik* 2 (1925): 842-58.

Fittbogen, Gottfried. "Deutsche Atlanten und neue Geographie." *Deutsche Arbeit* 24 (1925): 141-44.

Fox, Robert. "Die Forderungen des Verbandes deutscher Hochschullehrer der Geographie." *Geographischer Anzeiger* 29 (1928): 70-71.

Frauenbund der Deutschen Kolonialgesellschaft, ed. *Deutsche Jugend und Deutsche Kolonien. Was unsere Jugend über Deutsche Arbeit in unseren Kolonien wissen muss.* Aachen, 1932.

Friedrichsen, M. "'Deutschland' als 'natürliche' Grosslandschaft Mittel-Europas." *Zeitschrift für Geopolitik* 4 (1927): 423-30.

Gayl, W. Freiherr von. "Die Bedeutung des Ostens in der deutschen Volkspolitik." *Volk und Reich* 4 (1928): 566-68.

"Geburtenrückgang." *Süddeutsche Monatshefte* 25 (1927): 155-90.

Gehl, Walther. *Geschichte für höheren Schulen. 4. Heft.* Breslau, 1925-26.

————. *Geschichte für Mittelschulen. 5. Heft.* Breslau, 1927.

Geisler, Walter. "Politik und Sprachen-Karten. Ein Beitrag zur Frage des 'polnischen' Korridors." *Zeitschrift für Geopolitik* 3 (1926): 701-13.

————. *Schlesien als Raumorganismus.* Breslau, 1932.

Geistbeck, A. "Die Bedeutung der Erdkunde und erdkundlicher Bildung für das deutsche Volk in der Gegenwart." In *Reformvorschläge des deutschen Geographentages für den erdkundlichen Unterricht an den höheren Schulen,* ed. Deutscher Geographentag, 1-29. Lübeck, 1909.

"Geographische, ethnographische und verwandte Vorlesungen in deutscher Sprache an den Hochschulen Mitteleuropas im Sommerhalbjahr 1924." *Petermanns Mitteilungen* 70 (1924): 81-83.

"Geographische, ethnographische und verwandte Vorlesungen in deutscher Sprache an den Hochschulen Mitteleuropas im Winterhalbjahr 1928/29." *Petermanns Mitteilungen* 74 (1928): 296-97.

Georg-August-Universität zu Göttingen. Verzeichnis der Vorlesungen. Winterhalbjahr 1933/34 (Göttingen, 1933).

Gerstenberg, Kurt, and Ernst Krüger. *Geschichtswerk für höheren Schulen.* Vol. 9. Munich, 1933.

Godav, Kurt. "Die Notwendigkeit der Kolonien." *Deutsche Arbeit* 28 (1929): 233-35.

Golcher, Hans. "Grenzstruktur und Staatlicher Organismus." *Zeitschrift für Geopolitik* 4 (1927): 811-19.

Grabowsky, Adolf. "Genf und Wir." *Die Tat* 20 (1928): 696-701.

———. *Der Neger. Tragische Komödie in 3 Akten.* Berlin, 1926.

———. *Die polnische Frage.* Berlin, 1916.

———. "Der Primat der Aussenpolitik." *Zeitschrift für Politik* 17 (1928): 527-42.

———. "Das Problem der Geopolitik." *Zeitschrift für Politik* 22 (1932-33): 765-802.

———. "Remarque und Russland." *Reichsflagge,* 11 July 1929, 1.

———. "Soll Deutschland Kolonialpolitik treiben? Eine Umfrage." *Europäische Gespräche* 5 (1927): 638.

———. *Staat und Raum. Grundlagen räumlichen Denkens in der Weltpolitik.* Berlin, 1928.

———. "Völkerbund, Weltorganisation und Pazifismus." In *Jenseits der Grossmächte,* ed. Karl Haushofer, 448-77. Berlin, 1932.

Graf, Georg Engelbert. "Geographie und materialistische Geschichtsauffassung." In *Der lebendige Marxismus. Festgabe zum 70. Geburtstage von Karl Kautsky,* ed. O. Jenssen, 563-87. Jena, 1924.

Grimm, Hans. "Die neue Furcht vor Kolonien." *Grossdeutsche Blätter* 4 (1928): 262-65.

———. "Einleitung." In *Deutsche Jugend und Deutsche Kolonien. Was unsere Jugend über deutsche Arbeit in unseren Kolonien wissen muss,* ed. Frauenbund des Deutschen Kolonialgesellschaft (Aachen, 1932), 1-3.

———. "Übervölkerung und Kolonialproblem." In *Die neue Front,* ed. Moeller van den Bruck, Heinrich von Gleichen, Max Hildebert Boehm, et al. 329-51. Berlin, 1922.

"Grosse koloniale Kundgebung." *Reichsflagge,* 11 June 1924, 4.

Grotjahn, Alfred. "Geburtenhäufigkeit." *Berliner Tageblatt,* 13 December 1927, 12.

Günther, Erich. "Künstlerische Geographie." *Die Tat* 16 (1925): 824-30.

Haack, Hermann. Review of *Der Rhein,* by Karl Haushofer. *Geographischer Anzeiger* 29 (1928): 348.

———. *Zwischeneuropa. Physikalische Karte* (Gotha, 1932).

Hansen, Jorgen. "Sinn und Methode des erdkundlichen Unterrichts auf der Grundlage der Heimatkunde." In *Die Neue Geographie in der Schule. Ausgewählte Aufsätze zur gestaltenden Erdkunde,* ed. Jorgen Hansen, 12-20. Braunschweig, 1931.

Harms, H. *Fünf Thesen zur Reform des geographischen Unterrichts. Ein Vortrag.* 7th ed. Leipzig, 1921.

Harmsen, Hans, and Karl Christian von Loesch, eds. *Die Deutsche Bevölkerungsfrage im europäischen Raum.* Berlin-Grunewald, 1929.

Harmsen, Hans, Karl Christian von Loesch, and Franz Lohse, eds. *Bevölkerungsfragen.*
Bericht des Internationalen Kongresses für Bevölkerungswissenschaft, Berlin, 21 August–1 September 1935. Munich, 1936.

Harmsen, Hans. "Die deutsche Bevölkerungsfrage als Problem der völkischen Schutzarbeit." In *Die deutsche Bevölkerungsfrage im europäischen Raum,* ed. Hans Harmsen and Karl Christian von Loesch (Berlin, 1924), 1–9.

———. "Das deutsche Volk hat aufgehört ein wachsendes Volk zu sein!" *Volk und Reich* 4 (1928): 385–87.

———. "Ziele und Möglichkeiten deutscher Bevölkerungspolitik. Die Familie ist Grundlage aller Bevölkerungspolitik." *Zeitschrift für Geopolitik* 10 (1933): 207–13.

Hassinger, Hugo. *Geographische Grundlagen der Geschichte.* Freiburg im Breisgau, 1931.

Haushofer, Albrecht. "Bemerkungen zum Problem der Bevölkerungsdichte auf der Erde." *Zeitschrift für Geopolitik* 3 (1926): 789–97.

———. "Der Staat Danzig." *Zeitschrift der Gesellschaft für Erdkunde zu Berlin* 7–8 (1926): 335–50.

———. *Pass-Staaten in den Alpen.* Berlin, 1928.

———. Review of *The Revolt against Civilization,* by Lothrop Stoddard. *Deutsche Rundschau* 51 (1925): 54.

———. Review of *Volk unter Völkern. Bücher des Deutschtums,* ed. Karl Christian von Loesch and A. Hillen Ziegfeld. *Zeitschrift der Gesellschaft für Erdkunde zu Berlin* (1926): 206.

———. "Was ist ein Korridor." In *Deutschland und der Korridor,* ed. Friedrich Heiss and A. Hillen Ziegfeld, 202–20. Berlin, 1933.

Haushofer, Karl. "Ausstrahlungen politischer Geographie." *Deutsche Rundschau* 52 (1926): 70–73.

———. "Die Bedeutung der südlichen Grenzzone für die volksdeutsche Arbeit." *Grenzdeutsche Rundschau* 6 (1929): 155–60.

———. "Bevölkerungsdruck und Verstädterung im Lichte west-pazifischer Erfahrung." *Zeitschrift der Gesellschaft für Erdkunde zu Berlin* (1930): 287–300.

———. "Das deutsche Volk und sein Südsee-Inselreich." *Zeitschrift für Geopolitik* 3 (1926): 201–6.

———. "Das erwachende Asien." *Süddeutsche Monatshefte* 24 (1926): 97–123.

———. "Eurasien." *Süddeutsche Monatshefte* 21 (1924): 190–93.

———. "Geographische Grundzüge auswärtiger Politik." *Süddeutsche Monatshefte* 24 (1927): 260–62.

———. "Zur Geopolitik der Donau." *Volk und Reich* 1 (1925): 161–73.

———. *Geopolitik der Pan-Idee.* Berlin, 1931.

———. *Geopolitik des Pazifischen Ozeans. Studien über die Wechselbeziehungen zwischen Geographie und Geschichte.* Berlin, 1924.

———. "Geopolitik und Geojurisprudenz." *Zeitschrift für Völkerrecht* 14 (1928): 564–68.

———. "Geopolitik und Kaufmann." In *Bausteine zur Geopolitik,* ed. Karl Haushofer, Erich Obst, Hermann Lautensach, and Otto Maull. 270–85. Berlin, 1928.

———. *Grenzen in ihrer geographischen und politischen Bedeutung.* Berlin-Grunewald, 1927.

———. "Grundlagen, Wesen und Ziele der Geopolitik." In *Bausteine zur Geopolitik,* ed. Karl Haushofer, Erich Obst, Hermann Lautensach, and Otto Maull. 29–48. Berlin, 1928.

———. *Der Nationalsozialistische Gedanke in der Welt*. Munich, 1933.

———. "Der Ost-Eurasiatische Zukunftsblock." *Zeitschrift für Geopolitik* 2 (1925): 81-87.

———. "Politische Erdkunde und Geopolitik." In *Bausteine zur Geopolitik*, ed. Karl Haushofer, Erich Obst, Hermann Lautensach, and Otto Maull. 49-80. Berlin, 1928.

———. "Soll Deutschland Kolonialpolitik treiben? Eine Umfrage." *Europäische Gespräche* 5 (1927): 638-39.

———. "Die suggestive Karte." In *Bausteine zur Geopolitik*, ed. Karl Haushofer, 343-48. Berlin, 1928.

Haushofer, Karl, Erich Obst, Hermann Lautensach, and Otto Maull, eds. *Bausteine zur Geopolitik*. Berlin, 1928.

Haushofer, Max. *Bevölkerungslehre*. Leipzig, 1904.

Heck, Karl. "Preussische Schulreform und Erdkunde." *Geographischer Anzeiger* 27 (1928): 20-21.

———. "Wo stehen wir heute in der Schulgeographie?" *Geographischer Anzeiger* 34 (1933): 242-48.

Hedin, Sven. "Die russiche Gefahr." *Reichsflagge*, 16 April 1925, 3.

Helbok, Adolf. "Unterbauung der grenz- und auslandsdeutschen Geschichtswissenschaft durch Landesgeschichte auf Grund gesamtdeutscher Siedlungsforschung." *Deutsche Rundschau* 52 (1926): 248-51.

Hennig, Richard. "Geopolitische Enflüsse auf Deutschland als Wirtschaftsgebiet und als Staat." *Geographischer Anzeiger* 33 (1932): 81-83.

———. "Geopolitische Wirkungen des beginnenden Weltluftverkehrs." *Geographische Zeitschrift* 34 (1928): 581-86.

———. "Italien am geopolitische Scheideweg." *Zeitschrift für Geopolitik* 4 (1927): 241-46.

———. *Terrae Incognitae. Eine Zusammenstellung und kritische Berwertung der wichtigsten vorcolumbische Entdeckungsreisen an Hand der darüber vorliegenden Originalberichte*. Leiden, 1953.

———. *Weltluftverkehr und Weltluftpolitik*. Berlin, 1930.

Hennig, Richard, and Leo Korholz. *Einführung in die Geopolitik*. 4th ed. Leipzig, 1934.

Herfurth, Christoph. *Geschichte und Geographie (Geopolitik)*. Langensalza-Berlin-Leipzig, 1938.

Herre, Paul. *Spanien und Portugal*. Weltpolitische Bücherei: Berlin, 1929.

Hertzberg, H. "Die Deutschen, ein Kolonialvolk." *Geograpischer Anzeiger* 16 (1925): 68-71.

Hettner, Alfred. Review of *Deutschland und das Weltbild der Gegenwart*, by Adolf Grabowsky. *Geographische Zeitschrift* 34 (1928): 308.

———. *Das europäische Russland. Eine Studie zur Geographie des Menschen*. Leipzig, 1905.

———. "Methodische Zeit- und Streitfragen." Pt. 5, "Die Geopolitik und die politische Geographie." *Geographische Zeitschrift* 35 (1929): 332-36.

———. Review of *Landschaft und Seele*, by Ewald Banse. *Geographische Zeitschrift* 34 (1928): 626-28.

———. Review of *Weltpolitische Bücherei*, ed. Adolf Grabowsky. *Geographische Zeitschrift* 35 (1929): 299-300.

Hochholzer, Hans. "Zur Geopolitik des Flugwesens." *Zeitschrift für Geopolitik* 7 (1930): 243-54.

Hodann, Max. "Anthropogeographie." *Sozialistische Monatshefte* 32 (1926): 333.

———. "Bevölkerungspolitik." *Sozialistische Monatshefte* 34 (1928): 529-30.

Hofmann, Albert von. *Das deutsche Land und die deutsche Geschichte.* Stuttgart, 1930.

Hoffmann, Karl. "Zwischen zwei Zeitaltern." In *Die neue Front,* ed. Moeller van den Bruck, Heinrich von Gleichen, and Max Hildebert Boehm, 359-77. Berlin, 1922.

Huber, Wilhelm. *Politische Geographie. Eine Auswahl, zusammengestellt zur Einführung in geopolitisches Denken.* Munich, 1927.

Ittameier, C. "Geopolitische Einflüsse auf die Erhaltung und Vermehrung der Eingeborenen Bevölkerung Ostafrika in Alter und Neuer Zeit." *Zeitschrift für Geopolitik* 1 (1924): 497-509.

Jäckh, Ernst. *Deutschland. Das Herz Europas.* Stuttgart, 1928.

Janson, Gerhard von. "Raumwirtschaft." *Grossdeutsche Blätter* 4 (1927): 107-10.

Jung, Edgar Julius. *Die Herrschaft der Minderwertigen. Ihr Zerfall und ihre Ablösung durch ein Neues Reich.* 1929. Reprint, Berlin, 1930.

Kästner, A. "Das Problem einer Geo- und Ethnojurisprudenz." Ph.D. diss., Leipzig University, 1931.

Kehr, Eckart. "Englandhass und Weltpolitik." *Zeitschrift für Politik* 17 (1928): 500-526.

Kellermann, Bernhard. *Der Tunnel.* Berlin, 1913.

Key, H. "Die Folgen der amerikanischen Einwanderungspolitik." *Zeitschrift für Geopolitik* 2 (1925): 261-71.

Kjellén, Rudolf. *Die Grossmächte vor und nach dem Weltkriege.* 2d ed. Leipzig, 1932.

———. *Der Staat als Lebensform.* Trans. Margarethe Langfeldt. Leipzig, 1917.

———. "Studier öfver Sveriges politiska gränser." *Ymer* 9 (1899): 283-332.

Klesse, Max. "Mehr sozialistische Bevölkerungspolitik." *Sozialistische Monatshefte* 34 (1928): 314-19.

Klute, Fritz. "Die Lehrpläne der Geographie an den höheren Schulen." *Geographischer Anzeiger* 28 (1927): 351-59.

Knieper, Franz. *Politische Geographie (Geopolitik) für den Unterrich.* Bochum, 1933.

Kohl, Louis von. "Biopolitik und Geopolitik als Grundlagen einer Naturwissenschaften vom Staate." *Zeitschrift für Geopolitik* 10 (1933): 308-14.

———. *Ursprung und Wandlung Deutschlands. Grundlagen zu einer deutschen Geopolitik.* Berlin, 1932.

Köhler, Julius Paul. "Pan-Europa." *Deutsche Arbeit* 24 (1925): 225-29.

Köllreuter, Otto. Review of *Politische Geographie,* by Otto Maull. *Archiv des öffentlichen Rechts* 48 (1925): 11.

Koloniale Reichsarbeitsgemeinschaft, ed. *Wesen und Ziele der deutschen Kolonialbewegung. Verkündigung eines Allgemeinen Deutschen Kolonialprogramms der Kolonialen Reichsarbeitsgemeinschaft am 22. Juni 1928 in Köln a. Rh.* Berlin, 1928.

Kotthaus, H. "Die Grossmächte nach den Weltkrieg (Nach Kjellén Haushofer)." *Reichsflagge,* 16 May 1931, 5.

Krahmann, Max. "Kapital, Technik und Geopolitik." *Zeitschrift für Geopolitik* 4 (1927): 859-61.

Kranold, Herman. "Aussenkolonisation." *Sozialistische Monatshefte* 38 (1932): 196.

———. "Frankreich und die koloniale Aufgabe Europas." *Sozialistische Monatshefte* 37 (1931): 975-83.

———. "Nach dem Youngplan." *Sozialistische Monatshefte* 36 (1930): 9-17.

Krause, Kurt. "Zwischeneuropa." *Geographischer Anzeiger* 33 (1932): 378-86.

Krause-Wichmann, Georg. "Saargebiet und Locarno." *Zeitschrift für Geopolitik* 3 (1926): 227-33.

Krebs, Norbert. Review of *Geopolitik,* by Richard Hennig. *Geographische Zeitschrift* 37 (1931): 557.

Krug, Hans Ludwig. "Was bestimmt Europas Grenzen?" *Zeitschrift für Geopolitik* 9 (1932): 2-7.

Krüger, Bruno. "Von Deutschlands Weltpolitischer Aufgabe." *Zeitschrift für Geopolitik* 3 (1926): 807-17.

Kupfer, Paul. "Alles fängt mit dem Lande an." *Übersee und Kolonial-Zeitung* 42 (1930): 325-26.

Lampe, K. "Versuch einer Politischen Geographie der Polargebiete." *Geographischer Anzeiger* 31 (1930): 105-10.

Langenbeck, R. "Die Lehrziele, die Lehrmethode und die Lehrpläne des erdkundlichen Unterrichts." In *Reformvorschläge des Deutschen Geographentages für den erdkundlichen Unterricht an den höheren schulen,* ed. Deutscher Geographentag, 12-32. Lübeck, 1909.

Langenmaier, Theodor. "Die Reform des Geographie-Unterrichts im Sinne der Willensbildung." In *Freie Wege vergleichender Erdkunde,* ed. Erich von Drygalski, 371. Munich, 1925.

Langhans, Paul. "Die 21. Tagung des Deutschen Geographentages zu Breslau in der Pfingstwoche 1925," *Petermanns Mitteilungen* 71 (1925): 145-52.

———. "Die 24. Tagung des Deutschen Geographentages zu Danzig." *Petermanns Mitteilungen* 77 (1931): 195-99.

Langhans-Ratzeburg, Manfred. *Begriff und Aufgaben der geopolitischen Rechtswissenschaft (Geojurisprudenz).* Berlin, 1928.

———. *Die grossen Mächte geojuristisch betrachtet.* Munich, 1931.

———. "Das japanische Reich geojuristisch betrachtet." *Zeitschrift für Geopolitik* 7 (1930): 68-77.

———. "Rechtliche und tatsächliche Machtbereiche der Grossmächte." *Petermanns Mitteilungen* 70 (1924): 1-7.

———. "Karte des Selbstbestimmungsrechtes der Völker." *Petermanns Mitteilungen* 72 (1926): 1-9.

———. "Die strittigen Gebiete der Erde." *Petermanns Mitteilungen* 75 (1929): 10-11.

———. *Die Volgadeutschen. Ihr Staats- und Verwaltungsrecht in Vergangenheit und Gegenwart.* Berlin, 1929.

Lauen, Harald. "Das entschlusslose Mitteleuropa." *Grossdeutsche Blätter* 3 (1926): 5-11.

Lautensach, Hermann. "Berichterstattung über erdumspannende Vorgänge." *Zeitschrift für Geopolitik* 2 (1925): 595-602.

———. "Deutschland und Frankreich." *Zeitschrift für Geopolitik* 2 (1925): 149-60.

———. "Erich Obsts 'England, Europa und die Welt.'" *Geographischer Anzeiger* 28 (1927): 320-28.

———. "Geopolitik und Schule." In *Bausteine zue Geopolitik,* ed. Karl Haushofer, Erich Obst, Hermann Lautensach, and Otto Maull, 307-25. Berlin, 1928.

———. "Geopolitik und Schule." *Geographischer Anzeiger* 28 (1927): 341-48.

———. "Geopolitik und Staatsbürgerliche Bildung." In *Bausteine zur Geopolitik,* ed. Karl Haushofer, Erich Obst, Hermann Lautensach, and Otto Maull, 286-306. Berlin, 1928.

———. "Landschaft und Seele. Gedanken zu Ewald Banses gleichbenanntem Buch." *Zeitschrift der Gesellschaft für Erdkunde zu Berlin* (1930): 301-2.

Leyden, Friedrich. *Review of Politische Geographie,* by Otto Maull. *Zeitschrift der Gesellschaft für Erdkunde zu Berlin* (1926): 364-66.

Lindeiner-Wildau, Hans von. "Zur Führerfrage." *Zeitschrift für Geopolitik* 3 (1926): 196-99.

Linhardt, Hans, and Gottfried Vogenauer. *Die Strukturskizze im geographischen und historisch-geopolitischen Unterricht.* Munich, 1925.

Lips, Julius. "Ethnopolitik und Kolonialpolitik." *Koloniale Rundschau* (1932): 530-38.

Littig, Friedrich, and Hermann Vogel. *Geographie für höhere Lehranstalten. Die geographischen Grundlagen der Staatenbildung und weltpolitischer Fragen mit besonderer Beziehung auf Deutschland.* 3d ed. Munich, 1923.

Loesch, Karl Christian von. "Die grösseren Zusammenschlüsse. Paneuropa." In *Jenseits der Grossmächte,* ed. Karl Haushofer, 387-416. Leipzig, 1932.

———. "Der Kampf für das Recht im Osten." *Zeitschrift für Geopolitik* 7 (1930): 29-41.

———. "Polen." *Deutsche Rundschau* 51 (1925): 199-206.

———. "Schutzarbeit und Schutzbundtagung 1927." *Grenzdeutsche Rundschau* 4 (1927): 2-3.

Loesch, Karl Christian von, and Arnold Hillen Ziegfeld. *Volk unter Völkern. Bücher des Deutschtums* (Breslau, 1925).

Löwenberg, J. *Die Entdeckungs- und Forschungsreisen in den beiden Polarzonen.* Leipzig and Prague, 1886.

Lukas, Georg A. "Geopolitische Fragen im Geographie-Unterricht: 7 [Part 7]. Die Südtirole Frage." *Geographischer Anzeiger* 29 (1928): 187-92.

———. "Geopolitische Fragen im Geographie-Unterricht: 10 [Part 10]. Mitteleuropas geopolitische Achse." *Geographischer Anzeiger* 32 (1931): 302-5.

———. "Geopolitische Fragen im Geographie-Unterricht: 11 [Part 11]. Die Einheit der deutschen Ostfront." *Geographischer Anzeiger* 34 (1933): 346-50.

Maas, Walther. Review of *Die Grossmächte vor und nach dem Weltkriege,* ed. Karl Haushofer. *Sozialistische Monatshefte* 37 (1931): 267.

Mackinder, Halford J. *Democratic Ideals and Reality.* New York, 1962.

Mahan, A. T. *The Influence of Sea Power upon History 1660–1783.* 1890. Reprint, Boston, 1941.

———. *The Problem of Asia.* Boston, 1900.

Mannhardt, Johann Wilhelm. *Hochschule, Deutschtum und Ausland. Neue Wege deutscher politischer Wissenschaft und Erziehung.* Marburg, 1927.

———. *Südtirol. Ein Kampf um deutsche Volkheit.* Jena, 1928.

———. "Zum Tode Robert Siegers." *Deutsche Welt* 4 (1927): 96-97.

'Martellus.' "Politische Rundschau." *Deutsche Rundschau* 52 (1926): 261-63.

Martens, Herbert. Review of *Volk ohne Raum,* by Hans Grimm. *Deutsche Rundschau* 53 (1926): 294-97.

März, Josef. *Landmächte und Seemächte.* Berlin, 1928.

———. *Die Ozeane in der Politik und Staatenbildung.* Breslau, 1931.

———. "Das Schicksal überseeischer Wachstumsspitzen (Die Stutzpünkte der grossen Mächte. Grundlagen und Entwicklung)." In *Zur Geopolitik der Selbstbestimmung,* ed. Karl Haushofer, 165-468. Munich, 1923.

Maschke, Erich. "Der geopolitische Film." *Zeitschrift für Geopolitik* 5 (1928): 275-78.

Maull, Otto. "Freidrich Ratzel zum Gedächtnis." *Zeitschrift für Geopolitik* 5 (1928): 617.

———. *Politische Geographie.* Berlin, 1925.

———. Review of *Geopolitik,* by Richard Hennig. *Zeitschrift der Gesellschaft für Erdkunde zu Berlin* (1929): 61.

————. Review of *Grenzen in ihrer geographischen und politischen Bedeutung,* by Karl Haushofer. *Zeitschrift der Gesellschaft für Erdkunde zu Berlin* (1929): 62.

————. "Über politischgeographisch-geopolitische Karten." *Bausteine zur Geopolitik,* ed. Karl Haushofer, Erich Obst, Hermann Lautensach, and Otto Maull. 325-42. Berlin, 1928.

————. "Die Umwertung des menschlichen Lebensraumes in näher und ferner Zukunft." *Zeitschrift für Geopolitik* 5 (1928): 79-88.

Mayr, Otto. "Die räumliche Ausdehnung des abendländischen Kulturkreises in Oswald Spenglers 'Untergang des Abendlandes'." *Zeitschrift für Geopolitik* 1 (1924): 807-10.

Merk, Walther. *Wege und Ziele der geschichtlichen Rechtsgeographie.* Berlin, 1926.

Meyer, Hans. "Geopolitische Betrachtungen über Deutsch-Ostafrika (Tanganyika territory) Einst und Jetzt." *Zeitschrift für Geopolitik* 3 (1926): 161-74.

Ministerium für Wissenschaft, Kunst und Volksbildung. "Bestimmungen über die Mittelschulen in Preussen." *Zentralblatte für die gesamte Unterrichts-Verwaltung in Preussen* 67 (1925): 13-14.

————. "Erdkundlicher Unterricht in den höheren Lehranstalten." *ZgU* 66 (1924): 134.

————. *Richtlinien für die Lehrpläne der höheren Schulen Preussens.* Amtliche Ausgabe. Berlin, 1925.

————. "Richtlinien für einen Lehrplan der Deutschen Oberschulen und Aufbauschulen." *ZgU* 66 (1924): Beilage.

————. "Richtlinien zur Aufstellung von Lehrplänen für die Grundschule." *ZgU* 63 (1921): 185-88.

Mischke, Lothar. "Der polnische Staat als europäisches Problem." *Zeitschrift für Geopolitik* 2 (1925): 303-10.

'Mitarbeiter.' "Deutschlands Weg aus der Einkreisung." *Die Tat* 22 (1931): 929-57.

Mühlestein, Hans. "Deutschland in der Ost-West Spannung." *Zeitschrift für Geopolitik* 3 (1926): 1-7.

Müller, K. A. von, and P. R. Rohden. *Knaurs Weltgeschichte von der Urzeit bis zur Gegenwart.* Berlin, 1935.

Müller-Ross, Friedrich. "Verschlossene Welt." *Übersee und Kolonial-Zeitung* 44 (1932): 134.

Muris, Oswald. "Banses Buch der Länder." *Geographischer Anzeiger* 30 (1929): 130-31.

Naumann, Friedrich. *Mitteleuropa.* Berlin, 1915.

Obst, Erich. "Berichterstattung aus Europa und Afrika." *Zeitschrift für Geopolitik* 3 (1926): 58-65, 410-19.

————. "Berichterstattung aus Europa und Afrika." *Zeitschrift für Geopolitik* 4 (1927): 921-27.

————. "Geographie." In *100 Jahre Technische Hochschule Hannover. Festschrift zur Hundertjahrfeier am 15. Juni 1931,* ed. University Rector and Senate, 108-9. Hannover, 1931.

————. "Die Krisis in der geographischen Wissenschaft." *Preussische Jahrbücher* 192 (1923): 16-28.

————. "Sowjetische Aussenpolitik." *Zeitschrift für Geopolitik* 2 (1925): 1-9.

————. "Wir fordern unsere Kolonien zurück!" *Zeitschrift für Geopolitik* 3 (1926): 151-60.

Oppermann, E. "Neue Lehrpläne in Braunschweig." *Geographischer Anzeiger* 29 (1928): 160.

Osse, Hans. "Geopolitik und Volkserziehung." *Deutsche Rundschau* 58 (1932): 33-36.

Ostwald, Paul. "Deutschland und Japan." *Zeitschrift für Geopolitik* 3 (1926): 620-24.

Papenhausen, Friedrich. "Geopolitische Erwagungen zum Deutsch-Österreichischen An-schlussgedanken." *Zeitschrift für Geopolitik* 4 (1927): 319-25.

Pechel, Rudolf. "Karl Haushofer. Zu seinem 60. Geburtstag." *Deutsche Rundschau* 55 (1929): 167-68.

Penck, Albrecht. "Deutscher Volks- und Kulturboden." In *Volk unter Völkern. Bücher des Deutschtums,* ed. Karl Christian von Loesch and A. Hillen Ziegfeld, 62-73. Breslau, 1925.

'Pertinacior.' "Politische Rundschau." *Deutsche Rundschau* 51 (1925): 95.

Pfeil, Elisabeth. "Die deutschen Juden als Beispiel für das Aussterben bei Verstädterung." *Zeitschrift für Geopolitik* 10 (1933): 113-18.

Pleyer, Kleo. "Sudetenraum und Deutsch-Österreich." *Zeitschrift für Geopolitik* 5 (1928): 394-402.

Pollog, Carl Hanns. "Wahrer Völkerbund und Schein-Völkerbund." *Zeitschrift für Geopolitik* 2 (1925): 465-73.

Pommrich, Rudolf. "Geopolitische Ziele in der Luftpolitik." *Zeitschrift für Geopolitik* 4 (1927): 558-59.

Posse, E. Review of *Die grossen Mächte, geojuristisch betrachtet,* by Manfred Langhans-Ratzeburg. *Kölnische Zeitung,* Beilage, 10 May 1931.

Programm der Technischen Hochschule zu Hannover. Hannover, Studienjahr 1925-26, Studien-jahr 1926-27.

Quessel, Ludwig. "Die Aussenpolitik des Reichstags." *Sozialistische Monatshefte* 33 (1927): 265-70.

————. "Die Bilanz unserer Aussenpolitik." *Sozialistische Monatshefte* 35 (1929): 11-17.

————. "Kurze Chronik." *Sozialistische Monatshefte* 28 (1924): 315.

————. "Rhein und Weichsel." *Sozialistische Monatshefte* 62 (1925): 264-69.

————. "Youngplan und Reichsschuld." *Sozialistische Monatshefte* 35 (1929): 482-88.

Raschhofer, Hermann. "Ein Ostpreussen-Atlas." *Deutsche Arbeit* 30 (1931): 110-12.

Rathjens, Karl. "Das Hamburgische Weltwirtschaftsarchiv und seine Bedeutung für die Geographie." *Petermanns Mitteilungen* 73 (1927): 161-62.

Ratzel, Friedrich. *Anthropo-Geographie oder Grundzüge der Anwendung der Erdkunde auf die Geschichte.* 2 vols. Stuttgart, 1882.

————. *Der Lebensraum, eine biogeographische Studie.* Munich, 1901.

————. *Das Meer als Quelle der Völkergrosse. Eine politisch-geographische Studie.* Munich, 1900.

————. *Politische Geographie.* 3d ed. Munich, 1923.

————. "Die Wolken in der Landschaft." *Deutsche Rundschau* 112 (1902): 22-50.

"Redner des Weltwirtschaftsinstituts." In *Weltwirtschaftsdämmerung. Festschrift zum 10jährigen Bestehen des Weltwirtschafts-Instituts der Handels-Hochschule Leipzig,* ed. Karl Haushofer and Walther Vogel, 128-32. Stuttgart, 1934.

Reichwein, Adolf. Review of *Geopolitik,* by Richard Henning. *Sozialistische Monatshefte* 35 (1929): 449.

Rein, Adolf. "Grundzüge der Weltpolitik der letzten hundert Jahre. Eine raumpolitische Betrachtung." *Zeitschrift für Geopolitik* 1 (1924): 605-12, 671-78.

Reinhard, Rudolf. *Weltwirtschaftliche und politische Erdkunde.* 5th ed. Breslau, 1925.

Riedel, Otto. "Die deutschen Kolonien der Südsee." *Zeitschrift für Geopolitik* 1 (1924): 626-35.

Ross, Colin. "Die Einschaltung des Irrationalen in die Rationalisierung." *Zeitschrift für Geopolitik* 7 (1930): 855-60.

Rüdiger, Hermann. "Geographie und Deutschtumskunde." *Verhandlungen des Deutschen Geographentages* 25 (1934): 87-95.

Saenger, K. "Die Statistik im Rahmen der Geopolitik." *Zeitschrift für Geopolitik* 7 (1930): 255.

Sarre, Ernst. "Das Saargebiet und der 10. Januar 1925." *Zeitschrift für Geopolitik* 2 (1925): 10-17.

Schaefer, Albert. "Zur Behandlung geopolitischer Fragen im Erdkundeunterricht der Primen." *Geographischer Anzeiger* 34 (1933): 144-49.

Scheer, Albert, ed. *Fischer-Geistbeck Stufenatlas für höhere Lehranstalten.* Bielefeld, 1927.

Scheil, Erich. "Politisch Geographie im Rahmen eines gegenwartsbetonten Unterrichts." *Neue Bahnen* 44 (1933): 220-25.

Schiele, G. W. "Wo liegt das deutsche Kolonialland?" *Eiserne Blätter,* 16 May 1926, 335-36.

Schillmann, Fritz. "Deutschland und die Welt." *Grossdeutsche Blätter* 2 (1925): 235-38.

Schmalz, Heinz. "Politik im Luftraum." *Zeitschrift für Politik* 19 (1929-30): 786-92.

Schmidt, M. "Eine geopolitische Weltkarte." *Geographischer Anzeiger* 34 (1933): 141-44.

Schmidt, M., and H. Haack. *Geopolitischer Typen-Atlas. Zur Einführung in die Grundbegriffe der Geopolitik.* Gotha, 1929.

Schmitthenner, Heinrich. Review of *Landschaft und Seele,* by Ewald Banse. *Geographische Zeitschrift* 36 (1930): 100-103.

Schnee, Heinrich. "Braucht Deutschland Kolonien?" In *Deutschland in den Kolonien. Ein Buch deutscher Tat und deutschen Rechtes,* ed. Deutche Kolonialgesellschaft and Inter-fraktionelle Vereinigung, 156. Berlin, n.d.

———. "Die Koloniale Schuldlüge." *Süddeutsche Monatshefte* 21 (1924): 93-125.

Schnee, Heinrich. [Dr. H. S., pseud.] "Kolonialpolitischer Jahresrückblick." *Deutsche Arbeit* 32 (1932): 194-97.

Sieger, Robert. "Die geographische Lehre von den Grenzen und ihre praktische Bedeu-tung." *Verhandlungen des Deutschen Geographentages,* 200-203. Berlin, 1926.

Simmer, Hans. *Grundzüge der Geopolitik in Anwendung auf Deutschland.* Munich and Berlin, 1928.

Sölch, Johann. *Die Auffassung der 'natürlichen Grenzen' in den wissenschaftlichen Geographie.* Innsbruck, 1924.

———. "Raum und Zahl. Die Zukunftsfrage des deutschen Volkes." *Geographischer An-zeiger* 34 (1933): 40-42.

———. Review of *Grenzen in ihrer geographischen und politischen Bedeutung,* by Karl Haus-hofer. In *Geographische Zeitschrift* 34 (1928): 626.

Sörgel, Herman. "Europa-Afrika. Ein Weltteil." *Sozialistische Monatshefte* 37 (1931): 983-87.

Spahn, Martin. "Böhmen und das deutsche Volk." *Grossdeutsche Blätter* 3 (1926): 63-65.

———. "Die deutsche Sendung im mitteleuropäischen Raum." *Süddeutsche Monatshefte* 21 (1924): 159-64.

———. "Grossdeutsch." *Grossdeutsche Blätter* 2 (1925): 171-78.

———. "Mitteleuropa." *Volk und Reich* 1 (1925): 2-38.

———. "Völkerbund und Sicherheitsfrage." *Süddeutsche Monatshefte* 24 (1927): 280-85.

Springenschmid, Karl. *Die Staaten als Lebewesen. Geopolitisches Skizzenbuch.* Leipzig, 1933.

Stössinger, Felix. "Für den Anschluss Deutsch-Österreichs." *Sozialistische Monatshefte* 62 (1925): 335-39.

Supan, Alexander. *Leitlinien der allgemeinen politischen Geographie: Naturlehre des Staates.* 2d ed. Berlin, 1922.

Tamss, Friedrich. "Die Lebensaussichten des deutschen Volkes." *Petermanns Mitteilungen* 79 (1933): 60-62.

Thies, Johann. "Die Geopolitik als nationale Staatswissenschaft und ihre Eingleiderung in die deutschen Volksschule." *Neue Bahnen* 45 (1934): 208-14.

————. *Geopolitik in der Volksschule. Eine methodische Einführung zur nationalpolitischen Erziehung der deutschen Jugend.* Berlin, 1932.

————. *Die Staaten als völkische Lebensräume. Für den Erdkunde- und Geschichtsunterricht bearbeitet.* Dresden, 1933.

Thorbecke, Franz. "Die Stellung der Hochschullehrer zum geographischen Unterricht." *Geographischer Anzeiger* 28 (1927): 292-95.

————. "Warum Kolonien?" *Kölnische Zeitung,* Beilage, 24 April 1934.

Tiessen, Ernst. "Die Eingrenzung der Geographie." *Petermanns Mitteilungen* 73 (1927): 1-9.

————. "Der Friedensvertrag von Versailles und die Politische Geographie." *Zeitschrift für Geopolitik* 1 (1924): 203-20.

Trampler, Kurt. "Der Lebensausgleich zwischen Staat und Volk." *Deutsche Rundschau* 58 (1932): 161-65.

Traub, G. "Der Young-Plan." *Eiserne Blätter* 11 (1929): 490-92.

Tzedtwitz, E. von. "Deutschland und Russland. Sowjetrussland, Sicherheitspakt und Völkerbund." *Eiserne Blätter,* 13 September 1925, 188-91.

Ueberschaar, Hans. "Die japanische Staatskultur und ihr neues Verhaltnis zur Union der Sozialistischen Sowjet-Republiken." *Zeitschrift für Geopolitik* 3 (1926): 17-32.

"Die Ukraine und Deutschlands Zukunft." *Süddeutsche Monatshefte* 21 (1924): 153-58.

Ule, W. Review of *Bausteine zur Geopolitik,* ed. Karl Haushofer, Erich Obst, Hermann Lautensach, and Otto Maull. In *Petermanns Mitteilungen* 75 (1929): 41.

Ullmann, Hermann. Review of *Volk ohne Raum,* by Hans Grimm. *Deutsche Arbeit* 26 (1927): 176-78.

Verzeichnis der Vorlesungen. Philipps-Universität Marburg. Marburg, 1926.

Vogel, Walther. "Die Bilanz des staatlich-völkischen Lebensraumes." In *Weltwirtschafts-dämmerung,* ed. Karl Haushofer and Walther Vogel, 88-89. Stuttgart, 1934.

————. *Das neue Europa, und seine historisch-geographischen Grundlagen.* 3d ed. Bonn, 1925.

————. Review of *Jenseits der Grossmächte,* ed. Karl Haushofer. *Petermanns Mitteilungen* 78 (1932): 150-51.

————. "Rhein und Donau als Staatenbildner." *Zeitschrift für Geopolitik* 1 (1924): 63-73.

————. "Ziele und Wege der Auslandstudien." *Koloniale Rundschau* (1925): 73-83.

Volz, Wilhelm. "Gutachten über den Ullsteinatlas." *Deutsche Arbeit* 24 (1925): 241.

————. "Lebensraum und Lebensrecht des deutschen Volkes." *Deutsche Arbeit* 24 (1925): 169-74.

————. "Locarno und Oberschlesien." *Reichsflagge,* 10 December 1925, 10.

————. *Die Ostdeutsche Wirtschaft. Eine wirtschaftsgeographische Untersuchung über die natürlichen Grundlagen des deutschen Ostens und seine Stellung in der gesamtdeutschen Wirtschaft.* Berlin, 1930.

Vorlesungsverzeichnis der deutschen Hochschule für Politik. Berlin, 1925.

"Vorstand." *Verhandlungen des Vorstandes des Kolonial-Wirtschaftlichen Komitees* 1 (1932): 1-3.

Wagner, Paul. *Erdkunde für höhere Lehranstalten. Nach der Erdkunde von Fischer-Geistbeck unter Anlehnung an die neuen Lehrpläne.* Munich, 1926.

———. "Sächsische Schulreform und Erdkunde." *Geographischer Anzeiger* 28 (1927): 22-23.

Waibel, Leo. "Südwestafrika." *Zeitschrift für Geopolitik* 3 (1926): 187-200.

Waitz, Theodor. *Introduction to Anthropology.* New York, 1975. Originally published as *Anthropologie der Naturvölker* (London, 1863).

Wätjen, H. "Nachruf auf Walther Vogel." *Historische Zeitschrift* 158 (1938): 673-74.

Wegener, Georg. *Die geographischen Ursachen des Weltkrieges.* Berlin, 1920.

Wiedenfeld, Kurt. "Von der Geopolitik." *Deutsche Rundschau* 259 (1939): 151.

Wiesemann, Ewald. "Vereinigte Staaten von Europa?" *Reichsflagge,* 10 February 1927, 1.

Wiesing, Giselher. *Zwischeneuropa und die deutsche Zukunft.* Jena, 1932.

"Wir wollen Grossdeutschland." *Grossdeutsche Blätter* 1 (1924): 1-4.

Wittfogel, Karl. "Geopolitik, geographischer Materialismus und Marxismus." *Unter dem Banner des Marxismus* 3 (1929): 698-735.

Wolff, Georg. "Das Qualitätsproblem in der Bevölkerungspolitik." *Sozialistische Monatshefte* 37 (1931): 145-49.

Wolkan, Rolf. "Grossdeutschland und Paneuropa." *Deutsche Arbeit* 26 (1926): 33-37.

Wopfner, Hermann. "Entstehung und Eigenart des tirolischen Volkstums." *Deutsche Hefte für Volks- und Kulturbodenforschung* (1930-31): 290-96.

Wunderlich, Erich. "Das heutige Polen. Eine geographischauslandkundliche Skizze." *Osteuropa. Auslandkundliche Vorträge der Technischen Hochschule Stuttgart* 5 (1933): 7-32.

———. *Das moderne Polen in politischgeograpischer Betrachtung.* 2d ed. Stuttgart, 1933.

Wütschke, Johannes. "Geopolitik und europäische Luftverkehr." *Zeitschrift für Geopolitik* 1 (1924): 221-22.

———. *Der Kampf um den Erdball.* 2d ed. Munich, 1935.

———. *Unsere Erde. Erdkundliches Lehrbuch für höhere Schulen auf der Grundlage des Arbeitsunterrichts.* Leipzig, n.d.

Zeck, Hans F. "Europäische Aussenpolitik." *Zeitschrift für Geopolitik* 3 (1926): 577-85.

Zeiss, Heinz. "Die Notwendigkeit einer deutschen Geomedizin." *Zeitschrift für Geopolitik* 9 (1932): 474-84.

Ziegfeld, A. Hillen. "Die deutsche Kartograpie nach dem Weltkriege." In *Volk unter Völkern,* ed. Karl Christian von Loesch, 429-45. Breslau, 1925.

———. "Karte und Schule." In *Staat und Volkstum. Bücher des Deutschtums,* ed. Karl Christian von Loesch and A. Hillen Ziegfeld, 705-29. Berlin, 1926.

———. "Neue Atlanten—Neue Wege!" *Grenzdeutsche Rundschau* 7 (1930): 51-54.

———. "Schlesien." In *Deutschland und der Korridor,* ed. Friedrich Heiss and A. Hillen Ziegfeld, 164-70. Berlin, 1933.

"Zusammenfassender Bericht." *Berichte der Deutschen Hochschule für Politik* 4 (1926): 9-11.

Zweig, Arnold. *Der Streit um den Sergeanten Grischa.* Potsdam, 1928.

Secondary Literature

Abendroth, Wolfgang. "Die deutschen Professoren und die Weimarer Republik." In *Hochschule und Wissenschaft im Dritten Reich,* ed. Jörg Tröger, 11-25. Frankfurt am Main, 1986.

Aly, Götz, and Susanne Heim. *Vordenker der Vernichtung. Auschwitz und die deutschen Pläne für eine neue europäische Ordnung.* Frankfurt am Main, 1993.

Aly, Götz, and Karl Heinz Roth. *Die restlose Erfassung. Volkszählen, Identifizieren, Aussondern im Nationalsozialismus.* Berlin, 1984.

Anderson, Benedict. *Imagined Communities: Reflections on the Origin and Spread of Nationalism.* 2d ed. London, 1991.

Ante, Ulrich. *Zur Grundlegung des Gegenstandsbereiches der politischen Geographie. Über das 'Politische' in der Geographie.* Stuttgart, 1985.

Arbeitsgruppe Pädagogisches Museum, ed. *Heil Hitler, Herr Lehrer. Volksschule 1933–1945— Das Beispiel Berlin.* Reinbek bei Hamburg, 1983.

Auerbach, Inge, ed. *Catalogus Professorum academiae Marburgensis. Die akademischen Lehrer der Philipps-Universität Marburg.* Marburg, 1979.

Bagrow, Leo. *Die Geschichte der Kartographie.* Berlin, 1951.

Bakker, Geert. *Duitse Geopolitiek, 1919–1945: Een imperialistische ideologie.* Utrecht, 1967.

Bartov, Omer. *Hitler's Army: Soldiers, Nazis and War in the Third Reich.* Oxford, 1992.

Bassin, Mark. "Friedrich Ratzel, 1844-1904." *Geographers: Biobibliographical Studies* 11 (1987): 123-32.

———. "Imperialism and the Nation State in Friedrich Ratzel's Political Geography." *Progress in Human Geography* 11 (1987): 473-95.

———. "Race Contra Space: The Conflict between German *Geopolitik* and National Socialism." *Political Geography Quarterly* 6 (1987): 115-34.

Beck, Hanno. *Hermann Lautensach—führender Geograph in zwei Epochen. Ein Weg zur Länderkunde.* Stuttgart, 1974.

Behrendt, Armin. *Wilhelm Külz. Aus dem Leben eines Suchenden.* Berlin, 1968.

Bendersky, Joseph W. *Carl Schmitt: Theorist for the Reich.* Princeton, N.J., 1983.

Benjamin, Walter. "Das Kunstwerk im Zeitalter seiner technischen Reproduzierbarkeit." In *Schriften,* ed. T. Adorno. 1:388-99. Frankfurt am Main, 1955.

Bergmann, Klaus. *Agrarromantik und Grossstadtfeindschaft.* Marburger Abhandlungen zur Politischen Wissenschaft, Meisenheim am Glan, 1970.

Berman, Marshall. *All That Is Solid Melts into Air: The Experience of Modernity.* New York, 1982.

Berndt, Roswitha. "Wirtschaftliche Mitteleuropapläne des deutschen Imperialismus (1926-1931)." In *Grundfragen der deutschen Aussenpolitik seit 1871,* ed. Gilbert Zeibura, 305-34. Darmstadt, 1975.

Betz, Hans-Georg. "Mitteleuropa and Post-Modern European Identity." *New German Critique* 43 (1990): 173-92.

Beyer, Rüdiger. "Ewald Banse, 1883-1953." *Geographers: Biobibliographical Studies* 8 (1984): 1-3.

Birken, Lawrence. *Hitler as Philosophe: Remnants of the Enlightenment in National Socialism.* Westport, Conn., 1995.

Bloch, Charles. "Der Kampf Joseph Blochs und der 'Sozialistischen Monatshefte' in der Weimarer Republik." *Jahrbuch des Instituts für Deutsche Geschichte* 3 (1974): 257-88.

Blouet, Brian W. *Halford Mackinder: A Biography.* College Station, Tex., 1987.

Bormann, Alexander von, and Horst Albert Glaser, eds. *Deutsche Literatur. Eine Sozialgeschichte.* Vol. 9, *Weimarer Republik-Drittes Reich.* Reinbek bei Hamburg, 1983.

Bracher, Karl Dietrich. *Die Auflösung der Weimarer Republik.* 2d ed. Stuttgart, 1957.

Broszat, Martin. *Zweihundert Jahre deutsche Polenpolitik.* Frankfurt am Main, 1972.

Bruch, Rüdiger vom. *Weltpolitik als Kulturmission. Auswärtige Kulturpolitik und Bildungsbürgertum in Deutschland am Vorabend des Ersten Weltkrieges.* Paderborn, 1982.

Brunn, S. D., and K. A. Mingst. "Geopolitics." In *Progress in Political Geography*, ed. Michael Pacione, 60–89. London, 1985.

Brunzel, Hans-Paul. "'Die Tat' 1918–1933. Ein publizistischer Angriff auf die Verfassung von Weimar innerhalb der 'konservativen Revolution'." Ph.D. diss, Bonn, 1952.

Burleigh, Michael. *Germany Turns Eastward: A Study of Ostforschung in the Third Reich.* Cambridge, 1988.

Burleigh, Michael, and Wolfgang Wippermann. *The Racial State: Germany 1933–1945.* Cambridge, 1991.

Buttmann, G. *Friedrich Ratzel. Leben und Werk eines deutschen Geographen, 1844–1904.* Stuttgart, 1977.

Carr, William. *A History of Germany, 1815–1945.* 2d ed. New York, 1979.

Chickering, Roger. *We Men Who Feel Most German: A Cultural Study of the Pan-German League, 1886–1914.* Boston, 1984.

Childers, Thomas. "The Social Language of Politics in Germany. The Sociology of Political Discourse in the Weimar Republic." *American Historical Review* 95 (1990): 331-58.

Clemens, Garbiele. *Martin Spahn und der Rechtskatholizismus in der Weimarer Republik.* Mainz, 1983.

Conze, Werner. *Die Zeit Wilhelms II. und der Weimarer Republik. Deutsche Geschichte 1890–1930.* Stuttgart, 1964.

Craig, Gordon. *Germany, 1866–1945.* New York, 1978.

Crone, G. R. *Maps and Their Makers: An Introduction to the History of Cartography.* 4th ed. London, 1968.

Dickinson, Robert E. *The Makers of Modern Geography.* London, 1969.

Diner, Dan. "'Grundbuch des Planeten.' Zur Geopolitik Karl Haushofers." *Vierteljahrshefte für Zeitgeschichte* 32 (1984): 1-28.

Dingman, Roger. "Japan and Mahan." In *The Influence of History on Mahan,* ed. John B. Hattendorf, 49–66. Newport, R.I., 1991.

Dorpalen, Andreas. *The World of General Haushofer: Geopolitics in Action.* New York/Toronto, 1942.

Dowling, Timothy Charles. "Quixotic Crusade: Count Richard Nicolas Coudenhove-Kalergi and the Pan-European Union." Master's thesis, University of Virginia, 1987.

Düwell, Kurt. *Deutschlands Auswärtige Kulturpolitik 1918–1932. Grundlagen und Dokumente.* Cologne, 1976.

Eksteins, Modris. *Rites of Spring: The Great War and the Birth of the Modern Age.* New York, 1989.

Engelmann, Bernt. *Im Gleichschritt marschen. Wie wir die Nazizeit erlebten, 1933–39.* Vol. 1. Cologne, 1982.

Faber, Karl-Georg. "Zur Vorgeschichte der Geopolitik. Staat, Nation und Lebensraum im Denken deutscher Geographen vor 1914." In *Weltpolitik, Europagedanke, Regionalismus. Festschrift für Heinz Gollwitzer,* ed. Heinz Dollinger and Horst Grunder, 389-406. Münster, 1982.

Fesser, Gerd. "Die Mutterlauge der Nazis." *Die Zeit,* 8 July 1994, 54.

Feuchtwanger, Lion. *Erfolg. Drei Jahre Geschichte einer Provinz.* Munich, 1955.

Fink, Carole. "Defender of Minorities: Germany in the League of Nations, 1926-1933." *Central European History* 5 (1972): 335-58.

Fisher, Peter S. *Fantasy and Politics: Visions of the Future in the Weimar Republic.* Madison, Wis., 1991.

Fletcher, Roger. *Revisionism and Empire: Socialist Imperialism in Germany 1897–1914.* London, 1984.

Fritzsche, Peter. *A Nation of Fliers: German Aviation and the Popular Imagination.* Cambridge, Mass., 1991.

Frommelt, Reinhard. *Paneuropa oder Mitteleuropa. Einigungsbestrebungen im Kalkül deutscher Wirtschaft und Politik 1925–1933.* Stuttgart, 1977.

Gay, Peter. *Weimar Culture: The Outsider as Insider.* New York, 1970.

Geissler, Rolf. *Dekadenz und Heroismus. Zeitroman und völkisch-nationalsozialistische Literaturkritik.* Stuttgart, 1964.

Gerstenberger, Heide. *Der revolutionäre Konservatismus. Ein Beitrag zur Analyse des Liberalismus.* Berlin, 1969.

Geyer, Michael. *Aufrüstung oder Sicherheit. Die Reichswehr in die Krise der Machtpolitik 1924–1936.* Wiesbaden, 1980.

Godlewska, Anne, and Neil Smith, eds. *Geography and Empire.* Oxford, Eng., 1994.

Gollwitzer, Heinz. *Geschichte des weltpolitischen Denkens.* Göttingen, 1982.

Gowan, Peter. "The Return of Carl Schmitt." *Debatte* 2 (1994): 82–127.

Graham, Loren R. "Science and Values: The Eugenics Movement in Germany and Russia in the 1920s." *American Historical Review* 82 (1977): 1133–64.

Gruchmann, Lothar. *Nationalsozialistische Grossraumordnung. Die Konstruktion einer 'deutschen Monroe Doktrin'.* Stuttgart, 1962.

Grunder, Horst. *Geschichte der Deutschen Kolonien.* Paderborn, 1985.

Grundmann, Karl-Heinz. *Deutschtumspolitik zur Zeit der Weimarer Republik.* Hannover, Beiträge zur baltischen Geschichte, 1977.

Haffner, Sebastian. *Von Bismarck zu Hitler. Ein Rückblick.* Munich, 1987.

Harbeck, Karl-Heinz. "Die 'Zeitschrift für Geopolitik' 1924-1944." Ph.D. diss, Kiel, 1963.

Harke, Hellmut. "Die Legende vom mangelnden Lebensraum." In *Auf den Spuren der Ostforschung,* ed. Claus Remer, 59–105. Leipzig, 1962.

Harley, J. B. "Deconstructing the Map." *Cartographica* 26 (1982): 1–19.

———. "Maps, Knowledge and Power." In *The Iconography of Landscape,* ed. D. Cosgrove and S. Daniels, 277–312. Cambridge, Eng., 1988.

———. "Silences and Secrecy: The Hidden Agenda of Cartography in Early Modern Europe." *Imago Mundi* 40 (1988): 57–76.

Hauschild, Thomas. "Völkerkunde im Dritten Reich." In *Volkskunde und Nationalsozialismus. Referate und Diskussionen einer Tagung,* ed. Helge Gerndt, 245–60. Munich, 1987.

Heinemann, Ulrich. *Die verdrängte Niederlage. Politische Öffentlichkeit und Kriegsschuldfrage in der Weimarer Republik.* Göttingen, 1983.

Henze, Dietmar. "Ewald Banse und seine Stellung in der Geographie auf Grund seiner Schriften, Tagebücher und Briefe." Ph.D. diss., Frankfurt am Main, 1968.

Hepple, Leslie W. "The Revival of Geopolitics." *Political Geography Quarterly* 5, supplement (1986): 521–36.

Herb, G. Henrik, "Persuasive Cartography in *Geopolitik* and National Socialism." *Political Geography Quarterly* 8 (1989): 289–303.

Herf, Jeffrey. "Comments on Reactionary Modernist Components of Nazi Ideology." In *The Rise of the Nazi Regime: Historical Reassessments,* ed. Charles S. Maier, Stanley Hoffmann, and Andrew Gould, 35–40. Boulder, Colo., 1986.

———. *Reactionary Modernism: Technology, Culture and Politics in Weimar and the Third Reich.* Cambridge, Eng., 1984.

Hermand, Jost. *Der alte Traum vom neuen Reich. Völkische Utopien und Nationalsozialismus.* Frankfurt am Main, 1988.

Hermand, Jost, and Frank Trommler. *Die Kultur der Weimarer Republik.* Frankfurt am Main, 1988.

Herwig, Holger H. "The Influence of A. T. Mahan upon German Sea Power." In *The Influence of History on Mahan,* ed. John B. Hattendorf, 67-84. Newport, R.I., 1991.

Heske, Henning. "German Geographical Research in the Nazi Period: A Content Analysis of the Major Geography Journals, 1925-1945." *Political Geography Quarterly* 5 (1986): 267-81.

——. "Karl Haushofer: His Role in German Geopolitics and in Nazi Politics." *Political Geography Quarterly* 6 (1987): 135-44.

——. *. . . und morgen die ganze Welt. Erdkundeunterricht im Nationalsozialismus.* Giessen, 1988.

——. "Political Geographers of the Past III: German Geographical Research in the Nazi Period: A Content Analysis of the Major Geography Journals, 1925-1945." *Political Geography Quarterly* 5 (1986): 267-81.

Hess, J. C. *"Das ganze Deutschland soll es sein." Demokratischer Nationalismus in der Weimarer Republik am Beispiel der Deutschen Demokratischen Partei* (Stuttgart, 1978).

Heyden, Günter. *Kritik der deutschen Geopolitik. Wesen und soziale Funktion einer reaktionären soziologischen Schule.* Berlin, 1958.

Hildebrand, Klaus. *Vom Reich zum Weltreich. Hitler, NSDAP und koloniale Frage 1919-1945.* Munich, 1969.

Hillgruber, Andreas. *Hitlers Strategie. Politik und Kriegführung 1940-1941.* Frankfurt am Main, 1965.

——. "Kontinuität und Diskontinuität in der deutschen Aussenpolitik von Bismarck bis Hitler." In *Grossmachtpolitik und Militarismus im 20. Jahrhundert.* Düsseldorf, 1974.

——. "Unter dem Schatten von Versailles—die aussenpolitische Belastung der Weimarer Republik: Realität und Perzeption bei den Deutschen." In *Weimar. Selbstpreisgabe einer Demokratie,* ed. Karl Dietrich Erdmann and Hagen Schulze, 51-62. Düsseldorf, 1980.

Hochhuth, Rolf. *Eine Liebe in Deutschland.* Hamburg, 1978.

Höltje, Christian. *Die Weimarer Republik und das OstLocarno Problem 1919-1934. Revision oder Garantie der deutschen Ostgrenze von 1919.* Würzburg, 1958.

Hübner, Heinz-Werner. "Vom Feldzug zum Krieg." *Die Zeit,* 14 June 1991, 12.

Hughes, Michael L. *Paying for the German Inflation.* Chapel Hill, N.C., 1988.

Huhn, Michael. "'Europäische Gespräche'—Eine aussenpolitische Zeitschrift der Weimarer Zeit." In *Wissenschaftliche Verantwortung und Politische Macht,* ed. Klaus Jürgen Gantzel, 65-185. Berlin, 1986.

Iggers, Georg G. *The German Conception of History: The National Tradition of Historical Thought from Herder to the Present.* Rev. ed. Middletown, Conn., 1983.

Jäckh, Ernst, and Otto Suhr. *Geschichte der deutschen Hochschule für Politik.* Berlin, 1952.

Jacobsen, H.-A. "Auswärtige Kulturpolitik als 'geistige Waffe.' Karl Haushofer und die Deutsche Akademie (1923-1927)." In *Deutsche Auswärtige Kulturpolitik Seit 1861,* eds. Kurt Düwell and Werner Link (Vienna, 1981): 218-55.

——, ed. *Hans Steinacher, Bundesleiter des VDA 1933-37.* Boppard am Rhein, 1970.

————. *Karl Haushofer. Leben und Werk.* Vol. 1. Boppard am Rhein, 1979.

————, ed. *Karl Haushofer. Leben und Werk.* Vol. 2, *Ausgewählter Schriftwechsel 1917–1946.* Boppard am Rhein, 1979.

Jarausch, Konrad. *Deutsche Studenten 1800–1970.* Frankfurt am Main, 1984.

————. *The Unfree Professions: German Lawyers, Teachers and Engineers 1900–1950.* New York, 1990.

Jones, E. L. *The European Miracle: Environments, Economies and Geopolitics in the Histories of Europe and Asia.* 2nd ed. Cambridge, Eng., 1987.

Kennedy, Paul. *The Rise and Fall of the Great Powers.* New York, 1987.

Kern, Stephen. *The Culture of Time and Space, 1880–1918.* Cambridge, Mass., 1983.

Kessler, Heinrich. *Wilhelm Stapel als politischer Publizist. Ein Beitrag zur Geschichte des konservativen Nationalismus zwischen den beiden Weltkriegen.* Nürnberg, 1967.

Kimmich, Christoph. *Germany and the League of Nations.* Chicago, 1976.

Klessmann, Christoph. "Osteuropaforschung und Lebensraumpolitik im Dritten Reich." In *Wissenschaft im Dritten Reich,* ed. Peter Lundgreen, 350-83. Frankfurt am Main, 1985.

Knodel, John E. *The Decline of Fertility in Germany, 1871–1939.* Princeton, 1974.

Kocka, Jürgen. "Kritik und Identität. Nationalsozialismus, Alltag und Geographie." *Die Neue Gesellscahft. Frankfurter Hefte* 33 (1986): 890-97.

Koehl, Robert Lewis. *RKFDV: German Resettlement and Population Policy, 1939–1945.* Cambridge, Mass., 1957.

Korinman, Michel. *Quand l'Allemagne pensait le monde: Grandeur et décadence d'une géopolitique.* Paris, 1990.

Kost, Klaus. "Begriffe und Macht. Die Funktion der Geopolitik als Ideologie." *Geographische Zeitschrift* 74 (1986): 14-30.

————. *Die Einflüsse der Geopolitik auf Forschung und Theorie der Politischen Geographie von ihren Anfängen bis 1945. Ein Beitrag zur Wissenschaftsgeschichte der Politischen Geographie und ihrer Terminologie unter besonderer Berücksichtigung von Militär- und Kolonialgeographie.* Bonn, 1988.

Krekeler, Norbert. *Revisionsanspruch und geheime Ostpolitik der Weimarer Republik. Die Subventionierung der deutschen Minderheit in Polen.* Stuttgart, 1973.

Krockow, Christian Graf von. *Die Deutschen in ihrem Jahrhundert.* Reinbek bei Hamburg, 1992.

Kruck, Alfred. *Geschichte des Alldeutschen Verbandes.* Wiesbaden, 1954.

Krüger, Peter. *Die Aussenpolitik der Republik von Weimar.* Darmstadt, 1985.

————. *Versailles. Deutsche Aussenpolitik zwischen Revisionismus und Friedenssicherung.* Munich, 1986.

Kuczynski, Jürgen. *Studien zur Geschichte des deutschen Imperialismus. Vol. 2. Propagandaorganisationen des Monopolkapitals.* Berlin, 1950.

Lamb, Stephen, and Anthony Phelan. "Weimar Culture: The Birth of Modernism." In *German Cultural Studies: An Introduction,* ed. Rob Burns, 53–99. Oxford, 1995.

Lange, K. "Der Terminus 'Lebensraum' in Hitlers 'Mein Kampf.'" *Vierteljahreshefte für Zeitgeschichte* 13 (1965): 425-37.

Laqueur, Walter. *Weimar: A Cultural History 1918–1933.* New York, 1974.

Leach, Barry A. *German Strategy against Russia 1939–1941.* Oxford, 1973.

Lebovics, Herman. *Social Conservatism and the Middle Classes in Germany, 1914–1933.* Princeton, N.J., 1969.

Lee, M. M. "Gustav Stresemann und die deutsche Völkerbundspolitik, 1925-1930." In *Gustav Stresemann,* ed. M. M. Lee and Wolfgang Michalka, 350-65. Darmstadt, 1982.

Lehnert, Detlev. "'Politik als Wissenschaft': Beiträge zur Institutionalisierung einer Fachdisziplin in Forschung und Lehre der Deutschen Hochschule für Politik (1920-1933)." *Politische Vierteljahresschrift* 30 (1989): 443-65.

Leopold, John A. *Alfred Hugenberg: The Radical Nationalist Campaign against the Weimar Republic.* New Haven, Conn., 1977.

Lipgens, Walter. "Europäische Einigungsidee 1923-1930 und Briands Europa-Plan im Urteil der Deutschen Akten." *Historische Zeitschrift* 203 (1966): 46-89, 315-63.

Livezey, William E. *Mahan on Sea Power.* Norman, Okla., 1981.

Livingstone, David N. "Climate's Moral Economy: Science, Race, and Place in Post-Darwinian British and American Geography." In *Geography and Empire,* ed. Anne Godlewska and Neil Smith, 132-54. Oxford, Eng., 1994.

Lohalm, Uwe. *Völkischer Radikalismus. Die Geschichte des Deutschvölkischen Schutz- und Trutz-bundes 1919-1923.* Hamburg, 1970.

Lowe, James Trapier. *Geopolitics and War: Mackinder's Philosophy of Power.* Washington, D.C., 1981.

Mann, Erika. *School for Barbarians,* trans. Muriel Rukeyser. New York, 1938.

Mann, Golo. *Deutsche Geschichte des 19. und 20. Jahrhunderts.* Frankfurt am Main, 1958.

Matern, Rainer. "Karl Haushofer und seine Geopolitik in den Jahren der Weimarer Republik und des Dritten Reiches. Ein Beitrag zum Verständnis seiner Ideen und seines Wirkens." Ph.D. diss., Karlsruhe, 1978.

Matznetter, Josef. "Johann Sölch, 1883-1951." *Geographers: Biobibliographical Studies* 2 (1978): 117-25.

———, ed. *Politische Geographie.* Darmstadt, 1977.

Mauersberger, Volker. *Rudolf Pechel und die 'Deutsche Rundschau' 1919-1933. Eine Studie zur konservativ-revolutionären Publizistik in der Weimarer Republik.* Bremen, 1971.

Meyer, Henry Cord. "Der 'Drang nach Osten' in den Jahren 1860-1914." *Die Welt als Geschichte* 17 (1957): 1-8.

———. *Mitteleuropa in German Thought and Action, 1815-1945.* The Hague, 1955.

Meynen, Emil. "Albrecht Penck, 1848-1945." *Geographers: Biobibliographical Studies* 2 (1978): 101-7.

Monmonier, Mark. *Drawing the Line: Tales of Maps and Cartocontroversy.* New York, 1995.

Mosse, George. *The Crisis of German Ideology. Intellectual Origins of the Third Reich.* New York, 1964.

Muris, Oswald. *Der Globus im Wandel der Zeiten.* Berlin, 1961.

Neumann, Siegfried. *Nacht über Deutschland. Vom Leben und Sterben einer Republik.* Munich, 1973.

Norton, Donald H. "Karl Haushofer and the German Academy, 1925-1945." *Central European History* 1 (1968): 80-98.

Noyes, John. *Colonal Space: Spatiality in the Discourse of German South West Africa 1884-1915.* Chur, 1992.

Oberkrome, Willi. *Volksgeschichte. Methodische Innovation und völkische Ideologisierung in der deutschen Geschichtswissenschaft 1918-1945.* Göttingen, 1993.

O Tuathail, Gearoid. "The Language and Nature of the 'New Geopolitics'—The Case of U.S.-El Salvador Relations." *Political Geography Quarterly* 5 (1986): 73-85.

Parker, Geoffrey. *Western Geopolitical Thought in the Twentieth Century.* London, 1985.

Parker, W. H. *MacKinder: Geography as an Aid to Statecraft.* Oxford, 1982.

Paterson, J. H. "German Geopolitics Reassessed." *Political Geography Quarterly* 6 (1987): 107–14.

Pechel, Rudolf. *Deutscher Widerstand.* Zurich, 1947.

Peet, R. "The Social Origins of Environmental Determinism." *Annals of the Association of American Geographers* 75 (1985): 309–33.

Perry, Peter J. "Thirty Years On: Or, Whatever Happened to Wittfogel?" *Political Geography Quarterly* 7 (1988): 75–80.

Petzina, Dietmar, Werner Abelshauser, and Anselm Faust, eds. *Sozialgeschichtliches Arbeitsbuch.* Vol. 3, *Materialen zur Statistik des Deutschen Reiches 1914–1945.* Munich, 1978.

Petzold, Joachim. *Wegbereiter des deutschen Faschismus. Die Jungkonservativen in der Weimarer Republik.* Cologne, 1978.

Peukert, Detlev. *Die Weimarer Republik. Krisenjahre des Klassischen Moderne.* Frankfurt am Main, 1987.

Proctor, Robert. "From *Anthropologie* to *Rassenkunde* in the German Anthropological Tradition." In *Bones, Bodies, Behavior: Essays on Biological Anthropology,* ed. George W. Stocking, Jr., 138–79. Madison, Wis., 1988.

———. *Racial Hygiene: Medicine under the Nazis.* Cambridge, Mass., 1988.

Rammstedt, Otthein. *Deutsche Soziologie, 1933–1945. Die Normalität einer Anpassung.* Frankfurt am Main, 1986.

Ravenscroft, Trevor. *The Spear of Destiny.* New York, 1973.

Reichel, Peter. *Der schöne Schein des Dritten Reiches. Faszination und Gewalt des Faschismus.* Frankfurt am Main, 1993.

Reif, Wolfgang. "Exotismus und Okkultismus." In *Deutsche Literatur. Eine Sozialgeschichte. Bd. 9 Weimarer Republik—Drittes Reich,* ed. Alexander von Bormann and Horst Albert Glaser, 155–67. Hamburg, 1983.

Rich, Norman. *Hitler's War Aims: Ideology, the Nazi State and the Course of Expansion.* Vol. 1. New York, 1973.

Riekhoff, Harald von. *German-Polish Relations, 1918–1933.* Baltimore, Md., 1971.

Ringer, Fritz K. *Education and Soceity in Modern Europe.* Bloomington, Ind., 1979.

Ritter, Ernst. *Das Deutsche Ausland-Institut in Stuttgart 1917–1945. Ein Beispiel deutscher Volkstumsarbeit zwischen den Weltkriegen.* Wiesbaden, 1976.

Rössler, Mechtild. *"Wissenschaft und Lebensraum." Geographische Ostforschung im Nationalsozialismus.* Berlin, 1990.

Rüger, Adolf. "Der Kolonialrevisionismus in der Weimarer Republik." In *Drang nach Afrika,* ed. Helmuth Stoecker, 243–72. Berlin, 1977.

Sahlins, Peter. "Natural Frontiers Revisited: France's Boundaries since the Seventeenth Century." *American Historical Review* 95 (1990): 1423–51.

Samuel, R. H., and R. Hinton Thomas. *Education and Society in Modern Germany.* London, 1949.

Schivelbusch, Wolfgang. *Intellektuellendämmerung. Zur Lage der Frankfurter Intelligenz in den Zwanziger Jahren.* Frankfurt am Main, 1982.

Schmokel, Wolfe W. *Dream of Empire: German Colonialism 1919–1945.* New Haven, Conn., 1964.

Schoenberner, Franz. *Confessions of a European Intellectual.* New York, 1946.

Schulze, Hagen. *Weimar. Deutschland 1917–1933.* Berlin, 1982.

Schultz, Hans-Dietrich. "Deutschlands 'natürliche' Grenzen. 'Mittellage' und 'Mittel-europa' in der Diskussion der Geographen seit dem Beginn des 19. Jahrhunderts." *Geschichte und Gesellschaft* 15 (1989): 248–81.

———. "Die Situation der Geographie nach dem Ersten Weltkrieg. Eine unbekannte Umfrage aus dem Jahre 1919, historisch kommentiert." *Die Erde* 108 (1977): 75–102.

Schumann, Willy. *Being Present: Growing Up in Hitler's Germany.* Kent, Ohio, 1991.

Schütz, Erhard. *Romane der Weimarer Republik.* Munich, 1986.

Schwierskott, Hans-Joachim. "Arthur Moeller van den Bruck und die Anfänge des Jungkonservativismus in der Weimarer Republik. Eine Studie über Geschichte und Ideologie des revolutionären Nationalismus." Ph.D. diss, Erlangen, 1960.

Seidel, Rita, Horst Gerken, Oskar Mahrenholtz, Karl-Heinz Manegold, Cord Meckseper, and Gerhard Schlitt, eds. *Festschrift zum 150jährigen Bestehen der Universität Hannover.* Vol. 1. *Universität Hannover 1831–1981.* Stuttgart, 1981.

———, eds. *Festschrift zum 150jährigen Bestehen der Universitat Hannover.* Vol. 2, *Catalogus Professorum 1831–1981.* Stuttgart, 1981.

Sills, David L., ed. *The International Encyclopedia of the Social Sciences.* New York, 1968. S.v. "Environmentalism," by O. H. K. Spate.

Slowe, Peter. *Geography and Political Power.* London, 1990.

Smith, Woodruff D. *The Ideological Origins of Nazi Imperialism.* New York, 1986.

———. *Politics and the Sciences of Culture in Germany 1840–1920.* New York, 1991.

Sontheimer, Kurt. *Antidemokratisches Denken in der Weimarer Republik. Die politischen Ideen des deutschen Nationalismus zwischen 1918 und 1933.* Munich, 1968.

Speier, Hans. "Magic Geography." *Social Research* 8 (1941): 310–30.

Sprout, Margaret Tuttle. "Mahan: Evangelist of Sea Power." In *Makers of Modern Strategy: Military Thought from Machiavelli to Hitler,* ed. Edward Mead Merle, 415–45. Princeton, N.J., 1944.

Takeuchi, Keiichi. "The Japanese Imperial Tradition, Western Imperialism and Modern Japanese Geography." In *Geography and Empire,* ed. Anne Godlewska and Neil Smith, 188–206. London, 1994.

Troll, C. "Die geographische Wissenschaft in Deutschland in den Jahren 1933 bis 1945. Eine Kritik und eine Rechtfertigung." *Erdkunde* 1 (1947): 3–47.

Tucholsky, Kurt. "Sieg im Atlas." In *Gesammelte Werke, Bd. II, 1925–1928,* ed. Mary Gerold-Tucholsky and Fritz J. Raddatz. Reinbek bei Hamburg, 1960, 1258.

Turner, Henry Ashby, Jr. "Fascism and Modernization." *World Politics* 24 (1971–72): 547–64.

———. *Stresemann and the Politics of the Weimar Republic.* Princeton, N.J., 1972.

Ullmann, Hermann. *Hermann Ullmann. Publizist in der Zeitwende.* Munich, 1965.

Ulmen, G. L. *The Science of Society: Towards an Understanding of the Life and Work of Karl August Wittfogel.* The Hague, 1979.

Vogel, Barbara. "Der Verein für das Deutschtum im Ausland (VDA) an der Hamburger Universität in der Weimarer Republik." *Zeitgeschichte* 16 (1988): 12–21.

Voigt, Gerd. "Aufgaben und Funktion der Osteuropa-Studien in der Weimarer Republik." In *Studien über die deutsche Geschichtswissenschaft.* Vol. 2, *Die bürgerliche deutsche Geschichtsschreibung von der Reichseinigung von oben bis zur Befreiung Deutschlands vom Faschismus,* ed. Joachim Streisand, 369–99. Berlin, 1965.

Warmbold, Joachim. *"Ein Stückchen neudeutsch Erd'. . ." Deutsche Kolonial-Literatur. Aspekte ihrer Geschichte, Eigenart und Wirkung, dargestellt am Beispiel Afrikas.* Frankfurt am Main, 1989.

Waugh, Evelyn. *When the Going Was Good.* London, 1946.

Wehler, Hans-Ulrich. *Bismarck und der Imperialismus.* Cologne, 1969.

Weigert, Hans. *Generals and Geographers: The Twilight of Geopolitics.* New York, 1942.

Weinberg, Gerhard L. *The Foreign Policy of Hitler's Germany: Diplomatic Revolution in Europe, 1933–36.* Chicago, 1970.

Weindling, Paul. *Health, Race and German Politics between National Unification and Nazism, 1870–1945.* Cambridge, Eng., 1989.

Wheeler-Bennett, J. W. *Brest-Litovsk: The Forgotten Peace, March 1918.* New York, 1936.

Whittlesey, Derwent. "Haushofer: The Geopoliticians," in *Makers of Modern Strategy: Military Thought from Machiavelli to Hitler,* ed. Edward Mead Merle, 388-414. Princeton, N.J., 1944.

Wittfogel, K. A. *Oriental Despotism: A Comparative Study of Total Power.* New Haven, 1957.

Wulf, Stefan. *Das Hamburger Tropeninstitut 1919 bis 1945. Auswärtige Kulturpolitik und Kolonialrevisionismus nach Versailles.* Berlin, 1994.

Yahil, Leni. *The Holocaust: The Fate of European Jewry, 1932–1945.* New York 1990.

Zimmermann, Ludwig. *Studien zur Geschichte der Weimarer Republik.* Erlangen, 1957.

Zimmermann, Peter. "Kampf um Lebensraum. Ein Mythos der Kolonial- und der Blut- und-Boden-Literatur." In *Die deutsche Literatur im Dritten Reich,* ed. Horst Denkler and Karl Prümm, 165-82. Stuttgart, 1976.

Zitelmann, Rainer. *Adolf Hitler. Eine politische Biographie.* Göttingen-Zürich, 1989.

Index

Africa, and Africans: as objects of German colonial policy, 199-200, 211-12, 231-34; in writings of Ewald Banse, 78-79, 81-82, 91, 101; in writings of Arthur Dix, 94-95. *See also* Race, and racialist theories

André, Fritz, 155

Anschluss, 115, 163, 224-25

Antiurbanism. *See* Cities

Arbeitsgemeinschaft für Geopolitik, vii

Asia, and Asians: unfit for colonization, 212; in writings of Ewald Banse, 78, 80

Aviation, 50. *See also* Technology

Banse, Ewald, 93, 106; career in National Socialist era, 242-33; and "expressionist" geography, 56, 63, 75-84; and geographical education, 131, 133; as geopolitical propagandist, 22

Battaglia, Otto Forst de, 43, 57

Bäumer, Gertrud, 89

Behrmann, Walter, 38, 139

Benjamin, Walter, 55

Berlin Geographic Society *(Gesellschaft für Erdkunde zu Berlin),* 92

Berman, Marshall, 73

Birthrate decline. *See* Population, and demographic change

Bloch, Joseph: and *Sozialistische Monatshefte,* 69, 210

Boden, 154, 161; as key component of *Raum,* 27; in writings of Friedrich Ratzel, 9

Boehm, Max Hildebert, 67; and *Hochschule für nationale Politik,* 162, 164

Boelitz, Otto, 135-36, 138, 159

Borders, 224-25; as component of geopolitical thought, 30-32; "natural" borders, 10; stable and unstable borders, 41; in Weimar textbooks, 142-43; in writings of Adolf Grabowsky, 100-101

Brackmann, Albert, 158

Briand, Aristide, 217

Brüning, Kurt, 285n

Burgdörfer, Friedrich, 95, 205, 223, 236; and birthrate decline, 36, 84-92; bureaucratic career under National Socialism, 242-44; and German Protective League *(DSB),* 67; and impact of Raum upon demographic change, 35

Center Party *(Zentrum),* 90, 160

Childers, Thomas, 192

Cities: geopolitical hostility toward, 37, 52, 88; in writings of Albrecht Haushofer, 54. *See also* Modernism

Class, Heinrich, 15

Cohen-Reuss, Max, 92, 210

Colonial Institute, Hamburg, 152, 155

Colonialism: divisions among geopoliticians over, 92-97, 132; Karl Haushofer on, 262n. *See also* Dix, Arthur

Colonial Women's Aid *(Koloniale Frauenhilfe),* 203

Conservative People's Party *(Konservative Volkspartei),* 91

Coudenhove-Kalergi, Richard N., 231-35. *See also* Pan-Europa

Craig, Gordon, 62
Curtius, Julius, 240

Darré, Walther, 210
Darwinism: and geopolitical views of
    European imperialism, 196; in the works
    of Friedrich Ratzel, 7-8; in the works of
    Rudolf Kjellén, 11, 19, 29, 87
Dernburg, Bernhard, 229
Deutschtumspolitik, 225-28
Dix, Arthur, x, 17, 20, 64, 68, 106, 153, 196,
    218, 223, 242-43; and aviation, 51; and
    German campaign for colonies, 38, 90-97,
    204-5, 211-12; and "global village," 50
Drygalski, Erich von, 12, 52, 106; and
    "expressionist" geography, 83
Duems, Eric, 202, 204

Eckert, Max, 83
Economic Party *(Wirtschaftspartei),* 228
Environmental determinism, 53; evolution
    of, in geopolitical theories, 41; in
    geopolitical thought after World War I,
    17; impact of environment on races and
    states, 32, 33-34; in Weimar textbooks,
    146-47. *See also* Race, and racialist
    theories
Erfüllungspolitik, 227
Ernst, J., 154
Etscheit, Alfred, 195

Fehn, Richard, 206
Feuchtwanger, Lion, 109
Filchner, Wilhelm, 52
Fischer, Alois, 37
Fischer, Eugen, 208
Foundation for Research on German Ethnic
    and Cultural Soil *(Stiftung für deutsche
    Volks- und Kulturbodenforschung,* SDVK),
    151, 158-59. *See also* Volk, and volkish
    theories
Friedrichsen, M., 64

Gayl, Wilhelm Frhr. von, 62, 63; and
    German Protective League, 67
Geistbeck, Alois, 130
Geography: reform of discipline in Germany,
    128-35

Geopolitics: Allied views of after World
    War II, vii-viii; differentiated from
    political geography, 258n; maritime and
    continental theories of, 39; meanings
    of, 44; and National Socialist foreign
    policy, 246-47; origin of term, ix; and
    Weimar modernism, 25
German Academy (Munich), 244
German Colonial Serviceman's League
    (Deutscher Kolonialkriegerbund), 203
German Colonial Society *(Deutsche
    Kolonialgesellschaft,* DKG), 160, 191, 192,
    202, 203
German Democratic Party *(Deutsche
    Demokratische Partei,* DDP), 168; and
    birthrate decline, 89; and colonies, 92; use
    of geopolitical themes and rhetoric by,
    229, 237
German Farmers' Party *(Deutsche
    Bauernpartei),* 90
German Geographic Congress *(Deutscher
    Geographentag),* 20, 90
German National People's Party
    (Deutschnationale Volkspartei, DNVP), 20,
    164, 195; and campaign for colonies, 203;
    and Republican foreign policy, 227-28
German People's Party *(Deutsche Volkspartei,*
    DVP), 217, 237
German Protective League *(Deutscher
    Schutzbund,* DSB), 85; and Republican
    foreign policy, 225-26; use of geopolitical
    cartography, 168-69; use of geopolitical
    themes in border revisionist propaganda,
    65-67; and Weimar academic life, 160.
    See also Volk, and volkish theories
German State Party *(Deutsche Staatspartei),*
    229
German Students' Congress *(Deutscher
    Studententag),* 264
German University for Politics *(Deutsche
    Hochschule für Politik,* DHP), 211, 243;
    Adolf Grabowsky and, 104-5; geopolitical
    ideas in curriculum, 159-61
Grabowsky, Adolf, viii, x, 1, 60, 73, 92, 106,
    159; career and writings during Weimar
    years, 97-105; impact of World War I on
    his ideas, 16; League of Nations and, 239;
    in National Socialist era, 242; and political

propaganda during Weimar, 68; and
Republican foreign policy, 218
Graf, Georg Engelbert, 68, 70-71
Grimm, Hans, 92, 191, 197; and birthrate
decline, 87; and colonialism, 38; and
campaign for German colonies, 202,
204
Grossdeutschland: Friedrich Naumann and,
63; in volkish propaganda, 229
Grotjahn, Alfred, 89
Gruchmann, Lothar, 194
Günther, Erich, 56, 83

Hänisch, Konrad, 135
Harms, Hans, 129
Harmsen, Hans, 85, 86, 243
Hassinger, Hugo, 58, 84, 154, 242; and
environmental determinism, 34; Ewald
Banse and, 82, 83; and political propaganda
during Weimar, 68
Haushofer, Albrecht, 92, 223; and birthrate
decline, 35; and cities, 54; death in Nazi
era, 245; and distinction between political
geography and geopolitics, 22
Haushofer, Karl, x, 54, 58-59, 118, 128, 142,
150, 154, 215, 218, 221; and Albrecht
Haushofer, 22; Allied perceptions of,
vii-viii; and colonies, 38, 194-95; and
education during Weimar, 159, 160, 165;
and "expressionist" geography, 82; and
geojurisprudence, 111-12; Hans Grimm
on, 197-98; and ideas of Mackinder and
Mahan, 5; impact of World War I, 18; and
Marxism, 43; during National Socialist
era, 241, 242, 244; opaque literary style, 19,
258n; political propagandizing, 67, 68,
105-9; Raum in theories of, 28
Hedin, Sven, 224
Heidegger, Martin, 57
Heiss, Friedrich, 223
Hellpach, Willy, 89
Hennig, Richard, 58, 99, 204; and colonies,
196; definition of geopolitics, 20; and
education, 154; polar regions in geo-
politics, 52; Raum in writings of, 29
Herré, Paul, 58
Hess, Rudolf, 106, 244; and links with Karl
Haushofer and Hitler, vii

Hettner, Alfred, 58, 83, 112, 122; critic of
geopolitics, ix, 41-42; cultural geography
and, 12; distinction between political
geography and geopolitics, 18
Hitler, Adolf, 149, 194, 242, 246; and links
with Karl Haushofer, vii, 106, 277n
Hochholzer, Hans, 50-51
Hochhuth, Rolf, 241, 248
Hoetzsch, Otto, 114, 159, 164
Hoffmann, Albert von, 58, 112
Hoffmann, Karl, 162
Hugenberg, Alfred, 228
Humboldt, Alexander von, 166

Institute for Border and Foreign
Germandom (*Institut für Grenz- und
Auslandsdeutschtum,* IGAD), 151, 154-58.
See also Mannhardt, Johann Wilhelm
Institute for Foreign Policy, Hamburg, 194
Institute for Geopolitics: myth of, vii,
253n
Institute for International Law, Göttingen,
243
Institute for Maritime Exchange and World
Economics, Kiel, 154
Interallied Control Commission, 238
Interfractional Colonial Coalition
(Interfraktionelle Koloniale Vereinigung),
203

Jäckh, Ernst, 60; and geopolitical theories,
104-5; and German University for
Politics, 160, 164
Jaeger, Fritz, 122
Jews, and Judaism, 122, 247; as aliens in
Germany, 55, 120; response to environ-
ment in ancient times, 100
Jung, Edgar Julius, 60, 63
Juniklub, 161

Kehr, Eckart, 102
Kellermann, Bernhard, 47
Kjellén, Rudolf, 100, 118, 122, 140, 142, 153,
155, 209; and geopolitical thought before
World War I, 2; and origin of key geo-
political concepts, 6; and term
"geopolitics," ix
Knieper, Franz, 149-50, 172

Koch-Weser, Erich, 92
Kohl, Louis von, 53, 209
Köllreuter, Otto, 111
Kolonial-Wirtschaftliches Komitee, 92
Krahmann, Max, 48-49
Kranold, Herman, 210
Kraus, Herbert, 243
Krebs, Norbert, 21, 92, 242
Kulturboden, 148, 159, 171; origins of term
    and concept, 65-66; and volkish theories,
    162-63. See also Penck, Albrecht
Külz, Wilhelm, 207
Kunst und Wissenschaft, 57, 76
Kupfer, Paul, 206

Langhans-Ratzeburg, Manfred, 29, 109-16
Lautensach, Hermann, 58, 83, 106, 134, 141,
    218-19; and distinction between political
    geography and geopolitics, 20
Laws of geopolitical theory, 8, 11, 58-59, 95
League for Colonial Renewal (Bund für
    koloniale Erneuerung), 203
League for Germandon Abroad (Verein für
    das Deutschtum im Ausland, VDA), 155,
    172, 225; Raum in propaganda of, 28; and
    volkish movement, 65
League of German University Teachers of
    Geography, 55, 134
League of Nations, 40, 103-4, 221;
    geopolitical views of, 236-40
Lebensraum, 120; and birthrate decline, 86;
    and colonies, 198; definitions of, 10;
    evolution of concept, 245-46; in Karl
    Haushofer's theories, vii, 107; and Raum,
    27; in teaching, 136; and volkish theories,
    29
Lindeiner-Wildau, Hans-Erdmann von, 228
Lips, Julius, 208, 295n
Littig, Friedrich, 145
Locarno Treaties (1925), 215, 219-20, 237
Loesch, Karl Christian von, 222, 225, 244;
    and birthrate decline, 85; and links to
    goverment, 65; and volkish propaganda,
    159, 160, 167, 168
Lukas, Georg A., 134

Mackinder, Halford, 2, 4, 5, 255
McLuhan, Marshall, 50, 93

Mahan, Alfred Thayer, 2, 3, 4, 5, 12
Mann, Golo, 74
Mannhardt, Johann Wilhelm, 68, 243; and
    Institute for Border and Foreign
    Germandom, Marburg, 154-59
Marxism, and geopolitics, 68-69, 71,
    120-21
März, Josef, 99, 172, 196; and maritime
    geopolitical theories, 39-40
Maschke, Erich, 49
Maull, Otto, 58, 99, 111, 122, 150, 153, 154,
    159; distinction between political
    geography and geopolitics, 20; Friedrich
    Ratzel and, 12; and geopolitical
    cartography, 172; practical use of
    geopolitics, 21; Raum in writings of, 27;
    and Zeitschrift für Geopolitik, x
Meinecke, Friedrich, 130
Mitteleuropa, 225, 229, 234, 300n; in
    geopolitical critique of foreign policy,
    217-19; Naumann and, 16; Ratzel and, 8;
    technology, impact upon concepts of, 49;
    and volkish theories, 61, 63
Modernism, geopolitics and, 44-48,
    267n
Moeller van den Bruck, Arthur, 60, 161
Mühlestein, Hans, 55
Müller, Hermann, 211, 240
Müller, Karl Valentin, 211
Muris, Oswald, 67, 83, 133
Mussolini, Benito, 87

National Liberal Party (Nationalliberale
    Partei), 91
National Socialism, 82, 85, 164; and
    colonies, 209, 214; and education, 127;
    foreign policy and ideology, role of
    geopolitics in, xi, 23, 241-52; and
    geopolitical cartography, 173-74; Karl
    Haushofer and, 108
Naturvölker, 11
Naumann, Friedrich, 16, 63, 38-39
Naval League, 3, 12
Nietzsche, Friedrich, 55
Nonrationalism, in geopolitical theories,
    54-55
Notgemeinschaft der deutschen Wissenschaften,
    122

Obst, Erich, 56, 58, 150, 159, 196, 204; and colonies, 38; and education, 130, 133, 141; and "expressionist" geography, 82, 84; and foreign policy, 218, 229, 237; and National Socialism, 242; at Technical University of Hannover, 151-53

Pahl, Walther, 99
Pan-Europa, 25, 40; geopolitical critique of, 230-36
Pan-German League, ix, 8, 15, 192
Pechel, Rudolf, x, 105; on Karl Haushofer, 61-62; and volkish propaganda, 67, 68
Penck, Albrecht, 31, 64, 92, 135, 159; and cartography, 167, 170; and *Kulturboden,* 65; and volkish theory, 67, 68
Perthes, Justus, 166
Petermann, August, 166
Peukert, Detlev, 45, 73, 217
Poland, 145, 162; and Polish "corridor", 221-22, 223; and demographic "threat" to the Germany, 88; in writings of Adolf Grabowsky, 98-99
Polar Regions, 51, 265n
Political Science Union *(Staatswissenschaftliche Vereinigung),* 92
Population, and demographic change, 84-85, 223-24, 270n, 273n; fear of decline, 25; Friedrich Ratzel on, 256n; geopolitical perspective on causes of growth, 10; impact of Raum upon, 35; Lebensraum, colonies and, 206-7
Prussian Ministry for Science, Art and Public Education *(Ministerium für Wissenschaft, Kunst und Volksbildung),* 155, 158, 171, 296n

Quessel, Ludwig, 52, 210

Raab, Gerhard, 227
Race, and racialist theories, 54, 62, 78, 162; and colonies, 207-8; in Ewald Banse, 81-82; geopolitical theories, links to, 56-58; and geopolitics in National Socialist era, 247-48; and German expansion, 38; in Kjellén and Ratzel, 9, 11; and Pan-Europe movement, 234-35. *See also* Africa, and Africans
Rathjens, Karl, 16

Ratzel, Friedrich, 6, 11, 56, 64, 122, 242; and Adolf Grabowsky, 100; borders and, 10; and environmental determinism, 34; his *Politische Geographie,* 7; and maritime power, 12; and *Mitteleuropa,* 15; and prewar geopolitics, 2; race, Boden and, 9
Raum, 63, 154, 161; and Adolf Grabowsky, 99-103; and Carl Schmitt, 29; and conflict with racial theory, 266n; ethnic groups, interaction with, 33; in geopolitical theory, 26-28; and population, 87-88; technology and, 47; volk, relationship to, 61
Raumforschung, viii, 20
Reich Colonial Task Force *(Koloniale Reichsarbeitsgemeinschaft,* KORAG), 203, 204
Reinhard, Rudolf, 143
Rheinbaben, Frhr. von, 228
Richthofen, Ferdinand von, 212
Ritter, Karl, 208
Rohrbach, Paul, 212
Ross, Colin, 55-56
Ruprecht, Crown Prince of Bavaria, 203

Saenger, K., 86, 205
Sapper, Karl, 196
Schmitt, Carl, 28, 29, 111
Schnee, Heinrich, 97, 160, 191; and colonial revisionist campaign, 204-6, 212; and German Protective League, 67
Schultze-Jena, Leonhard, 154-55
Sieger, Robert, 154, 155; and borders, 32-32; and volkish theories, 68, 69
Simmer, Hans, 198
Slavs, 148, 167, 170; as demographic threat, 88-90, 115; and German expansion, 222-23; and Mitteleuropa, 62-63; in Weimar textbooks, 144-46. *See also* Race, and racialist theories; *Zwischeneuropa*
Smith, Woodruff, 25, 196
Social Democratic Party *(Sozialdemokratische Partei Deutschlands,* SPD), 23, 26, 60, 68, 135, 210
Sölch, Johann, 24, 39, 88
Southwest Africa, German colony in, 192
Spahn, Martin, 63, 218, 221, 236; and German University for Politics, 160-62; and volkish propaganda, 68

Spann, Othmar, 57, 60, 119
Spengler, Oswald, 52, 266n
Spreitzer, Hans, 285n
Springenschmid, Karl, 173
Stahlhelm, 29
State, organic theories of, 8, 9, 30, 52, 101-3, 236; in Weimar texts, 142, 147
Stresemann, Gustav, 215, 226, 236, 240
Supan, Alexander, 142, 143, 152
Swift, Jonathan, 166

Task Force for Foreign and Colonial Technology (*Arbeitsgemeinschaft für Auslands- und Kolonialtechnik,* AKOTECH), 212-14
Die Tat, 56, 83
Technology, in geopolitical theories, 47, 79, 93-94; and colonies, 200-201; in Weimar texts, 147
Thies, Johann, 127
Thorbecke, Franz, 99, 139, 196
Tirpitz, Alfred, 3, 85
Traub, Gottfried, 68
Traub, Gottlob, 195
Tucholsky, Kurt, 289-90n
Turner, Frederick Jackson, 2

Ullmann, Hermann, 167
Ullstein, Franz, 167
University for National Politics (*Hochschule für nationale Politik,* or *Politisches Kolleg*), 161-63

Versailles, Treaty of, 24, 100, 114, 216, 224; Arthur Dix critique of, 21; and borders, 10; and population changes in Germany, 36; resentment against, as source of geopolitical appeal, 16, 41
Vogel, Hermann, 145
Vogel, Walther, 58, 99, 112, 150, 153, 167, 242, 243; Raum, in writings of, 116-24; and volkish propaganda, 68
Volk, and volkish theories, 60-61, 161, 234; Adolf Grabowsky and, 100; and environmental determinism, 33; Friedrich Ratzel on, 9; and law, 109; Martin Spahn and, 63
Volz, Wilhelm, 56, 84, 167, 219, 224; and education, 154, 158; Raum as political force, in writings of, 27; and volkish propaganda, 64-65, 68
Vowinckel, Kurt, 68, 86

Wagner, Paul, 135, 140, 145
Waibel, Leo, 197
Waugh, Evelyn, 275n
Weltpolitik, 7, 196-97
Westarp, Kuno Friedrich Graf von, 238, 240
Will, as geopolitical force, 54, 120
Wittfogel, Karl, 68, 71-72
Workgroup of German Journals (*Arbeitsgemeinschaft deutscher Zeitschriften*), 65, 67
World War I, 14, 24
Wunderlich, Erich, 154
Wütschke, Johannes, 171

Young Plan, 70, 217, 228

Zehrer, Hans, 224
Zeitschrift für Geopolitik, founding and circulation, ix
Ziegfeld, A. Hillen, 65, 67, 168-69
Zwischeneuropa, 220, 144-48

THE HEROIC EARTH

was composed in 11/13.5 Bembo

on a Power Macintosh using QuarkXpress 3.32

at The Book Page;

printed by sheet-fed offset

on 50# Glatfelter Supple Opaque Natural stock

(an acid-free paper),

notch case bound over binder's boards

in ICG cloth,

and wrapped with dust jackets printed in three colors

on 100# enamel stock finished with film lamination

by Braun-Brumfield, Inc.;

designed by Diana Dickson;

and published by

THE KENT STATE UNIVERSITY PRESS

Kent, Ohio 44242